INVITATION TO PEACE STUDIES

FIRST EDITION

Houston Wood

HAWAI'I PACIFIC UNIVERSITY

NEW YORK   OXFORD

OXFORD UNIVERSITY PRESS

Oxford University Press is a department of the University of Oxford.
It furthers the University's objective of excellence in research,
scholarship, and education by publishing worldwide.

Oxford   New York
Auckland   Cape Town   Dar es Salaam   Hong Kong   Karachi
Kuala Lumpur   Madrid   Melbourne   Mexico City   Nairobi
New Delhi   Shanghai   Taipei   Toronto

With offices in
Argentina   Austria   Brazil   Chile   Czech Republic   France   Greece
Guatemala   Hungary   Italy   Japan   Poland   Portugal   Singapore
South Korea   Switzerland   Thailand   Turkey   Ukraine   Vietnam

For titles covered by Section 112 of the US Higher Education
Opportunity Act, please visit www.oup.com/us/he for the
latest information about pricing and alternate formats.

Published by Oxford University Press
198 Madison Avenue, New York, New York 10016
http://www.oup.com

Oxford is a registered trademark of Oxford University Press

Library of Congress Cataloging-in-Publication Data
Wood, Houston, 1944-
   Invitation to peace studies / Houston Wood. -- First edition.
      pages cm
   ISBN 978-0-19-021713-6 (paperback)
   1. Peace--Study and teaching. I. Title.
   JZ5534.W66 2015
   303.6'6--dc23
                                                      2015008425

CONTENTS

PREFACE

Peace studies is part of an immense and often unnoticed transformation in human relations, a change that is encouraging more and more people to work to decrease the frequency of violence. *Invitation to Peace Studies* celebrates this ambitious transformation and invites readers to become more conscious and skilled participants accelerating the change.

The academic field of peace studies has two main goals: first, to understand peace, conflict, violence, and war and, second, to find ways to apply this knowledge to help create a more peaceful world. Peace research, the first goal, is pursued in many disciplines, including anthropology, economics, ethology, the health sciences, history, international studies and relations, legal studies, philosophy, political science, psychology, religious studies, and sociology. Research drawn from these disciplines forms the core of this book.

Turning research findings into practical actions, peace studies' second goal, distinguishes the field from the disciplines with which it shares research interests. In peace studies, *peace research is a form of peace search.* Peace studies thus more resembles professional fields such as accounting, education, engineering, nursing, law, and social work than it does more exclusively research-oriented disciplines. For example, just as engineering relies on chemistry, geology, mathematics, and physics to produce alterations in the physical world, peace studies draws on a comparatively diverse body of knowledge to help professionals and ordinary citizens build more peaceful societies.

Invitation to Peace Studies does not attempt an encyclopedic summary of everything associated with the field. The book instead contents itself with focusing mostly on current ideas and controversies; it emphasizes recent over older research and empirical over philosophical investigations. The application of a gender perspective is given particular prominence in thinking about the causes and cures of violence. Also, even though empirical research forms the core of most chapters, substantial attention is given as well to faith-based ideas, movements, and peace pioneers. In these pages I celebrate the multiplicity of peace promoters and invite readers to understand peace studies as an inclusive field that unites hundreds of thousands of people across Earth who are working to increase individual, group, and international peace.

As mentioned, *Invitation to Peace Studies* celebrates one of the most consequential social transformations the world has ever seen. Adapting ideas developed by Robert C. Johansen (1978), Timothy A. McElwee (2003), Kent D. Shifferd (*From War to Peace*, 2011), and others, I call this new phenomenon a *global peace network* (Wood 2014) and claim in these pages that this network links diverse ideas, individuals, groups, organizations, movements, and regions within a single dispersed and powerful interconnected web. Readers will find this book offers repeated invitations to readers to become more involved in helping the global peace network create a yet more peaceful world.

Invitation to Peace Studies consists of three major sections that invite sequential study. Nonetheless, these sections and each of the thirteen component chapters can also be read independently, enabling readers and instructors to sequence their explorations in multiple ways.

Invitation to Peace Studies is aimed at newcomers to the field of peace studies and thus seeks to present complex ideas simply, though not simplistically. Aids for readers include: Overviews for each of the three book sections as well as for each chapter; chapter-specific lists of key terms and people; illustrative cases studies; numerous tables and text boxes; bolded key terms; a glossary; end of chapter review guides, and also questions to spark critical thinking. Each chapter concludes with a list of texts, videos, and websites to help interested readers learn more.

ACKNOWLEDGMENTS

I am lucky to have spent the last eight years teaching multiple sections of an introductory peace studies course to students from all over the world at my university in Honolulu. In these classes, as in this book, I draw upon a perspective built upon my years of research in both the social sciences and the humanities, the two sometimes-estranged perspectives that guide most peace studies inquires. In my youth, too, I spent transformative months in Alabama in 1965 and in Mississippi in 1966, first following instructions from Martin Luther King Jr. and then from Stokely Carmichael, later known as Kwame Ture. Two subsequent decades exploring life in alternative communities on the island of Hawai'i further shaped my thinking.

Rich though they are, these diverse teaching, research, and personal experiences have left me far from able to master the many disciplines that make up peace studies as I conceive it here. I have thus tried to enlist as many helpers as I could to ensure the accuracy of these chapters. The mistakes that remain are mine, but there would be many more errors were it not for the assistance of my students at Hawai'i Pacific University who responded to iterations of this book during its six year gestation. Precious Binas, Anthony Bonilla Jr., Ambria Flippo, Jerome Mester, Manuel Lucas Nicolini, and Henrike Wolter saved me from some real "howlers." Mahalo plenty. Many thanks as well to my HPU colleagues, to Phyllis Frus, Laurie Leach, Tyler McMahon, Andy Opitz, Deborah Ross, and Mark Tjarks. UCSD Emeritus Professor Bud Mehan also offered suggestions, briefly renewing a collaboration we began with our first book decades ago. George Lakey and the researchers he supervises at the Global Nonviolent Action Database were the source of many of the examples provided throughout the book. I appreciate as well recommendations from Paul Chappell, Frans de Waal, Douglas P. Fry, Judith Hand, Michael Nagler, Rachel McNair, David Ragland, Michael Reisinger, Stephanie Van Hook, Kent D. Shifferd, David J. Smith, and Stephen Zunes. Editors Jennifer Carpenter and her assistants Matthew Rohal and Maegan Sherlock at OUP were professionally patient with my sometimes unprofessional impatience. Jennifer Knerr, at Paradigm Publishers, offered good advice on an early iteration of the manuscript. William Hamilton, long time director of the University of Hawai'i Press, bucked me up at crucial moments. Charlotte Wood served ably as my social media consultant. Anna Wood shared our office working furiously on her novel, *The Lands of Atelto*. Naomi Pueo Wood helped her father try to get the gender sections right even as she was working on her own book, *Brazil in Twenty-First Century Popular Media*, which beat this one into print. Susan Wood edited, encouraged, indulged, and teased. Mostly indulged.

I dedicate this book to the National Peace Academy, at whose founding summit at Case Western Reserve University in 2009 I first glimpsed the benign specter that is the global peace network. I have been exploring this network ever since.

Likewise, there are several others who are unaffiliated with the author and editors, who contributed to this book's shape and success as well. Much gratitude is thus owed to the following people, who reviewed the manuscript in various stages and provided valuable insight and ingenuity in the development of this book:

Deina Abdelkader
University of Massachusetts–Lowell

Clement E. Adibe
DePaul University

Paul Baggett
South Dakota State University

Walton Brown-Foster
Central Connecticut State University

Greg Carroll
Salem State University

Andrew Cole
University of Wisconsin–Milwaukee

Kathleen Lynch Conway
Wayne State College

Nancy Erbe
California State University–Dominquez Hills

Mariana Leal Ferreira
San Francisco State University

Andrea Grove
California State University–Channel Islands

Marike Janzen
University of Kansas

R. Averell Manes
Western Connecticut State University

Ekaterina Romanova
American University

Rosemary E. Shinko
Bucknell University

Edwin Taylor
Missouri Western State University

CHAPTER 1

INVITATIONS TO PEACE WORK

CHAPTER OVERVIEW

This chapter outlines the major goals associated with peace studies. It describes how Mohandas K. Gandhi and Martin Luther King Jr. became peace workers then reviews recent changes in attitudes toward violence and war. Wael Ghonim's work with digital media during the Egyptian uprising is used to illustrate how new technologies are influencing peace movements. The chapter concludes with a review of the differences between macro, meso, and micro studies of peace and with a discussion of the emerging field of peace ecology.

Key terms and people discussed include: Peace studies; peace; Mohandas K. Gandhi; Martin Luther King Jr.; attitudes toward war; Wael Ghonim; macro level of peace analysis; meso level of peace analysis; micro level of peace analysis; peace ecology.

> We must become the change we wish to see in the world.
>
> —MOHANDAS GANDHI (attributed by his grandson
> Arun Gandhi 2004, x)

The last one hundred years spawned an extraordinary change in many people's attitudes toward violence. In earlier centuries most humans assumed that little could be done to eliminate war, slavery, hereditary monarchies, genocide, and the violent oppression of the poor, women, and minorities. Today, however, there is a widespread belief that humans can reduce violence in most, if not all, of its forms. A peace-promoting network of beliefs, institutions, and organizations now stretches its increasingly powerful influence across much of the globe.

Peace studies is one part of this growing peace network. Peace studies is relatively small but spreads a big tent, welcoming diverse people and perspectives to assist with its work. Some people in peace studies specialize in research, some in practical action, and some in education.

Many combine specialties, believing that peace research is a kind of peace search that at its best combines evidence, education, and action. Virtually everyone in peace studies shares the view that more peace is possible when people possess the necessary knowledge and will.

Peace studies' diversity includes a diversity of definitions of the key term "peace." These different ideas are explored in later chapters but, as a start, we can adapt a definition first put forward by the Earth Charter and later refined by Tony Jenkins and the National Peace Academy (2012). Peace is built through right relationships and harmonious associations. This characterization makes clear that peace is more than the mere absence of direct, physical violence. Ending violence through truces, ceasefires, and mutual agreements is important but lasting peace also requires ethical, harmonious interactions in situations as small as personal relationships and as large as the global system of nations.

Increasing numbers of people are trying to extend the definition of peace even further to include relationships between humans currently alive and future generations to come, between humans and nonhuman animals, and between humans and the natural world. These latter relationships between humans and the natural world are often referred to as peace ecology, a perspective discussed in a later section below.

Peace studies invites people to seize opportunities to work for peace wherever they appear. Mohandas K. Gandhi and Martin Luther King Jr. continue to inspire many in the field so it is fitting to begin this invitation to peace studies with reminders of how each of these men found their way to peace work.

UNEXPECTED INVITATIONS

Mohandas K. Gandhi was a timid, twenty-four-year-old lawyer who had recently arrived in South Africa in 1893 when he refused to sit in third-class coach on an overnight train from Durban to Pretoria. Gandhi possessed a first class ticket but those seats were "for whites only" and, in the South African system, Gandhi was "colored." A police officer threw Gandhi and his suitcases onto the station platform. Gandhi sat outside all night, with no overcoat, shivering in the cold (Fischer 1954, 21).

As biographer Bhikku Pareth describes the scene, "The distraught Gandhi debated whether to return to India or stay and fight for his rights" (Pareth 2001, 5). The former choice seemed more likely as Gandhi had until then shown few signs of becoming a leader. He had been forced to accept his new, obscure job in South Africa in part because in India Gandhi had found himself too timid to practice law. At his first courtroom appearance there he had risen to examine a witness, found himself unable to speak, and so in embarrassment returned the fee to his client (Nanda 1958, 30). Nonetheless, something in the situation that night a year later in South Africa convinced Gandhi he had been issued an invitation to act, not only for himself but also on behalf of the thousands of Indians then living in South Africa.

Within a week Gandhi had convened a meeting in Pretoria where he haltingly offered the first public speech of his life. Gandhi's determination and eloquence grew in the following months as he struggled to build a social movement in South Africa. He had planned to remain abroad but a short time but instead stayed for twenty-two years working for equal rights for Indians. Finally, in 1915, Gandhi returned to India to become the leader of millions of people seeking their independence from British rule. By the time of his murder in 1948, the once-timorous, failed lawyer had become the most influential proponent of organized peaceful action the world has known.

In 1955, seven years after Gandhi's death, **Martin Luther King Jr.** was twenty-six years old and working in his first job as a minister at the Dexter Avenue Baptist Church in Montgomery, Alabama. King was never as shy or as unconfident as Gandhi, but he was a somewhat introverted young man who had often shown himself more interested in studying theology than in preaching. King had completed a PhD in theology from Boston University just seven months before being invited by the senior ministers in Montgomery to become the spokesperson for a bus boycott campaign several people had been planning for years. Because he was a newcomer and junior member of the city's small black ministers' community, King felt he had to accept this fraught invitation from his social superiors.

The boycott lasted for over a year. Participants were often attacked and King's house and four churches were bombed. King spent two weeks in jail, a place he would later visit often. "I was proud of my crime," King explained. "It was the crime of joining my people in a nonviolent protest against injustice" (King 1986, 149). By the time a federal court ordered an end to racial segregation on Montgomery's buses, King had become a leader in a nonviolent movement that would inspire people across the world.

Coretta King greets her husband, Martin Luther King Jr., after a court appearance during the 1956 Montgomery, Alabama, bus boycott.

Both Gandhi and King's invitations to become peace workers came suddenly and unbidden, as such invitations commonly do. Gandhi and King accepted their opportunities warily, only later developing commitments to continue the work their unexpected circumstances had led them to.

Most people today live much as Gandhi and King once did—as ordinary citizens, caught up in unremarkable lives, not knowing if or when a summons to become a peace worker will arrive. However, most of us enjoy one great advantage over Gandhi and King. They had to rely mostly on trial and error, improvising strategies as they went along. Today, in large measure because of what Gandhi, King, and their many successors have taught us, most people have access to considerable knowledge about how best to mount nonviolent actions. Peace studies collects and adds to this knowledge, helping people promote peace within their relationships, families, groups, nations, and the world. Peace studies also helps people recognize that invitations for peace work can be found in nearly every situation, for those with eyes ready to see.

CHANGING ATTITUDES TOWARD VIOLENCE

Peace studies is part of an emerging global peace network, a historically unprecedented web of peace-promoting beliefs, institutions, and organizations. The network began with a handful of groups that opposed slavery in the later eighteenth and early nineteenth centuries, then grew erratically and slowly until blossoming after the end of World War II (Cortright 2008). Many elements of the contemporary global peace network are described in later chapters but one key element, a change in attitudes toward war, deserves emphasis here. In many places public approval and support for war and other forms of violence is decreasing. The changed attitudes toward war of modern Europeans and North Americans illustrates this transformation.

For centuries, Europe suffered through frequent, horrific wars that aroused little public opposition. European men were regularly conscripted to fight and die on behalf of kings and aristocrats in conflicts that generally won wealth only for the already prosperous few. Peasants and workers—the majority of the population—had few rights and were often beaten, driven from their ancestral lands, forced into exile, and imprisoned at the whim of their propertied and entitled "betters." Governments staged public executions for minor offenses. Women and girls were considered the property of their fathers, older brothers, and husbands. European nations also invaded and colonized peoples across the world, often assisted by brutal massacres and genocides. Slavery was legal, profitable, and widely thought to reflect the immutable will of God.

Violence was similarly commonplace during the same centuries in Europe's North American settler colonies. In the United States, for example, but one hundred and fifty years ago, excited spectators assembled on hillsides near Centerville, Virginia, to watch an early battle between Union and Confederate soldiers. People cheered at the sound of gun and cannon fire much as fans do today while watching sporting events. One observer reported, "A lady with an opera glass who was near me was quite beside herself when an unusually heavy discharge roused the current of her blood. 'That is splendid. Oh my! Is it not first rate?'" (quoted in Burgess 2011). By this war's end, however, such public celebrations had stopped and legal slavery in the United States was at an end.

Attitudes toward war and violence in Europe and North America steadily evolved across the following decades until, in the twenty-first century, a majority of people in these and many other regions prefer that conflicts be settled through negotiation rather than through violence. In the first few months of 2003, for example, an estimated 36 million people took part in almost three thousand protests across the globe against the impending Anglo-American invasion of Iraq. Three million gathered in a single demonstration in Rome, another million in both London and Madrid. These were the largest transnational outpourings of antiwar sentiment the world had ever seen.

The demonstrations did not stop the Iraq war. And frequent wars and glorifications of violence continue, in the media, in speeches by politicians, and in private conversations. Nonetheless, the length of time that governments can keep their citizens enthusiastic about fighting a "good war" seems generally to be getting shorter. Dying young in battle or in any way may appear more tragic now than it did a few centuries ago when life expectancies were much shorter. Like famines and pandemics, wars in the first decades of the twenty-first century are as often met with calls for better preventive measures as with the unquestioning enthusiasm or stoic acceptance that they once more commonly aroused.

Attitudes toward many other types of violence have also dramatically changed. Dueling was for centuries considered not just an acceptable but a preferred and honorable way to settle personal disputes. Vice President of the United States Aaron Burr killed one of the country's founders, Alexander Hamilton, in a duel in 1804, just one of the more famous of many thousands of dueling fatalities. However, as psychologist Steven Pinker points out, today the expression "Take ten paces, turn, and fire" is associated more with comic books and cartoons than with "men of honor" (Pinker 2010, 23).

A similar shift seems to be underway in public attitudes toward the use of government-sanctioned violent punishments. Eighteenth-century English children and adults were executed for over two hundred different crimes, including pickpocketing and other minor thefts. Attitudes have now changed so much that England outlawed capital punishment entirely in 1998, as have fifty-seven other countries. Another thirty-five countries still have capital punishment in their statutes but are enacting de facto moratoriums, having executed no one in over ten years. The growing opposition to gender-based violence illustrates yet another example of a decreasing tolerance for a type of cruelty that was long thought inevitable. (See Case 1-1, "Declining Public Violence.")

Changing attitudes toward war and violence helped create the global peace network described in Chapter 3. The steady growth of this network has, in turn, further strengthened public confidence in many places that it may be possible to resolve most, maybe even all, conflicts without killing.

CASE 1-1   DECLINING PUBLIC VIOLENCE

Psychologist Steven Pinker presents many examples of the callous attitudes most people in earlier centuries had toward violence in his widely-read study, *The Better Angels of Our Nature: How Violence Has Declined* (2010). For example, the famous English diarist Samuel Pepys wrote casually of visiting a public execution on October 13, 1660:

> To my Lord's in the morning, where I met with Captain Cuttance, but my Lord not being up I went out to Charing Cross, to see Major-General Harrison hanged, drawn, and quartered; which was done there, he looking as cheerful as any man could do in that condition. He was presently cut down, and his head and heart shown to the people, at which there was great shouts of joy.

Pepys continues with recollections of the rest of his ordinary day, describing his dinner with friends and further traversing his city. Watching a man be "drawn and quartered," that is, disemboweled, castrated, and made to look at his own internal organs as he died, earns but a brief reference in Pepys' reporting on his day.

Little had changed a century later. Pinker quotes this first-hand account of a public pillorying of two men in England:

> One of them being of short stature could not reach the hole made for the admission of the head. The officers of justice nevertheless forced his head through the hole and the poor wretch hung rather than stood. He soon grew black in the face and the blood issued from his nostrils, his eyes and his ears. The mob nevertheless attacked him with great fury. The officers opened the pillory and the poor wretch fell down dead on the stand of the instrument. (Quoted in Pinker 2010, 145)

Public torture and executions have become increasingly less common not only in England but across most of the rest of the world over the last few hundred years.

Though now rare, public floggings and similar public humiliations were once common throughout Europe and much of North America.

DIGITAL INVITATIONS TO PEACE

Sudden, unexpected invitations to become a peace worker continue to arrive for people today much as they did for Gandhi and King decades ago. (See Case 1-2, "An Invitation to Bid.") Because communication technologies have changed, however, these invitations now often appear through electronic media. Wael Ghonim's cyber work during the Arab Awakening illustrates how new media are altering some of the way that peace work is done.

Wael Ghonim was a thirty-year-old Egyptian living in Qatar in June 2010 when he saw a picture on Facebook of the battered body of Khaled Mohamed Said, killed by Egyptian police in Alexandria on June 6. The image of Said so moved Ghonim that he created a new Facebook page named "Kullena Khaled Said" (We Are All Khaled Said). Ghonim's first post said, "Today they killed Khaled. If I don't act for his sake, tomorrow they will kill me" (Ghonim 2012, 60). Within an hour, the page had three hundred members; in twenty-four hours, it had 36,000.

Ghonim had built previous web and Facebook pages for commercial and religious purposes. He used those skills to draw traffic to the Said page, emphasizing images more than words and writing primarily in the first person, "as though Khaled Said was speaking from his grave" (Ghonim 2012, 61). By September, the Said Facebook page had 250,000 members and visitors were being encouraged to try to think of ways to move their virtual commitments to honor Said's sacrifice out into the physical world.

Toward the end of 2010, Ghonim joined with other groups to use the Said page to urge participation in a mass demonstrations scheduled for January 25, 2011, Egypt's National Police Day. Then, in mid-December, the Internet exploded with images of Mohamed Bouazizi setting himself on fire in Tunisia and, subsequently, with reports of Tunisians taking to the streets to protest the conditions that had driven Bouazizi to despair. The size of the demonstrations in Tunisia swelled almost daily until Zine El Abidine Ben Ali, the country's dictator for twenty-four years, was forced into exile on January 14, less than a month after Bouazizi set himself on fire and but eleven days before the scheduled Egyptian National Police Day demonstrations.

The hope that a similar nonviolent revolution could transform Egypt pushed membership on the Said Facebook page to 365,000 by mid-January. Ghonim's instructions on how to act respectfully and nonviolently at this demonstration were downloaded from Google docs 50,000 times. Ghonim was simultaneously offering directions and comments to four thousand Twitter followers. During this build-up, until just two days before the January 25 demonstration, Ghonim remained with his wife and children in Qatar. Few knew his real identity; fewer still that he was participating in the Egyptian uprising remotely, from computers one thousand miles away.

Ghonim returned to Egypt on January 23 but nothing was heard from him on the Said Facebook page or Twitter from January 27 until February 7. Later the world learned that Ghonim had been secretly imprisoned by Egyptian State Security personnel. He was kept blindfolded in a dungeon for ten days and interrogated repeatedly as demonstrations across Egypt grew large enough to break Hosni Mubarak's thirty-year grip on power.

By the time Ghonim was released, the Said Facebook page had 640,000 users and Ghonim had 30,000 Twitter followers. These numbers hardly mattered anymore, however, because as Ghonim writes in his memoir, *Revolution 2.0*, "The momentum had been transferred from the virtual world to the real world, and the virtual world would from now on serve, at best, as a commentator, with limited influence" (2012, 268).

There were hundreds of other influential promoters of the Egyptian uprising. Still, Ghonim's example illustrates how cyberspace can offer people momentous invitations for peace work, even if they are far away from the actual place where oppression is taking place. As Ghonim remarks, a computer keyboard can sometimes work as effectively as "a machine gun, firing bullets with every keystroke" (2012, 285). Ghonin need not have ever moved from the virtual to the physical world—from Qatar to Egypt—to have had the impact he did.

CASE 1-2 AN INVITATION TO BID

Tim DeChristopher was a twenty-seven-year-old senior majoring in economics at the University of Utah in 2008 when he received an unexpected invitation to become an influential environmental activist.

DeChristopher learned that the United States Bureau of Land Management was auctioning oil and gas leases on 116 parcels of Utah public land in wilderness areas surrounding Arches and Canyonlands National Parks. DeChristopher was familiar with the area from his own recreational hiking and from previous work as a wilderness guide for troubled and at-risk youth. He believed the area should be preserved and that the Bureau of Land Management had failed to complete an unbiased environmental assessment as required by law. DeChristopher attended the auction unsure if there was anything he could do. He imagined he might find the courage to make a speech and temporarily disrupt the proceedings. However, outside the room the person managing the sign-in desk asked, "Are you here to bid?" Without quite understanding the consequences, DeChristopher answered that he was. He was handed auction paddle "70" and proceeded inside to win bids on fourteen parcels of land totaling 22,500 acres at a combined lease cost of $1.8 million. Of course, DeChristopher had no plan to actually drill the parcels and had no funds to pay even a small portion of the cost of the leases he had won.

DeChristopher's ruse was discovered and he was taken into custody by federal agents and later indicted and charged with two felony counts: one for violating the Federal Onshore Oil and Gas Leasing Reform Act by "scheming to disrupt the auction," and a second for making false statements. By the time of his trial two years later, DeChristopher had become well known throughout the North American environmental movement. During the trial, DeChristopher argued that his unfunded bids were necessary because the government had failed to obey its own laws and procedures that, if followed, would have kept the Utah lands from being leased for drilling. In early 2009, a federal judge and the United States Interior Secretary Ken Salazar offered similar opinions that the Bureau of Land Management had recklessly rushed to lease these Utah public lands without due diligence. Most of the leases granted when DeChristopher had offered his own bids were nullified, accomplishing what DeChristopher had wished.

However, the Interior Secretary's opinion did not help DeChristopher. He was convicted and served a total of twenty-one months in federal prison, from July 2011 through April 2013. During the trial, DeChristopher declared his hope that his actions would help many others "understand that we are on a path toward catastrophic consequences of climate change. They know their future, and the future of their loved ones, is on the line. And they know we are running out of time to turn things around."

DeChristopher is often referred to as "Bidder 70" as this was the number on his bidder card during the lease auction. Bidder 70 is also the name of the official DeChristopher news and support website, Bidder70.org, and is now as well the title of a documentary depicting DeChristopher's actions and his influence on the contemporary climate justice movement.

DeChristopher had earned his BA in economics before the trial. In the fall of 2013 he began studies at the Harvard School of Divinity.

Source: Goodell 2010.

Of course, digital peace work will never replace physical action. Nonetheless, new media make it possible for citizens to organize and participate in peaceful campaigns without leaving their homes, offices, or coffeehouses. Ghonim points out that these new social media are not just one way but in many circumstances in fact the very best way to "to organize, act, and promote ideas and awareness" (Ghonim, 2012, 51). During the Arab Awakening, eye-catching images helped inspire tens of thousands to overthrow long established violent regimes that seemed unassailable in the pre-Internet era. Without Facebook, Twitter, and mobile phones, Tunisia's Ben Ali and Egypt's Hosni Mubarak would likely have remained in power.

LEVELS OF PEACE RESEARCH AND WORK

Though they come in many forms, invitations to undertake peace work tend to involve one of three different types of activities, often associated with what are known as the macro, meso, and micro levels.

Peace work at the **macro level** focuses on conflict and violence associated with nation-state relations and global systems. This is the broadest unit of analysis used in the social sciences. Macro analysis dominated peace studies during its first decades in the middle of the twentieth century when the field focused primarily on international relations and interstate wars.

The **meso level** of peace work and research emphasizes intrastate conflict, particularly violence within nations and between groups and ethnic regions. Focus on the meso level swelled in the 1980s and then grew even greater after the end of the Cold War as most of the world's new armed conflicts then rose out of ethnic and sectarian tensions. Peace work and research at the broader, macro level now shares the field with activities highlighting conflicts at the group and sub-national level.

The **micro level** of peace studies emphasizes individual and interpersonal conflicts. This is the sphere of personal peace and intimate, familial, and acquaintance relationships. Micro level violence received scant attention among peace researchers and workers until

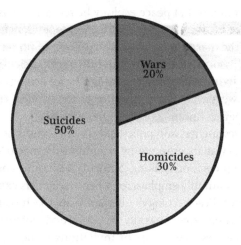

FIGURE 1.1   Causes of Direct Violence Global Deaths.

recently even though about 80 percent of all fatal non-accidental violence occurs at this level. Research by the World Health Organization (2010) indicates that in most years interstate (macro) and intrastate (meso) wars and insurrections generate about 20 percent of all global deaths by direct violence. Interpersonal homicides account for more, about 30 percent of the annual total deaths. Suicide, another micro level phenomenon, is consistently the largest single cause, producing about 50 percent of all non-accidental violent deaths each year. See Figure 1.1, "Causes of Direct Violence Global Deaths" for a summary of these causes.

Peace studies' earlier overemphasis on the macro and meso levels was abetted by a simultaneous overemphasis on male-based perspectives. Peace studies was thus mirroring similar biases found in history, philosophy, and the social sciences where violence and wars were also commonly supposed to be the business of men. Males annually perpetrate about 95 percent of the violence in the world and so many people assumed that men should also take the lead in seeking to understand peace and violence. For decades, women were severely underrepresented both among those doing peace research and among those implementing peace-promoting projects.

This systematic underrepresentation of women was especially unfortunate as women are disproportionately often the victims of male violence. In most recent wars women and children have been killed, wounded, and displaced from their homes at higher proportions than non-combatant men. Women are also the targets of intimate partner violence far more often than men. Including women in equal proportions as men in peace studies and throughout the global peace network is beneficial not only because it ensures gender equity but also because women are often more effective peace promoters than men. It may be as Elise Boulding (2000, 109), one of peace studies' most important pioneers, explains, that "women's knowledge and experience worlds have equipped them to function creatively as problem solvers and peacemakers in ways that men have not been equipped."

PEACE ECOLOGY

Some researchers recommend that peace ecology be recognized as a fourth level of analysis (Amster 2009). **Peace ecology** focuses on the interdependencies that connect the separate elements found at the macro, meso, and micro levels of human activity. Peace ecology is holistic and closely associated with the environmental sciences; both emphasize the mutual constitution of living and nonliving things. Peace ecology differs from most environmental sciences, however, by foregrounding peace studies' traditional emphases on nonviolence and on creating human communities at peace.

Most contemporary researchers and policymakers still focus mostly on one level at a time. They look for the causes of war, for example, by examining the macro level of nation-states or by studying meso-level group decision-making. Similarly, economic conditions or, alternatively, psychological states are commonly emphasized when researchers explain rates of homicide or intimate personal violence. Peace ecology's alternative approach seeks instead to understand war and violence through analyzing networks of cultural and biological relationships.

Peace ecology encourages new forms of invitations to peace work mostly unknown even a generation ago. Just how people can best manifest this ambitious, holistic perspective is still far from decided. Nonetheless, many of the problems facing humans today do seem to require ecological thinking that goes beyond the single focus on either the interpersonal, group, regional, or nation-state levels common to most other approaches to peace. Such contemporary problems as rising temperatures, resource scarcities, mass extinctions, pandemics, human trafficking, international crime and terrorism, and weapons proliferation may require a broader, ecological approach.

THE PLAN OF THE BOOK

Most people regularly contribute to keeping the peace in their families and communities and among their friends. *Invitation to Peace Studies* aims to help readers become more aware of their common everyday peace work while also encouraging everyone to seek further peace building opportunities, as a career or as a volunteer.

The book is divided into three parts intended to be read in sequence but sufficiently independent to be explored in other ways. Part One contains four chapters describing fundamental ideas and controversies associated with peace studies. It also reviews the origins and key elements that make up the global peace network, explores some major trends in contemporary violence, war, and terrorism, and details the crucial role that women play in making the world more peaceful.

Part Two examines the changing nature of contemporary interstate and intrastate wars and explains why collective violence so often fails. Chapters in this section also describe the origins and increasing power and sophistication of nonviolent movements as well as the role of religion in promoting both war and peace. Part Three presents key findings about peace, violence, and war associated with three different research disciplines, biology, psychology, and sociology. These chapters review evidence drawn from the micro, meso, macro, and ecological levels of peace research that suggest diverse strategies for decreasing violence. A final chapter offers a guide to help readers boost their personal levels of inner and outer peace.

FOR REVIEW

1. How does peace studies define "peace"?
2. What unexpected events transformed Gandhi and King into peace activists?
3. Describe some of the chief differences between predigital nonviolent campaigns like those led by Gandhi and King and later digital campaigns like that Ghonim helped lead.
4. Contrast the types of discoveries about peace, violence, and war likely to emerge from research at the macro, meso, and micro levels of analysis.
5. Explain why a peace ecology perspective may be increasingly needed to solve contemporary problems.

THINKING CRITICALLY

1. Building on the discussion in this chapter, how would you personally define "peace"?
2. Is it correct to describe Gandhi and King as ordinary men who were unexpectedly thrust into extraordinary circumstances?
3. What were probably the most important causes of the shift in public attitudes toward war and violence that occurred over the last few hundred years?

4. Is Ghonim accurate in his claim that new technologies and social media can transform societies as effectively as violent weapons?

5. What changes might cause a contemporary society to honor its peacemakers as often and as widely as its military heroes?

6. Which level of analysis—the macro, meso, or micro—seems most likely to produce significant findings about the causes of peace and violence? Does one of the levels seem significantly less promising for researchers than the other two?

7. What are the main problems people face in trying to develop a peace ecology perspective?

RECOMMENDED RESOURCES

Adolf, Antony. *Peace: A World History* (Malden, MA: Polity, 2009). Explores in a single volume the full spectrum of peace and peacemaking from prehistoric to contemporary times. Includes descriptions of key periods, events, people, ideas, and texts.

Ghonim, Wael. *Revolution 2.0, The Power of the People is Greater than the People in Power* (Boston: Houghton Mifflin Harcourt, 2012). A riveting memoir by one of the digital leaders of the Egyptian uprising of 2011. Ghonim describes how he and others used social media to draw millions of Egyptians first to an online and later to a physical campaign for regime change. See also Ghonim's TED Talk video lecture, "Inside the Egyptian Revolution," at http://www.ted.com/talks/wael_ghonim_inside_the_egyptian_revolution.htm

Horgan, John. *The End of War* (San Francisco: McSweeney's Books, 2012). Offers a wide-ranging but compact review of the growing body of research that treats violence as a solvable scientific problem.

McCarthy, Colman. "The Class of Nonviolence." Materials for an eight-session class based on classics in the peace and justice literature. Available at http://salsa.net/peace/conv/index.html

Nagler, Michael. PACS 164A. "Introduction to Nonviolence." This online course provides an excellent introduction to peace studies through a series of lectures first presented at the University of California, Berkeley in 2006. Free course reading materials and video lectures are provided. Available at the Metta Center for Nonviolence at http://mettacenter.org/research-education/pacs164

Stearns, Peter N. 2014. *Peace in World History* (New York: Routledge). Examines peace and war making across human history to explain why peace building sometimes fails and sometimes succeeds. Stearns offers suggestions for how best to build a stable peace in the twenty-first century.

Three Short Films about Peace. Directed by Erroll Morris. 2014. Documentaries produced by the New York Times and offered on its website that profile (1) the Liberian peace activist and Nobel Peace Prize winner Leymah Gbowee, (2) the former Polish president and Nobel laureate Lech Walesa, and (3) Irish musician and activist Bob Geldof.

United States Institute of Peace Global Peacebuilding Center. This rich website provides resources for both students and teachers in the areas of global conflict, building peace, teaching peace, and training for peace. The United States Institute of Peace is funded by the United States Congress but in most matters operates as an independent agency. Available at: http://www.buildingpeace.org

1

THE GLOBAL
PEACE NETWORK

The four chapters in Part One introduce the major ideas, controversies, and trends associated with peace studies. Chapter 2 examines the fundamental concepts and explores disagreements about the meaning of peace and how it can best be created and sustained. Chapter 3 describes the emerging global peace network, a historically unprecedented web of norms, institutions, and organizations helping to transform the modern world. Chapter 4 analyzes recent trends in violence, terrorism, and war. Chapter 5 focuses on the important role that women play in strengthening and expanding conditions that foster peace.

CHAPTER 2

PEACE CONCEPTS, DISPUTES, AND CONFUSIONS

CHAPTER OVERVIEW

This chapter introduces many of the concepts used in peace studies. It explains the differences between direct and indirect violence and between negative and positive peace. Structural and cultural violence, two types of indirect violence, are also described. Tensions over whether it is best to emphasize negative or positive peace are explored, as well as policies associated with the doctrine of peace through strength and with just war doctrine. The chapter concludes with an examination of the benefits and hazards of emphasizing personal peace.

Key terms discussed include: direct violence; negative peace; indirect violence; structural violence; cultural violence; positive peace; peace through strength; peace through peace; just war doctrine; and personal peace.

> Every time we use violence to solve a problem we send
> the signal that violence is the way to solve problems.
>
> —MICHAEL NAGLER (2004, 92)

Peace promotion and research is frequently complicated by disagreements over several basic ideas. There is often even debate over the very meaning of "peace." One founder of peace studies, Kenneth Boulding, once suggested, "Peace is a word of so many meanings that one hesitates to use it for fear of being misunderstood" (Boulding 1977, 3). Consider, for example, that people in war zones associate peace with ceasefires and a cessation of violent hostilities. On the other hand, non-combatants often associate peace with personal feelings of well-being; yet others think of peace as an ending to family arguments, or as ensuring social justice, or as the embrace of some specific religion. Peace means all of these as well as many other ideas.

Finding a common definition for violence causes similar problems. And, in peace studies, peace and violence are interconnected ideas. They are bound together like day and night, like light and shadow. This chapter begins with a discussion of violence, the shadow, before following Michael Nagler's advice to look to the light, to peace, to understand what makes violence dark (2004, 47).

DIRECT VIOLENCE AND NEGATIVE PEACE

Much thinking in peace studies draws upon a distinction between direct and indirect violence, and between the related concepts of negative and positive peace. Each of these four ideas is discussed at length below.

Direct violence refers to overt, human-initiated physical harm. Direct violence is the violence of rapes, assaults, gang fights, armed insurrections, police states, and wars. Direct violence occurs at the macro level when states or insurgent armies commit collective violence. At the meso level, direct violence manifests as ethnic, sectarian, and large-scale gang violence. Meso level direct violence also includes violent attacks and imprisonments undertaken by military, police, and security forces on behalf of nation-states. Direct violence at the micro level is associated with interpersonal, familial, and intimate partner assaults and murders, including injuries perpetrated by both acquaintances and strangers. Direct violence also occurs at the intrapersonal level through acts of self-harm and suicide. (See Table 2.1, "Types of Direct Violence.")

The absence of direct violence is known as **negative peace**, a condition that Mohandas Gandhi (2006, 132) once described as "armed peace." Martin Luther King Jr. used the phrase negative peace in his "Letter from Birmingham Jail" then elaborated on the idea in his 1964 Nobel Peace Prize lecture. King declared, "We will not build a peaceful world by following a negative path. It is not enough to say 'We must not wage war.' It is necessary to love peace and sacrifice for it. We must concentrate not merely on the negative expulsion of war, but on the positive affirmation of peace."

TABLE 2.1   TYPES OF DIRECT VIOLENCE

Type	Description	Examples	Features
Macro level collective violence	Large formal and informal groups physically harm other large groups and individuals	Wars, revolutions, insurrections, rebellions	A frequent topic of Western history, epics, and patriotic celebrations
Meso level collective violence	Mid-sized groups physically harm other mid-sized groups and individuals	Ethnic, sectarian, and gang violence; small-scale police and military actions	The most common type of new collective violence since the end of the Cold War
Micro level interpersonal violence	Individuals or small groups physically harm others	Fights, murders, intimate partner violence, rapes	Often exaggerated and sensationalized in fiction, films, and news media
Micro level intrapersonal violence	Individuals physically injure themselves	Substance abuse, bulimia, self-mutilation, suicide	Victims are sometimes also victims of other forms of violence

Negative peace can be achieved through ceasefires and treaties, as well as by putting violent people into restraints, prisons, or some other forms of social isolation (Galtung 1969; 1985). The Cold War is an example of an international condition of negative peace that went on for decades. Hiding someone's intimate partner from a would-be abuser is negative peace manifesting at the micro, interpersonal level.

Periods of negative peace have become increasingly common over the last fifty years and, some researchers claim, even over the last five hundred years. In aggregate, both the number of wars and the number of war casualties seems to be decreasing. In addition, Manuel Eisner (2003) estimates that across Europe from the fifteenth to the twentieth century direct interpersonal violence became at least ten times and perhaps as much as fifty times less frequent. In the decade of the 1990s alone serious assaults and murders declined by about 40 percent across most regions of North America (Zimring 2007).

Chapter 4 provides more scrutiny of the evidence for these and other positive trends in the reduction of direct violence. It is important to note immediately, however, that not all contemporary developments are positive. According to the World Health Organization (2011), the global suicide rate may be increasing, and almost certainly is not decreasing, even as war, group, and interpersonal casualty rates fall in many regions. Also, though new intrastate wars remain rare, several old, once-quiescent intrastate violent conflicts flared back up in the first decade of the new century (Hewitt 2011). These recurrences included

Demonstrations like this one in Egypt in 2011 often include demands for an end both to direct and to indirect violence.

wars in Azerbaijan, Central African Republic, Chad, Sri Lanka, and Myanmar. In addition, over the last ten years global spending on war personnel and weapons has increased almost 50 percent. The public availability of small arms, weapons that can be carried and operated by a single person, has also surged. The Small Arms Survey (2012) estimates that more than 875 million small arms are now in circulation, with millions more being manufactured and distributed every year in what is approximately a $6 billion annual business.

These worrisome trends caution against unbridled optimism. It is important to remember as well that the hopeful trends producing decreasing rates of new war outbreaks, war casualties, assaults, and murders are based on aggregate statistics. Clearly not all groups, regions, and countries are experiencing increasing levels of negative peace. And the future could produce reversals in even the longest and strongest positive trends. Nonetheless, in determining how peace workers and citizens can best forge a desirable future it is essential to begin with an accurate picture of current trends in direct human violence. And, as later chapters show, there is strong evidence to support the view that most types of direct human violence are decreasing. As political scientist Joshua S. Goldstein summarizes the evidence in *Winning the War on War: The Decline of Armed Conflict Worldwide*, "The world is going from worse to bad, from the fire to the frying pain. Good news—unless you are freaked out by the frying pan and so upset by the 'bad' coming at you constantly in the news that you cannot compare it with anything" (2012, x).

INDIRECT VIOLENCE

Direct acts of harm are absent in conditions of negative peace but many other forms of violence often continue. Peace studies uses the concept of **indirect violence** to refer to these less visible harms and, following a suggestion first made by Johan Galtung (1990), distinguishes between two types of indirect violence, structural and culture violence.

Structural violence, also sometimes called institutional violence, is indirect violence caused by inequitable customs, traditions, systems, and laws. Gandhi targeted these structural injustices, Galtung (1985) points out, to avoid blaming the individuals perpetrating them. Instances of structural violence include unequal childhood mortality and malnutrition rates, hunger in societies with plenty, mass incarceration, slavery, segregation, and any other systematic discrimination based on age, gender, group membership, ethnicity, income, religion, or race. Structural violence can be perpetrated by norms and laws that apply equally to the rich and the poor but that adversely impact the poor. Rules that create school or college fees for everyone, for example, systematically make education less available to the poor. Voting laws that require payment of a tax, proof of the ownership of property, or specific types of government-issued picture identification cards make it difficult for less affluent groups to vote. Similarly, laws that make it illegal to sleep in a public place, or remove food from dumpsters, or sell goods without a license, lead to many arrests of the poor but few of the rich.

People in inferior social positions often experience indirect, structural violence even when they are not subjected to direct violence. For example, a person who has been born a slave may be well fed and even loved by her owners. Still slaves suffer indirect violence in not being free. A woman married to a man who will not allow her to speak, or travel, or to own property, or to work as she wishes is a victim of structural violence. Poor people who cannot afford or are provided with inferior schools are often compelled to take dangerous and low-paying jobs that satisfy the needs of those with more wealth. Any group systematically denied equal access to basic human needs, for example, to food, education, clean air and water, or health care, suffers from indirect, structural violence.

Galtung (1990) compares structural violence to a virus. No symptoms may be visible even as the virus, structural violence, severely damages the patient, society. Advanced stages of both diseases and structural violence can produce great harm, even death, although no overt symptoms of direct violence or illness were earlier observed. In aggregate, structural violence produces many more fatalities than direct violence. Nonetheless, direct violence monopolizes mass media accounts of violence in part because structural violence usually creates its damage more slowly. Structural violence is not as dramatic or visually compelling as violence associated with assaults, murders, insurrections, and wars.

Cultural violence, the second type of indirect violence, is caused by aspects of culture that justify direct and structural violence (Galtung 1990). Any ethnic, ideological, political, or religious belief that excuses or normalizes structural inequalities supports cultural violence. For example, beliefs about the supposed inferior intelligence of Africans and women helped maintain slavery and misogyny for many centuries. Stereotypes of minorities or of the poor as lazy or immoral support rules and laws that make structural violence seem just.

Cultural violence is symbolic and works even more indirectly than structural violence. Cultural violence is maintained through stories told by families, friends, written histories, literature, the media, religions, and schools, in short by any means of transmitting a culture's attitudes and beliefs. Though much less publicized than direct and even structural violence, cultural violence may be the most basic of all three violence types. It is the foundation upon which justifications for direct and structural violence are built.

Because the effects of both structural and cultural violence are often unobservable, rates of both these types of indirect violence are much more difficult to track than rates of direct violence. Sometimes indirect violence's effects do not manifest for months or even years. Still, it is clear that many parts of the world have seen reductions in several forms of indirect violence over the last few hundred years. Rates of slavery, malnutrition, hunger, and discrimination according to gender and sexual orientation, for example, have fallen from earlier proportions across much of the industrialized world. However, many nonindustrialized regions have seen little progress and some even increases in structural and cultural violence. And, in the industrialized world, rates of structural violence built on income inequalities have been increasing for the last thirty years (Judt 2011).

Both armed and unarmed popular movements seek to oppose indirect violence as often as they oppose direct violence. For example, although the British perpetrated much direct violence in India, the main focus of Gandhi's campaigns was on the colonial culture of inequality, the indirect, structural violence that had transformed Indians into second-class citizens in their own country. Similarly, though direct violence such as assaults, rapes, lynching, and imprisonment were common in the American South in the 1950s and 1960s,

TABLE 2.2   TYPES OF INDIRECT VIOLENCE

Type	Description	Examples	Features
Structural violence	Systematic, unequal distribution of resources leading to harm to people without access to the goods and services enjoyed by others; issues of justice and human rights	In-country differential rates of child and maternal mortality, malnutrition, slavery, segregation, apartheid, lack of civil and women's rights, employment discrimination	Slow, often unnoticed processes of structural violence are difficult to personalize and sensationalize
Cultural violence	Words, symbols, stories and media that legitimize and encourage both direct and indirect violence; issues of fair representations and stereotyping	Race theories, dehumanized "enemies," media representations of unbelievers, and of black and Muslim men	Many cultural stories depict violence as inevitable, natural, and necessary

the primary aim of the Civil Rights movement was to end the structural and cultural violence that kept black Americans from equal educational, economic, and political opportunities. Most recent nonviolent movements such as those associated with the Philippines' People Power campaign, Europe's various color revolutions, and the Arab Awakening of 2011 also aimed at securing equality of opportunities—ending indirect violence—as much and sometimes even more than they aimed at stopping state-supported direct violence.

POSITIVE PEACE

Negative peace, described above, aims to end or decrease direct violence. This is what Nagler (2004) describes as the dark or shadow side of peace studies. As Robin J. Crews (2002, 73–74) points out, studying negative peace is what "peace studies and peace research has been engaged in, to a fairly significant extent, for the past half-century." These studies of negative peace should correctly be called violence studies, Crews argues, not peace studies. Peace studies properly understood focuses less on darkness than on light, on right relationships and harmonious associations, the definition of peace introduced in Chapter 1.

Right relationships and harmonious associations are sometimes called structural but more often **positive peace**, yet another concept pioneered by Johan Galtung (1964; 1969). Galtung reasoned that for most people peace means more than the mere absence or significant reduction of direct and indirect violence. Positive peace names this more ambitious condition where people flourish while living in equitable, nonviolent communities. People cooperate for mutual benefit without being coerced by threats of violence or war. The inequalities associated with structural and cultural violence are rare. Albert Einstein was referring to the condition of positive peace when he said, "Peace is not merely the absence of war but the presence of justice, of law, of order . . ." (1968, 371). This is the peace defined by the Earth Charter as "right relationships and harmonious associations."

Galtung (1985) compares negative peace and positive peace to the health sciences' concepts of cure and prevention. Negative peace works to cure already present direct violence while positive peace prevents further occurrences of violence. Negative peace stops an ongoing harm, much as an effective medicine cures a disease. Positive peace, on the other hand, creates healthy social conditions that will prevent future onsets of violence. (See Table 2.3, "Negative and Positive Peace.")

It may be necessary to establish negative peace, for example, to stop a war or end inequitable social practices, before working to create the broader conditions necessary to

TABLE 2.3   NEGATIVE AND POSITIVE PEACE

Type	Description	Examples	Features
Negative peace	Absence of direct physical violence; peace through coercive means	The Cold War, ceasefires, treaties, balance of power and mutually assured destruction strategies	Can be achieved by police states and military victories, and through compulsion and totalitarianism
Positive peace (also known as structural peace)	Right relationships and harmonious associations; absence of institutional and cultural violence; peace through peaceful means	Communities and groups with an equal distribution of power and resources; social justice	Achieved through unforced cooperation, through free pursuit of mutual and equal benefit

The World Health Organization estimate of 4000 violent deaths a day does not include deaths from indirect violence.

build positive peace. Still, it is clear, stopping some ongoing direct violence does not by itself guarantee future prevention. Negative peace does not automatically lead to positive peace, any more than treating the symptoms of one disease leads to lasting health. Positive peace must be pursued separately. This perspective is often associated with a slogan attributed to Pope Paul VI, as well as to Gandhi and others. "If you want peace, work for justice," the saying goes. The best path to peace in this formulation depends upon creating strong communities with little or no structural and cultural violence.

Peace ecologists and many environmentalists insist that positive peace must also include harmonious relationships between humans and the natural world. They assert that peaceful human societies must be built on sustainable economic systems that leave the Earth habitable for future generations. In this view, working for peace requires working for justice for ecosystems as well for people.

TENSIONS BETWEEN NEGATIVE AND POSITIVE PEACE

People sometimes disagree about whether negative or positive peace should be the primary focus for peace researchers and workers. As David Cortright (2008) shows in *Peace: A History of Movements and Ideas*, this difference in emphasis had already emerged among peace promoters early in the nineteenth century. Some then and now have focused primarily on ending violence, on negative peace, while hoping to leave their societies otherwise unchanged. Others seek to create positive peace by transforming social structures, sometimes radically, sometimes even while condoning the temporary use of violence. The former position counseling an emphasis on negative peace was represented early in twentieth-century America by powerful industrialists such as Andrew Carnegie and Henry Ford, both of whom funded efforts to end war while explicitly denying that the United States and other industrial nations needed any fundamental cultural, economic, or social changes. The Carnegie Endowment for International Peace, founded in 1910, continues its founder's advocacy for negative peace and is ranked as one of the most influential foreign-policy think tanks in the world (McGann 2012). The contemporary Ford Foundation, with a current endowment of over $10 billion, pursues similar goals.

An alternative position emphasizing the need for radical changes to create positive peace was also embraced by many in the first half of the twentieth century. Three women in the United States with very different ideas illustrate the range of perspectives that sometimes still provoke tensions among peace workers today. Jane Addams, the first American woman to win the Nobel Peace Prize, promoted women's and children's rights. Addams helped create the settlement house movement and sought to build positive peace from below in the face of what Addams saw as indifference and hostility from elites governing from above. Dorothy Day, another early twentieth-century American peace promoter, was the co-founder (with Peter Maurin) of the Catholic Worker Movement, based in part on Day's belief that people should live in nonviolent, sharing communities of equals, as Christian communities often lived in the first few centuries after Jesus. Emma Goldman, a third proponent of positive peace, championed anarchism, atheism, and sexual freedom.

Goldman's peace promotion led to multiple imprisonments, the longest for two years for opposing the United States Selective Service Act requiring all males between twenty-one and thirty years of age to register in preparation for a military draft.

Despite the examples of Addams, Day, Goldman, and thousands of others, most peace promoters and researchers have tended to seek much more modest levels of social change. Kenneth Boulding (1977) offered one influential rationale for emphasizing the promotion of negative peace and for de-emphasizing the need for building positive peace. Boulding maintained that direct violence is too different from indirect violence for the two to be effectively joined together within the single research field of peace studies. Boulding pointed out that the causes that guide leaders to order troops to wars or that provoke criminals to attack their victims are very different from the indirect, structural causes that lead billions to live in poverty year after year. The types of bodily harms that result from direct and indirect violence are usually also very different. Those who directly harm others act for different reasons than those who make decisions in offices and meetings creating social policies that perpetuate structural inequalities.

Boulding concluded that peace researchers and workers should focus mostly on establishing negative peace. There are, Boulding maintained, daunting challenges enough for people in trying to stop direct violence without also trying to transform societies and end both structural and cultural violence. Seeking positive peace can sometimes encourage people to attempt so much that they accomplish very little. Societies will always include some indirect, structural violence, it might be argued, so a focus on positive peace is likely better left for utopian idealists than for peace workers undertaking practical actions.

Boulding is certainly correct that those who promote positive peace tend to have more expansive interests than do those who concentrate primarily on negative peace. Positive peace is often associated, for example, with individuals and groups committed to faith-based approaches built on sacred texts or to political prophecies of a substanially better world. Positive peace has also often been promoted by people who trace their intellectual origins back to nineteenth-century socialists and social theorists. The Brazilian Pablo Freire (e.g., 2007) is an example of a prominent twentieth-century thinker who has inspired many people to seek to create and promote ambitious visions of positive peace.

The divergences between those who emphasize negative or positive peace have so far proven more invigorating than debilitating for most peace promoters across the world. Each approach offers something valuable. People who stress negative peace focus on ending the horrific direct violence that causes so much death and suffering. People who emphasize positive peace and social justice help build societies where both direct and indirect violence will be increasingly rare. Decreasing indirect violence can weaken the causes of much direct violence. Simultaneously, building negative peace can help create the conditions necessary for the long, slow work of building positive peace. Pioneering peace educator Betty Reardon (1988, 12) has helped convince many that negative and positive peace are "complementary and inseparable." And this is how they are understood throughout this book.

PEACE THROUGH STRENGTH

As will be explained in Chapter 6, many nations include positive peace among their foreign policy goals, a strategy associated with the promotion of human security and the use of soft power. However, foreign policies that emphasis "hard power" still dominate among countries that aim to use their military and diplomats to create states of negative peace with other nations. The hard power strategy of peace through strength has long been and remains among the most common ways countries pursue their international goals.

Peace through strength is a strategy that seeks to create negative peace through preparing for and sometimes starting wars. The strategy of peace through strength leads nations to create militaries that they can use as negotiating or coercion tools to create ceasefires, détente, surrenders, and treaties. Ronald Reagan explained his rationale for following a foreign policy based on peace through strength in a speech to the nation in 1986. Reagan said:

> We know that peace is the condition under which mankind was meant to flourish. Yet peace does not exist of its own will. It depends on us, on our courage to build it and guard it and pass it on to future generations. George Washington's words may seem hard and cold today, but history has proven him right again and again. "To be prepared for war," he said, "is one of the most effective means of preserving peace." (Reagan 1986)

Seeking negative peace through preparing for and embarking on wars remains common even though in the contemporary world this strategy fails more often than it succeeds. Iran, Iraq, Israel, the Soviet Union, and the United States are well-known examples of countries that recently failed to achieve their goals even though they vigorously pursued strategies of peace through strength. The Iran-Iraq War lasted eight years and killed around half a million soldiers without altering borders or relations between the two countries. Israel possesses overwhelming military superiority over those several countries and groups it has been fighting off and on for half a century yet few of Israel's large and small wars have much increased the sense of peace felt by Israeli citizens. The Soviet Union and United States achieved little if any substantial gains in peacefulness for their citizens through their separate ten-year wars against Afghanistan. The United States' dominating use of military force in both Vietnam and Iraq similarly did not noticeably increase the United States' level of peace.

These and other examples presented in later chapters suggest that the strategy of peace through strength as often leads to increased violence as to negative peace. In fact, some historians calculate that well-armed states throughout the modern era have been significantly more likely than weaker states to participate in wars (e.g., Kennan 1987). It may be that the very activity of preparing for war more often produces war than peace. As retired U.S. Army colonel and political scientist Andrew Bacevich explains, the "belief in the efficacy of military power almost inevitably breeds the temptation to put that power to work. 'Peace through strength' easily enough becomes 'peace through war'" (Bacevich 2010).

Wars often spread in the manner of an infectious disease. Wars expand geographically, as neighboring countries and groups feel threatened and so prepare for and enter wars to protect themselves. Barbara Ehrenreich (1998) demonstrates that wars tend to extend across time as well as geography. Past battles create anger, memories, and bellicose habits that lead to yet later wars. World War I, for example, widely thought to have been launched for no substantial policy reasons, created conditions that led to World War II, an even more catastrophic war. World War II, in turn, helped spark the Cold War, the Korean War, the Vietnam War, the Soviet War in Afghanistan, and several other deadly so-called proxy wars in Africa, Asia, and Central and South America. Though World War I was touted at the time as the ultimate peace-through-strength war, as "the war to end all wars," it became instead a principal cause for subsequent wars that killed hundreds of millions.

The doctrine of peace through strength persists not because it often works but, in part, because it is strongly supported in many countries by influential constituencies committed to promoting their national militaries. Modern war and preparing for war provides employment for many who do not see the possibility of finding equivalent, alternative jobs. The doctrine of peace through strength also persists because most people want their country to be strong and "strength" for many is synonymous with physical force, coercion, and violence (Fellman 1998). Many believe that those who oppose their country's preparation for and sometimes use of lethal violence against people designated enemies are unpatriotic or, sometimes worse, are traitors to the nation-state. The Buddha, Jesus, Gandhi, King, Desmond Tutu, the Dalai Lama, and millions of others who have championed nonviolent over violent actions are considered to be poor guides for designing foreign policies. Acts of cooperation, negotiation, forgiveness, love, and reconciliation are commonly judged to be irrelevant or even an impediment to creating "a strong nation" by those who believe peace is best achieved through coercive and violent strength.

Peace studies promotes an alternative approach that can be summarized as a strategy of **peace through peace.** This strategy reflects the view that, as A. J. Muste said, "There is no way to peace; peace is the way" (cited in "Debasing Dissent" 1967). In both foreign and domestic conflicts, peaceful means tend to lead to peaceful ends, while violent means tend to produce violent ends. Studies of the modern era described in Chapters 4 and 6 demonstrate that diplomacy and negotiation create negative peace between nations more often than the use of armed attacks. Nations that seek to build peace through threatening and harming others tend to provoke threats and harms in return. On the other hand, like war, peace, too, tends to spread both territorially and temporally: Peace in one place tends to spread into adjoining places; peace in the present tends to generate more peace in the future.

Much peace studies research seeks to understand exactly how peace through peace works and to develop effective strategies that encourage more peace through peace. Chapters 5, 7, 8, and 11 describe many of the practical discoveries associated with this research. Also see Case 2-1, "Reconciliation: Peace Through Peace."

CASE 2-1   RECONCILIATION: PEACE THROUGH
PEACE

Nelson Mandela was imprisoned for twenty-seven years
then, after the end of racial oppression in South Africa in
1994, he was elected president. Mandela invited one of
his white jailers to be his honored guest at the inaugura-
tion, "the first of many gestures he would make in his
spectacular way, showing his breathtaking magnanimity
and willingness to forgive" (Tutu 1999, 10).

For many generations the white minority in South Africa
relied on violence to control black and Asian South Africans.
Once the black majority gained power through the first
open, democratic elections, it seemed at first as if there
were only two possible ways to deal with the country's violent past. One was to follow the model of the post–World
War II Nuremberg Trials and impose a "victor's justice" on
members of the earlier minority white government and its
various security forces. Those found guilty of human rights
abuses and other crimes would be punished. Alternatively,
a blanket amnesty could be offered that legally dismissed
all possible criminal charges committed by the white-minority
regime. South Africa instead chose a third way; it established a public Truth and Reconciliation Commission (TRC)
to collect testimony from both victims and perpetrators.

The TRC had the principle aim of hearing and recording details of the various human rights abuses that had
occurred during the period of minority white rule. It was
charged to expose "the awfulness, the abuse, the pain,
the degradation, the truth" (Tutu 1999, 270). The TRC
could also prescribe appropriate acts of reparation and
rehabilitation and had the further authority to grant amnesty to individuals in exchange for their full disclosure of
the crimes for which amnesty was being sought.

Desmond Tutu, the first black South African Anglican
Archbishop of Cape Town, acted as chair of the TRC. In
No Future without Forgiveness (1999), Tutu offers several
reasons why an emphasis on reconciliation rather than on
retribution best served South Africa's interests. Imposing
"victor's justice" on losers, Tutu explains, would likely
have created further resentment and continued the familiar cycles of reprisal and counterreprisals. Offering routes
to restorative justice instead helps people "move on to
forgiveness" (260), thus encouraging the trust necessary
for modern nations to prosper. This is the path of peace
through peace.

Tutu argues that denial of what had happened in
South Africa, or attempts to ignore or feign forgetful-
ness, would have made it harder for both victims and perpetrators to forge healthier lives. The TRC instead made
it possible for victims to publicly acknowledge their
losses and pain, a necessary step for psychological healing, even though in the short run this sometimes made
people feel much worse. The TRC simultaneously fos-
tered a wider social healing, decreasing violence and the
likelihood of a civil uprisings by creating ways for victims
and their families to address the injuries the apartheid
regime had inflicted.

The example of South Africa's TRC has helped fuel a
growing worldwide interest in what is commonly called
reparative or, more often, restorative justice. Retributive
justice, the most common alternative to restorative justice,
relies on violence or the threat of violence, for example,
on fines, physical coercion, imprisonment, and execution.
Restorative justice instead builds peace through peace.

Source: Tutu 1999.

JUST WAR DOCTRINE

Unlike the doctrine of peace through peace, the doctrine of peace through strength sometimes encourages the initiation and continuation of wars. The horror of these wars has
long been acknowledged and so people across many centuries have proposed schemes attempting to make the pursuit of peace through war less frequently barbaric. Some concern
over the ethics of war can be found among the ancient Greeks and Romans but, in the
Western tradition, a perspective first developed in the fourth century CE by Augustine,
Christian Bishop of Hippo, has been the most influential.

just war principles

jus ad bellum

principles of war

Meta Peace Team practices peace through peace by offering medical assistance to a wounded Ku Klux Klan demonstrator during a 1998 KKK rally in Ann Arbor, Michigan.

Augustine created what is now usually referred to as a **just war doctrine**, a set of principles that specifies two sets of the conditions, those under which it is ethical to begin a war and the ways, once begun, a just war should be fought (Guthrie and Quinlan 2007). Table 2.4, "Just War Principles," provides a summary of these principles. The ethical conditions for going to war are known in Latin as *jus ad bellum*. In modern formulations, these conditions include that war must be chosen only as a last resort after all reasonable nonviolent alternatives have been exhausted. *Jus ad bellum* also specifies that the decision to go to war must be made by the established leaders of the nation. A third principle states that a just war can only be fought to redress an injury already suffered. Wars to protect against an existing armed attack can thus be just; preemptive wars to prevent suspected future attacks are not just.

Another principle states that a just war must be winnable. Undertaking a war unlikely to be won is not permitted. A final *jus ad bellum* principle maintains that a just war must have a good chance of establishing postwar conditions that are better than those in place before the war.

TABLE 2.4   JUST WAR PRINCIPLES

Jus ad bellum principles	Last resort
	Decisions by legitimate leaders
	To redress injuries
	Winnable
	Improves prewar conditions
Jus in bello principles	Proportional violence used
	Discriminate between combatants and non-combatants

Source: Guthrie and Quinlan 2007.

A second set of principles guides how a just war should be fought. These principles, *jus in bello* in Latin, maintain that the level of violence used against an enemy should be proportional to the violence the enemy itself uses. In practice, this means that decisions must be made about how many enemies can justly be killed to save the life of one or a few of one's own combatants. Is killing two enemies for each of one's own soldiers' casualties proportionate? Is killing at a rate of ten to one so disproportionate that the war is no longer just?

These are not idle questions since, for example, the proportion of enemy to friendly casualties has varied greatly in recent wars initiated by the United States. In Vietnam, some estimates suggest the United States killed eighteen Vietnamese combatants for every American soldier killed (White *Source List* 2011). If civilian deaths are included in the calculation, the ratio is about one American fatality for every fifty-three Vietnamese killed. In Iraq, a war against a non-state insurgency with no traditional military organization, the ratio was about nine enemy combatants killed for every American soldier (Iraq Body Count 2013). In the first Gulf War, approximately sixty-four Iraqi soldiers died for every American (CNN 2001). If sixty-four to one is considered morally proportionate, perhaps one hundred to one or two hundred to one might also be, and the criteria of proportionality would seem to have become so flexible as to lose moral force. (See Table 2.5, "Estimated Deaths in Recent United States Wars.")

Discrimination, the second principle associated with *jus in bello*, maintains that noncombatants should not be directly targeted. It is acceptable to kill civilians during a just war, but their deaths should not be intentional. Like all just war principles, the prohibition against targeting civilians has often been ignored. In fact, in the final phase of World War II, many more civilians than combatants were intentionally killed by most national militaries participating in the conflict. The Germans systematically murdered millions in concentration camps while the United States and its allies targeted hundreds of thousands through the aerial bombing of such cities as Dresden, Hamburg, Tokyo, Osaka, Hiroshima, and Nagasaki.

The distinction between enemy combatants and non-combatants is difficult to maintain in modern wars when a civilian economy has been retooled to support military activities, as happened among the major participating nations in World War II. Avoiding civilian deaths has also become more difficult in recent times with the development of ever more powerful weapons. The just war doctrine of discrimination between combatants and non-combatants has little force among nations prepared to use nuclear weapons and other devices of mass destruction in their pursuit of peace through military strength.

TABLE 2.5   ESTIMATED DEATHS IN RECENT UNITED STATES WARS

War	U.S. Military Deaths (Allied Deaths)	Estimated Enemy Combatant Deaths	Estimated Non-Combatant Deaths
Vietnam	58,000 (200,000 to 250,000)	1.1 million	1.5 to 3.8 million
Gulf War	294 (200)	100,000	35,000
Iraq	4,500 (310)	40,000	120,000
Afghanistan	2,155 (1,080)	No reliable estimates	12,000 to 14,000

Sources: CNN 2001; Fisk 2006; Iraq Body Count 2013; Iraq Coalition Casualty Count 2013; Shenon 1995; Tirman 2012; and White *Source List* 2011.

Although just war principles are often ignored, the principles have helped reduce the barbarities of some wars. For example, just war principles helped inspire the creation of the Geneva Conventions on prisoners of war first adopted in 1929 and substantially updated in 1949. Prisoners of war are considered no longer to deserve the status of combatants and prisoner of war agreements establish rules that aim to keep captured ex-soldiers healthy until war's end. The just war tradition sometimes even influences contemporary militaries that are systematically and intentionally targeting non-combatants; most militaries now commonly try to deny such actions or at least attempt to keep the scope of civilian casualties secret. For example, the United States' recent use of thousands of lethal drone attacks in Afghanistan, Pakistan, Somalia, Syria, and Yemen has been accompanied by repeated official government claims that few civilians are being killed, claims generally contradicted by independent analysts (e.g., CNN Wire Staff 2012). The importance of just war principles in the contemporary world was also illustrated in 2003 when the United States' preemptive war in Iraq provoked strong objections across the world.

Despite their benefits, however, just war principles can sometimes provide decision-makers with moral-seeming justifications that make mass killing easier. People throughout the global peace network commonly promote alternatives to war—peace through peace—rather than principles for choosing and conducting supposedly just wars.

PERSONAL PEACE

Inner or personal peace is also a focus of peace studies, though not nearly as often as either negative or positive peace. **Personal peace** refers to individual feelings of mental or spiritual well-being. Personal peace is worthwhile in itself but some people believe that it is also a prerequisite for effective peace work. Since people with high levels of personal peace may be better able to persevere in the face of challenges and disappointments, it is suggested, peace workers should concentrate first on raising their levels of inner peace before tackling the difficult problems associated with negative and positive peace. Important advocates for nonviolence, such as David Cortright (2009), on the faculty at the Kroc Institute for International Peace Studies at Notre Dame University, and Michael Nagler, founder and president of the Metta Center for Nonviolence, follow the example of Gandhi in maintaining that it is not just practically but also morally correct to seek personal peace before or, at least, simultaneous with advocating for negative and positive peace.

For decades, many people in peace studies deemphasized or ignored personal peace in part because its advocates sometimes seemed to be aiming to achieve inner peace as an individualistic end in itself. Peace studies has resisted the inclusion of the topic of personal peace as well because the acquisition of individual peace does not seem directly related to the goals of promoting negative and positive peace. However, this inattention to personal peace may now be easing. Many people in the global peace network have roots in faith-based traditions and share the perspective of the Dalai Lama, who claims: "Through inner peace, genuine world peace can be achieved. In this the importance of individual responsibility is quite clear; an atmosphere of peace must first be created within ourselves, then gradually expanded to include our families, our communities, and ultimately the whole planet" (quoted in Kraft 1992, 2). Similar claims for the primacy of personal peace can be found in most of the world's religions.

An increased emphasis on personal peace within peace studies is also being supported by secular voices. The National Peace Academy, a growing advocacy and educational organization founded in the United States in 2009, is one prominent promoter of this approach. As mentioned in Chapter 1, the National Peace Academy has adopted the Earth Charter's definition of peace as "wholeness created by right relationships with oneself, other persons, other cultures, other life, Earth, and the larger whole of which all are a part" (Earth Charter Initiative 2012). This approach views right relationships with oneself—personal peace—as equally important as the pursuit of negative and positive peace.

A stronger emphasis on personal well-being seems appropriate even for those who do not believe that people need to achieve a greater peace within themselves before turning outward to promote negative and positive peace. As previously mentioned, suicide is by far the most common type of non-accidental human harm in almost every region of the world today. And, while many other types of violence are declining, global rates of suicide seem to be rising. Some suicides are encouraged by direct, structural, and cultural violence, but others are also likely associated with deficiencies in personal peace. Peace studies concerns should be broad enough to include problems of self-harm and the related topic of inner or personal peace.

Differences between people who do or do not emphasize personal peace may mirror similar differences mentioned earlier between people who emphasize either negative or positive peace. Personal peace may seem less important for those who work primarily to foster negative peace. After all, little personal peace is required for people who intervene to end direct violence, for example, through their work as diplomats, humanitarian interventionists, security forces, police officers, and social service workers. These types of interventions are often provoked by emergencies and can sometimes be successfully resolved in a week or month or two. By contrast, people who work to promote positive peace, to lessen structural and cultural violence, seldom achieve quick successes. Diminishing indirect violence commonly requires changing long-established familial and societal patterns and cultural traditions. Many months and years, as well as patience, luck, and cleverness, are usually needed for success. Substantial levels of personal peace may be necessary to persevere through the frequent failures and frustrations associated with working for positive peace.

Chapter 13 offers yet more discussion of personal peace and of the choices of emphasis that both volunteer and professional peace promoters must make.

MAKING CONNECTIONS

Peace studies' growth has been dependent in part on the increasing sophistication and prestige of the health and social sciences. Religious people associated with many different faiths have also helped nourish peace studies. The field has greatly profited as well from the historic rise of the global peace network, a loosely connected web of hundreds of thousands of peace-promoting organizations and millions of individuals spread across the globe. Chapter 3 describes how these and other forces are shaping peace studies and the contemporary world.

FOR REVIEW

1. Summarize the major differences between negative and positive peace.
2. Describe some examples of both structural and cultural violence that shape your own society.
3. Evaluate the relative strengths and weaknesses of national policies built on principles of "peace through strength" and "peace through peace."
4. Using some of the just war principles, describe what conditions you believe would constitute an ethical, just war.
5. Create a definition of peace that combines elements of negative, positive, and personal peace.

THINKING CRITICALLY

1. Are the recent long periods of negative peace likely to continue into the decades ahead?
2. How effectively has the doctrine of peace through strength worked in international relationships since the end of the Cold War in 1990?
3. Is Boulding correct that direct and indirect violence are too different to be effectively studied together within the same research field?
4. What might be some advantages for peace studies of restricting the definition of peace to the absence of direct, physical violence? Some likely disadvantages?
5. Does the slogan, "If you want peace, work for justice," seem to be a good guide for promoting peace?
6. Which of the just war principles seem to be the most important guides for judging what constitutes a just war?
7. Choose a war to evaluate. Does applying the *jus ad bellum* and the *jus in bello* principles suggest this war was just?
8. What would be the likely consequences if most peace workers concentrated on achieving personal peace first before undertaking projects to promote negative and positive peace?

RECOMMENDED RESOURCES

Cortright, David. *Peace: A History of Movements and Ideas* (New York: Cambridge University Press, 2008). An ambitious examination of peace movements that provides both a chronological history and an in-depth analysis of eight themes often associated with these movements.

The Long Walk of Nelson Mandela. Directed by Cliff Bestall. 1999. A documentary that focuses on the story of Mandela's transformation into a nonviolent leader through the presentation of interviews with friends, fellow inmates, and jailers on Robben Island, the prison where Mandela was held for twenty-seven years. Available at: http://video.pbs.org/video/2365025027/

Mandela: Long Walk to Freedom. Directed by Justin Chadwick. 2013. A fictional film that is nonetheless based on factual published accounts that explore the personal sacrifices that Nelson Mandela made to end apartheid in South Africa. Traces Mandela's life from his childhood in a rural village to his work as a revolutionary, as a political prisoner, and as the first democratically elected president of South Africa.

Nagler, Michael L. *The Search for a Nonviolent Future* (Novato, CA: New World Library, 2004). Nagler explores peace studies concepts and issues from both a personal and political perspective. The book emphasizes the power of nonviolence and draws upon the spiritual tradition that inspired Gandhi, with an emphasis on the positive actions that Gandhi called "constructive programme."

Peace, Peacebuilding and Peacelearning: A Holistic Introduction. A free online series of lessons in peace work prepared by the National Peace Academy. Offers instructions to improve skills in both inner and outer peace and personal and professional peacebuilding. Available at the National Peace Academy: http://nationalpeaceacademy.us/edresources/study-guide/

Walzer, Michael. *Just and Unjust Wars: A Moral Argument with Historical Illustrations* (New York: Basic Books, 2006). This book examines the moral issues surrounding military theory, war crimes, and the spoils of war. It describes a variety of conflicts over the course of history, as well as the testimony of those who have been most directly involved—participants, decisionmakers, and victims. The introduction to the 2006 edition addresses the moral issues surrounding the war in and occupation of Iraq.

CHAPTER 3

PEACE NETWORKS: BENEFITS AND CHALLENGES

CHAPTER OVERVIEW

This chapter begins by examining the important role of science in contemporary peace studies. It also describes peace research associated with the humanities and the continuing importance of religion to many people in peace studies. The historic emergence of the global peace network is highlighted next, as the network's positive international, national, cultural, and technological developments are explored. The chapter then looks at how digital technologies are changing peace-promotion activities. It concludes by examining several challenges to peace, including trends in mass media, public pessimism, and possible new types of climate wars.

Key terms and people discussed include: Global peace index; Immanuel Kant; perpetual peace; faith-based peace studies; satyagraha; beloved community; Dalai Lama; global peace network; the international cluster, national cluster, and cultural and technological cluster of the global peace network; conflict resolution; digital activism; hacktivism; and climate wars.

> As the Ethiopian proverb has it, "When spider webs unite, they can halt even a lion." The hope of humanity lies in weaving a series of spider webs in order to halt the lion of war.
>
> —WILLIAM URY (2000, 196)

 Historians, philosophers, and religious thinkers have long been interested in peace and war, but the formal study of how to decrease violence and build peace did not begin until the mid-twentieth century. Changing attitudes toward violence helped spark this new research field, but it also grew out of the increasing maturity and ambition of the health and social sciences.

Though it is now rooted mostly in empirical research, peace studies remains deeply influenced by religious traditions that were involved in peace promotion before modern science arose. Both peace science and faith-based peace traditions now participate in a historically unprecedented global peace network that links hundreds of thousands of organizations and millions of people who, with varying degrees of commitment and frequency, are working to promote peace. Future obstacles to peace could present greater challenges than those faced by previous generations but the still-expanding global peace network may help people in many regions to maintain and strengthen peace.

THE SCIENCE OF PEACE

The academic field of peace studies emerged as a cry of pain in response to the horrors of World War II and to its disaster-threatening Cold War aftermath. In its first decades of work in the mid-twentieth century, peace studies focused mostly on nation-states, wars, insurrections, and civil disturbances. Gradually, however, peace studies has expanded to also include research and prevention programs focused on personal, domestic, and community violence.

Most peace research is grounded in the methods of the sciences. Fortunately, because the practice of science is much the same throughout the world, the accumulating knowledge about how to enhance peace and decrease violence can often be applied to conflicts everywhere. And even though peace studies began and continues to be practiced mainly in developed countries, its findings are increasingly used in responding to conflicts on every continent.

Hand washing, an example from the health sciences, illustrates how even small science-inspired changes can produce extraordinary results. Before the twentieth century, physicians and nurses produced harm as often as health (Riley 2005). The average life expectancy in Europe was only about forty-two years in 1900. Then medical practice became more rigorously scientific. The discovery of the pathogenic (germ) theory of disease proved especially consequential. This finding led to the practice of frequent hand washing and to the development of antibiotics, two early sources of the high level of prestige that the medical sciences enjoy across the world today. Life expectancy in Europe reached seventy-seven years in 2000 and newborns in much of the world can now expect to live well past eighty years.

Peace researchers based in the health, life, and social sciences are developing their own equivalents of the germ theory—evidence-based explanations of human violence. These analyses, in turn, suggest preventative practices to be further tested through research and experimentation. Several promising peace-promoting techniques discussed in later chapters are as simple to integrate into daily life as are regular hand washing and antibiotic consumption.

One of the most important contributions scientists have made is to show that human violence is not caused by human biology or genes. For example, neuroscience has recently made it clear that people are not born "hard-wired" for aggression or war (see Chapter 10). Another important set of social scientific studies has found that simply including women in decision-making groups tends to reduce levels of violence (see Chapter 5). There is also much evidence from yet other research to show that individuals, groups, and nation-states achieve their goals more often through discussion and negotiation than through violent force. Cross-cultural studies indicate that threats and coercion are usually ineffective even when a person or country possesses destructive powers many times greater than their opponents' (see Part Two). At least for conflicts over the last one hundred years, statistical analyses indicate that massive military campaigns more often create stalemates or disasters than successes.

These and other empirical findings guide contemporary peace promoters in their efforts to create and strengthen the right relationships and harmonious associations necessary for positive peace and peaceful communities. Medical, nursing, and public health schools are adding violence reduction and prevention to their research and training activities. The health science's embrace of peace studies' concerns signals the maturity of the field and suggests that the already brisk pace of knowledge production and application associated with peace studies is poised to further increase.

LEARNING MORE   THE GLOBAL PEACE INDEX

As it has become more evidence-based, peace studies has sought better ways to measure levels of peace and violence. One promising new measurement instrument, the **Global Peace Index,** provides an objective method for determining a country's level of peace. Scores on the global peace index can be used to look for trends over time, as well as to make comparisons among countries and regions.

Developed in 2007, the Global Peace Index combines twenty-three indicators in a complicated formula that measures both internal and external peace-related factors. Among others, these factors include: number of homicides and other violent crimes; per capita size of police and security forces; level of military spending; number of wars fought; relations with neighbors; and respect for human rights. The Index measures peacefulness annually, enabling researchers to compare trends across both nations and time.

In the 2011 assessment of 153 countries, Iceland rated as the country with the highest level of peace, followed in order by New Zealand, Japan, Denmark, and the Czech Republic (Institute for Economics and Peace 2011). On the other hand, Somalia ranked as the country with the least peacefulness, followed by Iraq, Sudan, Afghanistan, and North Korea. The United States ranked near the middle on the continuum, with the eighty-second highest score, indicating a country with an average level of peacefulness.

Other notable rankings included Canada as the eighth and the United Kingdom as the twenty-sixth most peaceful countries. Brazil ranked number 74 on the list, China was 80, Mexico was 121, India was 135, and Russia was 147.

The Global Peace Index can help measure how peace and violence influence national and world economies. In 2010, the Index indicated that violence reduced the total global economic output by over 10 percent, by about $8 trillion. Using the annual rankings, researchers have also determined that the more peaceful a nation becomes, the greater is its rate of economic growth. Even as little as a one point improvement in a nation's Global Peace Index score commonly is matched with a rise of about 1.5 percentage points in that country's annual economic growth (Institute for Economics & Peace 2009, 11). Deterioration in levels of peace have a correspondingly negative impact on gross national product. Countries that are more peaceful also tend to provide more equitable access to education and to operate with higher levels of government transparency and with lower levels of civil and commercial corruption.

Increasing peace pays, the Global Peace Index demonstrates, in gains in national wealth as well as in levels of individual well-being.

Sources: Institute for Economics & Peace 2009; Institute for Economics & Peace 2011.

THE HUMANITIES AND FAITH-BASED PEACE STUDIES

While the health, life, and social sciences are now central to peace studies, the field also depends upon two other traditions, the humanities and faith-based communities.

The formal study of peace originated in the humanities and many contemporary peace scholars continue to draw upon research in history, languages and literature, law, and philosophy. The German philosopher **Immanuel Kant** is usually credited with being the first thinker in the European intellectual tradition to propose that peace become a formal topic of study. Kant sketched the conditions necessary for what he called **perpetual peace** in an essay of that name published in 1795. Kant argued that an enduring global peace requires three conditions. Kant said that first the world needs to be made up primarily of democracies. Second, these democracies must enter into an international association also governed by democratic principles. Finally, citizens and, especially, leaders, must rise above their national parochialism and adopt cosmopolitanism, a perspective Kant called "universal hospitality" and that he identified with the then-radical idea that Earth belongs to the human race in common (Kant 2006).

Kant's vision of a world in perpetual peace seems less utopian now than when he wrote at the end of the eighteenth century. Kant's first condition has nearly been met: Close to a majority of Earth's countries are democratic, in name if not in reality. The United Nations in principle aspires to develop into a democratic association of nations like that Kant said was needed. And, aided by new forms of capitalism, electronic technology, and transportation, some people in many regions are moving toward cosmopolitanism, Kant's third condition. Nationalism and ethnocentrism continue to dominate most public policymaking, but some people everywhere increasingly consider themselves global citizens, people sharing one planet with others (Lane and Waqschal 2011).

Kant and other philosophers have been important to peace studies but perspectives based in religion have been even more influential than approaches based in the humanities. **Faith-based peace studies** builds on the religious or spiritual belief that not harming others is a moral good. Until the last decades of the twentieth century, most peace researchers and leaders had roots in faith traditions.

The first Christians generally interpreted the teachings of Jesus as an unequivocal endorsement of nonviolence, even in the face of deadly force (see Chapter 9). As a result, for several centuries most Christians were principled pacifists regardless of where they lived across the vast Roman Empire. Medieval Christianity later spawned dozens of influential monastic communities where believers similarly rejected the violent customs that had become common in the surrounding Christian societies. The Protestant Reformation produced many breakaway denominations that revived the earliest Christians' rejection of all personal and state-based violence. Several of these denominations survived centuries of persecution and, as the Church of the Brethren, Mennonites, and Quakers, played leading roles in nineteenth-century antislavery campaigns. Members of these denominations were also prominent in twentieth-century movements for women's rights, civil rights, nuclear disarmament, legally recognized conscientious objection to war, and many other peace-related actions. These faith-based campaigns helped spawn the contemporary global peace network. Religious believers were also prominent in the creation of the discipline of peace studies and many within the field today continue to ground their work in their faith.

TWENTIETH-CENTURY RELIGIOUS LEADERS

Almost all of the best known twentieth-century promoters of peace were also religious leaders. Gandhi, for example, was raised a Hindu and maintained throughout his life that his work was primarily spiritual, not political. Gandhi adopted the term **satyagraha**, meaning truth or soul force, to distinguish his nonviolent method from secular practices of resistance not rooted in religious beliefs. Gandhi argued that no secular movement or government could succeed at producing peace. Many people (e.g., Nagler 2004, 2006) within peace studies and the global peace network discussed below continue to promote Gandhi's view.

Abdul Ghaffar Khan, sometimes referred to as the "Frontier Gandhi," adapted Gandhi's methods to his own fervent Muslim faith in the 1930s as he created the largest and best-trained nonviolent army the world has ever known. Khan's army took the name Khudai Khidmatgar, a Pashtun word meaning "servants of God." Spanning remote mountainous areas in what are today Afghanistan and Pakistan, at its peak the Khudai Khidmatgar included over 60,000 uniformed volunteers. All completed nonviolent training and took an oath to respond to those who attacked them with nonviolence and forgiveness. They were frequently attacked by soldiers of the British Raj but, overwhelmingly, remained true to their vows. (Chapter 9 contains a fuller description of Khan and the Khudai Khidmatgar.)

Martin Luther King Jr. also grounded his campaigns in religion. While, as an American Baptist, his ideas about God were much different than Gandhi's and Khan's, King drew similar conclusions about the need for moral beliefs to take precedence over politics. His goal, King said on several occasions, was to create a **"beloved community,"** an association of caring, social equals like the one created by the early Christians and like the community that many Christians believe awaits them after death.

Numerous nonviolent campaigns since King's death have also been guided by religion. Catholic Cardinal Jaime Lachica Sin, for example, prominently invoked Christian beliefs as he helped lead the People Power uprising in the Philippines in 1986. Similarly, as discussed in Chapter 2, Anglican Archbishop Desmond Tutu played an important role in the anti-apartheid movement in South Africa and in the implementation of reconciliation practices across that country once apartheid ended.

The fourteenth **Dalai Lama,** a Tibetan Buddhist in the Gelugpa lineage of Tibetan Buddhism, is probably the best-known current peace worker guided by a religious tradition. Since his exile to India in 1959, the Dalai Lama has championed global interfaith dialogues aimed at reducing sectarian and ethnic conflicts. The Dalai Lama seeks to convince people that all the world's religions share the same core values of nonviolence and cooperation. Modern science and religion, the Dalai Lama maintains, agree fundamentally about how people should live.

Though religious belief and religious leaders remain important, both peace studies and peace movements have become more secular since Gandhi, Khan, and King led their nonviolent campaigns. The secular uprisings in the Baltics between 1987 and 1991 and in Czechoslovakia and East Germany in 1989, all associated with the collapse of the Soviet Union, are typical of nonviolent campaigns in the contemporary world. Religious beliefs similarly played but a small role in the first years of the present century in the unarmed insurrections in Serbia (2000), Georgia (2003), the Ukraine (2004), Kyrgyzstan (2005), Tunisia (2011), and Egypt (2011).

GLOBAL PEACE NETWORK

At first glance, peace studies' goal to promote negative, positive, personal, and ecological peace across the entire world may seem naïve or, at least, excessively ambitious. However, there are increasing reasons for optimism, including the change in attitudes toward violence and war described in Chapter 1. These changes are working in concert with an emerging **global peace network**, a non-hierarchical grid that currently links hundreds of thousands of peace-promoting organizations and millions of individuals spread across the globe (Wood 2014).

Historian Kent D. Shifferd surveys this unprecedented peace network (which he calls a "peace system") in *From War to Peace: A Guide to the Next Hundred Years* (2011). Shifferd points out that few of the components of the network existed during the first few thousand years of recorded history as humans suffered the consequences of living within what Shifferd calls a war and servitude system. These older societies seldom promoted ideals like those contained in the 1948 United Nations Universal Declaration of Human Rights. For example, Article Two asserts, "Everyone is entitled to all the rights and freedoms set forth in this Declaration, without distinction of any kind, such as race, colour, sex, language, religions, political or other opinion, national or social origin, property, birth or other status." This unprecedented mid-twentieth-century declaration could serve as a motto for the global peace network that soon after asserted its newly developing powers.

The first traces of what would become a global peace network began in the nineteenth century with citizen efforts to end slavery and with many different campaigns for a weakening or elimination of the divine right of chiefs, kings, and hereditary elites. Next came movements promoting the rights of women and an end to interstate wars (Cortright 2008). The network's growth accelerated after World War II to become an immense global web of interconnected beliefs, norms, institutions, and organizations, with no common leaders, plans, formal structure, or agreed upon name. Different elements within the network simultaneously work for negative, positive, personal, and ecological peace. These diverse elements gain and lose influence in different situations but, generally, grow more effective year after year.

The field of peace studies is but one of many thousands of nodes within the peace network. Though small, peace studies fulfills an important function as it seeks to map, research, and strengthen the much larger web within which it is but one part. As they ebb and flow, conflicts pulse bursts of energy to peace studies and to other nodes across the global network. Of course, nothing but death can stop people from continuing to struggle with one another, as they always have. Human disagreements and quarrels, in fact, often help produce much of what humans most value about their lives. Nonetheless, as anthropologist

Eleanor Roosevelt looks at the Declaration of Human Rights that she helped write.

William Ury (2000, 201) points out, though conflict is inevitable, "fighting, violence, and war are not." The global peace network aims not to end conflict but to transform how conflict is expressed, to divert potentially violent disputes into some of the many thousands of possible alternative nonviolent forms.

THE INTERNATIONAL AND NATIONAL PEACE NETWORK CLUSTERS

Shifferd (*From War to Peace*, 2011) points to three different types of activities coexisting within the global peace network. These clusters of activities mostly promote either (1) international, (2) national, or (3) cultural and technological trends. The clusters are summarized in Table 3.1, "The Global Peace Network."

The international cluster has helped drive at least five significant developments. These include the unprecedented expansion of international laws and treaties. For example, the World Court (also known as the International Court of Justice), established in 1945, has since been joined by regional courts in Europe and Latin America. The much newer International Criminal Court issued its first judgment in 2012 and now stands ready to investigate and try individuals for genocide, crimes against humanity, and war crimes. No such worldwide tribunal existed previously in human history. First-time international treaties have also been signed in the last half century banning the atmospheric testing of nuclear weapons and the use of child soldiers and of land and sea mines.

A second development within the international cluster of the global peace network is associated with the rise of transnational peacemaking. The United Nations, African Union, European Union, and Organization of American States are far from perfect but, as Shifferd points out, their goals of preventing war by nonviolent means represent a revolutionary development in relations among nation-states. These and other organizations reinforce a third unprecedented development, the use of neutral, international peacekeeping forces to intervene in violent conflicts and to maintain ceasefires. The United Nations, with by far the largest peacekeeping forces, had sixteen separate deployments in operation across the world in 2012. (A list of United Nations Peace Missions in the decades prior to 2010 can be found in Chapter 6, Table 6.5.)

The growth of international organizations promoting peace has been accompanied by an even more robust growth in nongovernmental international organizations. As will be explained more fully in Chapter 8, Mary Kaldor (2003) maintains that these organizations help constitute a potent new global civil society that is revitalizing politics from below. Global civil society groups include such well-known organizations as Oxfam (founded in 1942), at work now in ninety countries; Amnesty International (founded in 1961), with 6 million members; and Doctors without Borders (founded in 1971), supporting about 27,000 medical staff in over sixty countries. International groups of unarmed civilian peacekeepers are now also at work in many violent situations across the world. Just one of these, for example, the Nonviolent Peaceforce, in 2012 had civilian peacekeepers working in Myanmar, the Philippines, South Caucasus, South Sudan, and Sri Lanka (Nonviolence Peace-force 2012). (More information about the Nonviolent Peaceforce can be found in Case 13-3 in Chapter 13.) Other groups form what Jack Donnelly (1986) calls a human rights regime. These many groups work to advance the acceptance of universal human rights within both the international cluster and the national cluster of the global peace network.

Another international development associated with the global peace network is the rapid growth of global conferences that help coordinate peace, justice, and environmental efforts worldwide. The Earth Summit in 1992 inaugurated this development when it brought to-gether 2,400 representatives from hundreds of nongovernmental organizations. Now there are thousands of such conferences each year. These prominently include the series of World Social Forums that are held to counter the annual World Economic Forum conferences which are dominated by elites that exclude nongovernmental organizations and ordinary people.

Developments associated with the **national cluster** of the peace network include the rise of tens of thousands of volunteer groups committed to promoting peace within their countries. Several antislavery societies were pioneers in this work, forming in England and the United States in the early decades of the nineteenth century (Cortright 2008). Increasing numbers of groups promoting what are now known as civil and human rights appeared in the following two centuries. Today, one analyst (Hawken 2007) estimates there are likely close to 2 million volunteer organizations spread across the world promoting peace and environmental justice within their countries.

International Court of Justice (ICJ) in session in 1982.

The number of democracies is also trending upward, increasing the power of the emerging peace network in at least two ways. Democracies tend to support or at least tolerate both international and national civil society organizations more than do non-democracies. An increasing number of democracies also helps by decreasing the likelihood of war. As explained in Chapter 6, democracies fight non-democratic governments much more often than they fight each other. The diminishing number of non-democratic countries thus means there are fewer potential enemies for democracies to attack.

THE CULTURAL AND TECHNOLOGICAL PEACE NETWORK CLUSTER

These many developments in the international and national clusters intertwine with developments in the cultural and technological cluster. Shifferd describes almost a dozen such developments, including the rising economic and political power of women in most areas of the world. Women's increasing influence is strengthening elements within all the clusters of the emerging peace network. As Hudson et al. show in their pioneering *Sex and World Peace* (2012), countries with more gender equality tend to produce less domestic, group, and international violence. (The importance of women to peace is explored in Chapter 5.)

Other developments in the cultural and technological cluster include a change in attitudes toward war and violence and the emergence of the Internet and social media, developments discussed below and in Chapters 1 and 4. In addition, the growth of a shared global culture and economy may be making both men and women's xenophobic impulses less frequently violent. Other cultural trends in the peace network include the continuing growth of knowledge about how to mount effective nonviolent campaigns for social change, a trend described in both Chapters 7 and 8. Gandhi planned his campaigns almost entirely without models of similar actions; peace workers today have access to increasingly sophisticated databases that include analyses of all of Gandhi's strategies as well as records of the efforts of many thousands of others. For example, the online Global Nonviolent Action Database (available at http://nvdatabase.swarthmore.edu/), launched in 2010 by student researchers supervised by George Lakey, includes summaries of hundreds of nonviolent campaigns, beginning with a strike by Egyptian workers in 1170 BCE. The database is searchable by the movement's name, geographical location, methods used, associated campaigns, start year, and end year. This database creates research possibilities almost unimaginable but a generation ago.

The cultural cluster of the emerging peace network also includes the immense field of conflict resolution, another powerful element of the global peace network almost unknown

TABLE 3.1   THE GLOBAL PEACE NETWORK

Cluster	Elements
International	1. International law and treaties. E.g., World Court, the International Tribunal for the Law of the Sea, International Criminal Court 2. International parliaments. E.g., United Nations 3. International peacekeeping. E.g., African Union, United Nations, unarmed civilian peacekeepers 4. International nongovernmental organizations. E.g., Amnesty International, Fellowship of Reconciliation, Human Rights Watch
National	1. National peace societies. E.g., Southern Christian Leadership Conference, Code Pink, Mothers of the Plaza de Mayo 2. Rise of democracies. E.g., Bosnia, Egypt, Philippines, Serbia, Tunisia, South Africa 3. Increasing rights for women. E.g., educational, employment, property, marriage-choice, voting rights
Cultural/ Technological	1. Changed attitudes toward violence. E.g., end of legal slavery, of public punishments and executions, of legal forced child labor; shrinking acceptance of hereditary elite rule and of capital punishment; decline in popularity of violent ideologies such as those associated with nineteenth and twentieth century imperialism and colonialism 2. Recognition of long-term regions of peace. E.g., postwar Europe, North America, Scandinavia 3. Awareness of successful nonviolent movements. E.g., American civil rights movement, color revolutions, Arab uprising 4. Systemization of principles of nonviolent organizing. E.g., Global Nonviolent Action Database, International Center on Nonviolent Conflict, CANVAS (Centre for Applied Nonviolent Action and Strategies), Beyond Intractability Knowledge Base Project, Waging Nonviolence 5. Knowledge of conflict resolution strategies. E.g., mediation training, "win-win strategies" 6. Expanding global culture. E.g., global civil society, world film and popular music, Olympics, World Cup 7. Internet and social media. E.g., e-mail, Facebook, Instagram, Twitter, YouTube

a half century ago. Associated with but somewhat separate from peace studies, **conflict resolution** programs offer training in mutual-gain bargaining, non-adversarial negotiation, peer-mediation, and many other nonviolent techniques at businesses, nonprofit organizations, and schools across the world. These effective alternatives to violence are discussed in Chapter 12.

Shifferd's research into the dozens of developments associated with the emergence of the global peace network has made him cautiously optimistic. He points out, "The movement to abolish slavery, an institution as old as war and as deeply embedded in the economy, sanctioned by the Bible and considered to be inevitable, took about a hundred years to succeed. We can't be certain that this new story, the replacement of war with a peace network, will become the dominant mode of conflict management in the next hundred years, but it has a good chance" (Shifferd *Exploring Peace* 2011, 56).

DIGITALIZING THE GLOBAL PEACE NETWORK

New technologies change not only how people kill each other but also how people strive to stop killing. Wael Ghonim's use of Facebook and other digital tools described in Chapter 1 illustrates the power of some new media. The growing influence of the global peace network depends in part as well on the use of these same media.

Of course, communication technologies have always been important to people promoting peace. Gandhi relied a century ago on newspapers, letters, telegrams, and face-to-face meetings as he orchestrated his pioneering campaigns. Later organizers found great value in telephones, mimeographs, photocopiers and, even later, on inventions such as cassette tapes and fax machines. For many recent decades, however, broadcast television was the most important technology available to peace promoters.

Much of the American civil rights movement was organized with an eye to how it would appear in film clips on television. These mid-century broadcasts were seldom shown in real time until, in the 1970s, satellites made live reporting common. People on all continents were then able to watch public dissent erupt within the Soviet empire as Solidarity challenged Poland's communist rulers. Much of the world watched in amazement, too, as hundreds of thousands of Iranians swarmed the streets of Tehran in 1978 and 1979. Similar scenes were repeated on live television a few years later as the People Power revolution in the Philippines held the world's attention for a few memorable weeks in 1986. Images of Germans breaching, hammering, painting, and dancing upon the Berlin Wall in 1989 created televised visions of freedom that helped inspire later peoples' resistance movements in multiple countries.

Although broadcast and cable television, as well as many other older communication technologies, remain important, new digital technologies may be transforming civil resistance movements and the global peace network in fundamental ways. **Digital activism is the use of electronic technologies, especially social media such as Facebook, Instagram, Pintrest, Snapchat, Vine, Twitter, and YouTube to foment political and social change.** Digital technologies enable people to speed up communication among citizens at the same time that they make it easier to share information with large audiences.

Celebrants dismantle the Berlin Wall in 1989.

The Orange Revolution in Ukraine in 2004 offered an early example of the new potential of digital activism. Its organization largely depended on the use of early forms of social media and, especially, on mobile phones (Goldstein 2007). These digital tools also helped empower citizen resistance to violence in Kenya in 2007–2008 following a disputed presidential campaign (Goldstein and Rotich 2008). And, as was explained in Chapter 1, a single short video, posted on YouTube, showing Mohamed Bouazizi lighting himself on fire, helped spark a successful unarmed insurrection in Tunisia that, in the following months, encouraged further uprisings in over a dozen North African and Middle Eastern countries.

These latter insurrections, generally known as the Arab Spring or Arab Awakening, depended on digital technologies to varying degrees. For example, as Mary Joyce (2011) shows, in Egypt social media accomplished several tasks that would likely have been impossible to achieve without new media. Wael Ghonim and thousands of others used cameras, mobile phones, Facebook, Twitter, YouTube, and numerous websites to document the violence of the regime they opposed, as well as to digitally record their own resistance activities. Social networking tools were also used to share this information with a dispersed population that citizen resisters had little chance of reaching before.

In some places, citizens have begun turning to nonviolent hacking, sometimes called hacktivism. **Hacktivism** is a form of civil disobedience in which citizens access government

websites and conduct virtual-sits, institute website redirections, and create look-alike website parodies. Hacking becomes cyber warfare (discussed in Chapter 4) when the attacks cause significant damage to government-controlled computers and rely on computer viruses or denial-of-service attacks.

not w/ reader has w hacking.

The use of digital media will likely expand at least for a few more decades. (For example, see Case 3-1, "The Occupy Movement.") This expansion should prove especially useful for

CASE 3-1   THE OCCUPY MOVEMENT

Digital media had a powerful influence on the Occupy movement, which began modestly enough in New York City with a relatively small demonstration of between eight hundred and two thousand protestors. People walked through downtown Manhattan on September 17, 2011, before stopping at Zuccotti Park, a small private area in the city's financial district. Without prior planning, a few hundred demonstrators decided to spend the night in the park. The next day they were joined by others and, encouraged by blogs, Facebook, Instagram, Twitter, YouTube posts, and encouraging web pages, ever more participants arrived in the days and weeks that followed.

Additional protests sprouted in other parts of New York. Seven hundred protestors were arrested as they attempted to cross the Brooklyn Bridge on October 1. About 15,000 people marched from Foley Square to join Zuccotti Park on October 5. By mid-October, Occupy-inspired protests were ongoing or had taken place in over six hundred locations within the United States and in nearly one hundred cities across eighty-two countries. Hundreds of thousands of people had attended one or more Occupy rallies. Tens of thousands had slept on the streets and sidewalks for at least one night.

Municipal, state, and federal governments generally tolerated the movement at first but in November they began coordinating with one another to destroy all the overnight camps. Few were left by the end of 2011, three and a half months after the occupations began. Police harassment and arrests continued so that, by the middle of 2013, almost eight thousand people had been arrested at Occupy events in 122 cities in the United States and many more in other cities across the world.

Though Occupy has been removed from most city streets, the movement remains influential in at least three ways. First, Occupy helped manifest a new wave of economic populism built around the idea the "1 percent" is hoarding wealth and impoverishing the "99 percent." As one poster read, "Dear 1%. We were asleep. Now we've woken up. Signed, the 99%." The Occupy movement's focus on growing rates of income inequality influenced the political rhetoric of both the Obama and Romney presidential campaigns in Fall 2011 and continues to affect political debates within the United States and beyond.

The Occupy movement also made a lasting impact through its emphasis on means as ends. The encampments were generally organized as models of the same type of egalitarian societies that most in the movement wished to create. Decisions were made through long, often contentious discussions in group meetings, known as "general assemblies." There were no elected leaders and every person was accorded an equal right to talk. In a movement seeking to diminish the power of elites, decision-making by consensus offered daily examples of how an egalitarian form of social organization was immediately available to people willing to enact the new forms they were calling for.

Finally, the Occupy movement's legacy includes its creation of a new generation of citizens who have now directly experienced the power, exhilaration, and challenges of mass, popular action. Hundreds of thousands of people mostly younger than thirty created a movement that in a few weeks grew from one demonstration of one thousand into a mass campaign with manifestations in most major countries and cities across the world. Participants will likely not soon forget their time collaborating in consensus groups to promote justice for others and for themselves.

Just as politics in the United States over the last half-century was influenced by people associated with what are known as the "Civil Rights" and the "Sixties" generations, politics for the next half-century may be shaped by the Occupy generation.

Sources: Adam 2011; Earle 2012.

the global peace network which probably could not have become such an effective peace promoter without using electronic media to connect the network's tens of thousands of independent nodes. The network may grow still more powerful as new media become further integrated into the everyday lives of people in all regions of the world.

OBSTACLES TO PEACE

Substantial obstacles to peace exist in every part of the world. Much research reviewed in future chapters will detail how very difficult it is to foster right relationships and harmonious associations, even when the global peace network is working with great strength.

One obstacle may be created by the same new digital technologies that are currently facilitating citizen resistance and the global peace network. These same new media, after all, can be marshaled to strengthen repression as well as to oppose it. For example, governments are increasingly using digital monitoring to spy on their citizens' use of Facebook, YouTube, Twitter, and mobile texting, just as some citizens are using these same tools to document the government's actions against them. So far social media have commonly been more difficult for governments to control than are earlier communication technologies. Printing presses, landline telephones, and television can be monopolized and censored by states more easily than networked computers and mobile devices. Until now, at least, new communication technologies have favored resisting citizens somewhat more than nation-states.

Contemporary commercial mass media form yet another significant obstacle to peace as most of these media tend to present violence as normal and expected behavior (Lane and Waqschal 2011). Editors and producers declare, "If it bleeds, it leads," inspiring their staffs to fill books, newspapers, and magazines with stories of violence and misery. Ratings and revenues generally rise when commercial media increase people's fears. Stories celebrating everyday peacemaking citizens or describing contemporary trends toward an increasing peacefulness thus remain unknown to most people.

Movies and television have become especially dependent on using violence to attract audiences. Violent people killing others in the name of various "just" causes are presented as heroes. Meanwhile, peace workers in the mode of Gandhi, Khan, King, Nelson Mandela, Desmond Tutu, or the Dalai Lama seldom appear in novels, magazines, movies, and video games. Mass-market celebrations of influential female peace workers such as Jeannette Rankin, Jane Addams, Dorothy Day, Alice Paul, Rosa Parks, and Leymah Gbowee are even more difficult to find.

It is likely that people would still overestimate the frequency of violence even if contemporary media stopped encouraging them to do so. As psychologist Steven Pinker (2010) points out, people base their sense of present dangers in large measure on how well they recall examples of earlier dangers and, in general, past direct experiences and stories of violence are more likely to be stored in our memories than are memories of the much more common nonviolent occurrences that usually fill daily life. Pinker concludes, "No matter how small the percentage of violent deaths may be in absolute numbers there will always be enough of them to fill the evening news, so people's impressions of violence will be disconnected from the actual proportions" (2010, xxii). Our brains are accustomed to remembering the rare bad events and forgetting the much more frequent neutral and positive ones.

Pessimism also creates obstacles to peace. Modern mass media buttress this pessimism but its origins are much deeper and often grounded in cultural traditions that maintain human violence is inevitable. Numerous people believe, as is written in the Bible's New Testament (Mark 13:7), that "wars and rumors of wars" are unavoidable. Prominent thinkers in the twentieth century, including Sigmund Freud, Carl Jung, Raymond Dart, and Konrad Lorenz, promoted a similarly pessimistic view with their claims that civilization is made possible only through the harsh repression of so-called universal, biologically-based violent impulses. Robert Ardrey popularized this pessimism in his 1961 book, *African Genesis*, which argued that humans are "killer apes" who became a dominant species only once they evolved to be more successfully murderous than other primates. Believing that humans are naturally killer apes can work as a self-fulfilling prophecy; people who view humans as predisposed for violence by God or by their biological nature have less motivation to work to increase levels of peace.

Chapter 10 describes some of the massive body of scientific evidence against the pessimistic conviction that humans are biologically driven to be violent. Nevertheless, even many people who accept this scientific evidence sometimes shy away from supporting peace research and work because of yet another obstacle, the belief that peace seeking is for the weak. Peace in many societies is associated with fantasy, softness, timidity, and even cowardice. These characteristics are often claimed to be feminine and are associated with women, children, and other groups with little power. War and violence, on the other hand, are widely linked with realism, vigor, bravery, and a highly valued form of aggressive masculinity. Countries, groups, and leaders are more likely to be judged to possess "great strength" when they show themselves capable of using lethal violence on their own citizens and against other nations than when they choose to negotiate and cooperate in seeking their goals.

Gandhi himself frequently heard criticisms that he was asking his followers to be "womanish" and weak. In many speeches and writings, Gandhi thus repeatedly pointed out that in his experience, "The path of true nonviolence requires much more courage than violence" (Gandhi 2007, xxi). In fact, Gandhi wrote, "There is hope for a violent man to someday be nonviolent, but there is none for a coward" (xxii). Using weapons "implies an element of fear," Gandhi said, while using nonviolence is impossible "without the possession of unadulterated fearlessness" (xiii).

Unfortunately, the strength and courage shown by Gandhi, Khan, King, and hundreds of thousands of other participants in nonviolent movements has little altered the common association of peace promotion with fantasy, softness, and timidity. Heroes are still more often associated with the violent use of weapons than with the effective use of conflict resolution techniques. Peace studies and many others within the global peace network have tried to weaken this traditional association of strength with violence but there is much more work to be done.

CASE 3-2 NO TO KEYSTONE XL

Energy companies across the world currently own the rights to enough oil, gas, and coal to produce about 2,800 gigatons of atmospheric carbon. This is five times more carbon emission than scientists believe Earth can absorb before creating radical climate changes across most regions. Even if energy companies refine only half of these existing reserves, the global mean temperature will rise significantly more than the 3.6 degrees Fahrenheit (2 degrees Celsius) world leaders at the Copenhagen Climate Conference in 2009 set as the absolute maximum that the world could allow if it is to maintain the current levels of agricultural production. If all the existing oil, gas, and coal is extracted and burned, the resulting temperatures, changed weather patterns, and sea level rise will alter the planet more radically than any climate event since the last glacial period ended about 10,000 years ago.

The No Tar Sands Oil campaign is one of the most visible of many nonviolent efforts to try to force energy companies to keep much of their oil, gas, and coal reserves safely in the ground. The campaign has united hundreds of organizations around the common goal of stopping the completion of the Keystone XL oil pipeline, slated to run from Canada to the Gulf Coast of the United States, carrying over 500,000 barrels of oil a day. If completed, this pipeline system would facilitate the extraction of crude oil from a Canadian reserve estimated to be almost as large as that found under Saudi Arabia. About 240 gigatons of carbon could be released through burning this single oil source, an amount that by itself constitutes half of the entire maximum production that the Copenhagen Climate Conference declared should be permitted across the whole twenty-first century. James Hansen, head of NASA's Goddard Institute for Space Studies, has said that completing construction of the Keystone XL pipeline will mean "it's game over for the planet."

The No Tar Sands Oil campaign has employed the customary nonviolent methods used to influence governments, including public education, oil stock divestment drives, letter writing, petitions, meeting with elected officials and their representatives, and public demonstrations. Approximately 50,000 people attended a rally in February 2013 in Washington, DC, to protest construction of the pipeline, the largest climate change demonstration in United States history. Members of the No Tar Sands Oil campaign have also mounted nonviolent direct actions. Over 1,000 were arrested at a rally in August 2011 as they and a crowd of about 12,000 others formed a human chain around the White House while shouldering a long black inflatable replica of a pipeline. Hundreds of others have been arrested while undertaking civil disobedience at dozens of sites in Canada and the United States.

Success for the No Tar Sands Oil movement could create a model for yet more and larger efforts to reduce global use on fossil fuels. Failure, on the other hand, may in retrospect be seen to have signaled the end of hope that mass action could moderate a human-generated climate change disaster.

Sources: Mayer 2011; McKibben 2012.

ENVIRONMENTAL CHALLENGES TO PEACE

Many people fear that there will be cataclysmic climate wars as Earth becomes warmer in the decades ahead. (For example, see Case 3-2, "No to Keystone XL.") Books with titles such as *Climate Wars: What People Will Be Killed For in the 21st Century* (Welzer 2012) and *Climate Wars: The Fight for Survival as the World Overheats* (Dyer 2011) help sustain these fears. **Climate wars** are violent conflicts caused by disruptions in the availability in food, water, and other vital resources that could increase as Earth warms in the years ahead. Many think tanks and military strategists have already issued reports that explore the negative impact that a warming planet will likely have on national security strategies and plans.

Climate scientists agree on the broad outlines of the physical changes that lie ahead. Humans will burn increasingly more greenhouse gases that will be trapped for centuries within Earth's atmosphere. Ninety percent of the trapped heat will be stored in the ocean.

Warmer oceans will produce increasing ocean acidification, threatening the food supply of the close to one billion people who depend upon the sea for the bulk of their protein. Warmer oceans will also produce the thermal expansion of seawater, creating higher sea levels that increase coastal erosion and flood coastal regions. Melting polar caps and glaciers will raise sea levels even more. In just the last thirty-three years, for example, the Arctic sea ice has already shrunk by one-third.

Surface warming will create still more changes. Mass species extinctions, losses of biodiversity, and new disease vectors are already observable. Changed weather patterns, creating droughts and deluges, tornadoes and hurricanes, will become more common. Some rich waterways are likely to dry up. Some currently fertile soils will become barren. Michael T. Klare (2001) argues in *Resource Wars: The New Landscape of Global Conflict* that these many climate changes will almost surely create new tensions and instabilities in many regions of the world. The positive trends associated with emerging global peace networks could be reversed as climate change produces significantly more global competition for critical resources such as arable land, natural gas, oil, water, and key industrial minerals.

There are no historical precedents to look back on to help foresee what will happen as the climate noticeably warms across most of our interconnected world. Chapter 4 describes the work of some climate historians who have found that past rising temperatures did not increase rates of war in pre-industrial European and Chinese societies. These findings provide some grounds for hope. Nonetheless, there is ample reason to worry. Rising land and sea temperatures, ocean acidification, and changing weather patterns may plunge some parts of the world back toward levels of violent conflict like those common across much of Europe and Asia in the first half of the twentieth century.

MAKING CONNECTIONS

The single best predictor of the immediate future is the immediate past. And, as is detailed in Chapter 4, at least since the 1950s much of the world has been trending toward the use of alternatives to violence and war. It seems possible that the global peace network will continue strengthening and, along with other forces, provide effective nonviolent solutions to most future conflicts over resources and much else. Chapter 5 provides yet more reasons for optimism as it details the critical role that women are playing in building more peaceful societies across the world.

FOR REVIEW

1. Explain how a science-based approach to understanding conflict and violence may increase global peacefulness.
2. Analyze some problems that arise when peace-promotion is guided mainly by religious beliefs.
3. Evaluate the relative importance of each of the three clusters of the global peace network.
4. Explore how digital activism is changing peace-promoting campaigns.
5. Evaluate which of the obstacles and challenges to peace discussed in the chapter's final sections seems more likely to encourage violence in the decades ahead.

THINKING CRITICALLY

1. Are future scientific discoveries more likely to increase the destructiveness of wars than to increase levels of peace?
2. What is the significance of the creation of the Global Peace Index?
3. Are there elements of Kant's vision of perpetual peace that are becoming true?
4. Does the shift away from faith-based toward more secular-based peace campaigns make peace more, or less, difficult to achieve?
5. Which of the three clusters of the global peace network is likely to be the strongest promoter of peace over the next fifty years?
6. Can you find evidence in your own life of the influence of the global peace network?
7. Will future new communication technologies likely further enhance the power of citizens or instead increase the power of nation-states?
8. Was Gandhi correct that it takes more courage to practice nonviolence in dangerous situations than to use weapons such as guns?
9. What changes might cause a contemporary society to honor its peacemakers as often as its military heroes?

RECOMMENDED RESOURCES

Alliance for Peacebuilding. A membership organization of more than seventy influential groups and over 15,000 individuals that seeks to strengthen network connections and coordinate global efforts to build sustainable peace and human security. Many resources are available at http://www.allianceforpeacebuilding.org

Center on International Cooperation. *Annual Review of Global Peace Operations 2013* (Boulder, CO: Lynne Rienner Publishers, 2013). A comprehensive yearly survey of all military and civilian peace operations. The book describes 130 missions in place in 2012.

Hawken, Paul. *The Blessed Unrest: How the Largest Movement in the World Came into Being, and Why No One Saw it Coming* (New York: Penguin Books, 2007). A visionary overview of the explosive growth of civil society organizations across the world that are networked, non-hierarchical, and frequently integrating concerns about the environment, justice, and peace.

How Facebook Changed the World: The Arab Spring. Produced by BBC Current Affairs. 2011. A 100-minute, two-part documentary that explores the Arab Awakening's revolutionary use of video, blogging, Facebook, and Twitter as the movement spread from Tunisia to Egypt, Libya, Bahrain, and Syria. Emphasizes video and photos made by the participants.

Shifferd, Kent D. *From War to Peace: A Guide to the Next One Hundred Years* (Jefferson, NC: McFarland, 2011). This book examines the war system that Shifferd claims dominates the foreign policies and cultures of many nations. Shifferd also describes a parallel emerging peace system that has arisen to challenge and perhaps one day replace the war system. See also, the online lecture, "The Evolution of the Global Peace System 2.0," where Shifferd describes many elements in the global peace network, at http://youtu.be/f1HMRAZNQd8

Ury, William. *The Third Side: Why We Fight and How We Can Stop* (New York: Penguin, 2000). Mixes theory and practice to review evidence that humans are at root a cooperative and not a violent species and then presents ten roles that people can formally and informally adopt to help communities thrive.

CHAPTER 4

TRENDS IN VIOLENCE, TERRORISM, AND WAR

CHAPTER OVERVIEW

This chapter reviews historic trends in peace, violence, terrorism, and war, with an emphasis on patterns that emerged after World War II. It begins with a description of long-term decreases in the incidence of murder. This is followed by evidence that over the last seventy years there has also been a diminishing in both the frequency and deadliness of war. Differences between trends in interstate and intrastate wars are explored. The chapter next describes contemporary threats from both state-sponsored and domestic terrorism, before analyzing why terrorism seldom achieves its goals. Effective methods for countering terrorism from below are reviewed. Attention is then given to threats created by biological, chemical, and cyber weapons, as well as by lethal autonomous weapons such as aerial drones. The chapter concludes with a discussion of whether climate change is likely to increase violence and war.

Key terms include: Great power wars; industrialization of warfare; interstate wars; intrastate wars; civilian casualties; terrorism; terrorism from above; state-sponsored terrorism; terrorism from below; biological and chemical weapons; cyber warfare; lethal autonomous weapons; and drone warfare.

> Violence has declined over long stretches of time, and today we may be living in the most peaceable era in our species' existence.
>
> —STEVEN PINKER (2010, xxi)

[handwritten: @ — Wht is there still so much violence if we are trendly downward? —]

Violence and war continue to be terrible scourges, frequently killing over a half a million people each year across the world (Geneva Declaration 2008). Nonetheless, compared to earlier periods of history, most contemporary humans are living in a remarkably peaceful age. Murders and assaults have declined dramatically, at least in most of those

[handwritten: World is more peaceful & less violent.]

parts of the world with reliable records. Wars are now generally much less frequent. A person born in 1900 was three times more likely to die from violence as a person born in 1950 (Eisner 2003; Leitenberg 2006).

Exploring the generally decreasing global rates of violence and war is important since so many people incorrectly believe that direct violence is increasing or, at the least, occurring at rates like those common in earlier centuries. Learning the good news about these trends should not encourage complacency, however, but rather help bolster our confidence that even more can be done to reduce both direct and indirect violence.

TRENDS IN HOMICIDE

More people die each year from intrapersonal violence—suicide—than from all other forms of direct violence combined. As mentioned in Chapter 2, despite other positive trends, global rates of suicide seem to be stable or perhaps even rising (World Health Organization 2011).

After suicide, murder is overwhelmingly the world's worst violence problem. Homicide accounted for about 400,000 deaths annually across the world in recent years, a rate eight times higher than the rate associated with deaths from insurrections, terrorism, and wars combined (Geneva Declaration 2008). Fortunately, for centuries in many regions of the world the frequency of murder has been in decline.

Homicide rates differ markedly from country to country and, in many places, homicide statistics are unreliable, if they are kept at all. However, accurate historical data is available for much of Europe as most municipalities in this region have been keeping careful count of murders since the end of the Middle Ages. Criminologist Manuel Eisner examined thousands of these records and found that the murder rate in Europe ranged from 30 to 100 per 100,000 per year in 1500. The municipal records in the following centuries then show a steady decline until homicides reached their current historically low rate across Western Europe. In this region today there are on average between one and two killings per 100,000 people per year, fifteen to thirty times less than during the late Middle Ages. (See Table 4.1, "Homicide Rates in Europe.")

The composite rate for all contemporary nations is about nine murders per year per 100,000 people. That is close to six times higher than Europe's current murder rate. Nevertheless, even

TABLE 4.1 HOMICIDE RATES IN EUROPE, THIRTEENTH THROUGH TWENTIETH CENTURIES

Years	Average Homicide Rate per 100,000
Thirteenth and Fourteenth Centuries	32
Fifteenth Century	41
Sixteenth Century	19
Seventeenth Century	11
Eighteenth Century	3.2
Nineteenth Century	2.6
Twentieth Century	1.4

Source: Eisner 2003, Table 2, 99.

the highest murder rates found today, for example, those found in Columbia, the Congo, Jamaica, South Africa, and Venezuela, are low compared to the homicide rates common across late medieval Europe.

The United States has a relatively high murder rate for an advanced industrialized nation, currently averaging about five homicides per 100,000 people each year. By contrast, Australia, Denmark, Germany, Italy, Norway, Japan, Spain, Sweden, and a few others have a rate of one or fewer murders per 100,000. But even the United States' homicide rate has dropped significantly, from approximately twenty-five murders per 100,000 in 1800 to a rate close to 80 percent less today. There was a noticeable rise in homicides in the United States from the late 1960s into the 1980s, but in the decade of the 1990s murders (as well as other violent assaults) declined by about 40 percent (Zimring 2007).

People's tolerance of murder has also decreased with each new century of the modern era. Changed public attitudes toward the morality of intentional killing has now forced even state-sponsored executions to become less frequent and less gruesome. For millennia governments in many parts of the world tortured and publicly dismembered their citizen-victims, often without trials, evidence, or appeals. Small offenses such as criticizing the king, refusing to pay taxes, or petty theft were sometimes treated as capital offenses.

Fewer and fewer contemporary governments assert a right to execute their citizens. Even those countries such as the United States that continue practicing capital punishment tend to use this penalty increasingly less often. In addition, governments across the world now generally kill citizens only after trials that at least make a pretense of being evidence-based. And government-sponsored executions are generally carried out in private, using methods such as injections or firing squads that many believe reduce the victim's suffering. These efforts to make capital punishment fairer, less gruesome, and more private demonstrate there is a diminishing public support for the right of nations, as well as of individuals, to end human lives.

TRENDS IN THE FREQUENCY OF WARS

On average, there has been about one great power war per decade for the past five hundred years. **Great power wars** are violent conflicts among prominent countries that impact other nations beyond the warring powers themselves. Both the frequency and the duration of great power wars are decreasing. There were only three such wars in the twentieth century and all occurred before 1950: the Russo-Japanese war (1904–1905), World War I (1914–1918), and World War II (1939–1945). (Some analysts also describe the Korean War as a conflict between China and the United States, thus making it a fourth twentieth-century great power war.) The last sixty years are the longest period of negative peace among major powers in five centuries (Levy & Thompson 2010).

The decrease in frequency and duration of great power wars has been accompanied by the industrialization of warfare, a less positive trend. The **industrialization of warfare** allows countries to use modern technology, production methods, and bureaucratic organization to intensify their violent conflicts. These and other modern developments have tended to increase the destructiveness of wars, raising the rate of battlefield deaths (McNeill 1982). Levy and Thompson (2010) estimate that the death rate for combatants has been rising for thousands of years. They argue that the rate more than doubled in the two thousand years leading up to the fourteenth century. Then, with the growing application of new methods of warfare, Levy and Thompson believe the rate of death more than doubled again in just the next five hundred years. By 2000, combatants were more than ten times more likely to die in battle than combatants had been in 1800 (Levy & Thompson 2010, 11).

The increasing industrialization of warfare has made combat so deadly that some major powers now possess weapons of mass destruction capable of destroying most of the population and infrastructure of their "enemies." These circumstances may be acting as a deterrent to further major power wars since using weapons of mass destruction on other major powers is likely to produce a counterattack that leaves both sides more devastated than they would have been by the weapons used in earlier wars.

Like great power wars, smaller wars both between and, to a lesser extent, within nations are similarly becoming less common. It is useful to distinguish between **interstate wars**, primarily cross-border conflicts between countries, and **intrastate wars**, mostly involving groups within the borders of one country. Both types of wars are trending downward but the decrease in interstate wars has been especially dramatic. Joshua Goldstein's data from multiple sources indicate that the number of interstate wars, which he defines as 1,000 or more fatalities per year, has been decreasing for decades and, probably, for centuries (Goldstein 2012). Intrastate wars, on the other hand, increased after World War II, during the period of decolonization. Once this period of upheaval passed, however, the rate of new intrastate wars again declined.

There is at least one significant recent counter-trend. The total number of interstate and intrastate wars declined sharply from a high of thirty-eight in 1990 to twenty in 2004 but then the number jumped back up to twenty-seven in 2005 and has since remained fairly stable (Hewitt 2011). Most of the recent increase is not associated with new wars, however, but rather with recurrences of old wars whose truces or pauses have broken down. By historical standards, the pace of outbreaks of new wars remains low. As J. Joseph Hewitt explains, "Since 2000, there have been five years with no new conflicts at all. No decade since the end of World War II has witnessed so many years in which no newly triggered conflicts have been added to the roster of active conflicts" (2011, 18).

TRENDS IN WAR CASUALTIES

The decline in the incidence of war has helped lead to a simultaneous decrease in the number of people annually killed in wars. The decline in major power and other interstate wars is the primary cause of this decrease in fatalities since interstate wars tend to be much more lethal than intrastate wars (Human Security Report 2011). Thus, even in recent years when the number of intrastate wars increased, because there were simultaneously less interstate wars fewer total combatant and non-combatant deaths occurred.

Milton Leitenberg (2006) estimates about 241 million people died either directly or indirectly from interstate and intrastate wars between 1900 and 1999. Almost 80 percent of these, about 190 million, died before 1946, mostly from World Wars I and II. Horrible

mass violence continued after World War II, but the pace of killing fell dramatically. Approximately 3 million died in the Korean War and another 4 million in the Indochina War, beginning in 1960 and ending in 1975. The continuing present-day war in the Congo region that began in 1996 is estimated by some to have caused as many as 5 million combatant and non-combatant deaths. Still, the absolute number of war-related deaths has declined sharply since 1945 even as the world population has more than doubled. (See Table 4.2, "Declining War Deaths, Combatants and Non-Combatants.")

Though declining, terrible interstate killing continues. The last decades of the twentieth century and beginning of the twenty-first century produced long, major interstate wars between the Soviets and Afghans, Iran and Iraq, and between the United States and both Afghanistan and Iraq. There have been as well long-running intrastate wars in Angola, the Central African Republic, the Congo, Cambodia, Mozambique, Somalia, Syria, and Sudan. Still, all these post-1945 interstate and intrastate wars have produced fewer deaths over the last sixty-five years than occurred in just the five-years-long World War II (Human Security Report Project 2011). The annual number of war deaths in the years since 2000 remains below the already historical low rates of the 1990s even though the total global population continues to rise (Geneva Declaration 2008). Of course, these decreases in wars and their fatalities are based on aggregate data and so do not apply equally to all nations or regions. The United States, for example, is an exception to many peaceful trends. The United States increased both the frequency and duration of its interstate wars across the twentieth century. No other nation has fought as many external wars or had to travel so far from home to pursue them. The duration of these American wars also shows a steady increase. The United States' engagement in the Spanish-American War at the end of the nineteenth century lasted just five months. The United States' active participation in World War I went on for one year and seven months, in World War II for a little less than four years, in Korea for three years, in Vietnam for eight years, in Afghanistan for twelve years, and in Iraq for eight years (or for seventeen years if this latter conflict is considered to have commenced with the Persian Gulf War in 1991).

It is likely in part because the United States has been so often an exception to recent peaceful trends that many in that country remain unaware that in many significant ways the world is becoming more peaceful. (See Case 4-1, "Europe, a Continent at Peace.")

Handwritten annotations:
P — of course it has deaths
(No WW's!) Really no major conflicts either between nations
Q — How skewed or off could the data be?
World flip data change your claims at all?

TABLE 4.2 DECLINING WAR DEATHS, COMBATANTS AND NON-COMBATANTS

Years	Duration	Estimated Fatalities
1900–1945	45 years	100 million
1946–1954	9 years	26 million
1955–2010	55 years	17 million

Sources: Goldstein 2012; Leitenberg 2006; White 2011.

Europe is more peaceful than ever!

CASE 4-1   EUROPE, A CONTINENT OF PEACE

During the first forty-five years of the twentieth century, Europe remained as it had been for many centuries, a continent plagued by frequent horrific wars. Miraculously, in the last half of the twentieth century, Europe became a continent at peace. Today, about 500 million people within the European Union (EU) produce almost 25 percent of the world's gross national product in twenty-eight countries highly unlikely to start wars. This transformation of an entire continent from frequent warring to a stable peace offers hope for other regions where war today remains as common as it was in Europe one hundred years ago.

Part of Europe's transformation resulted from its exhaustion with war. Over 60 million died from wars and other state-sponsored violence across the continent between 1900 and 1945. Still, though World Wars I and II were devastating, other regions in other parts of the world have suffered analogous catastrophes without then transforming themselves into regions of peace. Other factors are responsible for Europe's pacification, including transformations in politics, economics, and culture.

Politically, Europe has become a continent of democracies that aspires to use democratic forms in its foreign policy relations with one another. Such important countries as Greece, Portugal, and Spain made the transition from dictatorships in the decades shortly after WW II. Then, after the fall of the Berlin Wall in 1989, still more European countries transitioned from communism to democracies, driven in part because this transition was a requirement for joining the EU. The European Court of Human Rights, European Court of Justice, and European Parliament now adjudicate disputes between countries and across the region's hundreds of inter-regional agencies. They enforce the "Four Freedoms" stipulated by the Treaty on the Functioning of the European Union. The treaty-mandated rights include the freedom of the movement of goods, people, services, and capital. The EU's free trade zone is now larger than the United States' economy and over twice the size of China's (European Commission 2012).

Beyond the EU stands the separate and larger Council of Europe, with forty-seven member states and 800 million members, including Russia. The Council of

EU!

4 Freedoms

Europe aims to promote the "fundamental values of human rights, democracy, and the rule of law" even within states that are not members of the more exclusive EU.

A growing sense of common culture and identity has also helped turn Europe into a continent at peace. People still strongly identify with their particular countries, regions and, sometimes, ethnicities, but they also increasingly include "European" as a part of their identity. This includes the shared experience for many of using the euro as a common currency. European schools and universities offer similar curricula; stores sell similar consumer goods. The sense of a pan-European identity is further strengthened by Europe's linked railroads and highways that enable millions of people to move quickly and with few border impediments as they learn more about one another.

Football (known as soccer in the United States) may be a further accelerator of an emerging pan-European identity. Devotion to local teams remains rabid, but these teams are increasingly made up of players and led by managers who have been traded back and forth across the continent and beyond. In addition, inter-European competitions among countries are common. A massive pan-European television audience for these games generates a carnival nationalism that is often fervent but seldom violent.

Comparable peace-promoting political, economic, and cultural factors are also at work transforming some other regions of the world. Canada, Mexico, and the United States already form an almost continent-sized region of peace built on democratic, economic, and legal institutions like those found in Europe. Central and South America may similarly be on the way to establishing a region of peace based on transnational democratic governance, economic integration, and the rule of law. A common language (except for Brazil) and a shared colonial history could facilitate the growth of a common Latin American identity as well.

Europe's twentieth-century transformation "from a continent of wars to a continent of peace" (as the Nobel Peace Prize Committee chair Thorbjørn Jagland phrases it) may foreshadow Earth's future.

Sources: Buchanan 2012; Judt 2006; Middelaar 2013; thanks for suggestions from Manuel Lucas Nicolini.

Council of Europe

Civilians were the primary target of the September 11
terrorist attack on the World Trade Center.

TARGETING CIVILIANS

As mentioned, the broad trend toward fewer wars has led to fewer civilian as well as to
fewer military fatalities. Of course, the rate at which non-combatants die varies greatly by
war, as does the rate of combatant fatalities. World War II was especially lethal for civilians, much worse than World War I or most wars since. Still, though the data will always
remain incomplete, most researchers agree that the proportion of **civilian casualties** in
wars has probably remained about the same, at about 50 percent, throughout the modern
period. In wars since 1700, at least, non-combatants and combatants have tended to die in
about equal proportions (Eckhardt 1992, Goldstein 2011).

Military strategists sometimes target non-combatants, especially when they conceive
their wars to be as much about subduing civilians as about winning resources and territories. If people's willingness to resist can be crushed, their material wealth is then thought
to follow. So the Germans bombed civilian London, the Japanese bombed civilian China,
and the Allies bombed both civilian Germany and Japan, all hoping that indiscriminate

killing of non-combatants would demoralize the citizenry, preparing the survivors to submit to their attacker's will.

The United States expanded the strategy of targeting civilians in its war in Korea to such an extent that it dropped more bombs across the Korean peninsula than had been used across the entire continent of Europe in World War II. Around 2 million non-combatant Koreans were killed (Cumings 2010). A decade later in Southeast Asia, the United States dropped about four times more tons of explosives than it had throughout all of World War II, again mostly on civilians. Across Cambodia, Laos, and Vietnam, the United States flew 3.4 million aircraft sorties, exploded 30 billion pounds of munitions, wounded approximately 5 million, and killed between 1.5 and 3 million more (Turse 2013).

Despite its frequent use, targeting civilians usually produces opposite results from those planned. The English did not become more willing to obey the Germans in 1940 and 1941 because of the German Blitz that included bombing London for fifty-seven consecutive nights, destroying or damaging a million houses while killing over 43,000 civilians. The Germans, similarly, did not grow significantly more amenable to yielding to foreign desires because of the massive Allied attacks on German cities, nor did the Chinese surrender after the Japanese killed a half million civilians. The later American killing of millions of Koreans and Southeast Asian civilians, too, generally did not lead to the submission of large portions of the surviving civilian populations.

A once-secret U.S. Department of Defense report concluded in 1967 that it is a "well-documented" fact established from previous bombing campaigns, as well as those then underway in Southeast Asia, that "a direct, frontal attack on a society tends to strengthen the social fabric of a nation, to increase popular support of the existing government, to improve the determination of both the leadership and the populace to fight back, to induce a variety of protective measures that reduce the society's vulnerability to future attack and to develop an increased capacity for quick repairs" (quoted in Young 2008, 164–65). Targeting civilians, in short, is usually not just an immoral but also a very ineffective strategy.

LEARNING MORE   AMERICAN EXCEPTIONALISM

The United States military has attacked about two dozen countries since World War II (Zunes 2009). These include: Afghanistan, Bosnia, Cambodia, Cuba, Haiti, Iraq, Korea, Kuwait, Laos, Libya, Panama, Pakistan, Philippines, Somalia, Syria, Vietnam, Yemen, and Yugoslavia-Serbia. The United States has also undertaken covert attacks and assassinations in several additional countries, including Chile, Columbia, Guatemala, Iran, and Somalia.

The United States' willingness to kill people in countries far beyond its own borders arises from many factors. These include the unusual circumstance that the United States has fought multiple recent wars without simultaneously suffering significant casualties on its own soil. The multiple military assaults on other countries launched by

the United States in reaction to the September 11, 2001, attacks arose in part because the country was so unaccustomed to having its own non-combatants targeted at home. About 2,400 were killed in the Japanese attack on Pearl Harbor in 1941, but less than 100 of these were civilians. Seven people were killed in the first attack on New York's Twin Towers in 1993. The Oklahoma City bombing of 1995 left about 168 non-combatants dead. Prior to 2001, these were the only major attacks causing civilian fatalities that Americans had endured on their own soil.

The shock generated by the number of casualties from the September 11 attacks helped government leaders persuade the American public that the customary legal way of responding to terrorism, with policing, indictments, and criminal trials, was insufficient.

Despite the customarily dismal chances of success, countries with air forces, missiles, and now drones continue to target non-combatants, especially when the probable victims live in countries with little capacity to retaliate by similarly killing civilians in the attacking country. The use of this tactic comes with increasing risks, however, and so most countries that target civilians now strive to hide the damage they do or, when confronted, tend to lie about how many non-combatants have been killed. Fortunately, government cover-ups are becoming increasingly difficult to maintain as many groups within the global peace network, assisted by social media and mobile imaging, help non-combatants publicize deaths that in earlier times would likely have remained unacknowledged and unknown.

FOUR TYPES OF TERRORISM

Terrorism has received much attention since the September 11, 2001, attacks in the United States. Surprisingly, despite this rising awareness, rates of terrorist violence and fatalities have shown few clear patterns over the last fifty years. In a study of 87,000 attacks since 1970, LaFree and Dugan (2012) found that terrorism across the world has ebbed and flowed with no direct association to the factors that have decreased the frequency and deadliness of interstate and intrastate wars.

Terrorism is premeditated violence directed primarily at non-combatants. It aims to produce fear—terror—and so, it is hoped, to advance a political cause. Unlike military violence, which seeks to force opponents to surrender or obey, terrorists use violence mainly to try to change public opinion, governmental policies, or both. As Bruce Hoffman reported to the United States Congress, terrorism is thus a form of psychological warfare "used to create unbridled fear, deep insecurity, and reverberating panic" (Hoffman 2002). Terrorism impacts individuals but then, through them, can have repercussions throughout entire countries and regions, altering patterns of everyday life and economic, governmental, and social institutions.

Most people associate terrorism with rebellious civilians but governments also frequently use violence to produce fear for political ends. In much of the world people have long been more likely to be victims of government-based rather than civilian-based terrorism. In the twentieth century, governments terrorized and killed many millions more of their citizens than have been killed by all civilian-based terrorists throughout human history. Governments led by murdering tyrants such as Joseph Stalin, Mao Tse-tung, Pol Pot, and Idi Amin gave their citizens much more to fear than did the nongovernmental groups—the so-called citizen terrorists—that sometimes violently opposed them.

Following a suggestion first made by Haig Khatchadourian (1998), government-initiated terrorism can be called **terrorism from above** or **state-sponsored terrorism** to distinguish it from civilian-based terrorism, known as terrorism from below. As indicated in Table 4.3, each type of terrorism may focus on creating fear either in domestic or in international populations. Terrorism from above is focused on domestic targets when a government uses violence to intimidate its own citizens. Terrorism from above becomes international when governments sponsor attacks on civilians in foreign lands aimed at changing psychological more than military conditions.

Contemporary North Korea provides a clear, current example of the effective use of domestic terrorism from above. Historical examples of large-scale international terrorism

TABLE 4.3 FOUR TYPES OF TERRORISM A IP

Source	Domestic	International
From above, also known as state-sponsored	Success rate: Declining. E.g., Hosni Mubarak's reign	Success rate: Low. E.g., U.S. 2003 shock and awe attacks on Iraq
From below, also known as civilian-based	Success rate: Very low. E.g., Timothy McVeigh's attack on an Oklahoma federal building	Success rate: Extremely low. E.g., September 11, 2001, attacks

from above include the Japanese air attacks on civilian Chinese during the Second Sino-Japanese War and German air attacks on civilians in Great Britain in 1940–41. Later bombing by the Americans of Dresden, Hiroshima, and Nagasaki were similarly aimed primarily at producing widespread fear among the Germans and Japanese. Much of the later American war against Vietnam and Cambodia also targeted non-combatants in an attempt to lessen their support for independence. Decades later, before its planned invasion of Iraq in 2003, the United States launched a campaign of terror from above that was broadcast on international television and labeled by the U.S. military as a campaign of "shock and awe." The nearly 1,700 bombs and missiles then exploded in Iraq had a secondary military purpose but were aimed primarily at producing feelings of disorientation and helplessness among the Iraqi people and so meet the definition of international terrorism from above.

Terrorism from below is undertaken by non-state actors and can also manifest in both domestic and international forms. Well-known instances of domestic terrorism from below include the Ku Klux Klan's decades-long campaigns of intimidation against black Americans and their supporters. Begun by groups of whites after the Civil War, these terrorizing acts of assault, torture, and murder continued intermittently across much of the United States until the middle of the twentieth century. The 1960s saw the emergence of many new domestic terrorist groups across the world, including the African National Congress in South Africa, the Tupamaros in Uruguay, the Red Army Faction in Germany, the Red Brigades in Italy, and the Red Army in Japan.

Another well-known example of domestic terrorism from below was the violent campaign of the Provisional Irish Republican Army in the United Kingdom begun in the 1970s. The Provisional Irish Republican Army used violence against civilians as well as against security personnel in an attempt to force the United Kingdom to relinquish sovereignty over Northern Ireland. More recently, in 1995 Timothy McVeigh acted as a terrorist from below when he killed 168 in an Oklahoma City federal building in an effort to undermine the legitimacy of the United States government. Another American terrorist from below, Eric Rudolph, killed two and injured about 150 others in attacks from 1996 through 1998, most through planting a bomb at the Centennial Olympic Park during the 1996 Atlanta Olympics. Norway, with a population of about five million, likely suffered modern history's worst loss from a single domestic act of terrorism from below on July 22, 2011 when a single attacker killed 78. This was a much larger proportion of a single country's population to die than had been killed in previous terrorist acts from below in other countries.

Search and rescue crews attend a memorial service for victims of the terrorist bombing of the Murrah Federal Building in Oklahoma City in 1995.

The fourth type of terrorism, international terrorism from below, occurs when civilians launch campaigns of fear beyond the borders of their own countries. The Palestinian Liberation Organization was among the first to internationalize terrorism from below when they murdered Israeli athletes on German soil during the 1972 Olympics. The 1990s saw much growth in international networks of terrorism from below. This expansion produced the 1992 World Trade Center truck bombing which killed six and injured more than a thousand. Almost a decade later, on September 11, 2001, a separate international terrorist network, al-Qaeda, orchestrated multiple commercial airline attacks on the World Trade Center and the Pentagon.

TERRORISM AS A LOSING STRATEGY

Whether applied from above or below, domestically or internationally, terrorism seldom works.

Domestic terrorism from above has produced the most successes among the four types but even this type of state-sponsored terrorism may be becoming increasingly difficult to

Domestic Terrorism has produced the most successes!

sustain. So, for example, Joseph Stalin and Mao Tse-tung were able to terrorize and control their citizens for long periods of time. Success with terrorism from above against their own citizens also later worked for years for Mohammad Reza Shah Pahlavi in Iran, Ferdinand Marcos in the Philippines, Augusto Pinochet in Chile, the white minority in South Africa, Charles Taylor in Liberia, Saddam Hussein in Iraq, Zine El Abidine Ben Ali in Tunisia, Hosni Mubarak in Egypt, and Mu'ammer al-Gaddafi in Libya. These leaders and regimes, however, were eventually driven from power in part by people's uprisings that exploited intrinsic weaknesses in governance built on terrorism from above.

Rule by fear works only as long as citizens remain intimidated. As the chapters in Part Two will show, once and if a committed minority of citizens refuses to be frightened, the effectiveness of domestic terrorism from above can deteriorate rapidly. The twenty-three-year reign of terror of Zine El Abidine Ben Ali in Tunisia collapsed in twenty-eight days and the thirty-year reign of Hosni Mubarak in Egypt ended in eighteen days, once large groups of citizens took to the streets to defy the threats of violence from above that their governments had for years used to terrorize them.

The record of success of international terrorism from above is even less robust than that of international terrorism from below. As mentioned earlier, although the bombing of civilians in London, Dresden, Hiroshima, Nagasaki, Cambodia, Vietnam, and Baghdad did create fear in the populace of the targeted countries, the tactic little altered the fundamentals of the associated wars. Civilians commonly increase their support for their existing governments when they are bombed by foreign powers. International terrorism from above thus more often solidifies status quo political policies than triggers the regime changes that the foreign terrorizers desire.

Terrorism from below in both its domestic and international manifestations also has a dismal record of success. In a pioneering study, Max Abrahms (2006) found that only two of the twenty-eight terrorist groups he examined achieved their goals. In a yet more comprehensive study of 648 non-state terrorists groups, Seth G. Jones and Martin C. Libicki (Jones and Libicki 2008) found a slightly higher but still anemic 10 percent of terrorist groups succeeded. Assaulting and killing civilians is seldom an effective way to change public attitudes and government policies in ways terrorists desire.

In fact, terrorism from below frequently makes the terrorists' goals even harder to attain. Consider, for example, that one of al-Qaeda's primary goals in its September 11 attacks was to produce insecurity and panic among Americans that would then inspire a reduction in Western interference in the economies and politics of the Arab world. The attacks did work to raise the level of fear among citizens of the United States and some of its allies. However, this increased terror did not reduce America's cultural, economic, or military presence across the Middle East. Instead, in the ten years after September 11, the United States poured hundreds of billions of dollars and hundreds of thousands of troops into the region attempting to bolster its influence even more.

Of course, terrorism from below does sometimes succeed. The Ku Klux Klan's violent campaigns of intimidation helped repress the civil rights of black Americans for many decades. More typical, however, are results like those produced by the violent terrorism against civilians perpetrated by the Provisional Irish Republican Army, Timothy McVeigh,

Eric Rudolph, the 2004 Madrid train bombings, the 2005 London transportation system bombings, the 2011 Norway attacks, and the 2013 Boston Marathon bombing. These efforts failed completely, as does about 90 percent of all terrorism from below.

COUNTERING TERRORISM FROM BELOW

Jones and Libicki's study of 648 terrorist groups included data on 268 groups that ended their violent campaigns between 1968 and 2006. Seven percent of them were defeated by military action while 10 percent won clear political or military victories. However, the vast majority of terrorism from below ended either through political negotiations (43 percent) or through police work (40 percent). (See Table 4.4, "How 268 Terrorist Groups Ended, 1968–2006.")

Domestic and internationally coordinated police action was nearly six times more effective in ending terrorism than military action. Successful military action is usually only possible when terrorists form large, well-armed, and well-organized insurgent armies. However, most terrorist groups remain dispersed, in part to thwart the effectiveness of hostile military action. Police work and, if possible, negotiation are by far the most effective methods of decreasing and ending terrorism from below.

Because they work so well, law enforcement and the criminal justice system are customarily used in response to terrorism in most parts of the developed world. For example, extensive domestic and international police work began in the United States immediately after the first World Trade Center bombing in 1993. Arrests were made within a month and four men were convicted in 1994 of charges that included conspiracy, explosive destruction of property, and interstate transportation of explosives. The man who planned the bombings and the driver of the truck carrying the bomb were convicted in a later trial in 1997.

Similarly, in 1995, after sarin gas killed thirteen and injured fifteen in the Tokyo subway system, the Japanese government launched an extensive, multi-agency criminal investigation, which eventually led to the indictment and trial of 189 members of Aum Shinrikyo. Other well-known police responses to terrorism include what was then the largest police investigation in European history mounted by the British in response to the 1988 terrorist bombing that brought down Pan Am Flight 103 in Scotland. These efforts led to the trial and conviction of two Libyan intelligence agents. The British later launched another widespread criminal investigation in 2005 after four bombs exploded in different areas of the London public transportation system, killing fifty-two civilians and four bombers, while injuring over seven hundred more. Spain reacted similarly with police action when explosions killed 191 and wounded 1,800 on multiple trains in Madrid in 2004.

TABLE 4.4   HOW 268 TERRORIST GROUPS ENDED, 1968–2006

Through political negotiations	43%
Through police work and the judicial system	40%
Through winning its goals	10%
Defeated through military action	7%

Source: Jones and Libicki 2008.

TABLE 4.5 MAJOR TERRORIST ATTACKS IN EUROPE AND NORTH AMERICA SINCE WW II

Year	Event	Casualties	Perpetrators	Response Type*	Response Results
1973	Pan Am Flight 110 over Italy	33 dead	International	Police	Negotiated release of 5 unindicted perpetrators
1974	Birmingham Pub bombings	21 dead	Domestic	Police	6 convictions later overturned
1985	EgyptAir Flight 648 over Greece	60 dead	International	Police	1 conviction
1985	El Descanso bombing	18 dead	International	Police	1 indictment but refused extradition
1985	Rome & Vienna airport attacks	19 dead	International	Police	No indictments
1987	Hipercor bombing—Barcelona	21 dead	Domestic	Police	4 convictions
1988	Pan Am Flight 103	270 dead	International	Police	2 convictions
1993	World Trade Center bombing	7 dead; 1,000+ injured	International	Police	6 convictions
1995	Oklahoma City bombing	168 dead	Domestic	Police	2 convictions
2001	Sept. 11 attacks	2,976 dead	International	Military	15,000 non-combatant Afghani fatalities; 3,000 coalition combatant fatalities
2004	Madrid train bombings	191 dead; 1,800 wounded	Domestic/ International	Police	21 convictions
2005	7/7; London bombings	52 dead; 700 injured	Domestic/ International	Police	Arrests; deportations
2009	Fort Hood shooting	13 dead; 30 wounded	Domestic/ International	Military police	1 conviction
2011	Norway attacks	77 dead; 319 injured	Domestic	Police	1 conviction
2013	Boston Marathon bombing	3 dead; 264 injured	Domestic/ International	Police	Awaiting trial in 2013

*Response Type—"police" may include use of multi-domestic and international agencies, but suggests the primary emphasis is on the criminality of the event and a reliance on existing criminal justice procedures.

Surprisingly, the United States chose not to mount a police-based response to the September 11, 2001, attacks. Instead, the United States declared that it was "at war" and launched a military invasion of Afghanistan that was later expanded into other countries, including Iraq, Pakistan, Somalia, and Yemen. By the end of 2012, the war in Afghanistan had by itself produced 12,000 more non-combatant deaths among Afghanis than were killed in the September 11 attacks. Hundreds of thousands more

Afghanis have been displaced from their homes. U.S. troops and their allies have suffered over 4,000 deaths and 15,000 serious wounds (see Chapter 2, Table 2.5).

A few of the people responsible for the September 11 attacks were killed in these wars but, according to analysts at the Rand Corporation, in the decade after the beginning of the Afghanistan war al-Qaeda greatly increased its global reach and was involved in many more terrorist attacks than in all the previous years of its existence (Jones and Libicki 2008, xv). The United States' military response helped al-Qaeda gather millions of new sympathizers, thousands of new recruits, and become a more dangerous enemy of the United States and its allies (Jones and Libicki 2008, xi). Spain and the United Kingdom, by contrast, relied on the customary policing option in response to their own separate, horrific terrorist attacks in 2004 and 2005. Their approaches created no new combatant or non-combatant deaths and seem to have been at least as successful at enhancing their citizens' security as did the much more lethal—and expensive—post-9/11 military approach that the United States embraced.

In future decades, the use of law enforcement and the criminal justice system is likely to continue to be the most effective response to terrorism from below. (See Table 4.5, "Major Terrorist Attacks in Europe and North America Since WW II.")

BIOLOGICAL AND CHEMICAL WARFARE

New technologies alter how wars and terrorism are fought and how frequently people die. The American Civil War, for example, saw one of the first widespread deployments of single-shot rifles, which were more accurate and deadly than the muskets used in earlier wars. By World War I, most soldiers were carrying bolt-action rifles holding multiple bullets. The further industrialization of war also brought heavy artillery and machine guns into increasingly frequent and devastating use. World War II introduced aerial bombing by piloted planes and pilot-less missiles, then ended with the detonation of atom bombs on civilian populations in Hiroshima and Nagasaki. The manufacture of nuclear weapons followed along with, as mentioned earlier, a half century in which aerial bombing of civilian targets became a common means of warfare for countries such as the United States with planes that could mount such attacks.

Several other important weapons that have not yet become a routine part of violent conflicts could reverse current global trends toward decreasing rates of war-related fatalities. Three of these technologies deserve attention here: biological and chemical agents, cyber warfare, and unmanned drones and robots.

Biological and chemical weapons are human-made agents capable of killing millions, perhaps even billions, of people. Their potential harm may be even greater than that of nuclear weapons as biological and chemical weapons require much less money or scientific sophistication to produce. Only a handful of countries currently have the ability to produce and deploy nuclear weapons while many small groups and thousands of individuals could create lethal disasters using biological and chemical weapons. Iraq is thought to have killed approximately five thousand Kurds and as many as two thousand Iranians with chemical weapons during the Iran–Iraq war (Horvitz and Catherwood 2006). Large stockpiles of chemical weapons stored in Syria were used with fatal consequences during the civil war that began in 2011.

⑤ Treaties

The adoption of the Biological Weapons Convention in 1975, eventually signed by 165 nations, created the first multilateral disarmament treaty that banned the production of an entire category of weapons. Later, in the 1990s, a similar Chemical Weapons Convention outlawing chemical weapons was adopted by even more nations. These two treaties demonstrate that the international community can make itself safer, when the will and conditions permit.

CYBER WARFARE

Treaties like those associated with biological and chemical weapons are only as effective as their signatories wish them to be. And new technologies can render earlier agreements and treaties ineffective. Computers offer a vivid example of unexpected changes in weaponry as they are already weakening the long association of war with physically harming opponents and with seizing territories. Countries increasingly occupy virtual, nonphysical spaces where they manipulate information essential to their economic, military, political, and social activities. Groups are thus now beginning to battle in virtual worlds, in forms of conflict almost inconceivable but a half a century ago. **Cyber warfare**, the most common name for these virtual battles, include acts sponsored by nation-states, international organizations, or other non-state groups that aim to damage or destroy an opponent's information networks and communication capabilities. The most common methods of cyber warfare occur through disseminating computer viruses or denial-of-service attacks. DDOS !

Criminal, economic, entertainment-seeking, and political hackers have so far been responsible for most cyber assaults but sophisticated, well-planned attacks by nation-states are becoming more common. For example, a joint American-Israeli cyberattack damaged Iran's nuclear industry in 2010 using malware code-named Stuxnet (Sanger 2012). According to a former director of intelligence at the U.S. National Security Agency, this was just one of several cyberattacks the United States has launched, though neither the targets nor results have been made public ("US Launched Cyber Attacks" 2012). Many vital web servers in the country of Georgia were subject to cyberattacks during its 2008 conflict with Russia. Over a million computers were disabled in Estonia in 2007 by attacks thought to come from Russia. North Korea is suspected of launching cyberattacks against South Korea.

Incidences of cyber warfare will probably increase in the years ahead since it is much cheaper and easier to wage cyber than traditional warfare. Cyberattacks could even work to prevent physical wars by preemptively destroying weapons or command and control systems before hostilities break out. As philosopher Mariarosaria Taddeo concludes, cyber warfare "has the potential to be blood-free, but that's only one potentiality; this technology could just as easily be used to produce the kind of damage caused by a bomb or any other traditional weapon—just imagine what would happen if a cyberattack was launched against a flight control system or a subway system" (quoted in Anderson 2012). There will likely be increasingly frequent wars in cyberspace but no one knows whether this will lead to an increase or decrease in human fatalities.

DRONES AND ROBOTS

Lethal autonomous weapons, popularly known as drones and robots, are yet another technological advance with the potential to alter war and also terrorism both from above and below. **Lethal autonomous weapons** are unmanned devices designed to carry out killing missions with little or no human intervention. Non-lethal autonomous devices associated with surveillance and reconnaissance have been used increasingly for decades. The United States Air Force now trains many more drone than traditional pilots; most new military airplane designs assume they will be flown unmanned (Caryl 2011).

The United States is so far the only nation that frequently deploys autonomous weapons to kill people (Benjamin 2012). It used many of its army's 15,000 non-lethal ground robots in its recent wars in Afghanistan and Iraq and deployed lethal aerial drones increasingly as these conflicts dragged on. **Drone warfare** occurs when unmanned lethal autonomous weapons are used to kill either or both combatants and non-combatants. The use of the seven thousand remotely-controlled aerial drones currently possessed by the United States was expanded under President Barack Obama to include missions aimed at people in Libya, Pakistan, Somalia, Syria, and Yemen. From 2004 through September 2014 the New America Foundation (International Security 2014) estimates there were anywhere from 2,141 to 3,510 people killed by the United States' unmanned drones in Pakistan alone.

More than forty other countries are currently developing lethal drones and robots of their own (Caryl 2011). If they follow the United States' example, within a few years Brazil, Canada, China, France, India, Iran, Israel, North Korea, Russia, South Korea, the United Kingdom, and perhaps others could begin launching unmanned drones into foreign lands to kill people that their leaders believe pose current or potential dangers to their interests.

Several organizations within the global peace network are trying to create treaties that regulate the use of lethal autonomous weapons (Benjamin 2012). One prominent group, the International Committee for Robot Arms Controls (ICRAC), has issued warnings about the growing ability of robots to choose targets on their own, without human input. South Korea, for example, now deploys just such autonomous weapons, known as SGR-A1s, to patrol its border with North Korea. ICRAC also points to the catastrophic threat posed by autonomous weapons that could carry nuclear weapons.

Predicting trends in future deployment of lethal robots and drones is very difficult. Nevertheless, it is possible this practice will become widespread. If it does, the United States may come to regret pioneering the use of autonomous weapons to kill people in distant countries with which it is not at war.

RESOURCE WARS RECONSIDERED

As Chapter 3 reported, many people fear that climate change will increase violence and war. These fears may prove warranted but, so far, though they have looked carefully using multiple methods and time periods, researchers have found little evidence to support the claim that rising temperatures automatically or commonly produce rising rates of violence (e.g., Gartzke 2012; Scheffran et al. 2012).

In the largest study yet undertaken, Richard S. J. Tol and Sebastian Wagner (2010) found higher mean temperatures in pre-industrialized Europe did not correlate with increased rates of violent conflict. A similar absence of a pattern was found in a related study of the correlation between temperatures and violence in pre-industrial China (Zhang et al. 2006).

Tol and Wagner's study also looked at the lower mean temperatures associated with modern industrialization in Europe and found a clear correlation between lower temperatures and decreasing violence. They reasoned that people are generally less dependent on local temperature-based variations in agricultural, hunting, and fishing production in today's industrialized economies. If generally true, then our contemporary globalized economic conditions may help diffuse violent tensions in future periods of rising temperatures.

Climate change will likely help make some regions richer and others poorer, for example, by transforming what are fertile and what are unfruitful fishing areas and agricultural lands. However, such changes in the distribution of resources have historically not led to increases in violence and wars. World regions and localities already live under conditions built on extreme disparities. The United States and thirteen other countries, for example, currently possess an average wealth of over $50,000 per person while the world's fifty poorest countries have a per capita income of less than $5,000, ten times less. Within many rich countries, the disparity between the rich and poor is even larger and growing. Though such immense differences in wealth—and resource availability—may increase with climate change, history does not suggest such disparities necessarily trigger increases in violence.

Since so many future problems are global and cut across political borders, it is possible that future climate change challenges will lead to increased global cooperation rather than to increased violence. In addition, many elements in the global peace network described in Chapter 3 are already working to address environmental problems through movements building coordinated, transnational, ameliorative actions. Of course, these and other efforts may prove insufficient. Acidified, rising oceans, hotter temperatures across land and seas, mass extinctions, and extreme weather could lead to increased violence and war. If they do, however, it will not be because there is an automatic causal connection between climate conditions and human behavior. Human cultures and choices will be the primary causes of future levels of peace and violence, just as they were in the past.

MAKING CONNECTIONS

Chapter 5 continues this chapter's review of trends by looking at patterns of violence and peace associated with girls, women, and LGBT groups. The rising power of women may be the single most positive trend at work in the world today.

As was mentioned earlier, increasing awareness of positive trends in peacefulness can help bolster people's confidence that even more can be done to reduce both direct and indirect violence. Still, most trends described in this chapter have narrowly focused mostly on developments associated with decreasing direct violence and increasing negative peace. Trends in positive peace, in both structural and cultural violence, do not necessarily mirror trends in negative peace. Direct violence can decrease even as indirect violence increases. Inequitable distributions of wealth, for example, are growing worse in many parts of the world where direct violence is rare. Part Two will review the most effective contemporary strategies and groups that promote positive peace.

FOR REVIEW

1. Summarize the main trends in the frequency both of wars and of war casualties.
2. Review why targeting civilians during wars seldom succeeds.
3. Explain the principal differences between terrorism from above and terrorism from below.
4. Describe the different methods associated with the two major approaches to countering terrorism from below.
5. Explore how new technologies may be changing the nature of war.

THINKING CRITICALLY

1. What causes murder rates to differ so greatly from country to country?
2. What were the likely primary causes for the historic sharp decrease in the incidence of murders in Europe?
3. What are the main reasons that interstate wars are decreasing?
4. Is it likely that the increasing industrialization of warfare is making war so deadly that the rate of occurrence of new interstate wars will continue to decline?
5. Why does the targeted bombing of civilians remain so common?
6. What causes terrorism from below to be employed so often even though it so seldom succeeds?
7. Why did the United States not rely on law enforcement and the criminal justice system in response to the September 11, 2001, attacks?
8. Could either biological, chemical, or cyber warfare become a dominant form of future warfare?
9. Will drone warfare likely become much more common in the decades ahead?

RECOMMENDED RESOURCES

Benjamin, Medea. *Drone Warfare: Killing by Remote Control* (New York: OR Books, 2012). A history and analysis of the growing use of lethal drones, with an emphasis on their ethical and political implications, as well as a look at international efforts to curb their use.

Dirty Wars. Directed by Rick Rowley and Jeremy Scahill, 2013. Based on a book by Scahill by the same name, this documentary explores the United States' current, mostly unreported lethal campaigns against people in countries with which the United States is not publicly at war. The film examines the increasing secret use of lethal drones, details multiple instances of the killing of civilians, and considers whether these deaths are creating more enemies of the United States.

Goldstein, Joshua S. *Winning the War on War: The Decline of Armed Conflict Worldwide* (New York: Plume, 2012). Details the age of peacebuilding and the important role that United Nations peacekeeping missions have played over the last twenty years in making wars both less frequent and less deadly.

Hewitt, J. Joseph, Jonathan Wilkenfeld, and Ted Robert Gurr, editors. *Peace and Conflict 2012* (Boulder, CO: Paradigm Publishers, 2011). A biennial report that summarizes key findings in trends and causes of violence at all levels of analysis. The book contains numerous graphs, tables, and maps.

Pinker, Steven. *The Better Angels of Our Nature: Why Violence has Declined* (New York: Viking, 2010). A massive study by a well-known evolutionary psychologist that summarizes data from both the natural and social sciences to support one theory about why for millennia human violence has been in decline.

Richards, Jesse. *The Secret Peace: Exposing the Positive Trend of World Events* (New York: Book and Ladder Press, 2010). An accessible, entertaining summary of recent positive trends including declines in war and violence and rising levels of health and mortality. Richards argues humans will become even healthier and more peaceful in the decades ahead.

Vasquez, John A., editor. *What Do We Know about War?* (Boulder, CO: Rowman & Littlefield, 2012). A collection of sixteen separate articles that surveys contemporary research about the causes of and trends in contemporary interstate wars.

Wallensteen, Peter. *Peace Research: Theory and Practice* (New York: Routledge, 2011). An overview of peace research, from its beginnings in the 1950s until the present. Emphasizes such issues as the causes of war, conflict data, conflict diplomacy, nonviolent sanctions, and third-party diplomacy.

BUILDING GENDER SECURITY

CHAPTER OVERVIEW

This chapter examines gender- and sex-based violence as well as ways that women and others are working to decrease this violence. It begins by describing several major contemporary forms of violence, including war rape, maternal mortality, sex-selective abortion, female infanticide, intimate partner violence, female trafficking and circumcision, and the targeting of lesbian, gay, bisexual, and transgendered people. The chapter then details trends toward an increasing female empowerment and a diminishing of many types of gender- and sex-based violence. These trends include the expanding role of women in politics as well as in peacebuilding organizations and in commerce. The chapter next describes how women's advancement in education and the research sciences is transforming which topics get taught and studied. The chapter concludes with a review of some instances of violence perpetrated by women.

Key terms discussed include: Sex-based violence, gender-based violence; gender roles; war rape; missing women; maternal mortality; sex-selective abortion; female infanticide; intimate partner violence; human trafficking; heteronormativity; critical mass of women; women in peacebuilding; gender perspective; gender-equity profits; women in the research sciences; and violent women.

> The very best predictor of a state's peacefulness is not its level of wealth, its
> level of democracy, or its ethno-religious identity; the best predictor of a
> state's peacefulness is how well its women are treated.
>
> —VALERIE M. HUDSON (2012)

Being female is often dangerous. Girls and women across the globe are regularly targeted for harm simply because they are not male. One out of three women worldwide will be the victim of some form of male-on-female violence at least once in her life (World

Health Organization 2013). And nearly one out of eight women will be injured by men multiple times (United Nations Secretary-General 2006).

In addition to targeted violence against girls and women, many people with an unusual gender appearance or with a minority sexual orientation are also the frequent victims of violence. Few of these gender- and sex-associated types of violence were considered social problems as long as heterosexual men monopolized power. This indifference to gendered violence began diminishing in the industrialized world first in the nineteenth and then more swiftly in the twentieth century as women gained political and economic power.

The growing power of women and of LGBT-identified citizens has also strengthened many elements of the global peace network. And, much evidence shows, increasing the influence of women and of sexual minorities decreases not only sex- and gender-based violence but also many other forms of violence as well (Hudson 2012). Empowering women and gender and sexual minorities is an especially effective way to increase both negative and positive peace.

SEX- AND GENDER-BASED VIOLENCE

Though closely related, it is useful to distinguish between sex-based violence, associated with biological characteristics of males and females, and gender-based violence, associated with social roles.

Sex-based violence is physical or mental harm directed at people because of their biological appearance—or assumed appearance—as either female or male. "Sex" is a biological concept in this phrase and refers to physiological differences between females and males. Sex-based violence is sometimes directed at males but much more often at females (Geneva Declaration 2011). Because of their biological sex-based characteristics, females are aborted, beaten, neglected, starved, raped, denied freedoms and rights, and killed by their families, male friends, and communities. Girls and women are also often victims of sex-based violence during wars and insurrections and then again, once hostilities subside, when they are more often than males held responsible for the healing of their families and communities that mostly male combatants have damaged.

Gender-based violence is physical or mental harm directed at people on the basis of their gender role, social-sexual characteristics, or sexual orientation. Gender is a social and not a biological concept; while biological differences between females and males are much the same across the world, culturally expected feminine and masculine behaviors greatly differ. Women in many industrialized countries, for example, are expected to do more housework and caretaking of children and the elderly than are males. Males are expected to be more interested in sex, sports, violence, and war than are females. These are culturally created gender differences not required by sex-based biological differences.

Gender-based violence is still considered acceptable in many places across the globe. Fathers, husbands, and brothers are accorded the "right" to use physical and psychological violence to control girls and women. Women, in turn, are often defined by **gender roles** that render them unable to vote, deny their husbands sexual demands, seek a divorce, travel freely, or work wherever and at whatever they might choose.

Gender-based violence is often directed at LGBT people for behaviors that differ from traditional gender roles. Most European and North American governments long treated nonconforming sexual and gender behavior as crimes. Accused gender "deviants" were harassed, arrested, and imprisoned with varying degrees of frequency and harshness. In the United States, some state laws criminalizing consensual same-sex behaviors remained in effect until 2003. In many parts of the world, LGBT people continue to be prosecuted. According to Amnesty International (2013), there are thirty-eight African countries alone where same-sex conduct is illegal. Same-sex convictions may even carry the death penalty in Mauritania, Sudan, and Somalia. Previously, in twentieth-century Europe and North America, physicians and psychologists used drugs and aversive therapies, including electroshock, to try to cure a disease they named "homosexuality." Though this diagnostic category was removed from the official list of psychological disorders in 1973, "homosexual" continues to be used as a term of abuse.

Acts of gender- and sex-based violence often overlap. For example, female infanticide is mostly violence against a child because she is biologically female, but it is also caused in part by the low value many cultures place on the feminine gender role. Similarly, though intimate partner violence is often directed at women because their gender is thought to be worth less than that of men, some of the damage associated with intimate partner violence may occur because biologically-based secondary sexual characteristics tend to make men possess greater upper body strength than females. In general, stronger people can inflict more severe harms than weaker people.

Sex and gender are both factors in the types of violence to be considered now. These violence types are, in order discussed: war and war rape, missing women, intimate partner violence, human trafficking, female circumcision, and LGBT-based violence.

WOMEN AND WAR

Although women have often been the sexual spoils and physical victims of war, they have seldom been among the powerbrokers who make decisions about when and where women, and others, would die. Though infrequently direct combatants, women suffer disproportionately from war in several ways. They are more likely to become refugees and are also more likely than boys and men to be victims of war rape. Women and their dependent children are also more likely than adult males to be driven from their homes by civil disturbances and wars. Fathers, husbands, and brothers are more often part of insurgencies or armies, or have left their families seeking to survive on their own. Exact numbers of refugees who have crossed national borders or who are internally displaced persons (refugees within their own countries) fluctuate from year to year. The U.S. Committee for Refugees and Immigrants estimates there have been about 60 million cross-border and in-country refugees in most recent years. Well more than half, maybe as many as 80 percent, are women and children (McKay 1998).

Women commonly bear the primary responsibility for children, the sick and injured, the elderly, and the psychologically wounded. These responsibilities continue to be disproportionately theirs in refugee camps and in communities trying to rebuild once wars end.

Wars and their aftermaths tend to greatly increase the need for familial caregiving at the same time that they diminish the resources women can rely on to help provide care.

Women also suffer from wars as the frequent targets of sexual coercion instead of, or prior to, their murder by attacking insurgents and troops. **War rape** includes the sexual violation and assault of women and girls who reside in or are refugees from a conflict zone. The exact prevalence of war rape in earlier ages is impossible to gauge, but there are some useful estimates of the frequency of sexual violence against women in conflict zones in modern times. Japanese soldiers raped between 20,000 to 80,000 Chinese women after their capture of Nanking (Chang 2011). The Japanese also enslaved 200,000 or more other women from several countries to act as sex slaves for their men in arms. Fewer than half of these women survived the war, and "some were summarily executed or forced to commit suicide together with defeated Japanese soldiers" (Lentin 1997, 10).

About the same time, on the other side of the world, estimates of the number of rapes committed in various countries by Germans on the Eastern Front of World War II range as high as 2 million (Brownmiller 1993). Russian soldiers at the end of that war raped between 100,000 and 2 million German women. There were tens of thousands of rapes during the partition of India in 1947, but the chaos of those times makes accurate estimates very difficult to calculate. The later war during which East Pakistan broke away from West Pakistan to become Bangladesh included the rape of 200,000 to 400,000 women; an estimated 25,000 women became pregnant as a result (Brownmiller 1993).

MISSING WOMEN

In most years, avoidable maternal mortality, sex-selective abortion, and female infanticide account for more female deaths than all other types of gender-based violence combined. In 1990 Nobel Laureate Amartya Sen estimated that over 100 million women and girls were then "missing" from the world population because of the combined effects of female infanticide and selective abortion (Sen 1990). Subsequent studies have supported this estimate of **missing women**, determining that while health care for female infants has improved, sex-specific abortions aimed at terminating females have increased (Sen 2003). The World Bank (2012) calculates there are nearly 3.9 million new missing females each year. This suggests the cumulative total of excess female deaths in the twentieth century was significantly larger than the combined combat death toll for all the wars in those one hundred years (Hudson et al. 2012). As a result, there is currently an unbalanced sex ratio of about 101.3 men for every 100 women on the planet.

Hundreds of thousands of the missing women died unnecessarily during pregnancy or through childbirth complications. **Maternal mortality** rates vary greatly by country but currently worldwide almost 300,000 women die each year from preventable childbearing-related complications. According to the World Health Organization (2012), most of these avoidable deaths are caused by a lack of access to prenatal and birthing health services. Sometimes no such services are available in the community; sometimes services are present but cost more than the distressed mother can afford. Also, often family members and cultural customs keep a mother from accessing care, even when she or her child is dying.

LEARNING MORE SEX AND WORLD PEACE

In the first decade of the twenty-first century, Mary Caprioli and others created the free, online WomanStats Database. Their aim is to provide a way for researchers to test if there are empirically verifiable connections between gender- and sex-based violence and both national and human security. The WomanStats Database currently contains over 130,000 data points with information on 310 indicators of women's status in 174 countries. The first systematic interpretation of this data, *Sex and World Peace*, published in 2012, concluded, "The days when one could claim that the situation of women has nothing to do with matters of national or international security are, frankly, over. The empirical results to the contrary are just too numerous and too robust" (Hudson et al. 2012).

Some of the findings reported in *Sex and World Peace* include:

1. The best predictor of a country's peacefulness is its level of violence against women. Level of gender equity is an even better predictor of peacefulness than a country's level of wealth, level of democracy, or ethno-religious identity.
2. The more vigorously a country protects women within its own border, the more likely it is to honor international agreements and treaties.
3. The greater a country's gender inequities, the more likely it is to (a) be involved in intrastate wars, (b) be involved in interstate wars, (c) be an interstate aggressor, (d) use violence first in conflicts, and (e) escalate the use of violence in conflicts.

After scrutinizing their data, Hudson et al. (2012, 209) conclude, "Establishing gender equality in interpersonal relationships, in homes, in the workplace, and in decision-making bodies at all levels will change states and their behaviors, and in turn will bring prosperity and peace to the world."

Long before these empirical discoveries were made, many women (and some men) had argued that gender- and sex-based violence is at the root of most human violence at all levels. This claim was part of the originating vision of the Women's International League for Peace and Freedom founded in 1915. Decades later, Elise Boulding explored the central importance of gender to peace in *The Underside of History* (1976; rev. ed. 1992) and *Cultures of Peace* (2000). Betty Reardon offered related, influential examinations of the centrality of gender to building all forms of peace in *Sexism and the War System* (1985) and *Women and Peace* (1993).

Additional recent analyses of violence from a gender perspective include biologist Judith L. Hand's *A Future without War* (Hand 2006), sociologist Kathleen Lois Barry's *Unmaking War, Remaking Men* (2010), and several pioneering studies by political scientist Mary Caprioli and her collaborators (e.g., Caprioli 2000; 2003; 2005; Caprioli and Boyer 2001).

Many victims of maternal mortality live in rural, tribal areas in Africa and Asia where women's lives are valued less than men's.

In **sex-selective abortion** more female than male fetuses are terminated in utero. In some modern countries with strong preferences for males and wide access to prenatal imaging, the sex ratio of newborns has become unprecedentedly unbalanced. For example, estimates suggest that in contemporary China about 118 boy babies are now born every year for every 100 girls (Hudson et al. 2012). In 2005, abortion and associated gender-based factors had created total population ratios of about 107 males to 100 females in both India and China, and near 105 males to 100 females in Pakistan and Bangladesh (Guilmoto 2007). These four countries together make up about 40 percent of the world's total population.

Female infanticide is caused by active violence or neglect and causes the premature death of many more females than males. Current rates of infanticide are very difficult to determine since most perpetrators disguise their acts. History does show that female infanticide has been practiced at some time in most cultures while systematic male infanticide has been extremely rare. Gender-based neglect also produces higher rates of fatal disease for female children than for males, adding further to the phenomenon of unbalanced sex ratios. Girls in many places are regularly provided with less medical care, food, and social services than boys in the same circumstances. Girls are thus more likely to become sick and to die prematurely (Mazurana and McKay 2001).

INTIMATE PARTNER VIOLENCE

The devaluing of girls and women that produces elevated maternal mortality rates, sex-selective abortion, female infanticide, and gender-based neglect often encourages adult males to harm their female acquaintances and partners (Dutton et al. 2003).

Male-on-female intimate partner violence is the single most widespread type of interpersonal violence in the world. Also called domestic violence, **intimate partner violence** commonly takes the form of battering, assault, murder, rape and other types of sexual coercion, as well as acts of controlling behaviors such as isolating a partner from family and friends or restricting access to information and assistance. Intimate partner violence was long ignored, sometimes even encouraged. For example, in the United States until the last decades of the twentieth century, "most states retained marital exemptions from rape laws. In some states, this exemption was extended to common-law husbands and live-in partners" (Purdy 2004, 123). Murdering a woman if she had "dishonored" her husband remained legal in Brazil until 1991. In many parts of the world men still frequently physically and sexually abuse females with little threat of prosecution. A global review of the status of women found that even today, "The majority of women live in countries where laws prohibiting violence against women are either nonexistent or unenforced and where social norms do not define domestic violence, rape, and even murder as serious and accurately reported crimes" (Hudson et al. 2012, 209).

Accurate estimates of the rate of intimate partner violence are difficult to determine since it is likely that less than one in three female victims of violence report their victimization to the authorities (United Nations Secretary-General 2006). In the United States, one survey found that women report physical assaults by partners and acquaintances only 27 percent of the time and rapes even less often, at about a 17 percent rate (Dutton et al. 2003). The absence of data about intimate partner violence was seldom considered a problem until women gained sufficient power late in the twentieth century to begin pressuring male-dominated governments to develop a clearer understanding of the scope of domestic violence. Finally, in the first decade of the new century, five female researchers sponsored by the World Health Organization (WHO) completed the first comprehensive study aimed at filling the knowledge gap (Garcia-Moreno et al. 2006; Ellsberg et al. 2008).

These female WHO researchers interviewed over 24,000 women in ten countries who had had intimate male partners in their lifetimes. Women who told the interviewers that they had experienced physical abuse from their partners ranged from a low of 13 percent in urban Japan to a high of 61 percent in rural Peru. The WHO study also found that physical intimate partner violence was generally more common than sexual violence. Sexual intimate partner violence is still a frequent problem, however, as rape and other coercive sexual activity were reported by from 10 to 50 percent of the women in the sampled countries. A recent study of nine thousand women in the United States found that 10 percent had been raped by an intimate partner and that another 17 percent had experienced other forms of sexual violence by a partner (National Center for Injury Prevention and Control 2011).

If a woman is murdered, it is as likely to be by her intimate partner as by a stranger (Ellsberg et al. 2008). Data from Australia, the United States, Canada, Israel, and South Africa show that 40 to 70 percent of female murder victims were killed by their husbands or boyfriends. In the United States, by contrast, wives or girlfriends were responsible for only four percent of all murdered men. Many of these latter murders, too, were retaliatory, committed by women who had previously been assaulted multiple times by the men they subsequently murdered (Stolberg 2002).

Immediate physical injuries are often not the worst consequences of intimate partner violence. The WHO study identified multiple lingering physical problems, including difficulty with walking and completing other daily activities, chronic pain, memory loss, dizziness, and unusual vaginal discharges. Many women also reported significantly more psychological problems than non-abused women, including more emotional distress, suicidal thoughts, and suicide attempts (Ellsberg et al. 2008). Another study, focused only on the United States, found that victims of intimate partner violence were from three to five times more likely than non-victims to suffer from depression, suicide attempts, post-traumatic stress disorder, and substance abuse (Dutton et al. 2003, 157).

FEMALE TRAFFICKING AND CIRCUMCISION

Two very different additional forms of gender-based violence, female trafficking and circumcision, also deserve attention. Girls and women are disproportionately found among the estimated 4 million to 27 million people who newly become "human traffic" each year (Clawson et al. 2009). **Human trafficking** refers to recruiting, transporting, harboring, or employing a person through the use of force, coercion, or other means, for the purpose of exploiting him or her. Trafficked individuals sometimes accept offers from what appear to be legitimate sources and then find themselves trapped in situations where their documents are destroyed and they or their families are threatened with harm, or with large debts that they have no chance of repaying (Bales 1999; Dutton et al. 2003).

As Kevin Bales (1999) makes clear, human trafficking has become increasingly common in the global garment industry, on agricultural plantations, and among domestic laborers. Forced prostitution makes up another large type of human trafficking. Girls and women from poor families, as well as homeless individuals, runaway teens, abused wives, refugees, and drug addicts are especially likely to be targeted. Coerced, international sex workers are now found in most cities and even in some small towns across the United States (Hodge 2008).

Human trafficking is the fastest growing criminal activity in the world, second only to drug- and arms-trading in its revenue-producing size. With an estimated 27 million people currently living in this "modern form of slavery," as Hillary Clinton and others have named it, there are probably more enslaved people now on earth than at any other time in human history (U.S. Department of State 2009; Bale 1999). Two-thirds or more, around 20 million, are girls and women. Few local or national governments treat trafficking as a serious criminal issue. Some governments, in fact, encourage this exploitation for their own financial gain.

Female circumcision, also known as female genital cutting and mutilation, constitutes yet another form of sex-based violence. There are estimated to be about 2 million new female genital cuttings each year. UNICEF (2013) believes that about 125 million girls and women have undergone this practice in Africa, with about 27 million cases in Egypt alone. Male genital cutting (penile subincision) also occurs but it is neither as widespread nor as dangerous as female genital cutting, which requires the partial or total removal of the external female genitalia. Female genital cutting can produce death through excessive bleeding but more often leads to acute infections from inadequate sterilization of the instruments used. Other consequences include urinary and reproductive tract infections, infertility, cysts, and a lifetime of painful sexual intercourse.

VIOLENCE AGAINST LGBT PEOPLE

Lesbian, gay, bisexual, and transgendered people are also frequent targets of gender- and sex-based violence. The appearance and behaviors of LGBT people vary so greatly that it may at first seem unworkable to group them together into a single category. Unfortunately, despite their many differences, for centuries LGBT people have been victims of a similar violent response.

Gender and sexual minorities frequently suffer harassment, threats, assaults, and murders. Much of this violence is associated with **heteronormativity**, a worldview commonly supported by laws and customs that promote heterosexuality and dichotomous gender relations as the single acceptable form of gender and sexual expression. Violence is often directed at people who fail to present themselves as unambiguously female or male or who transition to a gender that does not match their sex at birth. People who participate in sexual activities that do not emphasize female-male foreplay or intercourse are also sometimes targeted.

Religious- and state-sponsored violence against gender and sexual minorities has been common for millennia. For example, Leviticus, the third book of the Hebrew Bible, which is also part of the Christian Old Testament, advises that a man who "has sexual relations with a man as one does with a woman" should be put to death (Leviticus 20:13). This advice was followed by many tribes and nations well into the twentieth century. Those not executed were likely to be banished, imprisoned, tortured, or mutilated. The Nazis initiated a plan to murder all sexual minorities in all parts of the world they might one day control. Shortly after the end of World War II, for the crime of "gross indecency," the United Kingdom chemically castrated Alan Turing, one of its most important war heroes and one of history's most extraordinary mathematicians.

Today same-sex activities are still considered serious crimes in about eighty countries. In Uganda in 2014, for example, new laws were passed mandating life imprisonment for convictions of some same-sex acts. Nonetheless, there are global trends encouraging many

TABLE 5.1 GALLUP POLL OF SEXUAL IDENTITY

Do you, personally, identify as gay, lesbian, bisexual, or transgender?

Age	Yes %	No %	Refused %
18 to 29	6.4	90.1	3.5
30 to 49	3.2	93.6	3.2
50 to 64	2.6	93.1	4.3
65+	1.9*	91.5*	6.5*
18 to 29 women	8.3*	88*	3.8*
18 to 29 men	4.6	92.1	3.3

*Some rows do not total 100 percent due to rounding.

Source: Gallup 2012.

governments to become less hostile to LGBT minorities. In the United States, for example, laws enforcing heteronormativity were found in all states but Illinois in 1969 but were eliminated entirely by a Supreme Court ruling in 2003 voiding Texas's laws against sodomy.

Much individual and group violence against gender and sexual minorities continues even when official government-sponsored violence declines. Nevertheless, rates of harassment, assault, and murder may be less now in most of the developed world than they were before the late twentieth-century rise of support for LGBT rights. On the other hand, violence against gender and sexual minorities could actually be increasing as fewer people hide their minority identities and so are more often openly challenging heteronormativity. There is insufficient data to accurately determine trends in the frequency of what are today called "hate crimes" against LGBT minorities. One hint there may have been a significant recent decrease in gender- and sex-based violence is found in a Gallup survey that found younger people in the United States between ages eighteen and twenty-nine years are more than three times as likely as people sixty-five and older to self-identify as LGBT (Gates and Newport 2012). The rates are 6.4 percent for people under thirty versus 1.9 percent for people over sixty-four. Table 5.1, "Gallup Poll of Sexual Identity," summarizes the results of this poll.

This trend toward an increasing self-identification as LGBT among younger people may indicate that they feel safer than their elders to publicly acknowledge their gender and sexual orientations. It is possible that violence against LGBT people has decreased sufficiently in North America and parts of the rest of the world across the last fifty years so that younger people feel better able to answer survey questions about their sexuality more honestly. Unfortunately, as mentioned, without solid statistical data on hate crimes from past decades it is very difficult to determine trends accurately. It is clear that violence against LGBT people is no longer systematically ignored by the criminal justice system or by mass media, as it once was. Some schools and other institutions support LGBT violence abatement programs. This suggests that efforts have begun to try to decrease hate crimes, even if these programs have not yet much reduced many of the dangers associated with being lesbian, gay, bisexual, and transsexual.

WOMEN AND LGBT MINORITIES IN THE GLOBAL PEACE NETWORK

Horrific gender- and sex-based violence persists in every part of the world. However, in many places the safety of girls, women, and LGBT minorities is improving and may continue to improve. Through participation in the global peace network and other organizations, women and LGBT people have gained influence in spheres where they were excluded for centuries. The work that women and others have done to publicize and decrease war rape illustrates the type of successes future decades may see.

War rape has been common in civil unrests and wars for thousands of years. The Bible, Homer, and Herodotus provide well-known though brief descriptions of this sex-based violence. However, in these and most other historical texts written by men, rape is seldom foregrounded. The suffering of female victims was not considered worthy of condemnation or analysis in these many chronicles focused almost exclusively on men. Then, in the last half of the twentieth century, newly empowered women produced a shift. Most of the information about the frequency of war rape presented earlier in this chapter came to light because of the efforts of women working both within and outside of the global peace network. These efforts also generated a particularly significant result in the 1990s when the global news media was pressured to report on the mass rapes then occurring in the wars in Yugoslavia and in Rwanda with a prominence never approached in previous wars (Aafijes 1998). Soon after, international tribunals and courts begin prosecuting war-related sexual violence, acts rarely thought worthy of legal consideration only fifty years before.

Another milestone was reached in 1998 when the newly established International Criminal Court began treating sexual violence as a war crime. This Court is now accepted by 111 countries, with thirty-eight additional nations awaiting local legislative approvals. Implementation of the Court's laws about sexual violence and much else remains weak, but the growing power of the global peace network to protect women and LGBT minorities is demonstrated by the fact that most leaders across the world now find it necessary to publicly declare that they oppose war associated sexual violence. Like slavery, another taken-for-granted violent custom that persisted practically unnoticed for centuries, war rape is now thought by most people to be a tradition that should end.

Women and LGBT minorities are participating in the global peace network in many ways but with particular effectiveness (1) through local, regional, and national politics and (2) through their increasingly prominent work in peacebuilding organizations. Women and LGBT minorities are further increasing their opportunities to lead by (3) acquiring greater economic autonomy and wealth, (4) achieving higher levels of schooling, and (5) attaining authority within most research sciences. Each of these five areas of empowerment is discussed separately below. Simultaneous gains in all five empowerment areas, as is now occurring in a few countries, raises the possibility that in some places many of the worst forms of gender- and sexual-based violence could end.

GENDERED POLITICS

Though women have been gaining political power for over one hundred years, few women secured positions of political leadership until the last few decades. In 2010 women made up about 20 percent of the more than 40,000 parliament members elected across the world, nearly double their representation but fifteen years before (Inter-Parliamentary Union 2010). The range of representation varies greatly by region, with women holding over 40 percent of the elected positions in parliaments in Nordic countries, about 22 percent in the rest of Europe and in the Americas, and around 10 percent in Arab states. Upward trends continue almost everywhere.

Increasing the proportion of elected and appointed women helps create democracies that truly represent their entire populations. Increasing the proportion of females in leadership positions is vital, too, for it takes a **critical mass of women** to change long-established policies associated with males. Studies show, for example, that legislatures require a critical mass to advocate for the end of gender- and sex-based violence and other so-called "women's issues." Maha Khatib, a female member of the national cabinet in Jordan, explains, "You need a group of women who can support each other. In 2007, there were four women in the cabinet together. Three of us were able to join together and push women-sensitive issues" (quoted in Pellegrino, D'Amato and Weisberg 2010, 15). Among other changes, these appointed female Jordanian ministers increased the rates of prosecution for "honor killers" and ended the long existing Jordanian practice of early release and pardon for men convicted of murdering their wives.

When women achieve a critical mass they tend to change policies that directly impact women and children. In Norway, female members of parliament organized around what they called "the politics of care," seeking legislation to improve child-care services, parental leave, and flexible work schedules (Hoare and Gell 2009). Similarly, in South Africa female parliamentarians introduced a system of "gender budgeting," a requirement that state spending be analyzed to assure that women's needs were being met equally with men's. A similar system of "gender audits" has been established by a critical mass of female legislators in the Philippines (Urgel and Tanyang 2008). For the first time, in 2013, female senators achieved a critical mass on the powerful United States Senate Armed Services Committee, making up seven of its twenty-six members. And for the first time this committee began investigating the United States military's long-standing failure to reduce the high rate of sex- and gender-based crimes perpetrated by members of its troops.

The number of female heads of state and women appointed to cabinet-level positions is also trending upward. More than thirty women have served as heads of state since 1995,

TABLE 5.2   FEMALE POLITICAL LEADERS

Year	Global Percentage of Female Members of Parliaments	Global Total Number Female Heads of State
1975	11%	3
1995	11%	8
2010	20%	20
2025	35%*	35*

Estimates—if current trends continue.

Jane Addams and other delegates en route from New York to the Women's Peace Conference at the Hague in 1915.

and many more have been appointed to cabinet positions. Eight women were newly elected as heads of state in 2010 alone, by far more women in one year than had been elected in any other year of the modern era. (See Table 5.2, "Female Political Leaders.")

A critical mass is best but including even one or a few women as members of a group generally raises the quality of the decisions made. Research shows that all-male groups tend to make more extreme and aggressive decisions than mixed-gender groups. Mixed-gender groups are also more likely to operate democratically and to include consideration of all stakeholders affected by decisions (Bear and Woolley 2011). One study even suggests that adding women to an all-male group increases the group's ability to brainstorm and solve both simple and complex puzzles (Malone and Woolley 2011).

WOMEN IN PEACEBUILDING ORGANIZATIONS

Women have been active in their own peace-promoting organizations for almost two centuries. These organizations were crucial to winning the right to vote for women and then subsequently in helping create the global peace network described in Chapter 3. Women's organizations continue to occupy a prominent role in promoting peace in most parts of the world.

The need to include women in peacebuilding was officially acknowledged in 1979 when the United Nations General Assembly adopted the landmark Convention on the

LEARNING MORE   WOMEN'S PEACE
ORGANIZATIONS

Women have been prominent in peace campaigns much
more often than in military campaigns. Many of the most
influential early peace movements depended on the
work of women even while they were denying them the
chance to lead. As a result, women formed their own organizations where they could pursue their goals without
opposition from men.

The first women's peace organization in the United
States was formed in 1820 and named the Female Peace
Society. In 1854, Fredrika Bremer, a Swedish novelist,
formed the first transnational peace group, the European
Women's Peace League. Bremer declared that if women
"extend our hands around the whole world, we should be
able to take the earth in our hands like a little child."

Many new international antiwar groups formed in the
1890s, influenced by the Austrian Baroness Bertha von
Suttner's widely read anti-militarism book, *Lay Down Your
Arms*. Von Suttner won the Nobel Peace Prize in 1905.

Most peace organizations founded by women have
been small and short-lived, but some have persisted for
decades. Many played important roles in the development of the global peace network. A few of the more
significant women's peace organizations include:

> *The Women's International League for Peace and
> Freedom* (WILPF). This is the oldest and largest
> women's peace and justice organization in the
> world. It was founded as the Women's Peace
> Party in 1915 by 1,300 women from Europe and
> the United States, then renamed in 1919 when
> Jane Addams became its first international presi-
> dent. WILPF currently has branches in thirteen
> countries. Two WILPF leaders received the Nobel
> Peace Prize for their work, Jane Addams in 1931
> and Emily Greene Balch in 1946.
>
> *Women Strike for Peace* (WSP; also known as
> *Women for Peace*). Founded in 1961 to protest
> atmospheric testing of nuclear weapons, WSP
> continued to be a significant voice in various anti-
> war efforts until the 1990s. Volunteers from WSP
> counseled over 100,000 men on their rights of
> conscientious objection during the United States–
> Vietnam war.
>
> *Mothers of the Plaza de Mayo* (Spanish: Asociación
> Madres de Plaza de Mayo). Several mothers
> began this organization in 1977 to protest against

Argentina's "dirty war." It achieved great influence
across South America with its emphasis on the
rights of mothers to keep their children safe.

> *Women's Peace Camps*. Protest encampments have
> a long history but were brought to international
> prominence by the Greenham Common Women's
> Peace Camp established outside an English Air
> Force base in 1981 to protest the siting of nuclear
> cruise missiles. Subsequent widely-publicized
> peace camps include Camp Casey, started in 2005
> by widowed war-mother Cindy Sheehan near the
> Texas ranch of President George W. Bush.
>
> *Women in Black*. This movement was started by
> Israeli Jewish women in support of Palestinians in
> 1988. Their tactic of wearing black and standing
> vigil in public places in opposition to violence and
> war has since been adapted by women in dozens
> of countries, including Australia, England, India,
> Italy, the Philippines, Serbia, South Africa, Spain,
> and the United States.
>
> *WomenAction 2000 Network*. This media-savvy
> group was founded in 2000 as a global informa-
> tion, communication, and media network to
> coordinate the many UN and nongovernmental
> organizations that are seeking to enhance wom-
> en's empowerment. WomenAction currently in-
> cludes member organizations that include most
> regions of the world.
>
> *Women's Learning Partnership for Rights, Develop-
> ment, and Peace* (WLP). WLP was begun in 2000
> and dedicated to women's leadership and
> empowerment. WLP works with twenty partner
> organizations in the Global South, particularly in
> Muslim-majority societies, to empower women
> to transform their families, communities, and
> societies.
>
> *Code Pink*. Founded in 2002 by women to oppose
> the then-proposed United States invasion of Iraq,
> Code Pink has become one of the largest and most
> active antiwar organizations in North America. It
> currently has about 250 local chapters in the United
> States and over a dozen international affiliates.
>
> *UN Women*. Created by the UN General Assembly
> in 2010 to accelerate the organization's goals of
> gender equality and the empowerment of
> women. UN Women merges and builds on the
> previously distinct sections of the UN system that
> were focused on women.

Elimination of All Forms of Discrimination against Women (CEDAW). CEDAW commits nations to ending customs and laws within their borders that foster both direct and indirect violence against women. Over 187 countries (though not the United States) have since acceded to or ratified the convention. CEDAW-accepting nations are expected to submit a public report every four years detailing their government-initiated actions to increase gender equity and also describing the major areas of inequity remaining. Of course, no country has ended all discrimination against girls and women but the fact that so many governments now officially acknowledge the need to end gender-based inequities signals an unprecedented historical change.

A later initiative, UN Security Council (SC) Resolution 1325 on Women, Peace, and Security, adopted in 2000, mandates that more women be included in all peacemaking missions. SC Resolution 1325 states that women must be equal participants "in all forums and peace activities at all levels, particularly at the decision-making level." New peace missions by UN member states are thus now obligated to make good-faith efforts to include women in proportions equal to men. In 2010 only 2 percent of UN peacekeepers and 8 percent of UN police were female, far less than the equity that SC Resolution 1325 demands (UN Office for the Coordination of Humanitarian Affairs 2010).

APPLYING A GENDER PERSPECTIVE

It is not enough merely to make sure that an equal number of men and women work together during negotiating and peacebuilding sessions. As SC Resolution 1325 itself proclaims, the desired balance in the gender ratio of participants must be accompanied by the use of a gender perspective. A **gender perspective** uses gender as a master lens through which to foreground differences between men and women's customs, expectations, experiences, opportunities, roles, status, and power (Jenkins and Reardon 2007). Peace workers employing a gender perspective pay particular attention to how conflicts and their aftermaths differentially impact females and males (Schirch and Sewak, "Women: Using the Gender Lens" 2005).

The effectiveness of women in peacebuilding has been amply demonstrated for decades in organizations not affiliated with the United Nations, CEDAW, or SC Resolution 1325. The work of the Abuelas de La Plaza de Mayo (Grandmothers of the Plaza de Mayo) in exposing repression in Argentina in the 1970s and 1980s is one dramatic example often noted. It was also mostly women, working through their organization, the Leitana Nehan Women's Development Agency, who brokered a peace settlement in Bougainville in 1998 between secessionists and the Papua New Guinean government. The women then refocused their efforts to promote postwar reconstruction, rehabilitation, and reconciliation, assuming functions the government could or would not ("Women Weaving Bougainville" 2005). In 2003, the Women in Peacebuilding Network helped force an end to the fourteen-year-long civil war in Liberia. Some of their efforts are chronicled in the documentary film *Pray the Devil Back to Hell.*

Muslim, Hindu, and Sikh women built joint initiatives through Women in Security, Conflict Management, and Peace (WISCOMP) to breach sectarian divides in Kashmir (DasGupta and Gopinath 2005). Similar cross-sectarian women groups are at work between

Liberian women demonstrate for an end to war in Monrovia in 2007.

Israeli and Palestinian women in organizations such as the Jerusalem Link and also Women in Black, as well as between Pakistani and India women in groups such as WISCOMP and Women's Initiative for Peace in South Asia (WIPSA) (Schirch and Sewak, "Role of Women" 2005).

Case 6-2 in Chapter 6 demonstrates how a gender perspective can be used to understand the causes of war. See also Case 5-1, "Sex Strikes."

TOWARD ECONOMIC EQUALITY

Across the world today, women's employment opportunities are steadily improving. And, as women gain greater occupational and economic equity, they tend to find increasing means to lessen the gender- and sex-based violence that targets them (Caprioli 2005; Hudson et al. 2012).

Women are still far from achieving economic equity, except in a few areas of northern Europe and among under-thirty workers in Japan. Women now make up nearly 40 percent of the global paid workforce but they earn only 26 percent of the world's income (Hoare and Gell 2009). Women are still steered more often than men toward low-status, low-wage, and low-benefit jobs, as well as toward work in the "informal economy" where low wages are frequently paid in cash and where employers try to remain unknown to government authorities.

CASE 5-1 SEX STRIKES

Gene Sharp (1973) includes sex strikes among the 198 nonviolent actions he defines in his pathbreaking *Politics of Nonviolent Action*. Sharp calls the collective withholding of sex "Lysistratic nonaction" in homage to an ancient Greek comedy by Aristophanes in which Lysistrata persuades women to refuse sex with their male partners until they end their current war. Lysistrata's fictional method has been used at least six times in real nonviolent campaigns.

The earliest known sex strike documented in the Global Nonviolent Action Database was undertaken by Iroquois women in the seventeenth century. These women vowed to stop having sex until they were granted more power in determining when Iroquois men would go to war. The women also restricted the men's access to food and other supplies and eventually succeeded in being granted veto power over future decisions to wage war.

More recently, withholding sex was used as part of a women's peace campaign in Liberia in 2003. Christian and Muslim women formed a single organization to insist negotiations begin to end a long civil war. Along with demonstrations and, later, sit-ins at the eventual peace talks held in Ghana, the women vowed to refuse sex with their partners until a peace agreement was signed. Once this goal was achieved, the women ended their sex strike and other nonviolent actions and began working to create honest elections. Liberia then elected its first female president, Ellen Johnson Sirleaf, in 2005.

The girlfriends of violent gang members organized yet another sex strike in Pereita, Colombia, in 2006. The strikers produced a rap song to promote their campaign to pressure their partners to reduce the frequency of murders in their town. The lyrics included: As women, we have great worth / a violent man will not impress us / because with them, we lose so much. / I will choose how, where, when I submit myself. / All together, we will win / against the violent ones, we close our legs. / Sex strike, / sex strike!

In 2009, women in the oldest and largest women's rights group in Kenya organized a one-week, nationwide sex strike to force an end to the post-election violence that had killed 1,500 and driven over half a million Kenyans from their homes. The week ended with a prayer session that brought the feuding leaders together and produced a public agreement to begin peace talks.

A fifth successful sex strike occurred in 2011 in Daho, a small town in the Philippines. A group of women in a sewing collective there struck when they found that they could no longer deliver their goods to market because violence among neighboring gangs and families had made the local highway too dangerous. The women vowed to withhold sex from their partners until the roads were safe. The affected men quickly organized, negotiated with each other, and within a week the road was violence-free.

Another successful sex strike motivated by a problem road occurred in Barbacoas, Colombia, also in 2011. Women there organized to pressure government authorities to improve conditions on the lone highway connecting Barbacoas to the outside world. Without a better road, the women argued, it would be unethical for them to bear more children, since children in the town could not receive needed medical care or access to the basic education, food, and other resources only a decent road could bring. The women announced a "crossed legs strike" animated by the slogan, "No more sex. We want our road." Their argument was supported by the memory of a pregnant woman in labor who had recently died while stuck in an ambulance on the highway as it tried to transport her to the nearest hospital seven hours away. After four months of Lysistratic nonaction, and helped by other nonviolent methods including marches and hunger strikes, funds were pledged, design work began, and the sex strike ended.

Like all the nonviolent actions that Sharp describes, to be effective sex strikes usually must be used in concert with other actions. But sex strikes do have one advantage: They tend to attract outsized media attention, a great asset for most nonviolent campaigns. As Leymah Gbowee (2011, 147), one leader of the 2003 Liberian campaign and a subsequent Nobel Peace Prize winner, reports, "Until today, nearly ten years later, whenever I talk about the Mass Action, 'What about the sex strike?' is the first question everyone asks."

Sources: Global Nonviolent Action Database, authors Hannah Lehmann, Nancy Liu, Kylin Navarro, Max Rennebohm, Samantha Shain, and Nicole Vanchieri. Spanish translation assistance by Naomi Pueo Wood.

Women in most countries are also commonly paid less for the same work as men even in the formal economy. And, at the highest levels, women remain seriously underrepresented both as owners and managers. Only about 3 percent of the largest one thousand multinational companies have women presidents or CEOs (Pellegrino et al. 2010). Fewer than 15 percent of the top level managers at the top five hundred companies in the United States are female (Catalyst 2010).

Nonetheless, an unprecedented transformation is underway. Women executives and CEOs receive almost equal pay with men in many nonprofit sectors, especially in service organizations where women were first concentrated when they entered the workforce in increasing numbers in the last third of the twentieth century. In addition, for-profit companies now frequently compete with nonprofits for senior female managers and members of boards of directors. Many for-profits look at the gender diversity of not-for-profit organizations as role models.

The increasing push for more females at the top levels of for-profit companies is in part a response to public pressure to end gender discrimination. But, probably even more significantly, this search for gender equity within for-profit companies reflects evidence that companies with more female board members tend to make larger profits than those with few or none. These **gender-equity profits** provide a significant incentive for businesses to recruit and retain females at high managerial levels. One study of Fortune 500 companies over a four-year period found that companies with the highest percentage of women on their boards produced 53 percent higher equity returns than companies with the fewest female members (Joy et al. 2007). Another study of eighty-nine companies in Europe with a high proportion of women in senior positions found these firms "enjoyed a higher return on equity, fatter operating profits and a more buoyant share price" than comparable companies with lower proportions of senior women ("Still Lonely at the Top" 2011, 61). Both studies discovered that having token female participation was insufficient. As in politics, a critical mass of women seems necessary to produce significant boosts in profit growth.

FEMALE EDUCATION

Increasing educational opportunities for girls and women is another effective way to empower females and decrease gender- and sex-based violence. Much evidence shows that educated women are "better able to control what happens to their bodies, better able to avoid oppression in marriage, better able to safeguard their own health and the health of their children, [and] better able to participate in the deliberations of human society" (Hudson et al. 2012).

Women college graduates in the developed world now exceed the number of male graduates. The Department of Education predicts that in the United States by 2016, women will earn over 60 percent of all associates, bachelor's, and master's degrees. It also predicts females will then be earning 58 percent of doctoral and professional degrees. Already nearly half of all new physicians are women, as are 45 percent of all new graduates from law schools. However, women still make up only about 30 percent of all new MBAs. China's trends in education gender ratios are similar to the United States. Only about a quarter of the student population at Chinese colleges and universities was female in 1978 but now the number is almost half. And so it is in most industrialized countries.

Educational gender equity is increasing even in many parts of the developing world. Changes in access to education in the Middle East and North Africa are emblematic. In this male-dominated region, access to primary school is now increasingly universal and gender differences in secondary school enrollments are decreasing. In addition, Middle Eastern women are increasing their presence in universities, reflecting official policies that seek to maximize the skills of all citizens in order to increase long-term economic growth (Roudi-Fahimi and Moghadam 2003). In Saudi Arabia, for example, where women have yet to win the right to drive a car, females now make up almost 60 percent of all university students. The country's first coeducational university opened in 2009 and Saudi women are for the first time being encouraged to earn law and engineering degrees.

In 2014 one young crusader for female educational rights, Malala Yousafzai, at 17 became the youngest person ever to win the Nobel Peace Prize. Yousafzai was shot and severely wounded in 2012 in her native Pakistan by an attacker attempting to discourage education for Muslim girls. After Yousafzai recovered, she became a widely known spokesperson insisting on the right to schooling for both boys and girls across the world. About her attacker, Yousafzai said, "I do not even hate the Talib who shot me. Even if there was a gun in my hand and he stands in front of me, I would not shoot him" (quoted in Johnston 2013).

Escalating educational opportunities for women helps further increase the political, organizational, and economic power of women. These gains in power in turn weaken cultural traditions of gender- and sex-based violence.

RESEARCH SCIENCES

Research plays a vital role in the global peace network, providing a growing body of knowledge about how people can most effectively build a lasting peace. This peace knowledge is increasingly shaped by the emergence of new critical masses of **women in the research sciences**. As in economics, organizations, and politics, a critical mass of females in a research area tends to change its priorities and policies.

The health sciences were among the first to experience a change in gender ratios. When medicine and its related sciences were almost exclusively male, the "normal" body was assumed to be male. Most research and clinical trials used males, assuming females were less important, were like males, or that female hormonal cycles could "distort" the findings (Verdonk et al. 2009). However, once they entered this research area, a critical mass of women insisted upon and often themselves carried out studies of health problems specific to girls and women. Another consequence of the entry of women into the health sciences is that intimate partner violence is now regularly included as a topic of study at most medical schools and in schools of public health.

The social sciences have lagged behind the health sciences but are now also being transformed by the emergence of critical masses of female researchers. Most of the empirical work this chapter reports was completed by women. Without their introduction of a gender perspective, the scope of the problems associated with gender- and sex-based violence would likely still be mostly unknown. In addition, without the arrival of a critical mass of women in the social sciences, peace studies itself might have remained as it was until recently, a field focused mostly on wars, insurrections, and men. A critical mass of women in peace studies is now bringing attention to the immense harm that war does to girls and women, as well as to the more frequent harms that gender- and sex-based violence inflicts on families and communities, even when no wars are being fought.

VIOLENT WOMEN

The increasing empowerment of women seems likely to decrease levels of violence against both men and women. Nonetheless, it is important to note that not all women oppose violence more than men. In some circumstances women encourage and even commit violence as much as and, occasionally, more than men. Women have participated in violent conflicts on all continents for at least the last few hundred years. Violent women are less common than violent men but history makes clear that women are not genetically or universally nonviolent, as some Western stereotypes maintain.

The west African kingdom of Dahomey (now known as Benin) supported a female regiment of soldiers from 1727 until 1892, when they were defeated and disbanded by the French. These women warriors had a reputation for both bravery and cruelty. It is well to remember as well that the first important modern act of Western terrorism from below was the work of a woman, Vera Zasulich, who shot the governor general of St. Petersburg in 1878. Three years later, several other women helped organize the successful assassination of Czar Alexander II. Russian and Yugoslav women fought on the front lines during World War II (Zarkov 2006). Women often joined men in combat during many subsequent anti-colonial struggles across the developing world. Women in the Italian Red Brigades, Nicaragua, Northern Ireland, South Africa, and Vietnam were especially active in their very different violent liberation campaigns. Similarly, Hindu women today hold prominent positions in the Rashtriya Swayamsevak Sangh (RSS) movement in India that for decades has promoted violence against Muslims (Zarkov 2006). Women have also played active roles in recent violent separatist movements in Assam, Chechnya, Kashmir, Nepal, Palestine, Punjab, and Sri Lanka. Some Rwandan women were tried for genocide at the International Criminal Tribunal.

Women have participated in nearly half of the documented terrorism from below groups active in the last two decades (Bloom 2007). About 220 women completed or attempted to complete suicide bombings between 1985 and 2006; women thus made up about 15 percent of all such bombers in that time.

Women legislators do not always use their critical mass to work for the empowerment of other women or for peace. Newly empowered women in Honduras, for example, sponsored legislation that encouraged traditions of violence against women (Matheu 2008). Pioneering female political leaders such as Indira Gandhi, Golda Meir, and Margaret Thatcher have even seemed, according to some, to be "the only men in their cabinets," that is, to be leaders more eager to choose violence than their male peers (Steinberg 2008).

Still, though women are capable of perpetrating violence, for decades females have tended more often than males to use their power to promote negotiation and cooperation rather than violence and war. This gendered tendency seems likely to continue as women acquire yet more influence in the decades ahead.

MAKING CONNECTIONS

In most places the rise of women has meant a rise in peace. Chapter 10 explores the biological basis for gender differences and whether a propensity for violence is hard-wired in human genes. First, however, Part Two offers four chapters that explore the recent history and contemporary prospects for peace and war. Just as the increasing empowerment of women tends to decrease violence so, too, does the increasing accumulation of knowledge about how to deal with conflicts without resorting to violence. The chapters in Part Two examine the contributions of Gandhi, King, and many others in creating a global peace network capable of reducing violence across the world. A final chapter in Part Two surveys the influence of religion on wars, violence, and peace.

FOR REVIEW

1. Explain the main differences between gender-based and sex-based violence.
2. Describe ways in which non-combatant women commonly suffer more from war than non-combatant men.
3. Review the leading causes that produce "missing women" across the world.
4. Analyze some of the changes that a critical mass of women creates in both politics and peacebuilding.
5. Review the impact that a critical mass of women has had in both business and the research sciences.

THINKING CRITICALLY

1. What are the main benefits from separating gender-based from sex-based violence? The main problems?
2. Which of the causes of missing women are likely to be most difficult to counteract in the coming decades?
3. How does empowering women tend to reduce the frequency of intimate partner violence?
4. Why has human trafficking become the fastest growing criminal activity in the contemporary world?
5. What factors led to the formation of the new concepts of heteronormativity and of LGBT minorities in the last half of the twentieth century?
6. Why did it take until the 1990s for war rapes to begin to be widely treated as war crimes?
7. Will international relations likely change if the majority of the world's nation-states are one day governed by parliaments containing a critical mass of women?
8. Why do new female college graduates in the developed world now exceed the number of male graduates?
9. Will the tendency for women to promote negotiation and cooperation more than men likely continue if women achieve near gender equality in the decades ahead?

RECOMMENDED RESOURCES

Girl Rising. Directed by Richard E. Robbins. 2013. An inspirational documentary that tells the story of nine girls from different parts of the world who manage to overcome such obstacles as arranged marriage, child slavery, and extreme poverty.

Half the Sky. Directed by Maro Chermayeff. 2012. Inspired by Nicholas Kristof and Sheryl WuDunn's book of the same name, this documentary travels to ten countries to detail how the oppression of women is being fought through increased opportunities to health care, education, and public economic activities. The film is part of the Half the Sky Movement (see http://www.halftheskymovement.org/) and is available in both four-hour and one-hour versions.

Hudson, Valerie M., Bonnie Ballif-Spanvill, Mary Caprioli, and Chad F. Emmett, *Sex and World Peace* (New York: Columbia University Press, 2012). A path-breaking book that uses a rigorous statistical approach to demonstrate that the best predictor of a country's peacefulness is how well its women are treated.

Iron Jawed Angels. Directed by Katja Von Garnier. 2004. Fictional account of the campaign for women's suffrage in the United States before and during World War I, with an emphasis on the work of Lucy Burns and Alice Paul.

My So-Called Enemy. Directed by Lisa Gossels. 2010. A documentary that follows six Palestinian and Israeli teenage girls who became friends at a camp in the United States in 2002. The film explores how their friendships complicate their lives back in the Middle East over the following seven years.

Pray the Devil Back to Hell. Directed by Gini Reticker. 2008. A documentary about the crucial role played by women in ending a long civil war in Liberia, leading up to the election of the country's first female head of state.

Rosa Parks Story. Directed by Julie Dash. 2002. A fictional account of the Montgomery bus boycott that focuses on the woman who refused to relinquish her seat and so helped energize campaigns for civil rights across the United States.

"When a Women is the Victim." *Global Burden of Armed Violence 2011.* The Geneva Declaration of Armed Violence and Development. 2011. A focused summary of the frequency and consequences of gender- and sex-based violence across the world. The summary is especially useful in comparing different regional trends. Available at http://www.genevadeclaration.org/fileadmin/docs/GBAV2/GBAV2011_CH4_rev_pdf

Women's Rights. Films for the Humanities & Social Sciences. 2010. A documentary that contrasts the struggle for women's rights in the United States with the status of women in China, Afghanistan, and Kenya. Focuses on nonconsensual marriage and domestic violence.

WomenStats Project and Database. Provides a continuously expanding compilation of information on the global status of women. The Project emphasizes studies of the linkage between the situation of women and the security of nation-states. Website at http://www.womanstats.org

UN Women: United Nations Entity for Gender Equity and the Empowerment of Women. Collects international resources focused on problems of violence against women, gender peace and security, and equal gender access to national planning and commerce. Website at http://www.unwomen.org

2

FROM VIOLENCE
TO NONVIOLENCE

The four chapters in Part Two describe the shifting roles that violence and nonviolence play in contemporary interstate, intrastate, and regional conflicts. Chapter 6 focuses on key developments moving nations away from cross-border wars toward foreign policies that emphasize nonviolent alternatives. Chapter 7 surveys the increasing prominence of nonviolent action as a popular form of political action. This chapter also reviews the recent upsurge in support for democracy, international peacebuilding organizations, and human rights. Chapter 8 looks at intrastate conflicts with an emphasis on how nonviolent strategies and methods can reduce group and regional violence. Chapter 9 explores the relationship between religion and violence while highlighting the importance of the ethic of reciprocity and also the historic influence of faith-based practitioners of nonviolence.

FROM VIOLENCE TO NONVIOLENCE

CHAPTER 6

INTERSTATE WAR AND PEACE

CHAPTER OVERVIEW

This chapter describes developments moving nations toward foreign policies that emphasize soft power. It explores several causes for this shift, including the recent history of multiple interstate war failures; the changing way nations win respect; the rise of democracies and global capitalism; the growing strength of peace-promoting international organizations; and an emerging perspective that winning popular consent, not resources or territory, is the key to success in most conflicts. The chapter concludes with a review of three obstacles to the trend toward increasing soft power: the military-industrial complex, domestic politics in democracies, and cultural and media traditions that encourage war.

Key terms discussed include: Interstate conflicts; hard power: soft power; motives for war; democratic peace; capitalist peace; globalization of production; globalization of markets; foreign direct investment; population is the prize; new wars; national security; human security; age of peacebuilding; military-industrial complex; and smart power.

> Throughout much of the time for which we have a record of human behavior, mankind can clearly be seen to have judged that war's benefits outweighed its costs, or appeared to do so when a putative balance was struck. Now the computation works in the opposite direction. Costs clearly exceed benefits.
>
> —JOHN KEEGAN (1993, 59)

The foreign policies of many countries seek to win the hearts and minds of foreign civilians rather than to destroy them. As the then United States secretary of defense Robert M. Gates explained, violent force is often less important to modern militaries than are "measures to promote participation in government, economic programs to spur development, and efforts to address the grievances that often lie at the heart of insurgencies and among the discontented" (Gates 2008).

TABLE 6.1   THE SHIFT IN STRATEGIC THINKING

Previous Emphasis	New Emphasis
Negative peace	Positive peace
Hard power	Soft power
Military power	Civil power
Force	Persuasion, negotiation, and cooperation

Peace researchers conceptualize this change in strategic thinking as a shift from negative toward positive peace, concepts introduced in Chapter 2. Military planners, international relations scholars, and political scientists have their own names for similar ideas. Some call this change in foreign policy a shift from hard toward soft power, the label used most in this chapter. This shift has also been described as a transition from military toward civil power, from industrial toward peoples' wars, and from national to human security. There are subtle differences associated with these different names but they all are informed by the same empirical observation that, in the contemporary world, wars seldom achieve their goals. Nations in conflict situations are thus increasingly relying on alternatives to the coercive military force that was once common for nations large and small. (See Table 6.1, "The Shift in Strategic Thinking.")

This chapter focuses mostly on trends in **interstate conflicts**, clashes between countries driven by causes working at the macro, international level of analysis. Chapters 7 and 8 look at related trends in intrastate conflicts, uprisings that take place among groups within countries.

FROM HARD TO SOFT POWER

Hard power refers to a foreign policy emphasis on economic coercion, military power, and other types of force. **Soft power** describes an alternative foreign policy perspective that stresses cooperation, negotiation, and persuasion. The distinction has been developed by many but is most often associated with an influential series of books and articles by Joseph S. Nye Jr. (e.g., 1991, 2005). Nye defines power as the ability to change the behavior of others to "get what you want." Hard power changes others through the use of economic and military coercion. By contrast, Nye says, soft power relies on attraction or co-optation, on convincing people to change their behavior through earning their acceptance, admiration, or respect.

The repeated military disappointments suffered by the Soviet Union and the United States in interstate wars over the last fifty years has helped drive the shift of emphasis toward soft power. The world had seldom seen two such disproportionately large empires wielding global power simultaneously on both the military and economic levels. Yet, for decades, the immense hard power of both the Soviets and Americans produced mostly bloody stalemates and outright defeats, seldom results that either nation could truthfully call victories.

At its height in the 1960s, the Soviet empire stretched across dozens of countries. Nationalist resistances against these mostly Russian imperialists ebbed and flowed, sometimes—as in Hungary in 1956 and in Czechoslovakia in 1968—forcing large, emergency military invasions to keep the Soviet empire enact. Despite such fearsome deployments of hard power force, challenges to Soviet rule still repeatedly appeared. The rise of the Solidarity movement in Poland around 1980 exposed a latent instability in most of the local regimes the Soviet military had established across its empire.

The weakness of hard power was further exposed in Afghanistan in the 1980s when the Soviets found its military unable to subdue a very poor, rural tribal population determined to resist. The return home from Afghanistan in 1988 of a defeated and demoralized Red Army helped create, or at least accelerate, the disintegration of the Soviet Union (Reuveny and Prakash 1999). Within a short time of that war's end, each of the many countries that had been coerced into the Warsaw Pact asserted their autonomy, revealing the fragility of most modern coalitions built on violent force.

The United States, with riches and a military capability even greater than the Soviets, was at about the same time providing further demonstrations of the weakness of hard power. Andrew J. Bacevich, a West Point graduate with twenty years' experience in the U.S. Army, summarizes the record. "Three times in the last sixty years, U.S. forces have achieved an approximation of unambiguous victory—operational success translating more or less directly into political success" (Bacevich "No Exit" 2010). These victories came in the Dominican Republic in 1965, in Granada in 1983, and in Panama in 1989, three cases where as Bacevich points out "the enemy has tended to be, shall we say, less than ten feet tall." Victories in these three countries were earned against relatively tiny resisting forces who had had little training, possessed few advanced weapons, and had scant reason to fight. On the other hand, the use of force produced defeat or stalemate for the United States in every major post–World War II interstate military campaign, first in Korea, then in Vietnam, Afghanistan, and Iraq. Bacevich maintains that even the first Gulf War, often touted as a hard power victory, "succeeded chiefly in drawing the United States more deeply into the vortex of the Middle East—it settled nothing" (Bacevich "No Exit" 2010).

The recent United States' wars in Iraq and Afghanistan are typical of the results that hard power deployments tend to produce in the contemporary world. The United States spent about $3.3 trillion in these two overseas wars and in enhanced domestic security in reaction to the 9/11 attacks. As David E. Sanger (2011) points out, "Put another way, for every dollar al-Qaeda spent to pull off the September 11, 2001, attacks, the cost to the United States was an astonishing $6.6 million." The return on this hard power investment has been quite small.

Jason Burke (2011) estimates that fatalities since the 9/11 attacks include about 7,000 American and allied soldiers, 40,000 cooperating local soldiers and police, and between 90,000 to 150,000 civilian deaths. In sum, the United States' hard power wars fought in reaction to the 9/11 events led to the death of fifty times more Americans, allies, and "friendly" non-combatant civilians than died in the 9/11 attacks themselves. In addition, there have been approximately 750,000 injuries to soldiers, security forces, and civilians and from one to two million Iraqis displaced. The 9/11 wars created these significant costs and lasted longer than previous United States' wars but failed to reduce global terrorism, establish new stable governments, or increase respect for human and gender rights in the two countries that the United States invaded.

The repeated failure of interstate wars over the last half-century helped convince the U.S. secretary of defense to announce in 2008 that the soft power promotion of indigenous civil societies and not military domination would henceforth guide United States foreign policy. Gates explained that the United States, like many other governments, now believes that "over the long term, we cannot kill or capture our way to victory" (Gates 2008). In fact, Gates later stated that "any future defense secretary who advises the president to again send a big American land army into Asia or into the Middle East or Africa should 'have his head examined'" (quoted in Shanker 2011).

WAR AND THE SEARCH FOR RESPECT

Recent hard power failures by the Soviet, American, and other militaries are but one of multiple causes for the current shift in international strategic thinking. Changes in how countries build influence and earn prestige in the contemporary world system are also important.

Richard Ned Lebow's (2010) analysis of ninety-four major interstate wars from 1648 to 2010 found that four primary reasons drive national leaders to undertake cross-border wars. These recurring **motives for war** include a desire by decision-makers (1) to access resources, (2) to sustain or increase national security, (3) to earn prestige, and (4) to seek revenge. The first two, the desire for resources and for security, are commonly assumed to be the most important. Indeed, national decision-makers themselves often publicly justify their decisions to go to war by invoking their country's resource and security needs. Lebow's data suggest, however, that at least for the last four centuries the most common motive for interstate war has been decision-makers' desires for prestige. The quest for prestige, often framed by leaders as a search for national respect, was the principal cause of almost two-thirds of the ninety-four wars that Lebow reviewed. Hard power quests for resources and security accounted for less than a third of the interstate wars that Lebow analyzed. Even the fourth motive, the desire for revenge, caused leaders to choose war more often than the quest for resources. And seeking revenge is also usually associated with a wish to regain lost prestige. Lebow's research is summarized in Table 6.2, "Motives for War, 1648–2010."

Lebow's study indicates that the desire for prestige continues to be the most frequent cause even for most recent interstate wars. However, Lebow argues, it is becoming

TABLE 6.2   MOTIVES FOR WAR, 1648–2010

Leaders' Motives	Number of Wars	Note
Resources	8	Common with 18th-century mercantilism
Security	19	Usually becomes primary only after a nation has been attacked
Prestige	62	Is declining as war increasingly fails to increase standing
Revenge	11	Usually associated with a quest to recover previously lost territory; often associated with prestige motive

Source: Lebow 2010.

increasingly difficult for national leaders to win prestige through military conquest since pursuing interstate wars in the post–Cold War era has more often led to humiliation than to increases in global respect. Countries in the twenty-first century can emphasize soft power and still be included among the world's most prestigious nations without incurring the costs in treasure and blood that hard power wars require. World admiration now flows to nations with cultural capital, strong economies, and a willingness to engage cooperatively with countries across multiple regions (Lane and Waqschal 2011). For example, France, Germany, the United Kingdom, and Japan topped a 2008 BBC World Service poll of 17,000 people in thirty-four countries that asked which countries the respondents thought were most exerting a positive influence on the world (BBC World Service 2008). The United Kingdom was the only one of these four leading nations that had recently participated in a cross-border war. World public opinion even viewed Russia more favorably than it did the United States. Russia's higher prestige relative to the United States seems likely to arise at least in part from the fact that Russia is no longer widely associated with either empire or the pursuit of wars far beyond its immediate borders. (See Case 6-1, "Prestige and the United States-Iraq War.")

CASE 6-1 PRESTIGE AND THE UNITED STATES–IRAQ WAR

The United States 9/11 wars illustrate both the continuing importance of the pursuit of prestige to nations and also how contemporary world affairs differ from the past. The United States' decision to initiate war against Iraq was in large measure driven by the desire for prestige, just as Lebow's data predict. The core of Bush's national security team had been advocating military action against Saddam Hussein for reasons of prestige since the mid-1990s (Badie 2010). Key presidential advisors such as Vice President Dick Cheney, Secretary of Defense Donald Rumsfeld, Deputy Secretary of Defense Paul Wolfowitz, and others had been members of the Project for the New American Century, a think tank that promoted what are often called neoconservative policies. These analysts jointly supported the view that the fall of the Soviet Union provided the United States with a unique opportunity to "restore the honor" it had lost through its defeat in Vietnam (Wallerstein 2006). Renewed honor and prestige could be won, these neoconservatives argued, through undertaking massive, unilateral, aggressive actions across the world.

An increased level of world prestige, the neoconservatives maintained, would enable the United States to better achieve its foreign policy goals (PBS Frontline 2003).

Rumsfeld thus asked the Department of Defense to begin planning a possible attack on Iraq only three days after September 11, 2001 (Badie 2010). An attack against an enemy like Iraq that possessed significant hard power was necessary, Rumsfeld asserted, because attacking a poor, weak, poorly armed country such as Afghanistan would not be sufficiently "confidence-inspiring" to the rest of the world to increase the United States' global prestige (quoted in Feith 2009, 95). A former senior official in the Bush administration would later explain, "The only reasons we went into Iraq . . . is we were looking for somebody's ass to kick. Afghanistan was too easy" (quoted in Baker 2013, *Days of Fire* xx).

Bush's neoconservative foreign policy team supervised their desired massive, long, and expensive military campaign in Iraq but this war failed to increase the United States' global prestige. Lebow (2010) speculates that the combined United States' humiliations in its wars in Afghanistan and Iraq may one day be seen as a major tipping point in modern international relations. These wars may have "delegitimized the unilateral use of force and foregrounded and encouraged alternative, peaceful means of gaining standing" (Lebow 2010, 21). The United States' wars in Afghanistan and Iraq may have the unanticipated consequence of accelerating the future use of soft power, by the United States as well as by others.

THE DEMOCRATIC PEACE

Democratically elected leaders seek respect from their citizens as well as from the international community. Autocratic leaders, on the other hand, commonly need to consider the opinion of significantly fewer people, often only their military, security commanders, and an elite circle of supporters. These differences in leadership needs have played a part in producing the **democratic peace**, a name for the finding that established democracies rarely, if ever, go to war against each other.

Few democracies fought each other throughout the entire twentieth century. One pioneering researcher even maintains there have been no such wars since 1789 (Babst 1972). Whether or not a potential target country is a democracy is more determinative of where wars erupt than are factors such as economic and power status, alliance memberships, and even physical proximity of the possible aggressive belligerents (Russett 2010). The democratic peace finding may be the closest thing to a law yet discovered in the field of international relations.

The democratic peace does not mean that democracies are more peaceful than non-democracies but that democracies overwhelmingly conduct their wars against autocracies (Russett 2010; Russett and Oneal 2001). Most research suggests that democracies tend to start interstate wars more often than autocracies; democracies also tend to win their wars more often than autocracies. In addition, some research suggests that democracies commonly continue wars longer, prolonging hostilities in situations where autocratic leaders would tend to seek a truce or even surrender and admit defeat (Russett and Oneal 2001).

Democratic leaders may choose war more often than autocrats in part because waging war often strengthens their holds on power. Electorates tend to want their countries to win contests against other countries and so waging a war tends to rally citizens behind a democratic leader even if he or she had weak political support before. Conversely, autocrats generally gain from wars only when it helps them supply their circle of supporters with the bounty they expect. Wars led by autocrats usually have more narrowly focused goals than those launched by democratic leaders.

The democratic peace may also result in part from the different methods that democratic and autocratic leaders use to maintain their power (Bueno de Mesquita et al. 1999). Democracies may tend not to fight other democracies because democratic leaders must convince many, sometimes even a majority, of their citizens that the proposed enemy

---

LEARNING MORE FEATURES
OF THE DEMOCRATIC PEACE

Democracies rarely go to war against each other

Democracies go to war about as often as autocracies

Democracies conduct their wars against autocracies

Democracies tend to start interstate wars more often than autocracies

Democracies tend to win their wars more often than autocracies

Some evidence suggests democracies tend to continue their wars longer than autocracies

Sources: Bueno de Mesquita et al. 1999; Russett and Oneal 2001; Russett 2010.

deserves to be killed. This is harder to accomplish if citizens in the proposed enemy nation elect their leaders. It is more difficult for democratic leaders to demonize an entire population of a democratic nation than to rally their citizens to seek to destroy nations led by "bad" autocratic decision-makers.

Democracies tend to win their wars more often than autocracies probably in part because democratic leaders risk more if they lose. Defeat on the battlefield can lead to defeat at the ballot box and thus a great loss of power for democratic war leaders. Democratic leaders may thus plan their wars more thoroughly and be more willing than autocrats to invest all the financial and human resources necessary to win. Dictators lose power much less often after a defeat since their survival depends less on successful public policies. Autocrats may be able to withdraw their troops at any time and still satisfy their core supporters with the distribution of the private goods that they expect.

For decades autocratic nations across the globe have been transforming themselves into democracies. Indeed, by 2010, democratically elected leaders led about half the world's nation-states. There are thus increasingly fewer autocracies for democracies to fight. If this democratization trend continues, the pool of potential non-democratic enemies may become so small that future democratic leaders find interstate wars very difficult to start.

THE CAPITALIST PEACE

Explanations for the democratic peace remain in dispute. Some researchers maintain that the increased peace among democratic governments derives from the empowerment of large groups of citizens like those associated with the global peace network. These citizens and their groups make it increasingly difficult for leaders to send people into wars. Other researchers offer explanations based on the global spread of norms that encourage respect for borders, laws, and human rights (Lane and Waqschal 2011; Mitchell 2012). Yet other researchers argue for a third position, maintaining that the absence of war between democracies is rooted more in economic than political or normative causes. As Erik Gartzke (2007) explains, these analysts believe the democratic peace should more accurately be called the capitalist peace.

The **capitalist peace** is thought to arise in part from capitalism's heavy reliance on contracts, which in turn encourage states of all types to depend increasingly on non-lethal dispute resolution practices. Market-based capitalism does tend to encourage democracies, analysts such as Michael Mousseau (2012) argue, but it is capitalism and not democracy that is primary. According to this view, the democratic peace could exist with many fewer democratic states, for example, in a world system dominated by autocratic but capitalist-leaning states like China, Hong Kong, Kuwait, Saudi Arabia, Singapore, United Arab Emirates, Vietnam, and Qatar.

Much evidence indicates that contemporary transnational capitalism works as a deterrent against interstate wars, at least among developed nations that actively participate in the global commercial system (Brooks 2005). Contemporary capitalism differs from earlier types of much more war-prone systems of capitalism in its emphases on (1) the globalization of production, (2) the globalization of markets, and (3) foreign direct investment.

Each of these related characteristics of contemporary capitalism tends to encourage the use of soft power more than hard power.

The globalization of production refers to dispersing the creation of goods and services across multiple borders. So, for example, American cars were once made in a single factory in Detroit from parts manufactured on site or nearby. Now "American" cars are assembled at multiple sites both inside and outside the United States from parts manufactured in dozens of countries spread across the world. Similarly, newer iconic American companies such as Apple and Nike manufacture their computers and shoes from parts assembled on multiple continents. Multinational companies based in all countries similarly depend on the geographic dispersion of production and so have a common interest in discouraging interstate wars in the countries that act as their suppliers. Multinational companies also have reason to discourage tensions that might disrupt the complicated sea and land transportation systems they depend upon.

The globalization of markets, a second characteristic of modern capitalism, further decreases incentives for interstate wars. The **globalization of markets** leads companies to sell their products all over the world. Earlier capitalist markets were mostly domestic, usually not even national but more often regional and even local. Today, instead, all large and many small businesses sell products and services to customers in many dozens of countries.

The globalization of markets was well underway before the invention of the Internet and wireless technologies, but these new media accelerated this trend. Access to global markets is now theoretically possible for even sole proprietor businesses in small, very poor countries. This means that products produced anywhere can be sold everywhere. It also means that the profits and jobs in one country are increasingly dependent upon the consumption patterns of people in distant countries. Interstate wars are likely to disrupt both production and consumption in unforeseen but economically devastating ways.

Foreign direct investment, a third prominent feature of contemporary capitalism, also tends to discourage interstate wars. **Foreign direct investment** occurs when a company makes an investment in buildings, machinery, or equipment in another country. Foreign direct investment can also include joint ventures and alliances, as well as investments in management services, technology, and intellectual property. These direct investments are different from so-called indirect portfolio investments in stocks or bonds. Indirect investments require less communication and commitment and so do much less than foreign direct investments to integrate the financial and strategic interests of nations.

Foreign direct investment has grown significantly in the past decade. According to the UN Conference on Trade and Development (2011), the world economy as a whole saw about $1.4 trillion to $1.6 trillion of direct foreign investment flow in 2011. This means that foreign direct investment was associated with almost one-fortieth of that year's total global $60 trillion economy. Most countries in all regions are now increasingly dependent on foreign direct investment. And, in general, the more foreign direct investment a state receives or sends to other states, the less likely that state is to participate in hard power disputes with their partner countries (Altincekic 2009).

China and the United State provide a stark example. China has invested about $1 trillion in United States treasuries and other indirect portfolio investments. China in addition currently also has about $16 billion in foreign direct investment in the United States; companies in the United States in turn have about $50 billion of direct investment in China. Iconic U.S. companies such as Apple, Caterpillar, General Electric, General Motors, and Walmart are banking on future growth overseas, especially in China, the soon-to-be world economy with the largest number of middle-class consumers. (India currently has the most.) General Motors already sells more cars and trucks through its joint ventures in China than throughout all of North America. A hard power war between China and the United States would devastate both nations' economies and precipitate a deep global recession.

The democratic-capitalist peace does not apply with great force to non-democratic countries in their relations with other non-capitalist economies (Hewitt and Wilkenfeld 1996). The democratic-capitalist peace thus does not signal the end of interstate conflicts either between non-capitalistic autocracies or between democracies and non-capitalistic autocracies. Still, as mentioned earlier, yet more countries seem likely to become democracies and participants in the world capitalist system in the decades ahead. The soft power strategies associated with the democratic-capitalist peace may then further expand. The rate of eruption of new interstate wars may continue its downward trend.

THE POPULATION IS THE WAR PRIZE

Waging an interstate war more often decreases than increases an invader's gross national product (Brooks 2005). Killing people and destroying infrastructure in cross-border wars in our current era is thus usually not as effective as finding ways to win over an opponent's "hearts and minds." Brigadier General Larry Nicholson, a Marine commander, explained this changed perspective to his troops in Afghanistan: "The population is not the enemy. The population is the prize—they are why we are going in" (quoted in Filkins 2010).

The **population is the prize** increasingly sought by both foreign and military policies. The trend among military strategists is thus toward seeking ways to assist in strengthening cooperative commercial and social relations between countries. One leading political scientist, Mary Kaldor (2007), maintains this new emphasis on civilian populations has created "new wars" different from most interstate wars that the world knew before. **New wars** still sometimes include elements of hard power wars but these new wars are fought to mobilize civilian populations at least as often as to capture their resources or territory. Rupert Smith (2007) explains this same shift as a change from an era of "industrial wars" to "war among the people." Smith served in the British army for forty years, including tours as commander of the UN forces in Bosnia and as NATO deputy supreme allied commander. He argues that his career overlapped with an earlier time when interstate wars focused on coercing opponents in order to control their resources and territories. These conflicts were like wars in the ages of mercantile and colonial capitalism when European countries used hard power to extract resources and enslave humans in the Americas, Asia, Africa, and Oceania.

Today, however, as mentioned earlier, great national wealth is more often created through the maintenance of complicated, multinational chains of global commerce.

TABLE 6.3 THE SHIFTING NATURE OF WAR

Traditional Wars	Contemporary Wars
Old wars, industrial wars	New wars, wars among the people
Hard power wars	Smart wars, using both hard and soft power
Wars for resources	Wars for access, relationships, trade agreements
Population as enemy	Population is the prize
Battlefield is territory	Battlefield is minds of the people
Linear, begins and ends	Recursive, continual
Media reports about	Media is used as a "weapon," as an instrument of persuasion

Sources: Kaldor 2007; Nye 2009; Smith and Rupert 2007.

Admiral Mike Mullen, Chairman of the Joint Chiefs and highest-ranking officer in the armed forces in the United States, pointed to the shift when he declared that for the military today, "the battlefield isn't necessarily a field anymore. It's in the minds of the people. It's what they believe to be true that matters" (Mullen 2010). When new hard power interstate wars do now erupt, their goals are likely to include strengthening conditions for successful capitalist production, marketing, and foreign direct investment. (See Table 6.3, "The Shifting Nature of War.")

FROM NATIONAL TO HUMAN SECURITY

The "old war" strategic emphasis on acquiring resources and territory is yielding to increasing concerns with protecting the people residing inside territories, a change often referred to as shift from national to human security. **National security** focuses on protecting national borders through the use of hard power threats, coercion, and force. By contrast, **human security** aims to protect and expand human rights through increasing cooperation among citizens within borders. Human security includes attention to the basic human needs for food, potable water, breathable air, shelter, and health care.

Basic human rights and needs play little or no part in traditional national security policies. Their aim is instead to preserve existing governments and their supporters, along with any territory that might enrich these groups. Governments thus frequently invoke national security to explain why they are using coercion not just against other countries but also against their own citizens, the terrorism from above described in Chapter 4. In fact, however, for the last one hundred years people have been killed much more often by their own governments than by interstate wars. Commonly these government-produced killings have been justified by the controlling elites as necessary to maintain "national security" (Human Security Report Project 2005).

The alternative human security perspective builds on this realization that people usually have more to fear from their own governments than from foreign enemies. Human security strategies reject the traditional national security assumption that government elites and their allies should be the primary decision-makers in questions of life and death. Human security aims to include all national groups in both internal and external security decision-making.

TABLE 6.4 NATIONAL AND HUMAN SECURITY

National Security	Human Security
Seeks secure states	Seeks secure people
Aims to protect national borders	Aims to protect citizens
Focuses on maintaining stability	Focuses on advancing human rights
Emphasizes nation-states	Emphasizes individuals and minorities
Emphasizes negative peace and stability	Emphasizes positive peace and justice
Assumes a hierarchical world	Assumes an interconnected, networked world
Managed from above by government organizations	Managed both by governments and from below by civil society and nongovernmental organizations

Source: Adapted from 3P Human Security, at http://3phumansecurity.org/site

Over the past few decades, people in every part of the world have created hundreds of thousands of grassroots civil society organizations that focus on issues of human security which their own governments cannot or will not address (Kaldor 2003). These organizations tend to emphasize long-term conflict transformations more than short-term conflict resolutions, a distinction explored further in Chapter 12.

National and human security perspectives can mutually support each other, in a relationship similar to that between negative and positive peace. Citizens may sometimes need protection from foreign attacks and intrastate conflicts. Governments that stress human as well as traditional national security concerns within their strategic plans are, however, less likely to oppress, harm, incarcerate, and murder their own people. (See Table 6.4, "National and Human Security" and Case 6-2, "Applying a Gender Perspective to War.")

THE AGE OF PEACEBUILDING

The rising strength of international judicial organizations described in Chapter 3 is yet another cause for the increasing use of soft power and human security strategies. Countries in most of the world now have the option to bring interstate disagreements to the Permanent Court of Arbitration (with 115 member nations), the International Court of Justice, the World Trade Organization, and many other intergovernmental organizations. Third-part mediation, arbitration, and adjudication are becoming common responses to potentially deadly international conflicts. Both democratic and non-democratic countries feel pressure from the international community to turn to nonviolent dispute resolution mechanisms rather than to threats or declarations of war (Mitchell 2012). When many nations are using war as a way to try to settle disputes, it is easier for other nations to join in (Ehrenreich 1998). When the majority of nations are turning to courts, arbitrators, and mediators, it becomes more difficult (though certainly not impossible) even for autocratic states to initiate interstate violence.

The 193-member United Nations has also helped decrease the frequency and deadliness of interstate wars (Goldstein 2012). The UN sent its first peacekeepers to broker the end of the Arab-Israeli War in 1948. During the Cold War in the following decades, however, the Soviet Union and United States used their Security Council vetoes to discourage

CASE 6-2 APPLYING A GENDER PERSPECTIVE TO WAR

Decisions to go to war are usually deeply gendered activities. The honor and prestige that decision-makers so often seek is frequently associated with their desire to appear "strong," in a physically aggressive, supposedly male-appropriate way.

Decision-makers who plan, prepare, and profit from wars are overwhelmingly male. It is also primarily men in countries both rich and poor who act as military officers and war planners, weapons designers and plant managers, and arms dealers and deliverers. When inter- or intra-state wars start, it is mostly other, younger, less educated, and poorer men that the male decision-makers send off to kill and be killed.

Men dominate both war preparation and the militaries that wage war in large part because war is associated with traditional masculine values that tend to glorify war and warriors. Traditional masculine values include a preference for hierarchical, top-down decision-making, the method preferred by militaries and the government agencies with which they are associated. Traditional masculine values also associate strength with force and coercion. Power, in turn, is perceived as a source of physical and psychological control.

These several traditional masculine values contrast with alternative traditional feminine values that prefer non-hierarchical, consensus decision-making, based on empathy, personal relationships, and reason. Traditional feminine strength and power is associated with interdependence and networking more than with force and control. Populations that embrace traditional feminine values are less accepting of war.

Of course, many men hold more traditionally feminine than masculine values and many women hold more traditionally masculine than feminine values. Nonetheless, in most societies boys and men choose war-associated entertainments and occupations more often than girls and women do. These persistent differences in values continue to fuel debates about whether women are "hard-nosed" enough to be "suitable or capable" for combat. Basic training drill sergeants declare their aim is to turn "boys into men." Recruits who stumble are shamed by being called "ladies," "girls," and other less flattering names suggesting they are not "real men." In business and sports, as well as in war, leadership is more often associated with toughness and force than with collaboration and care.

From a gender perspective, ending war requires changing the prevailing value system. Wars will not decrease even if women become more economically and politically equal to men if, simultaneously, women become more accepting of the masculine values of hierarchy, coercion, and control. These values encourage war preparation and participation, whether they are held by biological females or males.

Traditional masculine values have great merit. They are essential to healthy human societies. But so are traditional feminine values. War and other problems result in part from misbalanced societies in which masculine values dominate. A rebalancing is needed to combine equal measures of traditional feminine and masculine values. As Betty Reardon wrote in her pioneering *Sexism and the War System* (1985, 89), "As male and female genetic material converge in the conception of an individual human life, so must masculine and feminine perceptions, modes, and participation merge into a conception of a truly human society."

Sources: Enloe 1983, 1990; Jenkins and Reardon 2007; Reardon 1985.

peacekeeping operations in the many so-called proxy wars they were both sponsoring. Then the Cold War ended and between 1991 and 1994 the UN undertook "peacebuilding operations in revolutionary number and frequency" (Philpott 2010, 3). There were more missions in those four years of the early 1990s than in the previous forty-five years combined. The last few decades are sometimes referred to as the **age of peacebuilding** as during this period the United Nations and other organizations undertook an unprecedented wave of projects to end both interstate and intrastate violence. (Peacebuilding in this sense also includes both peacekeeping and peacemaking, though these three terms can also have distinct meanings, as is explained in Chapter 13.) Table 6.5, "UN Peace Missions," summarizes the growth in peacebuilding operations.

TABLE 6.5 UN PEACE MISSIONS

Decade	# of missions	Locations
1940s	2	Palestine; Kashmir
1950s	2	Egypt, Suez; Lebanon
1960s	6	Congo; West Irian; Yemen; Cyprus; Dominican Republic; Kashmir
1970s	3	Sinai; Golan Heights; Lebanon
1980s	5	Afghanistan-Pakistan; Iran-Iraq; Angola; Namibia; Nicaragua
1990s	38	Kuwait; Cambodia; Eritrea; Rwanda; Tajikistan; Albania; Guatemala; Kosovo; East Timor; Democratic Republic of Congo; and others
2000s	11	Ethiopia/Eritrea; East Timor; Liberia; Côte d'Ivoire; Haiti; Burundi; Sudan; Timor; Darfur; Central African Republic/Chad; Democratic Republic of Congo

Source: Dobbins et al. 2005, xxxi–xxxiv.

Precise rates of success of UN peacekeeping missions are difficult to compute, especially if one uses a definition of success that is more expansive than simply that an agreement was signed or that most violence was stopped. Still, though inexact, the evidence is clear: UN peace operations since the end of the Cold War have repeatedly helped end interstate and intrastate wars, genocides, and other violent crises. According to a study by the Rand Corporation, seven out of eight major UN missions conducted since 1988 left their targeted societies more peaceful; six of those eight societies have established democratic governance (Dobbins et al. 2005). These proto-democracies include: Bosnia, East Timor, Eastern Slovenia, Haiti, Kosovo, and Mozambique. In addition, according to this report, UN missions have been largely responsible for "a fivefold decrease in deaths from civil and international conflict," from an average of 200,000 in the early 1990s to 27,000 deaths per year a decade later (Dobbins et al. 2005, xxxvi).

This generally successful peace work has been done cheaply. All seventeen UN peacekeeping missions in 2013, using approximately 76,000 troops, cost only about $7 billion (UN Department of Public Information 2013). By contrast, the United States spent almost as much every month during the first eight years of its military occupation of Iraq. The total UN peacekeeping expense per year is about half of one percent of the world's aggregate annual military spending.

The UN's peace work is aided by the fact that, unlike its member nations, the UN has no specific territory, ethnic groups, electorate, or military traditions to defend. National leaders can sometimes support UN and other nongovernmental peace missions without risking being accused of weakness. Also, putting the UN in the forefront of the current ongoing shift toward soft power allows the UN rather than vulnerable nation-based politicians to bear the brunt of the consequences of failed missions, inevitable occurrences as new, nonviolent peacebuilding strategies are being developed.

There have been several spectacular disasters. These include the UN's failure to prevent the 1994 Rwandan genocide, a lack of effective intervention in the Second Congo War, impotence both in the face of the 1995 Srebrenica massacre and in the genocide in Darfur,

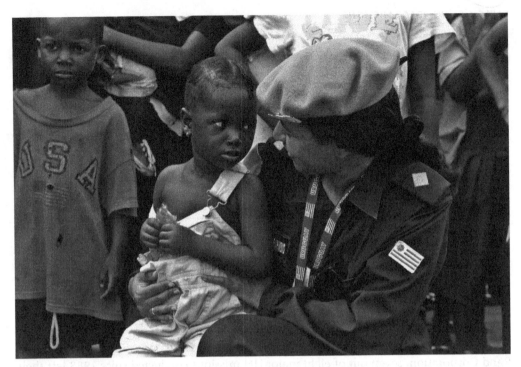

A UN peacekeeper from Uruguay offers assistance to a girl in Liberia in 2011.

as well as a lack of implementation of several Security Council resolutions related to the Israeli-Palestinian conflict. These and other failures have been much publicized. However, the fact that the UN is faulted in such cases demonstrates that there is now a widespread belief that massacres, genocides, and wars could be avoided, or at least greatly moderated, if only the right intervention plans were implemented.

Because of their frequent successes, the UN Security Council has become willing to authorize larger and more complex peace missions. These missions have, in turn, energized peacebuilding programs in other departments within the UN, for example, in the UN's Development Programme (UNDP) and in the High Commission for Refugees (UNHCR). The UN's success is also encouraging regional organizations such as the European Union, as well as nongovernmental organizations such as Médecins Sans Frontières (Doctors without Borders) and Oxfam to undertake ambitious projects that might have seemed unrealistic twenty years ago.

THE MILITARY-INDUSTRIAL COMPLEX

Some nations are shifting their foreign policy emphasis from hard to soft power. Still, there are many obstacles to decreasing most nations' traditional reliance on coercion and war. These impediments include: military-industrial complexes, the tendency for war to increase citizen approval of leaders, and cultural and media traditions that glamorize warriors. Each of these obstacles deserves attention.

Military-industrial complex is a phrase popularized by United States President Dwight D. Eisenhower to describe the disproportionate influence of professional soldiers and members of the commercial security sector on domestic and foreign policies. Eisenhower used his farewell speech at the end of his presidency in 1961 to caution that the goals of the military-industrial complex were likely to become increasingly antithetical to the nation's interests and that, unfortunately, the power of the military-industrial complex was growing.

The political influence of the military-industrial complex has increased even more than Eisenhower anticipated. Some maintain that the United States today is largely governed by a military-industrial-congressional-media-educational complex since the majority of people in Congress, the mass media, and public and private education commonly promote hard power strategies above all others (Giroux 2007). Many members of Congress receive much of their campaign funding from military contractors. The United States Department of Defense itself shapes public policy and opinion in favor of hard power by funding researchers at many of the country's most prestigious universities. The Department of Defense also spends over $200 million annually to support so-called "independent civilian" think tanks. The research at these centers is completed mostly by retired officers and government officials who have spent lifetimes studying hard power strategies but who know little about diplomacy, negotiation, and nonviolent persuasion.

Many Department of Defense–supported researchers write books and articles and appear on media outlets to present their opinions on foreign policy, even though they rarely acknowledge the biases that shape their ideas. An associated, influential circle of policy advisors to each president is drawn disproportionately from those whose careers and research has been supported by Department of Defense funds. Soft power experts are much less often supported, consulted, or heard.

The United States is not the only country with an influential military-industrial complex. However, the United States spends a higher proportion of its gross national product (GDP) on hard power preparation than any other large, industrialized country, about 4.7 percent of GDP in 2011 (Stockholm International Peace Research Institute 2011). (The second highest is Russia at 3.9 percent; South Korea is third at 2.7 percent. China spends about 2 percent of its GDP on its military.) Military spending in every country tends to foster a constituency with interests in championing further rises in military expenditures. In a democracy like the United States, where almost 5 percent of all economic activity is directly tied to hard power preparation, the constituency encouraging growth of the military-industrial complex constitutes roughly one out of every 20 who are employed.

In the United States as elsewhere there are no comparably influential constituencies joining together to promote alternatives to the hard power views sponsored by the military-industrial complex. Unfortunately, the 95 percent of the economy that profits more from soft than hard power preparations has not formed a peace-industrial complex to promote its financial interests in increasing funding for education, child, health and senior care, infrastructure, and positive peace. Such a group in the United States could claim to represent about 19 out of every 20 persons who are employed.

A few organizations within the global peace network are attempting to create a wider public awareness of what the Institute for Economics and Peace (2009) calls the "peace industry." These peace-sensitive industries prominently include the finance, insurance, retail, and tourism sectors, all of which generally suffer greatly when wars break out. The International Institute for Peace through Tourism (IIPT) has been promoting a similar message about the commercial importance of peace since 1986. In total, the Institute for Economics and Peace (2009) estimates that violent conflicts cost the world economy about $7 trillion a year, roughly 10 percent of the entire global domestic product. Peace is good for most businesses—about 19 out of 20 in the United States—and greater public awareness of this truth would be good for peace.

TWO OTHER OBSTACLES TO SOFT POWER

A second obstacle to soft power is the tendency of national leaders to promote wars or preparations for wars as a way to divert citizen attention away from domestic problems. Democratic leaders seem especially prone to this tendency since they commonly receive an immediate boost in their approval ratings when they send their militaries to war. For example, George W. Bush's public approval rating jumped eleven percentage points in March 2003 with the launch of the Iraq war (PollingReport 2013). Autocrats can also gain from launching interstate wars but only if they are thereby better able to provide material goods to their supporters. Because citizens tend to overlook their political differences and to rally around their leaders in times of a supposed threat, most leaders have an incentive to provoke wars or exaggerate supposed risks of domestic attacks when they want to distract public attention from domestic problems.

Cultural and media traditions that encourage war are a third obstacle to the increased use of soft power (Lane and Waqschal 2011). Many cultural traditions exalt military warriors as heroes while ignoring or sometimes even ridiculing people who work for peace. As Maciej J. Bartkowski (2013, 2) points out in his introduction to *Recovering Nonviolent History*, the memory of most nonviolent campaigns against oppression "have been misinterpreted or erased altogether from collective memory, buried beneath nationally eulogized violence, commemorative rituals of glorified death, martyred heroes, and romanticized violent insurrections." For example, people in the United States are frequently told about the presidents and generals who led them in wars (for example, Washington, Grant, Roosevelt, Eisenhower, Schwarzkopf, and Powell), but schools teach little about the people who led nonviolent campaigns to end slavery, regulate child labor, create a forty-hour workweek, establish workplace safety laws, or win for women the right to vote. These peaceful campaigns mobilized many tens of thousands and sometimes lasted for decades. Telling these stories, however, requires describing complexities that are generally less dramatic than the events of wars.

As mentioned in earlier chapters, contemporary popular media increasingly normalize and glorify violence. Newscasts, movies, documentaries, and electronic games frequently exaggerate the effectiveness of physical coercion while downplaying the more common successes of soft power. Violence is visually interesting; negotiations are not. Force produces abrupt, theatrical changes to onscreen characters and events. On the other hand, lengthy efforts at persuasion, conflict resolution, mediations, community organizing, educating for civic action, and most other nonviolent processes are difficult to present as entertainment, even by the most talented writers and directors. War and violence attracts audiences; peace and negotiation do not.

Cultural and media traditions supporting violence and war often also promote the bellicose masculine values discussed earlier in this chapter. The continuing dominance of these traditional war- and violence-supporting norms help explain why the repeated failures of interstate wars over the last fifty years have not led even more governments to emphasize soft power alternatives to military action. Nonetheless, the trends are clear: The military-industrial complex, political expediency, and cultural, media, and confrontational masculine traditions are slowing but not preventing the development of new foreign policies that rely more on persuasion than on violent coercion. We may be entering what Joseph S. Nye Jr. (2009) describes as an era of smart power. **Smart power** seeks to achieve foreign policy goals through relying first and foremost on soft power while nonetheless retaining the capability and willingness to sometimes also use hard power. Smart power emphasizes soft power persuasion because, as Nye points out, hard power's effectiveness is always limited and inevitably costly. On the other hand, soft power's benefits can be limitless and immensely profitable.

MAKING CONNECTIONS

Many forces are encouraging nations to ease away from foreign policies that emphasize their military's ability to kill and destroy. These forces for peace include the recent history of prominent interstate war failures, the changing way nations win respect, the rise of democracies and global capitalism, the new emphasis on the population as the prize, the rising strength of international organizations such as the United Nations, and the growing power of the global peace network.

The future is unknowable, of course, but there are many reasons to expect that the current global trend toward the increasing use of soft power will continue. The frequency and deadliness of intrastate insurrections, considered next in Chapter 7, are also in decline, though not as strongly or consistently as declines in interstate violence. The increasing sophistication of nonviolent movements, described in both Chapters 7 and 8, and the rising power of women, described earlier in Chapter 5, are further encouraging reductions in both interstate and intrastate wars across much of the world.

FOR REVIEW

1. Explain why a desire for respect is often more important for national decision-makers in starting wars than the pursuit of resources or security.
2. Analyze the key differences between using the idea of a "democratic peace" or of a "capitalist peace" to understand recent decreases in interstate wars.
3. Describe how foreign policies change when populations and not territory become the central prize.
4. Summarize what you believe is the strongest evidence presented in the chapter that there is a shift underway from an emphasis on hard to soft power.
5. Explain which one of the three obstacles discussed in the chapter is most likely to hinder the further expansion of soft power.

THINKING CRITICALLY

1. Are there reasons to believe that the era of large interstate land wars has likely come to an end?
2. Why does a desire for respect play such a large role in the decision-making of government leaders?
3. Can you find examples from one or more wars to explain the differences between the four motives that Lebow found shape most decision-makers' choices to wage war?
4. Does the idea of a "democratic peace" or of a "capitalist peace" better explain the finding that democracies rarely go to war against each other?
5. Is contemporary capitalism so different from pre-globalization capitalism that it is best understood as a new form of world commerce?
6. What would be the likely consequences for both countries of a hard power war between China and the United States?
7. How can nation-states simultaneously best achieve both their national and human security goals?
8. What are the major obstacles to increasing the rate of success of international peacekeeping missions?
9. Is the influence of the military-industrial complex declining—or rising—in the United States? In most of the rest of the developed world?

RECOMMENDED RESOURCES

The Human Security Gateway. Provides an extensive research and information database of electronic and bibliographic resources on human security. Website at http://www.humansecuritygateway.com

Kaldor, Mary. *New and Old Wars: Organized Violence in a Global Era*, 2nd edition (Palo Alto, CA: Stanford University Press, 2007). Offers a widely influential way of understanding contemporary war and conflict that goes beyond the traditional emphasis on nation-states.

Korengal. Directed by Sebastian Junger. Goldcrest Films, 2014. A sequel to *Restrepo* (described below), this documentary explores what war feels like and how it alters the young men who fight it. Based on the work of embedded filmmakers who recorded battles and their aftermaths, often from very close range.

Lane, Jan-Erik, and Uwe Waqschal. *Culture and Politics* (New York: Routledge, 2011). This ambitious textbook emphasizes the importance of culture in shaping societies and personal experiences. It foregrounds empirical work on the role of culture at the micro, meso, and macro levels of analysis.

Peace Portal. Resources presented by the international Global Partnership for the Prevention of Armed Conflict. Emphasizes networking, peacebuilding stories, and tools for building successful campaigns. Website at http://www.peaceportal.org/

Restrepo. Directors Tim Hetherington and Sebastian Junger. Outpost Films, 2010. A documentary, shot by embedded filmmakers, that offers an intimate examination of a platoon of U.S. soldiers at war in Afghanistan who must use both hard and soft power strategies. *Korengal*, described above, is a sequel to *Restrepo*.

Ricigliano, Robert. *Making Peace Last: A Toolbox for Sustainable Peacebuilding* (Boulder, CO: Paradigm Publishers, 2012). Describes why peace programs fail and what practical steps can be taken to make them work better.

Why We Fight. Director Eugene Jarecki. Sony Classics, 2005. A documentary with many illuminating interviews that examines the roles of the military-industrial complex, the Project for the New American Century, and other groups in shaping the United States' decision to wage war against Iraq.

CHAPTER 7

THE RISE OF NONVIOLENCE AND HUMAN RIGHTS

CHAPTER OVERVIEW

This chapter surveys the rise of nonviolence as both a popular idea and a form of political action. It describes the use of nonviolent action in pre–Revolutionary War America before examining Thoreau's idea of civil disobedience. Subsequent sections describe the upsurge of nonviolent movements across the first six decades of the twentieth century. Gene Sharp's concept of nonviolent action is explained, followed by a review of the nonviolent insurrections that filled the last decades of the twentieth century. Relationships between nonviolence and the increase in nation-state democracies are explored. Next comes separate looks at the peacebuilding role of international organizations, tribunals, and courts. The chapter concludes with a discussion of benefits and problems associated with nonviolent campaigns for human rights.

Key terms and people discussed include: Revolution in the minds of the people; Henry David Thoreau; civil disobedience; Mohandas K. Gandhi; Global Nonviolent Action Database; Martin Luther King Jr.; nonviolent action; satyagraha; rise of democracy; international tribunals and courts; human rights.

> Civilization is a stream with banks. The stream is sometimes filled with blood from people killing, stealing, shouting and doing the things historians usually record, while on the banks, unnoticed, people build homes, make love, raise children, sing songs, write poetry and even whittle statues. The story of civilization is what happened on the banks.
>
> —WILL DURANT (1950, 302)

In 1700, at the beginning of the modern period, governments everywhere were dominated by hereditary rulers as likely to enslave as benefit their citizen-subjects. Many humans then seemed to live in a "warre of every man against every man," the English philosopher Thomas Hobbes observed in the seventeenth century. This left ordinary people sometimes living lives "solitary, poore, nasty, brutish, and short."

Few in the developed world today find Hobbes' description persuasive. Rather than constant oppression by kings, chiefs, and nobles, people in over half the world's countries now more often choose candidates through different types of nonviolent election campaigns. Of course, decision-making in many democracies remains dominated by a very few. Those with money have much more influence almost everywhere. Nonetheless, the fact that fears about the fairness of democratic institutions exist today demonstrates how far humanity has traveled from the Hobbesian view that people must passively accept unchangeable, brutish, and short lives.

Harbingers of this new optimistic perspective on human life spread with radical consequences across England's Atlantic seaboard colonies in the decade before the American Revolutionary War. As this chapter will show, a similar faith in the power of ordinary people to shape their lives and governments is now found in almost all regions of the world.

REVOLUTION IN THE MINDS OF COLONIAL AMERICANS

England was a world colossus when a few thousand disaffected American colonists began resisting British rule in the 1760s. Against great odds, within a few years, England lost control of large portions of its empire on the eastern shore of North America. The rebels secured much of their independence through nonviolent actions before the shooting war started in 1775 (Conser 2013).

John Adams served as the first vice president and as the second president of the new nation called the United States of America. Thinking back in his retirement, Adams concluded that the most important events of the American Revolution transpired in the years before the signing of the Declaration of Independence, in the years before the violence began. A **revolution in the minds of the people** transformed the colonists into citizens able to view themselves as part of a new, democratic, sovereign nation. As Adams explained in a letter to Thomas Jefferson, the shooting war that came later "was no part of the revolution; it was only an effect and consequence of it. The revolution was in the minds of the people, and this was effected from 1760 to 1775, in the course of fifteen years, before a drop of blood was shed in Lexington" (Adams 1856, 172). In that earlier time, as Walter H. Conser (2013) shows, the colonists cobbled together their own independent economic, social, and political institutions, drastically reducing the power of British rule years before what Ralph Waldo Emerson later called the "shot heard round the world" was heard.

The pre-revolutionary colonists organized hundreds of acts of nonviolent noncooperation that grew bolder and more defiant year after year (Wood 1993). The Boston Tea Party remains best known. In Boston Harbor in December 1773, thirty to one hundred men boarded three ships and threw 342 chests of tea into the water, in protest against "taxation without representation." Most accounts agree that the rebels were careful to damage no property beyond destroying the imported tea (Schell 2003). Some historians maintain that a padlock broken on one ship was replaced later by participants to emphasize that they were not vandals but concerned citizens, determined to act with respect while making a symbolic statement about the tax on tea.

As Jonathan Schell (2003) explains, Adams points to another, earlier nonviolent campaign as the crucial turning point in the revolution in the minds of the people. In 1772, the English tried to re-establish their autocratic control of the judges on the Massachusetts Supreme Court; they ended their election by the Massachusetts House of Representatives. The House protested their loss of democratic power and voted to impeach the new judges. When the colony's English-appointed governor still would not yield, the colonists refused to serve on juries presided over by these disputed judges. Without jurors, there could be no court sessions. The judicial system and much of the power of English governance in the colonies thus ground to a halt even though not a single weapon had been fired or even threatened to be fired.

The early American nonviolent resisters also conducted numerous other campaigns that built cooperation across the thirteen diverse and geographically dispersed colonies. As Gandhi would later, the resisters even launched grassroots campaigns to encourage production of homespun cloth, to create alternatives to buying textiles from English mills. Through this and hundreds of other acts of nonviolence, Adams concludes, the colonists established their independence without firing a shot.

CREATING NAMES FOR NONVIOLENCE

Adams' claim that no shooting war was necessary to win independence from England because a revolution had already occurred in the minds of the people remains controversial. The colonists may still have been required to use some violence to earn independence in the 1780s rather than decades later. Still, most historians agree with Adams that multiple campaigns of what we today call nonviolent action transformed governance in the colonies between 1760 and 1775. Adams worried that memories of the effectiveness of the colonists' nonviolent prewar actions would be forgotten as the new nation forged myths of its origins built on tales emphasizing violence and war. And, just as Adams anticipated, Washington and his lieutenants, as well as those who fought in the Revolutionary army, have since been elevated to the status of "patriots," "freedom fighters," and "creators of the nation" while the many people who participated in the earlier nonviolent protests and who helped create independent economic, social, and political forms have mostly been forgotten.

Much of this forgetting grows from the tendency of historians to stress military history and to chronicle violence more than nonviolent resistance (Bartkowski 2013). But historians also ignored what happened before 1775 in part because they could not understand it. Until the last century or so there were few words to help people name and remember what Adams characterized as a revolution in the minds of the people. Historians thus continued emphasizing what they already knew most about: military strategies and campaigns, violent actions for which there have been abundant names since at least the time of the first Greek and Roman historians. Historians and the laypeople they informed could not memorialize nonviolent resistance since they possessed no words for these actions. They could not remember what they could not easily name.

[Handwritten margin notes: "Was Adams this peaceful? — seems peaceful..."]

This conceptual deficiency exists no more. The American essayist **Henry David Thoreau** was one of the earliest thinkers to invent ways to conceptualize the peaceable revolutions now familiar to many across the world. Thoreau's 1848 lecture, "The Rights and Duties of the Individual in Relation to Government," has become as famous as any text produced anywhere in the Americas in the nineteenth century. It was first published in 1866, four years after Thoreau's death, under the name by which it is now known, "Civil Disobedience."

Thoreau argues in this lecture that an individual's private moral judgment is likely to be superior to the judgment of governments. He coined the phrase **civil disobedience** to name a nonviolent, sometimes illegal act, undertaken by individuals or groups to oppose government actions that they believe are unjust. Thoreau maintained that individuals have an obligation to use civil disobedience to produce "a counter friction to stop the machine" of government when that government is in the wrong.

Thoreau pointed to the American war with Mexico and to slavery as examples of immoral government actions present at the time he was writing. Nonviolent civil disobedience was necessary to oppose these injustices, Thoreau insisted, for "under a government which imprisons unjustly, the true place for a just man is also a prison." Mere politicking and campaigning against government policies was insufficient, Thoreau argued:

> Cast your whole vote, not a strip of paper merely, but your whole influence. A minority is powerless while it conforms to the majority; it is not even a minority then; but it is irresistible when it clogs by its whole weight. If the alternative is to keep all just men in prison, or give up war and slavery, the State will not hesitate which to choose. If a thousand men were not to pay their tax bills this year, that would not be a violent and bloody measure, as it would be to pay them, and enable the State to commit violence and shed innocent blood. This is, in fact, the definition of a peaceable revolution, if any such is possible. (Thoreau 1980)

Thoreau's ideas remained little known for decades, even though, even in Thoreau's lifetime there were groups in the Americas and elsewhere struggling to organize nonviolent actions to clog the nineteenth-century machines of injustice. Few of these groups were aware of each other and so, for more than a half century after Thoreau's death, there was little sharing of experience and scant development of civil disobedience techniques. The two catastrophic world wars of the first half of the twentieth century, as well as the very violent revolutions in Russia and then China, even seemed to cast doubt on the possibility that revolutions in the minds of the people could produce radical changes in modern nations.

Then, in the last half of the twentieth century, a seismic shift took place. Ordinary citizens across the globe for the first time gained access to knowledge and a vocabulary that could help them plan nonviolent insurrections. Successful campaigns built on civil disobedience became epidemic. The more people learned about successes elsewhere, the better organized their own campaigns became. Each success spawned more knowledge and more imitators, followed by yet more knowledge and successes until nonviolent revolutions in the minds of the people became even more common than violent revolutions.

The very concept of revolution often now refers to unarmed insurrections like those that happened in the Philippines, Serbia, and Egypt as to the earlier bloodbaths in France, Russia, or China.

THE RISE OF NONVIOLENT CAMPAIGNS

As mentioned in Chapter 1, **Mohandas K. Gandhi** had few concepts and fewer examples to draw upon at the end of the nineteenth century when he found himself leading a campaign for justice for the Indian minority in South Africa. Gandhi thus had to improvise to fit circumstances as they unfolded. He proved a brilliant innovator, creating ever new ways to disrupt a repressive regime that found itself scrambling to discover how to destroy Gandhi's novel movement.

When he returned to India in 1915 after a decade of nonviolent experimentation in South Africa, Gandhi was forced to adjust his tactics to fit the very different conditions on the subcontinent. Gandhi began slowly, creating a mass movement focused first on promoting economic and political equality and then, finally, pushing for India's independence from England (Pareth 2001).

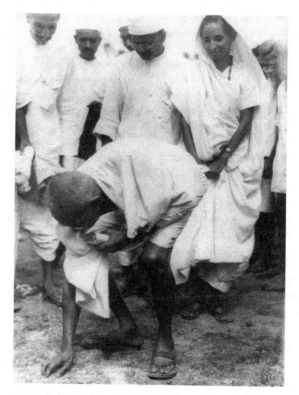

Gandhi picks up salt to break the law at the end of his 24-day, 240-mile march to the sea.

CASE 7-1 GANDHI'S SALT SATYAGRAHA
CAMPAIGN

Mohandas K. Gandhi's year-long salt satyagraha campaign remains among the best known and most influential nonviolent actions in history.

India had long been governed by Great Britain when Gandhi began his first sustained mass campaign in 1930. (Gandhi had begun and then aborted several earlier attempts at nationwide actions when he judged their likely participants were insufficiently trained.) Gandhi wrote the British ruling viceroy to announce his intention to lead a group of volunteers on a 240-mile march from Gandhi's home to the sea. Those assembled would then break the British law prohibiting the private manufacture of salt. Gandhi offered to stop the march if the Viceroy stopped taxing the private production of salt.

The Viceroy ignored Gandhi's letter and the then sixty-year-old Gandhi and dozens of others began their march on March 12, 1930. They walked for twenty-four days, pausing to explain their purpose in dozens of villages along the way. Gandhi's accomplices had alerted the national and international press and the march received increasing media attention the closer the marchers moved to the sea.

On April 6, 1930, Gandhi and hundreds of Indians gathered salt along the shore of Dandi, thereby publicly breaking the law and challenging the legitimacy of British rule. The British did nothing, reluctant to make arrests and create bad publicity for themselves. Seeking further attention, Gandhi decided to escalate his resistance. For a second time he wrote the Viceroy, this time announcing his intention to lead the marchers in seizing possession of the Dharasana salt works, twenty-five miles from Dandi.

The Viceroy ordered Gandhi and other leaders arrested. The raid took place anyway without Gandhi's presence and, for several days, hundreds of marchers walked toward the salt works and submitted to being assaulted by the police. Dozens were seriously injured.

Hundreds were arrested. But none of the marchers fought back as journalists from around the world observed, reported, and filmed. The *New York Times* reporter, Webb Miller, wrote:

> Suddenly . . . scores of native policemen rushed upon the advancing marchers and rained blows upon their heads with steel-shod lathis. Not one of the marchers even raised an arm to fend off the blows. They went down like ten-pins. From where I stood I heard the sickening whack of the clubs on the unprotected skulls. . . . Those struck down fell sprawling, unconscious or writhing with fractured pain or broken shoulders. . . . There was no fight, no struggle, the marchers simply walked forward until struck down. (quoted in Fischer 1954, 101)

Volunteers carried the wounded off on stretchers to receive first aid.

Even though Gandhi remained in jail, in the following months many additional nonviolent actions were launched. Over 60,000 people were eventually arrested. Though the Viceroy did not end the salt tax, Gandhi judged the salt campaign a success in several important ways. First and perhaps most importantly, it demonstrated that Indians could remain nonviolent even in the face of escalating British brutality. Second, the British had revealed to the world that their rule of India was immoral, based on force and not consent. Third, the campaign made it possible for previously fearful politicians and ordinary Indians to stand up to their oppressors and to go to jail. Finally, with the Salt Satyagraha Gandhi laid the groundwork for future nonviolent campaigns. He was ready now to try to create a new India that would not only be free of British imperial rule but also be built on a foundation of *sarvodaya*, a word Gandhi invented that roughly means "equal respect and uplift for all" (Mayton 2001).

Source: Global Nonviolent Action Database, authors George Lakey and Aden Tedla.

Gandhi's campaigns were widely publicized at the time and have been at the center of discussions of nonviolence ever since. However, this emphasis on Gandhi and India has unfortunately helped deflect attention from dozens of other civil resistance movements that also appeared across the world in the first half of the twentieth century. For example, in 1905, as Gandhi was organizing his first campaigns in South Africa, diverse forms of nonviolent action roiled Russia for months in reaction to soldiers killing one hundred peaceful demonstrators in St. Petersburg as they tried to present a petition to the Tsar (Ackerman and Duvall 2000; Sharp 2005). The nonviolent Russian Revolution of 1905 that followed produceed at its zenith more than a million workers on strike, numerous military mutinies, and major disruptons to railroads and communication networks across the country. Entire cities and ethnic regions set up alternative governments and police forces. The Tsar capitulated by issuing the October Manifesto calling for the establishment of an elected national assembly and other reforms that increased citizen rights. Most participants in the massive movement celebrated these changes as a sign of victory for their nonviolent efforts. Those who did not count the Tsar's concessions as a victory, however, increased their calls for the use of violence, a view that after World War I would help produce the now much better remembered bloody Russian Revolution of 1917.

In Asia, as Gandhi was growing the opposition to British rule in India, other important nonviolent campaigns emerged in areas that are now within the nations of Aghanistan, Pakistan, and Burma. Campaigns in regions of eastern Afghanistan and western Pakistan are particularly important to recall as they were undertaken by the ethnic Pashtuns (also known as Pastuns and Pathans), a tribal people often stereotyped by outsiders as brutal, militaristic, and vengeful (Raqib 2005, 113). The Pashtuns were in the news often in the first decade of the twenty-first century as they supplied the main support for the Taliban, a central foe of the United States' invasion and occupation of Afghanistan. Decades before, during the 1930s under the leadership of Khan Abdul Ghaffar Khan, the Pashtuns shunned the violent methods they later used against American soldiers to create instead the largest trained corps of nonviolent resisters the world has ever known.

These resisters were overwhelmingly Muslim and took the name of Khudai Khidmatgar, meaning "Children of God." At their peak, the Khudai Khidmatgar included over 60,000 volunteers who had completed a demanding nonviolent training. In nonviolent camps modeled on then-current military practices, volunteers drilled, paraded, and rehearsed nonviolent reactions to the violence that British troops and police would likely unleash upon them (Banerjee 2000). Each volunteer also took a pledge that included promises to "always live up to the principle of nonviolence," to "serve all humanity equally," and to perform their nonviolent efforts for God and not "for attaining rank or for show" (quoted in Raqib 2005, 117–18). The Khudai Khidmatgar's nonviolent actions included refusing to pay taxes or to participate in British-controlled civil and criminal courts, picketing, boycotting, and ostracizing collaborating village officials (Global Nonviolent Action Database 2009). The British responded with increasingly violent repression, including mass arrests and incarceration, forced labor, burning villages and food stores, rape, castration, torture, and summary executions. Through it all, most Khudai Khidmatgar remained true to their vows of nonviolence. (Chapter 9 looks at the role of religion in the work of Khan Abdul Ghaffar Khan and the Khudai Khidmatgar.)

Another massive Asian nonviolent movement has received even less notice than these Pashtun campaigns. In the 1920s and 1930s, tens of thousands of Burmese employed multiple civil resistant methods against their own British occupiers (Moser-Puangsuwan 2013). The many Burmese successes were later mostly forgotten even in Burma as subsequent indigenous regimes choose instead to glorify Burma's violent resistance to Japanese occupation during World War II. Leaders in Burma and elsewhere may discourage their citizens' learning about the effectivness of nonviolent campaigns in part to try to make sure these effective tactics are not used against current regimes.

REMEMBERING NONVIOLENT HISTORIES

As the frequency of nonviolent campaigns increased across the world in the last decades of the twentieth century, historians began searching for earlier instances of civil resistance like those of the Burmese and Pashtun that had previously been overlooked. Hundreds of such cases have now been identified and are beginning to be studied. One important result of this new research is *Recovering Nonviolent History: Civil Resistance in Liberation Struggles*, a collection of reports that describes fifteen early civil resistance movements on four continents and three islands. As the editor Maciej J. Bartkowski (2013) points out, these and many dozens of other civil society movements are usually ignored by historians who generally are more interested in foregrounding violent insurrections than in objectively evaluating the frequency and effectiveness of nonviolent actions.

Another new research project, the **Global Nonviolent Action Database**, aims to create a comprehensive searchable resource that includes every nonviolent campaign throughout history, from every part of the world. By early 2014 researchers had catalogued seventeen civil resistance campaigns situated in the nineteenth century. The database suggests that there was then an almost sixfold increase, to 107 such campaigns, between 1900 and 1950. The pace of new nonviolent actions accelerated further between 1951 and 2000, to total over four hundred separate campaigns.

The Global Nonviolent Action Database did not begin collecting cases until 2010, so it is likely that hundreds, perhaps thousands, more nonviolent campaigns from the early twentieth century and even from earlier centuries remain to be described. The current distribution of cases, as outlined in Table 7.1, is overrepresentative of more recent campaigns since historical traces of these are more plentiful than those of older nonviolent actions. Nonetheless, the exponential increase in nonviolent campaigns suggested in this table probably accurately indicates the general trend.

TABLE 7.1 THE RISE OF NONVIOLENT CAMPAIGNS

Years	Number of Campaigns*
Pre-1901	34
1901–1950	107
1951–2000	400
2001–2013	338

Source: Global Nonviolent Action Database (accessed March 16, 2014).

*A "campaign" is defined as collective nonviolent action in a concentrated period of intense activity aimed at achieving specific goals. Thus, for example, the American civil rights movement is not here counted as a single campaign but as a movement made up of several distinct campaigns.

THE POLITICS OF NONVIOLENT ACTION

Leaders of what would become the American civil rights movement were among the many visitors from all over the world who flocked to India in the 1930s and 1940s to try to figure out how they could adapt Gandhi's ideas to create their own nonviolent campaigns. James Farmer, William Stuart Nelson, Bayard Rustin, Howard Thurman, and Sue Bailey Thurman all spent time with Gandhi. Harris Wofford, later an advisor to Martin Luther King Jr., the Southern Christian Leadership Conference, and President John F. Kennedy, as well as a co-organizer of the Peace Corps, was an especially consequential visitor. With his wife, Clare, Wofford published *India Afire* in 1951. This book explained how Gandhi's nonviolent campaigns could be used to end racial discrimination in America. The example of the earlier American Revolution in the minds of the people had not yet been remembered but mass actions like those that Adams had recommended were now being widely discussed again in North America for the first time in almost two hundred years.

Crowds gather at the Washington Memorial during the Martin Luther King Jr-led 1963 March on Washington for Jobs and Freedom.

Many of his advisors and colleagues had already been to India so **Martin Luther King Jr.** made his own pilgrimage a decade after Gandhi's death. King explained in a letter written in 1959, "I returned to America with a greater determination to achieve freedom for my people through nonviolent means. As a result of my visit to India, my understanding of nonviolence became greater and my commitment deeper" (King Jr. 2005, 212).

King and others in the civil rights movement borrowed from Gandhi's repertoire of nonviolent actions while inventing new ones as well. Numerous reports of these methods appeared in media across the world in the middle of the twentieth century but it was not until 1973 that the first systematic manual for civil disobedience was published. This pioneering book, Gene Sharp's *The Politics of Nonviolent Action* (1973), has helped guide nonviolent revolutions across the world ever since.

Sharp wrote *The Politics of Nonviolent Action* based on almost twenty years of research into nonviolent campaigns stretching back to the Roman Empire. Sharp adopted the term **nonviolent action** rather than the simpler term "nonviolence" or the then more common "passive resistance" to emphasize the potency of the campaigns he was recommending. Sharp described dozens of historical instances where nonviolence worked more effectively than violent alternatives. "Nonviolent action is not an attempt to avoid or ignore conflict," Sharp wrote (1973, 64). Rather, this approach is a way to wage conflict without violence. "It is *action* that is nonviolent."

Sharp described 198 different nonviolent actions used in dozens of nonviolent campaigns across diverse societies and eras. Later researchers have discovered the use of even more actions to provide yet more tools for people who wish to mount nonviolent campaigns (e.g. Bartkowski 2013). Never again will people be, like the American colonists, Thoreau, or Gandhi, faced with inventing tactics on their own. No longer is it necessary for

---

LEARNING MORE   TERMS OF RESISTANCE

Henry David Thoreau's phrase "civil disobedience" is just the first of dozens of names that have been proposed to name citizen-based, unarmed movements promoting change. "Passive resistance" was popular for a time, but then generally rejected because of its false associations with submissiveness.

Gandhi began by using Thoreau's "civil disobedience" but then shifted to the phrase "civil resistance" as he thought this term better captured the range of both obstructive and constructive actions that he was using (Bartkowski 2013; Nagler 2006). Gandhi later preferred his own invented Sanskrit term, **satyagraha**, usually translated as "insistence on truth" or "soul force." Gandhi used this word to highlight his belief that nonviolent actors should possess an inner spiritual strength along with the courage to perform nonviolent acts.

Like Thoreau and Gandhi before them, people engaging in civil disobedience still often craft their own terms for what they are doing. As Maciej J. Bartkowski (2013) points out, the Polish Solidarity movement called its action "social self-defense." The Philippines uprising was often called "people power." The first Intifada in Palestine was named "popular resistance." Nonviolent action in Spain was known as "non-submission." Civil disobedience in Burma was named "political defiance" and in Ghana "positive action."

Contemporary researchers still sometimes use the phrase civil disobedience but the labels "civil resistance" and "nonviolent action" have become more common. Political scientists often use the phrase "unarmed insurrection" to create a contrast with violent armed insurrections. These terms all point toward a similar phenomenon: coordinated, collective, nonviolent acts aimed at changing economic, political and/or social forms.

Gene Sharp in his office at the Albert Einstein Institution in Boston, Massachusetts.

people like King and the Woffords to travel to other countries to learn how to nourish revolutions in the minds of the people.

THE REVOLUTION OF REVOLUTIONS

Sharp's mid-twentieth century books were translated into dozens of languages. Sharp himself sometimes traveled to present lectures and seminars offering practical lessons drawn from Gandhi's, King's, and dozens of other, less famous campaigns. Many other books and pamphlets also helped spark the unprecedented cascade of nonviolent campaigns that swept across the world. Table 7.2, "Major Nonviolent Campaigns, 1978–2011," offers a listing of the best known campaigns.

In Portugal in 1974, thousands of peaceful people took to the streets in support of military insurgents who had just overthrown a long-running dictatorship. Two years later these insurgents yielded to the democratic process which has guided Portugal ever since.

In 1977 in Argentina, a group of mothers, the *Asociación Madres de Plaza de Mayo*, began what would be a many-years-long white-scarfed demonstration in front of the presidential palace aimed at forcing their repressive government to account for thousands of kidnapped and murdered citizens. Once the military yielded power in 1983, the organization continued to gather and insist that subsequent democratic governments investigate and seek justice for the thousands still missing.

In Iran, a year of growing demonstrations and strikes in 1979 helped overthrow an autocratic regime that commanded a heavily armed police force and a sophisticated army backed by the United States.

The surprising triumph of the Polish workers movement Solidarity in 1980 and 1981 presaged many later successful nonviolent actions that helped dissolve the Soviet Union a decade later. Lech Walesa and other opposition leaders were arrested in a government crackdown in 1981. "At this moment, you lost," Walesa told his captors. "We are arrested, but you have driven a nail into your communist coffin. . . . You'll come back to us on your knees" (quoted in Ackerman and Duvall 2000, 1). And so it would be, as Walesa became president of Poland nine years later.

Civil resistance successes were also achieved in South Africa late in the 1980s assisted by a two-decades-old nonviolent international campaign against apartheid. Nelson Mandela's subsequent release after twenty-seven years of imprisonment, along with his much-publicized repudiation of violence, helped convince even more people that nonviolent techniques could succeed, even against a long-entrenched, race-based, militarized regime.

In 1986, the widely televised success of the People Power Revolution (also known as the EDSA Revolution) in the Philippines further raised awareness of the effectiveness of nonviolence. Dictator Ferdinand Marcos had ruled with the military assistance of the United States since 1965. His iron hand began to falter in 1983 when he is widely believed to have ordered the murder of an opposition leader, Benigno Aquino Jr. A three-year campaign culminated in a three-day series of massive, prayerful street demonstrations involving an estimated 2 million Filipinos. Marcos's armies disintegrated and Marcos fled to asylum in the United States.

Then came the watershed year of 1989 and the sudden, surprising, and peaceful collapse of the Berlin Wall. Masses of previously blockaded Germans sang, danced, and celebrated as at first small openings and then entire highways opened across the barrier that symbolized fifty years of nuclear tensions between NATO and the Warsaw Pact nations. Also in 1989, Solidarity took control of Poland, Czechoslovakia had its peaceful Velvet Revolution, and nonviolent mass demonstrations brought down a communist regime without bloodshed in Bulgaria. During this same period a series of mass singing demonstrations created what has been called "The Singing Revolution" across the Baltic states of Estonia, Lithuania, and Latvia.

In 1991, peaceful throngs in the streets of Moscow reversed a coup d'état that was seeking to discontinue democratic reforms. Around this time important unarmed insurrections also pushed changes in Burma, Chile, Indonesia, Iran (for a second time), Nepal, and the Philippines (also for a second time). In Africa in the 1990s, nonviolent demonstrators helped bring democracy—or at least a decrease in the power of dictators—in Benin, Cape Verde, Ethiopia, Gambia, Ghana, Madagascar, Mali, Mozambique, Senegal, Tanzania, Uganda, and Zambia. In 2003, a small group of determined women demonstrators at peace talks in Ghana forced the end to a fourteen-year civil war in nearby Liberia. One Liberian leader of the demonstrators, Leymah Gbowee, won a 2011 Nobel Peace Prize for her efforts.

THE SECOND WAVE OF NONVIOLENT INSURRECTIONS

A second wave of successful so-called "Color Revolutions" in former Soviet states and the Balkans in the first decade of the twenty-first century further demonstrated the power of nonviolence. In Serbia in 2000, Georgia in 2003, the Ukraine in 2004, and (though with

TABLE 7.2 MAJOR NONVIOLENT CAMPAIGNS, 1978–2011

Country	Peak Years	Outcome
Portugal	1974	Success
Iran	1978–1979	Success
El Salvador	1979–1981	Failure
Bolivia	1978–1982	Success
Pakistan	1983	Failure
Philippines	1983–1986	Success
Chile	1985–1988	Success
South Africa	1983–1990	Success
Sudan	1985	Success
Haiti	1985	Success
South Korea	1987	Partial success
Burma	1987–1988	Failure
Tibet	1987–1989	Failure
Panama	1987–1989	Failure
West Bank and Gaza	1987–1990	Failure
Baltic States	1987–1991	Success
China	1989	Failure
Czechoslovakia	1989	Success
East Germany	1989	Success
Nepal	1989–1990	Partial success
Bangladesh	1989–1990	Partial success
Mali	1989–1992	Success
Kenya	1989–1992	Failure
Niger	1991–1992	Failure
Madagascar	1991–1993	Success
Indonesia	1998	Success
Serbia	2000	Success
Philippines	2001	Success
Georgia	2003	Success
Ukraine	2004	Success
Kyrgyzstan	2005	Success
Lebanon	2005	Success
Burma	2007	Failure
Armenia	2008	Failure
Tunisia	2011	Success
Egypt	2011	Success

Sources: Nepstad 2011, Schock 2005, and Zunes 1994. For descriptions of each campaign, as well as dozens of others, see the online Global Nonviolent Action Database at http://nvdatabase.swarthmore.edu

some violence) in Kyrgyzstan in 2005, masses of ordinary people demonstrated to demand democratic reforms. Nonviolent action worked again in Lebanon in 2005, when nearly a million people took to the streets to defy a ban on public gatherings imposed by the Syrian sponsors of the soon-to-be-deposed Lebanese government.

The success in Lebanon suggested that large nonviolent campaigns could be mounted in the contemporary Middle East. The proof came in the form of the Arab Awakening of 2011 when demonstrations roiled the entire region. Civil disobedience led to new governments in Tunisia and Egypt and to significant unrest in Algeria, Bahrain, Iraq, Jordan, Libya, Morocco, Oman, Syria, and Yemen. Unfortunately, Egypt has struggled to establish political stability and the conflict in Syria developed into a fierce civil war which has spilled over into neighboring countries.

Leaders of contemporary nonviolent campaigns adopt for their own cultures ideas from what they glean from studying earlier movements. Some leaders in the color revolutions and Arab Awakening even met secretly with international organizations who trained them in nonviolent methods. Nonviolent research and training organizations continue to proliferate across the globe. They now include some government sponsored groups, such as the United States' National Endowment for Democracy and the United States Institute of Peace, as well as Britain's Westminster Foundation.

Nongovernmental organizations (NGOs) promoting nonviolent campaigns are even more plentiful and influential than government-sponsored organizations since activists in most countries want to avoid accusations of being "foreign agents." The Albert Einstein Institution, founded by Gene Sharp himself, is one of the oldest of these organizations. This institute and some other influential organizations promoting nonviolence are listed in the Appendix.

THE RISE OF DEMOCRACY

The spread of nonviolent campaigns across the world over the last half-century has been closely associated with the simultaneous **rise of democracy**. All large societies were ruled by kings, dictators, oligarchies, or rich elites until a few centuries ago. Now about ninety of the world's countries are democracies to some degree, an increase of more than fourfold since 1946 (Marshall and Gurr 2005). Economic and hereditary elites still exercise disproportionate power almost everywhere, but even dictators today commonly find it is necessary to pretend they are serving the interests of "the people."

As William Ury (2000, 156) points out, a strong democracy is "fundamentally a mechanism for nonviolent conflict resolution." Democracies tend to rely on peaceful methods to resolve their internal conflicts while non-democracies are more prone to use coercion and violence. Democracies spawn fewer intrastate wars, armed insurrections, and violent civil unrest. Unfortunately, as explained in Chapter 6, democracies have so far pursued interstate wars at least as often as non-democratic governments. Still, as the number of autocracies decreases, democracies are finding it more difficult to find non-democracies to fight. Europe may provide what could become a common model. Wars among autocracies and oligarchies raged across this region for centuries until first the western half and then almost the entire continent became democratic. Except for the violence associated with the dissolution of Yugoslavia in the early 1990s, there have now been no interstate wars among European democracies for almost seventy years. (See Case 4-1, Europe, "A Continent of Peace in Chapter 4.")

The United Nations, with over two hundred member-nations, aspires to model democratic cooperation for all of Earth's people. The creation of such an organization was considered impossible less than one hundred years ago. The League of Nations, convened in the aftermath of World War I, failed to attract a broad membership and disappeared meekly in the first skirmishes that led to World War II. Even when the United Nations was formed in 1945, few were ready to take seriously the idea that all nations should have votes equal to those of the few nations with the largest militaries. As a result, the United Nations was saddled with five veto-wielding, anti-democratic, permanent members on its Security Council.

No such misbalance in a new international forum aspiring to represent all nations would likely be so easily permitted today. Even within the United Nations as presently constituted, methods are increasingly being sought to mobilize the General Assembly, representing all member-nations, to counter the permanent Security Council's autocratic power.

The UN's democracy of nations, like all democracies, remains fragile, contentious, and prone to fracture from the domination of a powerful few. Still the formation of a General Assembly of the world's nations is one of the greatest accomplishments of modernity. The UN's peacekeeping missions since the end of the Cold War have become increasingly frequent and effective (Goldstein 2012; see Chapter 6). Few now doubt that the world is better off having an organization where all nations can talk about common problems, even though their efforts at cooperation sometimes fail.

RIGHTS AND THE RULE OF LAW

A historic rise in the belief in human rights is another potent element supporting the rise of nonviolent movements. **Human rights** are fundamental moral or legal entitlements that people possess at birth. These rights are claimed to apply to everyone regardless of nationality, gender, sex, national or ethnic origin, race, religion, language, or other social status.

The rise of human rights in the latter half of the twentieth century was sparked in large measure by adoption of the Universal Declaration of Human Rights by the United Nations General Assembly in 1948. This document led to two foundational treaties, the International Covenant on Civil and Political Rights and the International Covenant on Economic, Social, and Cultural Rights, both adopted by the United Nations in 1966. Subsequent agreements built on these two have separately addressed the prevention and punishment of genocide, rights of freedom from racial discrimination, from gender discrimination, and from torture, as well as the rights of children, the rights of persons with disabilities, and protections for migrant workers and their families. Dozens of nations, including the United States, have refused to endorse some or all of these agreements. Nonetheless, each covenant and convention was accepted by a majority of the members of the United Nations and even non-signatory countries frequently feel obligated to claim they support the variously described rights.

Numerous international tribunals and courts have been created as a result of the rising acceptance in human rights. **International tribunals and courts** apply the rule of law to the adjudication of human rights and other types of disputes, often in places where the local judicial system is either weak or corrupt. As mentioned in Chapter 3, significant examples of these institutions include the Commission on Human Rights (created in 1946), the World Court (created in 1946 and also known as the International Court of Justice), and the International Criminal Court (created in 2002).

The rule of law has been steadily extended to areas that often tend to provoke violence. The development of international treaty law has been especially effective. Treaties are used in the modern world not only to end wars but also to adjudicate an increasing number of otherwise potentially volatile issues. As Kent D. Shifferd (*From War to Peace*, 2011) points out, treaties in force today regulate the production and positioning of mines and of weapons of mass destruction, the treatment of war prisoners, the use of child soldiers, Antarctic land use, hundreds of national borders, fishing rights, the use of airwaves, air traffic control, banking, passports, international policing, disease control, satellite communications systems, and many other issues. In addition, in 2013 the United Nations General Assembly adopted an unprecedented Arms Trade Treaty aimed at stopping the flow of weapons such as small arms, tanks, combat aircraft and ships into conflict regions. Treaties can be broken, of course, but nations and their leaders tend to want to ensure future trust with other signatories. International treaty law has become a significant contributor to global peace.

EXPANDING HUMAN RIGHTS

The idea of "rights" entered European politics in the English document known as the Magna Carta created in 1215. This charter focused on protecting the privileges of a small minority, the so-called nobles, from abuses by hereditary monarchs. Political theorists such as Thomas Hobbes, John Locke, and others later refined the idea to support the assumption that those in the propertied classes also have "natural rights" to control the lives of people who do not own property (Howard 2000). Owners of slaves, of landless peasants, and of indentured servants, for example, were generally claimed to have the natural right to exploit their human property from birth to death, as people in many places across the world had done for thousands of years.

In London in 1787, nine Quakers convinced three Anglicans to join them in establishing the faith-based Society for Effecting the Abolition of the Slave Trade (D'Anjou 1996). These twelve were later joined by other small groups in places across Europe and North America that were similarly condemning the increasingly profitable global slave trade. For decades these protesters were generally ignored or mocked as eccentric fanatics too crazy to be listened to by "reasonable people." Then, through relentless hard work, less than one hundred years after that first meeting in London, legal slavery had disappeared.

Unfortunately, extra-legal slavery is still practiced in many places in the twenty-first century. Experts estimate there may be as many as 27 million people currently being forced to work without pay, under threats of violence or other forms of coercion, such as a denial of passports or wages earned (Dodson 2005). Still, many people on every continent now believe that slavery denies its victims of their basic human rights, an opinion that was quite rare everywhere just two centuries ago.

Each new generation since World War II has extended the idea of universal rights a little further. The first postwar generation focused on international relations, on national sovereignty, and on the elimination of colonialism and imperialism. The next generation introduced within-country concerns, seeking equal rights for groups, races, and women. A later generation pursued what was at first called "gay rights," seeking the elimination of discrimination against same-sex-preferring females and males. Now protection is being sought not just for same-sex relationships but also for bisexuals, transsexuals, and all people whose sexuality might be perceived as varying from the majority's gender norms.

The idea that public discussions about sexual minority rights could become commonplace seemed utopian to most of the pioneering gay rights activists who began public campaigns in the 1960s and the 1970s. Now discrimination against sexual minorities in employment, housing, and employee benefits has been outlawed in many places. The right to same-sex marriage has been debated in legislatures across the world and, by 2014, had been made legal in 17 countries, including Argentina, Brazil, England, Canada, Denmark, France, Iceland, Luxembourg, Norway, the Netherlands, New Zealand, Portugal, South Africa, Spain, Sweden, Uruguay, and Wales. Twenty-nine states in the United States permitted same-sex marriage by October 2014; together these include well over half of the country's total population.

Many governments are now extending equal rights to people with special physical and mental needs, people who are still now in many communities commonly institutionalized and discriminated against. There are as well campaigns to extend universal rights to children, to animals, and to the planet Earth itself. The work of peace ecologists described in Chapter 1 is an example of this latter extension of rights. Future generations may promote rights to end yet other inequalities that are mostly overlooked today. Table 7.3, "Types of Human Rights," surveys the most common kinds of rights that have been identified so far.

TABLE 7.3 TYPES OF HUMAN RIGHTS

Type	Application	Examples
Individual civic and political rights, mostly promoted by neoliberal capitalist governments	Individual bodily rights	Freedom from torture, unjust imprisonment, and execution
	Individual intellectual rights	Freedom to assemble, speak, write, and worship
	Individual political rights	Freedom to assemble, associate, and vote
Individual well-being, mostly promoted by state-socialist governments	Individual socioeconomic rights	Freedom to work and fair wage, right to education, food, clean air and water, housing, and medical care
State-level rights, newly proposed and controversial	Government responsibility to protect individuals	Duty for states to intervene to protect civilians in other states
Planet-level rights, associated with peace ecology and environmentalists	Individual and government responsibility to promote sustainable societies	Duty of states to reduce carbon dioxide emissions

THE LIMITS OF HUMAN RIGHTS

It is difficult to overstate both the historical novelty and the immense positive global impact of the human rights movement, especially in the years since the mid-1970s. So much has changed that most governments now sponsor entire human rights divisions with multiple groups of investigators. Thousands of diplomats and lawyers specialize in human rights. In addition to new human rights tribunals and courts, there are now numerous human rights foundations, organizations, and specialized advocates, authors, journalists, and researchers.

Nonetheless, despite its successes, the human rights movement has provoked much criticism. Some of the negative evaluations arise from just how very influential the human rights movement has become (Mutua 2002). As the dominant approach to so many global problems, human rights thinking crowds out alternative perspectives. So, for example, human rights campaigns generally ignore both traditional religious perspectives and also political viewpoints that are demanding decreases in the power of transnational corporations. Of course, every dominant perspective tends to discourage alternatives but the human rights movement is especially dismissive of other views since it often presents itself as "universal" and applicable to every location, culture, time, and problem. Human rights work is thus often represented as a comprehensive solution to contemporary problems rather than as just one possible approach among a diverse network of multiple solutions.

Since local religious, political, and social ideas not framed in the vocabulary of rights tend to be ignored, people are often forced to attempt to reframe their ideas to fit into the human rights vocabulary (Smith and Verdeja 2013). Environmental problems, for example, are now sometimes presented as a matter of the "people's right to a clean environment" rather than as problems that must be addressed more directly through broad economic, political, and social changes. Similarly, some analysts now speak of a "right to development," encouraging support for global capitalism and an increasing depletion of the world's material resources rather than for a search for alternatives that would slow development throughout the world (Kennedy 2004).

In addition, human rights law is nation-state centered. This encourages its advocates to treat nation-states as the most important units of governance and to de-emphasize the significance of local communities and of local political action. As David Kennedy points out, the human rights perspective thus "equates the structure of the state with the structure of freedom" (2004, 16). Because human rights adjudications validate the legitimacy of governments, they tend to leave existing power hierarchies unchanged.

In sum, it may be, as Kennedy (2004, 32) maintains, that human rights thinking spotlights "only the tips of icebergs" of the biggest problems facing the world today. Immense political work is needed to respond to cross-border challenges such as climate change, ocean acidification, polar cap melting, species extinctions, pandemics, rising global economic inequality, and increasing food and water insecurity. For most of these twenty-first century problems, Kennedy (2012) argues, solutions require increased focus on place-specific collective action rather than on civil and criminal cases based in human rights law. Many perspectives and types of cultural movements will be necessary to build negative and positive peace in the decades ahead (Smith and Verdeja 2013).

MAKING CONNECTIONS

As more people believe that every person has the right to "life, liberty, and pursuit of happiness," as the United States Declaration of Independence phrases it, violence and war have become less acceptable. Citizen-led nonviolence and human rights campaigns have provided people with ways to improve their lives without coercion and killing. Fortunately, too, as more people use nonviolent methods, more is learned about how to maximize their effectiveness. Chapter 8 examines both theoretical explanations of the power of nonviolence and specific research findings about which nonviolent methods work best. Chapter 9 traces some religious origins of violence, nonviolence, and peace.

FOR REVIEW

1. Evaluate the significance of what Adams described as the "revolution in the minds of the people" in the American colonies prior to 1775.
2. Describe some key events associated with the twentieth century's rise of nonviolent campaigns.
3. Explain how strong democracies replace violent with nonviolent conflict resolution practices.
4. Trace some important ways that the concept of "rights" has expanded since the United Nations Declaration of Human Rights was adopted in 1948.
5. Summarize the principle reasons people should be wary of further expanding the contemporary global emphasis on human rights.

THINKING CRITICALLY

1. How might the United States be different if it had achieved independence from England without violence, that is, by taking a path to self-governance like that taken by other English settler colonies such as Australia, Canada, and New Zealand?
2. What would be the consequences for societies if most citizens within a country adopted Thoreau's criteria for committing civil disobedience?
3. What were the probable principle causes of the increasing frequency of nonviolent campaigns across the twentieth century?
4. Were there key differences in the nonviolent revolutions that occurred before and those that erupted after the end of the Cold War?
5. Why do wars and violent insurrections commonly attract much more attention than nonviolent campaigns?
6. Is the rise of democracies across the world evidence of a continuing Western domination of the world system? Is the increasing focus on human rights similarly evidence of Western domination?
7. Do the rise of international organizations such as the United Nations and international tribunals and courts suggest that the power of individual nation-states is decreasing?
8. Should human rights abuses be treated primarily as an internal, local problem or as a problem to be addressed by international organizations?
9. What are the most important alternative perspectives to viewing contemporary economic, environmental, and political problems as issues of human rights?

RECOMMENDED RESOURCES

Amazing Grace. Directed by Michael Apted. 20th Century Fox, 2007. A fictional account of William Wilberforce's campaign to outlaw the British trans-Atlantic slave trade.

Amster, Randall and Elavie Ndura, Editors. *Exploring the Power of Nonviolence: Peace, Politics, and Practice* (Syracuse, NY: Syracuse University Press, 2013). A rich, wide-ranging collection of essays that explores the application of nonviolence philosophy and practice to historical and, especially, contemporary social problems. Topics include conflict resolution, climate change, education, ethics, indigenous perspectives, insurrections, and resource management.

Bartkowski, Maciej J., editor. *Recovering Nonviolent History: Civil Resistance in Liberation Struggles* (Boulder, CO: Lynne Rienner Publishers, 2013). A path-breaking collection of chapters exploring mostly forgotten nonviolence campaigns in Asia, Africa, Cuba, Europe, the Middle East, and the colonial United States.

Budrus. Directed by Julia Bacha. 2009. Film that documents the nonviolent actions taken by Palestinian residents in the early 2000s to protest the construction of an Israeli West Bank barrier designed to divide and encircle their small town.

A Force More Powerful. Directed by Steve York. 2000. Offers six thirty-minute documentaries with interviews and riveting archival footage from nonviolent campaigns in Chile, Denmark, India, Poland, South Africa, and the United States (Nashville, Tennessee). Available at some commercial video-on-demand sites. See also the companion book by Peter Ackerman and Jack Duvall, *A Force More Powerful* (New York: Palgrave, 2000).

Global Nonviolent Action Database. An active database that describes hundreds of cases of nonviolent action, stretching back to twelfth-century-BCE Egypt. The database can be searched in multiple ways, including by country, date, name, goals, and methods used. At http:// nvdatabase.swarthmore.edu

Kurlansky, Mark. *Nonviolence: Twenty-Five Lessons from the History of a Dangerous Idea* (New York: Modern Library, 2006). A sweeping yet concise history of nonviolence that moves from ancient Hindu times to present-day conflicts in the Middle East and elsewhere.

Nonviolent and Violent Campaigns and Outcomes (NAVCO) Data Project. Catalogues major nonviolent and violent resistance campaigns around the world since 1900 to help researchers and activists determine the principle causes of failure and success. Available at http://www .du.edu/korbel/sie/research/chenow_navco_data.html

Schell, Jonathan. *Unconquerable World: Power, Nonviolence, and the Will of the People* (New York: Holt, 2003). Schell uses the major events of modern history to argue that nonviolence has become increasingly more effective than military force in securing peace and prosperity. Schell argues that "violence is a method by which the ruthless few can subdue the passive many. Nonviolence is a means by which the active many can overcome the ruthless few."

Sharp, Gene. *Waging Nonviolent Struggle: 20th Century Practice and 21st Century Potential* (Boston: Porter Sargent Publishers, 2005). Includes both a summary of Sharp's influential theory of power as well as a guide to the dynamics of nonviolent action and suggestions for how best to organize a nonviolent campaign. In addition, the book describes twenty-four cases of twentieth-century nonviolent action drawn from campaigns across the world.

We Women Warriors. Directed by Nicole Karsin. Todos Los Pueblos Productions, 2012. A documentary that follows three native women caught in the crossfire of Colombia's warfare who use nonviolent resistance to defend their people's survival. The film interweaves character-driven stories about female empowerment, unshakable courage and faith in the survival of indigenous culture.

CHAPTER 8

NONVIOLENT POWER, METHODS, AND STRATEGIES

CHAPTER OVERVIEW

This chapter explores the increasing use of nonviolent alternatives to armed intrastate insurrections. It begins with an overview of the historical shift away from an almost exclusive reliance on violent revolutions, then describes recent research concluding that nonviolent campaigns are about twice as effective as violent ones. The chapter contrasts monopolistic and consent theories of power before exploring common strategies used to guide choices among nonviolent methods. Some frequent misconceptions about nonviolent action are described, followed by a discussion of some differences between obstructive and constructive campaigns. The chapter concludes by explaining the rising importance of civil society and of the movement of movements in which civil society organizations play a prominent part.

Key terms and people discussed include: Intrastate conflicts; state monopoly on the use of violence; success rate of nonviolence; Gene Sharp; consent theory of power; nonviolent methods; nonviolent strategies; paradox of repression; Children's Crusade; obstructive program; constructive program; civil society organizations; and the movement of movements.

> If there is no struggle there is no progress. Those who profess to favor freedom and yet deprecate agitation are men who want crops without plowing up the ground; they want rain without thunder and lightning. They want the ocean without the awful roar of its many waters.
>
> —FREDERICK DOUGLASS (1999, 367)

A wave of successful nonviolent uprisings in the final decades of the twentieth century called into question many assumptions about the necessity of using violence to create radical change. For centuries, political and social insurrections had been associated with bloodshed. The American (1776), French (1789), Russian (1917), Chinese (1949), and

Cuban (1953–59) revolutions were only among the best known of many dozens of horrific clashes that seemed to show that people must kill to produce substantial change. Then the extraordinary success of nonviolent campaigns like those described in Chapter 7 changed perceptions and expectations.

While Chapter 6 adopted a broad, macro level view to examine interstate conflicts between countries, this chapter focuses on internal, **intrastate conflicts**, the violent and nonviolent uprisings that take place between groups within countries. Intrastate wars are especially important because, since the end of the Napoleonic wars in 1815, intrastate wars have erupted about three times more often than interstate wars (Sarkees and Wayman 2010). The proportion of intrastate to interstate wars increased even more after 1990 (Wallensteen 2012).

As detailed in Chapter 4, even though the total number of wars being fought each year is generally in decline, the proportion of wars that occur within rather than between states is increasing. Nevertheless, the most recent increase in intrastate wars is due mostly to recurrences; since the end of the Cold War the number of brand new civil wars and armed insurgences has fallen off (Human Security Report Project 2011). Not coincidentally, during the same decades the frequency of nonviolent responses to crises has risen dramatically. The rate of violent campaigns fell in part because the use of nonviolent strategies rose (Chenoweth and Stephan 2011). This chapter explores why and how this occurred.

THE STATE MONOPOLY ON VIOLENCE

The communist revolutionary Leon Trotsky expressed what many already believed when he said that "every state is founded on force." Max Weber, a pioneering German sociologist, refined this idea to argue that modern nations exist because they maintain a **state monopoly on the use of violence.** Weber said that governments assert that they alone can legitimately harm and coerce their citizens. Governments and their supporters thus often brand others who use violence as criminals and terrorists. In a famous essay, "Politics as a Vocation," Weber wrote that in the modern era "the right to use physical force is ascribed to other institutions or to individuals only to the extent to which the state permits it. The state is considered the sole source of the 'right' to use violence" (2004, 33). According to Weber and others, states work to convince their citizens to accept that government-controlled police and militaries have the right to intimidate, injure, capture, and even kill people both inside and outside their borders. Governments often even maintain that they must perpetrate violence against citizens "for their own protection."

The Weberian view of state power encourages leaders to believe that intrastate civil disturbances are, at root, conflicts over which factions will monopolize the violence upon which governments depend. The state monopoly view of violence thus legitimates violent clashes by suggesting that whoever proves to be the most effective at harming others will also prove to be the most capable of successfully governing.

Many events seem to support the Weberian view of power. The victorious violent Chinese revolution in 1949 especially caught the world's attention and helped inspire further violent seizures of power in Algeria, Cuba, and elsewhere. A revolution is "an act of violence by which one class overthrows another," Mao (1972, 11–12) wrote in his widely circulated *Little Red Book.* Mao (1972, 61) also asserted the Weberian idea that "political power grows out of the barrel of a gun." Che Guevara (2009), the Argentine hero of the Cuban revolution, relatedly once claimed that revolutionary violence is an expression of love.

Discussions about the necessity of using violence to create change were common within the civil rights movement in the United States. Although the faction represented by Martin Luther King Jr., the Southern Christian Leadership Conference, and other established black advocacy groups rejected violence, the persuasiveness of this position decreased substantially among black Americans as the 1960s wore on. So, for example, the Student Nonviolent Coordinating Committee (SNCC), representing a younger constituency, stopped sponsoring regular workshops in nonviolence after the Harlem Riots of 1964. King's murder at age thirty-nine in April, 1968, and the murder of Robert Kennedy just two months later convinced many people of all races that, as Black Panther Party leader H. Rap Brown said, "violence is as American as cherry pie." It seemed to many that those with power killed their opponents. Those unwilling to kill seemed destined to be oppressed.

The view that political power depends upon violence has also been very prominent at the macro, interstate level. The view supports the doctrine of peace through strength discussed in Chapter 2. Both the United States and its allies and Russia and its allies justified their Cold War in the twentieth century in part as a struggle over who had the right to use violence wherever they chose to advance their interests all around the world. Each side aspired to coerce the other through violence in proxy wars on multiple continents, as well as through the deployment of weapons of mass destruction capable of destroying all human life.

Then, as explained in Chapter 7, first in a trickle and then in a flood, a widely publicized stream of unexpected nonviolent revolutions interrupted the final decades of the twentieth century. By the time of the wave of nonviolent campaigns associated with the Arab Awakening of 2011, popular understanding of the nature of political power had changed. The world was surprised at the timing and speed of the campaigns in 2011 that drove dictators out of Tunisia and Egypt but few people still doubted that, in the right circumstances, nonviolent action can produce revolutionary effects. Most researchers in intrastate conflicts now doubt the claims made by Marx, Mao, Castro, Guevara, and others that political and social change is best won from behind the barrel of a gun.

HOW OFTEN DOES NONVIOLENCE WORK?

The **success rate of nonviolence** is significantly greater than that of violence. This empirical finding has been repeatedly confirmed over the last few decades as researchers analyzed diverse historical records to determine how often and in what circumstances nonviolent movements succeed.

An important early analysis by Adrian Karatnycky and Peter Ackerman (2005) examined sixty-seven authoritarian regimes overthrown between 1972 and 2002. Karatnycky and Ackerman discovered that nonviolent movements were the driving force in 74 percent (50) of these successful insurrections. Their data showed, too, that an oppositional group's use of violence tends to have negative effects, commonly reducing the group's chances of later achieving both its short- and long-term goals.

Erica Chenoweth and Maria J. Stephan (2011) subsequently produced an even more comprehensive analysis of intrastate conflicts. These researchers examined 323 armed and unarmed intrastate insurrections that took place between 1900 and 2006. Chenoweth and Stephan found that nonviolent campaigns succeeded about 53 percent of the time while campaigns that relied on violence achieved their goals just 26 percent of the time. This data suggests that over the last century, nonviolence has been roughly twice as effective as violence.

Perhaps even more significantly, Chenoweth and Stephan found further support for Karatnycky and Ackerman's important discovery that even when they fail in the short term nonviolent campaigns tend to create conditions for later successes. By contrast, failed violent actions tend to increase the probability for yet more future failures. The coordination required to conduct a nonviolent campaign tends to encourage further collaborations when the immediate crises end; on the other hand, violent campaigns' initial failures discourage later cooperation. The difference is dramatic. In Chenoweth and Stephan's 323 cases, only four percent of the violent insurrections led to democracies five years after their conflicts ended; ten times more, 41 percent, of the nonviolent insurrections had become democracies by then.

Chenoweth and Stephan's data also demonstrate that civil resistance works well against both moderately and extremely repressive regimes. In addition, their analysis confirms that the more frequently nonviolent insurrections occurred over the last half of the twentieth century, the more often they tended to succeed. Successes breed further successes. Simultaneously, as the rate of success for nonviolent actions rose, the rate of success for violent campaigns declined. These rates are summarized in Table 8.1, "Success Rates of Violent and Nonviolent Campaigns."

In a related but separate study of 648 non-state terrorists groups, Seth G. Jones and Martin C. Libicki (2008) determined that terrorism from below succeeds about ten percent of the time, a high rate of failure discussed previously in Chapter 4.

Successful nonviolent movements usually require broad-base support across multiple sectors of their society. The more participation, the more power is dispersed and so the better prepared are victorious nonviolent movements to form new more representative governments. Successful violent campaigns, by contrast, win by forcing the old rulers to yield; insurgent violence is pitted against government violence. Broad-based popular support is thus seldom important to armed insurrections. It is estimated, for example, that less than two percent of the population took part in the French Revolution. By contrast, the nonviolent Iranian revolution that grew from 1977 to 1979 culminated with approximately a fifth of the adult population marching in the streets (Kurzman 2004).

The rare victorious violent movement commonly finds itself facing a population where it has fragile or little support. In these cases, too, violence has now been further legitimized as a "winning" strategy so additional violence or threats of violence commonly follow. As mentioned in Chapter 2, intrastate wars thus often spread like an infectious

TABLE 8.1 SUCCESS RATES OF VIOLENT AND NONVIOLENT CAMPAIGNS

Campaign type	Rate of success	Failed campaigns
Nonviolent	53%	Increase probability of future success
Violent	26%	Decrease probability of future success
Terrorism	10%	Decrease probability of future success

Sources: Chenoweth and Stephan 2011; Jones and Libicki 2008.

disease (Ehrenreich 1998). Once they start violent rebellions tend to extend into ever-larger segments of the population. Successful nonviolent campaigns can similarly spread, as they seem to have done across much of the world over the last forty years.

SHARP'S CONSENT THEORY OF POWER

The recent success of so many nonviolent movements has encouraged a search for new views of the nature of political power. Gandhi himself based his campaigns on one promising alternative perspective. Gandhi maintained, "No government can exist for a single moment without the cooperation of the people, willing or forced, and if people withdraw their cooperation in every detail, the government will come to a standstill" (Gandhi 2001, 157). This is true for all types of government, Gandhi argued, as "even the most powerful cannot rule without the cooperation of the ruled" (quoted in Sharp 1979, 29). **Gene Sharp** (1973) developed this perspective further in his path-breaking *The Politics of Nonviolent Action*, published in three volumes in 1973. Sharp advanced a **consent theory of power** built on the premise that state power ultimately depends not on violence but on the collaboration of ordinary citizens.

Sharp divides the people in modern societies into two groups, rulers and those they rule. The rulers control the state, including its bureaucracy, courts, police, and military. Rulers also frequently control economies and important cultural institutions such as the mass media. While Weber and others believed these state apparatuses ultimately draw their power from the state's monopoly on physical force, Sharp maintains that power instead depends "*intimately* upon the obedience and cooperation of the subjects [citizens]" (Sharp 1973, 12).

According to Sharp, nonviolent movements work because they reduce the people's collaboration with the state and thereby directly decrease the rulers' power. If the people withdraw their obedience and cooperation entirely, the ruler's power disappears entirely. Nonviolent action, Sharp says, should thus be understood as a process whereby citizens work together to lessen and, sometimes, to eliminate their obedience to and cooperation with rulers and policies they oppose.

Sharp's view of power deemphasizes the macro level of analysis. For example, Sharp's perspective does not directly address capitalism, democratization, globalization, imperialism, militarism, racism, sexism, or patriarchy, important concerns for many (Zunes and Kurtz 1999). Sharp's perspective also focuses mostly on negative peace, on stopping direct violence. So far it has been of limited use to those committed to building positive peace and to stopping indirect violence. Nonetheless, Sharp's view has become increasingly popular among citizens working to change their societies.

For example, Sharp's ideas were explicitly invoked by several organizers of the 2011 nonviolent campaign that ended the thirty-year Mubarak regime in Egypt (Mackay 2012). Some of these leaders had, in turn, been trained by Serbians who had themselves previously been taught Sharp's theories by Robert Helvey, a long-time Sharp collaborator. (Some of these connections are discussed in the documentary film, *How to Start a Revolution*, directed by Ruaridh Arrow and first released in 2011.) Though perhaps inadequate as a complete theory of governance, Sharp's idea that state power is fundamentally rooted in the consent of the governed has proven its usefulness in dozens of civil resistance campaigns while more complex theories have not.

LEARNING MORE GENE SHARP'S 198 NONVIOLENT METHODS

Gene Sharp identified 198 nonviolent methods, which he arranged into three categories: Protest and persuasion, noncooperation, and intervention.

Sharp lists fifty-four nonviolent methods associated with protests and persuasion. These include formal statements, such as public speeches and group petitions; communication with a wide audience, such as banners, books, and skywriting; public acts, such as wearing symbols and prayer; processions, such as marches and motorcades; withdrawals and renunciations, such as walk-outs and renouncing honors; and public assemblies.

Sharp lists 103 nonviolent methods associated with noncooperation. These are further divided into three types: social, economic, and political noncooperation.

Nonviolent acts of social noncooperation include social boycotts, student strikes, and protest emigrations. Nonviolent acts of economic noncooperation include consumer boycotts, trade embargoes, strikes, and refusal to pay fees, dues, debts or interest. Nonviolent acts of political noncooperation include election boycotts, sit-downs, breaking laws, and withholding of diplomatic relations.

Sharp lists forty-one nonviolent methods associated with interventions. These include fasts, occupations, stall-ins, land seizure, leaking information, seeking incarceration, and creating alternative economic institutions.

The open source database maintained at the Civil Resistance 2.0 website is collecting what it describes as "digital enhancements" to Sharp's original 198 methods.

Source: Sharp 1973. Also available at: http://www.aeinstein .org/nva/198-methods-of-nonviolent-action/

NONVIOLENT METHODS

Gene Sharp's consent theory of power suggests there are many ways to lessen government control. These **nonviolent methods** enable people to oppose government actions and policies through protests, resistance, and interference. The number and diversity of potentially effective nonviolent actions is huge. As mentioned, Sharp (1973) himself described 198 different methods in *The Politics of Nonviolent Action* and more have been developed in the decades since.

Using multiple methods and changing methods as a campaign unfolds increases the likelihood of success. If a movement relies too heavily on one or a few methods, the movement's failure can seem to signal the failure of the entire campaign. So, for example, when the Chinese protestors were driven from Tiananmen Square in 1989, the movement's demand for more freedom also largely disappeared. Among other strategic mistakes, the campaign had become too closely associated with the single tactic of mass demonstrations (Schock 2005).

Changing methods is also necessary as some methods may work early in a campaign and not later, and vice versa. The mass march on Washington led by Martin Luther King Jr. in 1963 employed a method that A. Philip Randolph had first proposed in 1941. (See Case 8-1, "The 1963 March on Washington.") This mass mobilization finally proved effective in the 1960s only because it had been preceded for over a decade by the use of dozens of other nonviolent methods across the American South. Most later mass marches on Washington have failed to achieve their goals in large measure because they have not similarly grown out of campaigns that have already employed many other nonviolent methods.

Different methods appeal to different groups of people with different levels of commitment to a campaign. Some people may be willing to boycott a store, for example, but not

An unknown man braves civil disobedience against a tank during the Tiananmen Square uprising in Peking, China in 1989.

to take part in a sit-in inside that store. Urging workers to participate in a slowdown at work demands less risk than asking workers to join a mass walkout or strike. Choosing methods requires monitoring the ever shifting situations and conditions among both the allies and opponents of a movement's goals. (See, for example, Case 5-1, "Sex Strikes" in Chapter 5.)

CASE 8-1 THE 1963 MARCH ON WASHINGTON

The March for Jobs and Freedom on August 28, 1963, was the largest, most reported and, probably, most successful one-day civic action ever undertaken in the United States. Yet, almost until it was over, the march seemed poised to fail.

The leaders who planned the march had conflicting ideas about both its goals and tactics. Some, like Roy Wilkins, head of the NAACP, mistrusted mass actions of every type. Others, especially the young leaders associated with the then not-yet-three-years-old Student Nonviolent Coordinating Committee (SNCC), wanted to include multiple disruptive acts of civil disobedience across the capital. Labor leaders Walter Reuther and A. Philip Randolph sought to focus the march on their plan to call for federal intervention to create a massive number of new jobs. Martin Luther King Jr. hoped the entire day would focus on federal civil rights legislation. Negotiations among these diverse leaders were often heated and seemed likely to break down.

Then, on July 2, less than two months before the planned march, a compromise final agenda was accepted. Promotion and recruitment was spread among many groups, largely under the leadership of Bayard Rustin. He coordinated what one historian describes as "the first mass-marketed protest in the history of demonstrations in Washington" (Barber 2002, 154). The organizers believed they needed at least 100,000 marchers to show up. President Kennedy himself told them that any fewer than 100,000 would suggest to the country that there was weak public demand for federal civil rights legislation.

(continued)

CASE 8-1 *(CONTINUED)*

Some officials in the Kennedy administration were afraid that the massing of large numbers of black people in the nation's capital would increase the country's resistance to civil rights. The FBI stoked these fears by releasing a series of alarming false reports to politicians and reporters claiming the march leaders were seeking to overthrow the government of the United States.

The FBI's intentional fearmongering convinced many that widespread violence would likely erupt on the march day. As precautions, District of Columbia schools were closed and the sale of alcohol was banned throughout the city. Hospitals canceled elective surgeries in anticipation of mass medical emergencies. Firefighters were forced to join the police to increase security on the streets. President Kennedy signed an executive order authorizing military force to be used as necessary. Army troops and 2,000 National Guardsmen massed nearby. Nearly 15,000 additional paratroopers in North Carolina were readied for quick deployment to Washington, if needed.

Many more marchers came than the 100,000 that had been predicted, about 250,000 by most estimates, more people than had ever before demonstrated on the streets of Washington. The day's activities went off smoothly, almost exactly as the leaders had planned. There was no violence. Images transmitted across the United States and the world showed an orderly, well-dressed, integrated crowd holding mostly professionally prepared signs facing the Lincoln Memorial listening to music and speeches.

The final speaker was Martin Luther King Jr. His words went out simultaneously over the three United States television broadcast networks and around the world on the newly launched Telstar satellite. King felt inspired by the moment to abandon his prepared speech to reprise instead ideas he had begun offering audiences earlier that year. King began, "I am happy to join with you today in what will go down in history as the greatest demonstration for freedom in the history of our nation," a bold prediction that would prove true. Later King offered what has become the most famous phrase in American oratory: "I have a dream," King said, "that one day this nation will rise up, live out the true meaning of its creed: 'We hold these truths to be self-evident, that all men are created equal.'"

King's interpretation of events as a proclamation of black-white unity was soon treated as the central message of the March on Washington, eclipsing alternative interpretations offered by the nine speakers who preceded him. King's speech, along with images of hundreds of thousands of marchers peacefully assembling and dispersing, helped galvanize public opinion and encouraged the Kennedy administration and its successor, the Johnson administration, to push for legislation that passed in the form of the Civil Rights Act of 1964.

Source: Barber 2002.

NONVIOLENT STRATEGIES

Because there are so many nonviolent methods to choose from, leaders must use strategies to help them select among the hundreds of possibilities. Careful deliberation is necessary because, as Sharon Erickson Nepstad points out, "The planning and execution of a nonviolent revolt is just as complex as planning a violent revolt" (2011, 137). **Nonviolent strategies** are plans, policies, and schemas that guide decisions about which methods to choose in conducting protests, resistances, and interventions.

Gandhi relied on numerous strategies and subsequent nonviolent leaders refined his ideas while developing new strategies of their own. Social science researchers have begun evaluating the many possible strategies to create empirical generalizations about which ones work best. The following describes several strategies for choosing among nonviolent methods that are often recommended by practitioners or that have strong empirical support.

GOALS

Nonviolent movements succeed more often when they pursue clear goals. These goals can then be used to help guide the selection of specific methods. Goals may range from small to large; they may be local, regional, national, or even global, as for example with the international movements to eliminate land mines and nuclear weapons. Goals may change as the campaign proceeds and circumstances change but some clear goals usually should be foregrounded to attract broad citizen support. The Polish Solidarity movement in 1980, for example, focused on the legalization of independent trade unions, a radical but precise goal that proved popular across Poland and, within years, also across much of the Soviet bloc. By contrast, both the 2011 Occupy Wall Street movements and most of its dozens of global spin-offs resisted associating their efforts with specific goals. Many analysts believe this lack of focus is largely responsible for the Occupy movement's general lack of concrete achievements. As sociologist Kurt Schock writes, the consensus among researchers is that "the more focused the goals of the challenging movement, the greater the likelihood of success" (Schock 2005, 164).

Figure 8.1 illustrates how goals can be considered a prerequisite for selecting among strategies, which in turn guide choosing methods. The influence goes both ways, however, as practical experience with methods will often lead to adjustments in strategy and, sometimes, even to a change in goals.

TIMEFRAME

Nonviolent campaigns work best when they strategize for the long term. Gandhi's campaigns went on for fifteen years in South Africa and for almost thirty years in India. Solidarity began its work in 1980, as mentioned, but did not achieve its primary goal until 1989.

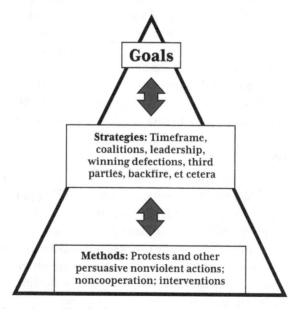

FIGURE 8.1 Goals, Strategies, and Methods

Even many nonviolent insurrections that seem to erupt spontaneously often turn out upon examination to be based on months and even years of planning. For example, the Egyptian uprising in late 2010 and early 2011 was built in part from elaborate and sophisticated organizing work begun by the April 6 Youth Movement in 2008. Short-term defeats do not necessarily signal long-term defeats, so strategies should be based on an understanding that a nonviolent movement may take years and even decades to achieve success.

COALITIONS

Nonviolent campaigns should choose goals and methods that attract many types of citizens. The evidence here is especially strong. Chenoweth and Stephan (2011) found in their 323 cases reviewed earlier that the higher the percentage of the society that participated in a movement, the more likely it was to succeed. Unsuccessful movements are usually those that involve only one population segment, for example, only young people, urban dwellers, the educated, or the working class. The American civil rights movement and South African anti-apartheid movements each built increasingly broad coalitions of supporters for over a decade before finally becoming large enough to succeed. The Chinese revolt in Tiananmen Square was weakened by the lack of coordination between students and workers (Nepstad 2011). The ever-widening support for both the Tunisian and Egyptian campaigns of the Arab Awakening helped produce their successes. Broad-based movements are much more difficult for governments to silence and repress. Including many representative segments of the society also helps prepare for more cooperative relations once a crisis is over.

LEADERSHIP

Nonviolent movements succeed more often when they have multiple leaders, dispersed like their supporters across multiple sectors of the society. A centralized command and control structure may be necessary in armed insurrections, as it seems to be in modern militaries, but authoritarianism is often a liability in civil resistance campaigns. A greater distribution of leadership makes it more difficult for governments to silence and repress the movement. Dispersed leadership also helps build support throughout the society and helps prepare for democratic institutions once the conflict ends. Campaigns run by autocrats are more likely to follow their success by replacing the old set of rulers with new autocratic rulers.

WINNING DEFECTIONS

Fracturing the unity among the rulers is often critical for success. The tipping point in many successful nonviolent movements comes when significant portions of the security forces refuse or even just momentarily hesitate to carry out orders to harm protesters. In 1989, when the Red Army soldiers based in Beijing were unwilling to attack their fellow residents in Beijing's Tiananmen Square, the Chinese rulers called in more obedient troops domiciled in distant provinces who did not share the sympathies of their Beijing colleagues. Had all the Red Army acted like those stationed in Beijing, the outcome of this nonviolent movement would likely have been very different.

Nepstad's analysis of six nonviolent campaigns demonstrates that security force defections can occur in many ways (Nepstad 2011). They may begin at the top, as they did in Chile in 1988 after a disputed plebiscite vote when military and police commanders refused to follow orders. Security defections can also begin at the grassroots and trickle up, as they did in East Germany in 1989 when low-ranking soldiers deserted or told their commanding officers they would not use force on protestors. Sometimes, as in the Philippines in 1986, there is a mutually escalating effect through independent actions by high- and low-ranking security forces.

Defections of members of governmental bureaucracies can also have a significant effect. A critical mass of defections disempowers rulers so much that they often capitulate or flee, as was the case, for example, with the Shah of Iran in 1979 and with both Zine al-Abidine Ben Ali and Hosni Mubarak in 2011. Studies by Nepstad (2011) and by Chenoweth and Stephan (2011) suggest that creating mass security force defections is often the single most important factor in producing nonviolent success.

THIRD PARTIES

Armed insurrections are often dependent on outside organizations and states to provide them with cash and weapons. However, nonviolent movements usually work best when they have little or no support from people outside the society. In fact, being publicly associated with external organizations or countries can greatly decrease a nonviolent insurrection's ability to recruit and retain sympathizers.

The Federal Bureau of Investigation spent much time and money in the 1950s and 1960s trying to convince the public and government leaders that the American civil rights movement was being funded by the Soviet Union and was therefore "subversive" and "un-American." Such dishonest efforts to discredit nonviolent campaigns are common. So, for example, the Mubarak government in 2011 tried to convince Egyptians that the Arab Awakening demonstrations were being led by one or both of two bitter enemies, the Muslim Brotherhood and the Israelis.

Strategists of civil resistance movements should be wary of accepting funds or other help from outside their countries. This advice has become easier to follow now that most of the information needed to plan and manage nonviolent movements is freely available through multiple electronic media.

GO DIGITAL

As explained in several earlier chapters, electronic technologies offer new ways to foment nonviolent political and social change. In the Arab Awakening and other recent uprisings, social media such as Facebook, Twitter, and YouTube made it faster, easier, and cheaper to share information with large audiences. Future civil resistant movements are likely to depend increasingly on the use of social media. Strategizing effective ways to adapt nonviolent methods to electronic technologies will be increasingly necessary for success. The website Civil Resistance 2.0, described earlier, is an especially rich source for finding the latest digital-based nonviolent methods.

THE PARADOX OF REPRESSION

be prepared for violence

One additional strategy deserves special attention. Nonviolent campaigns must plan for violence, both how to react to violence used against them and how to minimize their own members' attempts at violent retaliation. Refraining from retaliation is crucial as nonviolent movements tend to lose their popular appeal when they are perceived as employing violence against governments. Violence, even acts as mild as rock and bottle throwing, is often used by rulers as an excuse to take extreme measures to, as governments like to say, "preserve public safety." The government possesses great advantages if both parties act violently since it controls police and military forces equipped to win what will ordinarily be a very unequal fight.

The more effective a nonviolent campaign becomes, the more likely its targeted government will respond with escalating coercion and violence. This escalation of ruler repression often signals that the methods of civil resistance are threatening the stability of the regime. Enabling nonviolent participants to understand this can help dissuade them from reacting violently to state-sponsored violence.

When civil resistance movements stay nonviolent, they tend to provoke levels of state-sponsored repression so disproportionate that it increases rather than decreases the movement's power. Richard Gregg (1966) named this phenomenon political jiu-jitsu but it is now more often known as backfire (Martin 2005), backlash (Sharp 2012), or the paradox of repression (Smithey and Kurtz 1999), the term most used in this book. The **paradox of repression** occurs when oppressive violence by government forces or their allies backfires and increases public support for the nonviolent campaign. The use of state force then paradoxically weakens the regime that wields it. As Sharp (2012, 223) explains, the government's violence "produces shifts in opinion and power relationships favorable to the nonviolent group."

Paradoxical reversals have signaled turning points in many of the twentieth century's best-known nonviolent movements. Gandhi's arrest in South Africa on September 11, 1906, convinced many previously reluctant Indians to join his first campaign and revealed to Gandhi the power of a method he would use repeatedly thereafter. In part because the arrest of Rosa Parks for sitting on a bus was widely seen as an outrageously disproportionate response, the path-breaking Montgomery, Alabama, bus boycott attracted wide support.

Coup d'etat

Coup d'états can produce backfire, as one did in the Soviet Union in 1991 when conservative Communist Party officials seized the government to try to stop the process of democratization being promoted by Mikhail Gorbachev and Boris Yeltsin. The resulting massive nonviolent demonstrations were much larger than any that Russia had seen since the 1905 events described in Chapter 7. State-supported tortures and disappearances may also lead to the paradox of repression, as they did by inspiring the Mothers of the Plaza de Mayo movement in Argentina and the SERPAJ campaign against Pinochet in Chile.

assassination

Backfire from assassinations is also common. Benigno Aquino Jr.'s murder at the Manila airport in 1983 energized the People Power movement that led to the removal of a dictator and helped elect Aquino's wife, Corazon Aquino, president of the Philippines in 1986.

The paradox of repression often rises from the disproportionate use of force on nonviolent demonstrators. State-sponsored attacks on student demonstrators in Wenceslas Square in Prague were a galvanizing event in the 1989 Velvet Revolution in the Czech Republic.

CASE 8-2 PUSSY RIOT

Though often described as a Russian punk band, Pussy Riot is probably better understood as a loosely organized group of female performance artists. Around twelve women perform, while another fifteen or so men and women shoot and edit the group's videos. Music is only one of several elements in Pussy Riot's politically-oriented presentations which oppose authoritarian rule in Russia.

Members of the performance group Pussy Riot wearing their signature balaclavas in 2012.

Pussy Riot's first performance in late 2011 took place without warning or official permits atop a scaffold and subway cars in a Moscow subway. Members wore brightly colored dresses, tights, and face-hiding ski masks (bala-clavas), as they would in subsequent performances. The women ripped pillows apart, scattering feathers across the platform as they sang lyrics recommending Russians boycott the upcoming parliamentary elections. "Ballots will be used as toilet paper," the song proclaimed. And, "Egyptian air is healthy for your lungs/Turn Red Square into Tahrir," referring to the focal point of Egypt's earlier uprising against Hosni Mubarak.

Shots of the performance were edited into a music video and uploaded to YouTube on November 7, 2011, the anniversary of the 1917 Bolshevik revolution. Three subsequent Pussy Riot performances were similarly up-loaded to YouTube. Increasingly larger audiences viewed each one. Then, on February 21, 2012, inside Moscow's Cathedral of Christ the Savior, five members of Pussy Riot launched into yet another surprise, costumed performance. Guards stopped them less than a minute after they began. Later that day, Pussy Riot released footage of the performance and the guards' intervention as part of a music video entitled, "Punk Prayer, Mother of God, Chase Putin Away." The song's chorus exhorts, "Virgin Mary, Mother of God, put Putin away," and "Virgin Mary, Mother of God, become a feminist" (see English captioned version at http://www.youtube.com/watch?v=lPDkJbTQRCY). In later interviews, members of Pussy Riot explained they had targeted the Russian Orthodox Church because its

(continued)

CASE 8-2   *(CONTINUED)*

leaders were partners with Putin encouraging violations of human, women's, and LGBT rights.

Two of the five performers in the Cathedral escaped capture but the others were charged and convicted of "hooliganism motivated by religious hatred." All three were sentenced to two years in prison, though one later had her sentence suspended. The trial brought worldwide attention to Pussy Riot's political causes. Support groups and rallies appeared in dozens of countries. Many well-known international musicians, including Björk, Green Day, Paul McCartney, and Madonna, protested the trial and convictions. Some offered

to show their support by performing with Pussy Riot but a spokesperson for the group told an interviewer, "The only performances we'll participate in are illegal ones. We refuse to perform as a part of the capitalist system, at concerts where they sell tickets."

Pussy Riot's innovative performances and use of You-Tube suggest there are many new methods people can invent to draw attention to their nonviolent campaigns.

Sources: Kirilenko and Sindela, 2012; Mirovalev, 2012; Pussy Riot, 2013; Wikipedia, 2013; see as well, *Pussy Riot: A Punk Prayer*, a 2013 documentary directed by Maxim Pozdorovkin and Mike Lerner.

The televised images of people on horses and camels pummeling demonstrators in Tahrir Square helped increase Egyptian and world support for the 2011 anti-Mubarak campaign. See also the example of the paradox of repression presented in Case 8-2, "Pussy Riot."

PURPOSEFULLY PROVOKING VIOLENCE

The boost that state violence sometimes gives to nonviolence movements has encouraged some nonviolent strategists to intentionally invite disproportionate reactions. One especially consequential use of this strategy occurred in the United States in 1963 at a time when the civil rights movement had stalled. A long campaign to challenge segregation in Albany, Georgia, led personally by Martin Luther King Jr., had ended in failure in 1962 in large part because Albany officials were careful to use minimal force (Lewis 2013). The nonviolent civil rights movement, then a decade old, seemed in danger of being replaced with some of the more violent alternatives being proposed by younger black leaders.

King and his associates thus chose Birmingham, Alabama, as the site for their next campaign in part because they knew that the police there were controlled by Eugene "Bull" Connor, notorious for his fervent segregationist views and violent tactics (Torres 2003). King was arrested soon after the demonstrations began but, despite the eloquence of his now-famous letter from the Birmingham jail, this new campaign also stalled and seemed headed toward repeating the dismal results of the previous year in Albany.

One of King's SCLC colleagues, James Bevel, began encouraging Birmingham's black junior and senior high school students to join the demonstrations (Sandquist 2009). On the first day hundreds were arrested, creating some novel and dramatic pictures for the news media but no significant change in the campaign's momentum. On the second day about a thousand students began a new march. The jails were already filled with students arrested on the previous day so Connor decided to stop the march with police dogs and high pressure water hoses.

What happened then became known as the civil rights' **Children's Crusade.** Television in living rooms across the United States and much of the world showed images of teenagers and even pre-teen participants being dragged by dogs and thrown into police cars (Torres 2003). Nearby other students tumbled helplessly down roads and streets beneath the spray of water cannons. The horrified public reaction helped convince the Kennedy administration to

A dog attacks a young man in Birmingham, Alabama, in 1963, helping produce the paradox of repression.

involve the federal government in the business of making laws for Southern states. A year later the Civil Rights Act of 1964 was signed by Kennedy's successor, President Johnson. (The Children's Crusade is chronicled in *Mighty Times: The Children's March*, a documentary listed in the Recommended Resources at the end of this chapter.)

The Birmingham campaign's use of children was controversial among civil resistance strategists at the time and the tactic of using nonviolent methods to intentionally provoke violent responses has remained controversial ever since. Nonetheless, this strategy of inviting backfire, of exploiting the paradox of repression, continues to be in frequent use.

MISCONCEPTIONS, MISUNDERSTANDINGS, AND MYTHS

Nonviolent movements succeed best when participants learn how to employ nonviolent strategies and methods. This learning is made difficult, however, by many widespread misconceptions, including the belief that nonviolence is the refuge of the weak (Nagler 2004). Even Gandhi called his method "passive resistance" for a while and nonviolence has continued to be falsely associated with pacifism and passivity, concepts that suggest one should do nothing in the face of great need. As mentioned in Chapter 7, Gene Sharp chose the term nonviolent action in an attempt to correct the false view that nonviolence is a form of inaction.

Refusing to harm and even to murder others in the name of an ethnic, religious, or nationalistic cause is still thought to signal cowardice to many. The Old Testament's advice to take violent revenge on one's enemies, to extract "an eye for an eye," continues to guide much popular storytelling and political strategizing. Acts of civil resistance such as Rosa Parks' refusal to leave her seat on a segregated bus are not celebrated nearly as often as are decisions to enlist to fight in a war.

Gradually, however, the success of so many nonviolent campaigns across the world may be weakening the myth that participants in civil resistance movements are less patriotic or brave than the armed security forces who often attack them. Those who have filled both roles usually report that it requires at least as much courage to choose not to retaliate while being beaten or fired upon as it does to assault and kill others. Still, nonviolent organizers must find ways to counter the misconception that nonviolent action is a strategy for cowards.

 A related misconception imagines that nonviolent campaigners seek to avoid conflict. Often, in fact, nonviolent movements do the opposite; they purposefully escalate conflicts and crises. Gandhi devised his 240-mile march to the sea to gather salt, an illegal act in British India, precisely to escalate the dormant conflict between Indians and their occupiers. King's choice of Birmingham, Alabama, for what became the Children's Crusade was similarly based on a strategy of forcing a crisis.

 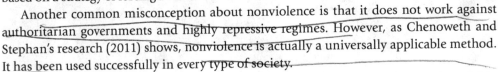 Another common misconception about nonviolence is that it does not work against authoritarian governments and highly repressive regimes. However, as Chenoweth and Stephan's research (2011) shows, nonviolence is actually a universally applicable method. It has been used successfully in every type of society.

Nonviolence can be used within every type of social movement; it contains within itself no intrinsic moral or ethical value. As Sharp pointed out decades ago, "There is nothing in nonviolent action to prevent it from being used for both 'good' and 'bad' causes" (1973, 71). For example, the Nazis organized economic boycotts of Jewish businesses, and in the United States it was long a common practice for banks to refuse to loan money to black Americans seeking to move into predominantly white neighborhoods.

Understanding the value-neutrality of nonviolent action corrects the misconception that nonviolence must be associated with moral commitments. The pioneering successes first of Mohandas Gandhi and then of Martin Luther King Jr. encouraged this misunderstanding as both prominently invoked religious principles. Since the 1960s, however, most nonviolent campaigns have had little or no explicit association with religious beliefs. Some people believe that disassociating nonviolence from religion is a mistake. Chapter 9 explores arguments for coupling nonviolence with faith-based perspectives.

OBSTRUCTIVE AND CONSTRUCTIVE PROGRAM

Civil disobedience as Thoreau conceived of it emphasized noncooperation with governments (see Chapter 7). Subsequent nonviolent movements have also similarly tended to focus on protests, resistance, and interventions that disrupt. But nonviolent campaigns also include at least the possibility of a second approach: They can oppose governments or public policies by building attractive alternative social forms.

Gandhi employed both approaches. He maintained that "cooperation with good" is just as important as "non-cooperation with evil" (Gandhi 2001, 165). Michael Nagler (2011) suggests that Gandhi's perspective can be understood "as a bird with two wings and a brain." One wing carries what Nagler calls **obstructive program**, the non-cooperation with evil associated with protests, resistance, and interventions, the methods of civil disobedience most commonly associated with nonviolent campaigns. The second wing carries what Gandhi called **constructive program**, cooperation with good through building a new, better society in the shell of the old or, as Nagler (2011) describes it, through "building what you want without waiting for others to give it to you." The brain in Nagler's metaphor refers to strategies like those discussed earlier that guide choices from among the hundreds of possible obstructive and constructive actions.

By the time he published *Constructive Programme: Its Meaning and Place* (1941), Gandhi had begun emphasizing constructive more than obstructive projects. Gandhi now believed that fundamental changes in India could not be created through a reliance mostly on obstructive actions. Instead, Gandhi thought, a free and peaceful society must be built through transforming cultural, economic, health, and spiritual institutions from the bottom up. "My real politics is constructive work," Gandhi said (cited in Nagler 2004, 129). And so Gandhi initiated projects to improve rural sanitation and health services, promote education, build food and clothing self-sufficiency, decentralize production, increase religious tolerance and cooperation, end caste untouchability, and empower women. His famous constructive project to free India from dependence on English textiles transformed the spinning wheel into a national symbol of freedom. Spinning was, Gandhi said, the "sun" in his solar system of many constructive projects (quoted in Nagler 2004, 166).

The revolution in the minds of the American colonists discussed in Chapter 7 provides an even earlier example of the power of constructive program. Growing nonviolent resistance to English rule from 1760 to 1775 led the colonists to create alternative economic, social, and political forms that severely undermined the official English-controlled institutions. Home spun cloth, later to be Gandhi's "sun," worked across the Eastern seaboard as a key economic element of resistance. John Adams concluded that through these constructive actions the colonists won the war for independence before "a single drop of blood was shed" (Adams 1856, 172).

Leaders of nonviolent movements face difficult choices about whether to emphasize obstructive or constructive projects. This further complicates the many strategic choices described earlier. Obstructions—protests, resistance, and interventions—commonly work best in confronting direct violence and creating negative peace. However, obstructive methods seldom change the cultural, social, and economic patterns of a society. Constructive program seeks to alter these patterns and build positive peace. Implementing successful constructive projects generally requires longer commitments and greater persistence than mounting obstructive actions.

The successful obstructive campaigns in Tunisia and Egypt during the Arab Awakening were not preceded by substantial constructive efforts to build alternative non-autocratic institutions. As a result, once obstructive civil resistance campaigns achieved their goals of deposing each country's dictator, both Tunisia and Egypt found themselves still governed by many of the same autocratic social forms and institutions the nonviolent demonstrators had wished to end. Gandhi might argue that constructive programs should have been instituted in Tunisia and Egypt for years, maybe even for decades, prior to the unleashing of nonviolent obstructive actions.

THE MOVEMENT OF MOVEMENTS

Campaigns promoting constructive projects are prominent within the global peace network described in Chapter 3. Much of this constructive work is undertaken by the many civil society organizations now active in most regions of the world.

Civil society organizations are voluntary associations that seek to advance common economic, political, social, or religious interests. They do not aim to make money or to operate as official government agencies and thus are often called nonprofit and nongovernmental organizations. Civil society groups may include family members but they differ from families by including people who are unrelated by blood or marriage. Influential civil society organizations include faith-based associations and religious groups, secular educational and research institutes, charities and philanthropic foundations, environmental groups, labor unions, local community groups, professional associations, and amateur sports clubs.

Naomi Klein has christened the contemporary global explosion of voluntary organizations as a "movement of movements—a coalition of coalitions" (2004, 220). The **movement of movements** is without leaders or hierarchy and this greatly inhibits the media's ability to report about it. Some of the organizations participate in obstructive projects but most pursue Gandhi's constructive program, without knowing about or using that name.

The movement of movements likely includes millions of nongovernmental, noncommercial organizations spread across the world (Hawken 2007). It is impossible to know precisely how many civil society organizations exist in part because most groups work so differently than did past movements that were trying to overthrow or replace their governments. Most contemporary civil society organizations do not mount either armed or unarmed, nonviolent insurrections. As a result, most local and global media seldom consider these organizations newsworthy.

The United States State Department estimates there are 1.5 million civil society organizations in the United States alone (U.S. Department of State 2012). India is estimated to have over 3 million (OneWorld South Asia 2010). These two estimates suggest there may be 10 million or so nongovernmental, noncommercial organizations currently at work across the world. WiserEarth maintains a searchable online database for organizations that register on their website. At the beginning of 2014, there were nearly 115,000 registered organizations, probably only around one or two percent of the global total, but still providing a glimpse at the many different sorts of work that civil society groups undertake.

Over 29,000 of the registered groups on the WiserEarth website describe themselves as focusing on human rights and another 13,000 emphasize peace and peacebuilding. About 8,000 additional organizations work mostly to promote democracy and fair voting and another 4,300 focus on conflict resolution. These groups together make up almost 40 percent of all the registered organizations, a proportion that if approximated by the organizations not in the database would suggest there are close to 40 million civil society groups across the world working on human rights, peace and peacebuilding, democracy and fair voting, and conflict resolution. It should be little wonder then that political scientist Mary Kaldor believes that global civil society now represents "an answer to war" (Kaldor 2003).

HOW CIVIL SOCIETY WORKS

Many organizations in the global civil society are very small, boasting a dozen members or less. Many, too, are rarely active. Some are ineffective even when they are at their peak. Still, as with the global peace network, with which it overlaps, the movement of movements' liquidity and breadth bolsters its strength. The dissolution or destruction of any single organization would likely little effect the strength of the whole.

As Chapter 9 explains, many of the pioneering organizations within the movement of movements grew out of religions. The Fellowship of Reconciliation is one of the oldest and best-known such organizations. It now has branches in forty countries. Some other large faith-based organizations include: the American Friends Service Committee, founded by Quakers in 1917 and a 1947 Nobel Peace Prize winner; Pax Christi, created after World War II to bring French and German Catholics together, now active in thirty countries; and the International Network of Engaged Buddhists, organized by Sulak Sivaraksa with assistance from Thích Nhất Hạnh, the Dalai Lama, and others, to promote social activism among Buddhists worldwide. There are many thousands of other similarly religiously based peace and justice organizations, as well as many thousands more that use their religious faith to guide work on environmental issues.

Though some religious-based organizations are better known, most civil society organizations are secular. What is today known as the Women's International League for Peace and Freedom, for example, was formed in 1915 to organize opposition to World War I under the name of the Woman's Peace Party (Plastas 2011). The organization has been opposing wars ever since and today has branches in thirty-seven countries. Amnesty International, a more recently formed and better known civil society organization, was founded in 1961, won the Nobel Peace Prize in 1977, and now has 2 million members in over 150 countries. Several organizations opposed to land mines are also well known, in part because of efforts by Diana, the late Princess of Wales. Some of the more prominent anti-land mine organizations include Adopt-a-Minefield, the International Campaign to Ban Landmines (ICBL), Landmine Action, and the United States Campaign to Ban Landmines. WiserEarth lists 150 organizations focused on eliminating land and sea mines.

Most civil society organizations were formed in the last few decades as the global peace network expanded and more people committed to increasing levels of positive peace within their countries. Gandhi's plans for constructive programs may not have transformed Indian society as he wished but, as Michael Nagler (2006, 257) says, Gandhi's pioneering discovery that "something positive can only be achieved by positive—constructive—means" has become a basic principle for millions across the world. In all regions people seeking change are now more likely to be involved in building alternative institutions than either in inciting violent revolutions or in supporting obstructive nonviolent campaigns.

The Appendix lists some of the more prominent secular civil society organizations dedicated to promoting peace and nonviolence.

MAKING CONNECTIONS

Gandhi had to stumble his way through modernity's first sustained nonviolent campaign without guides or guidebooks. Today, humans possess peacemaking institutions and techniques far superior to what was available just a century ago. Anyone with an Internet connection can quickly find how-to manuals prepared by experienced leaders of earlier nonviolent movements who have worked in diverse regions of the world. If challenged, most civil society organizations could swiftly transform themselves into nonviolent resistance movements with at least some hope of success.

Of course, the increasing number of successful nonviolent campaigns, continuing expansion of civil society organizations, and further strengthening of the global peace network do not guarantee a more peaceful future. However, they do provide the possibility of a greatly expanded global peace, a possibility that seemed highly unlikely but fifty years ago.

FOR REVIEW

1. Summarize the key research findings made about the relative success rates of violent and nonviolent campaigns.
2. Evaluate some of the strengths and weaknesses in both Max Weber's and Gene Sharp's theories of power.
3. Review how strategies can be used to guide choices among nonviolent methods.
4. Explore some of the factors likely to produce the paradox of repression.
5. Explain the criteria that leaders can use in choosing between emphasizing either an obstructive or constructive nonviolent program.

THINKING CRITICALLY

1. What arguments might governments offer to explain why they must maintain a monopoly on the right to use violence against their citizens?
2. What factors most commonly cause aggrieved groups to choose nonviolent rather than violent resistance?
3. How might empirical studies demonstrating the relative high success rate of nonviolent campaigns discourage future violent insurrections?
4. Which of the several nonviolent strategies described in the chapter seem likely to be the most important? Which seem likely to be the least important?
5. If you were a leader of a nonviolent campaign, what factors would cause you to encourage children to participate in an attempt to produce the paradox of repression?
6. Why do you think that violent campaigns usually receive so much more publicity than nonviolent campaigns?
7. What causes most nonviolent campaigns to emphasize obstructive projects more than constructive projects?

8. Why did the number of civil society organizations increase so rapidly in the last half of the twentieth century?

9. Explain how countries with a strong civil society are likely to differ from countries with a weak civil society.

RECOMMENDED RESOURCES

Bock, Joseph G. *The Technology of Nonviolence: Social Media and Violence Prevention* (Cambridge, MA: MIT Press, 2012). Details local uses of social media and other forms of technology to prevent violence. This includes five case studies that range from "low-tech" interventions to prevent ethnic and religious violence in India, to an anti-gang initiative in Chicago that uses Second Life to train its "violence interrupters."

Boycott. Directed by Clark Jackson. 2001. A fiction film that stays close to the historical record and interweaves archival footage to dramatize the story of the Montgomery bus boycott and of Martin Luther King Jr.'s transformation into a national leader.

Bringing Down a Dictator. Directed by Steve York. 2002. A documentary account of the Serbia campaign to remove Slobodan Milosevic. Emphasizes the role of the youth-led Otpor! nonviolent resistance movement whose success has since inspired other movements across the world.

Canvasopedia NonViolent Struggle Multimedia Library. A multimedia library for nonviolent campaigns that includes videos, how-to manuals, and news reports. Website at http://www .canvasopedia.org/library

Eyes on the Prize. Produced by Henry Hampton. 1987. A fourteen-hour documentary that includes historical footage as well as interviews with many of the central participants in the American civil rights movement. Many episodes explore how ordinary people made the movement effective.

Freedom Song. Directed by Phil Alden Robinson. 2000. A fiction film that explores tensions between generations of African Americans facing racial discrimination in the southern United States in the 1960s. The film explores the work of the SNCC as it focuses on ordinary people faced with extraordinary choices in locations far from the national spotlight and from assistance by national civil rights celebrities.

How to Start a Revolution. Director Ruaridh Arrow. 2011. A documentary that profiles the impact of Gene Sharp's ideas on nonviolent campaigns over the last forty years. Includes interviews with Sharp and those who have worked with him.

International Center on Nonviolent Conflict. A rich Internet portal that focuses on current nonviolent campaigns and news reported by bloggers from across the world. Also offers webinars. Available at nonviolent-conflict.org

Kaldor, Mary. *Global Civil Society: An Answer to War* (Malden, MA: Polity Press, 2003). A pioneering examination of the explosive growth of transnational civic networks after 1989, with a special emphasis on how global civil society is creating a new form of horizontal, bottom-up politics that avoids traditional state-centered approaches.

King: A Filmed Record . . . Montgomery to Memphis. Directed by Ely Landau, Joseph L. Mankiewicz, and Sidney Lumet. 1970. Long unavailable until rereleased in 2013, this documentary attempts no analysis but presents Martin Luther King Jr. directly, using his interviews, speeches, and private moments caught on film along with scenes from demonstrations, marches, and other events associated with the times and society in which King lived.

Mighty Times: The Children's March. Directed by Robert Houston. 2004. A documentary that uses archival footage, interviews, and reenactments to tell the story of the young people in

Birmingham, Alabama, who braved fire hoses and police dogs in 1963 in the battle to end segregation.

Nepstad, Sharon Erickson. *Nonviolent Revolutions: Civil Resistance in the Late 20th Century* (New York, Oxford University Press, 2011). A sociological study that takes a comparative approach to try to determine why nonviolent movements fail or succeed. Cases include movements in China, Chile, Germany, Kenya, Panama, and the Philippines.

Sir! No Sir! Directed by David Zeiger. 2005. This feature-length documentary explores the widespread resistance against the Vietnam War that rose up in the 1960s from within the U.S. military itself. Narrated by a diverse group of veteran Vietnam War resisters, the film also explores why the influential role of nonviolent action by soldiers has mostly been lost from public memory.

CHAPTER 9

RELIGIOUS INFLUENCES

CHAPTER OVERVIEW

This chapter explores the relationship between religion, peace, and violence with a special emphasis on shifting interpretations of the ethic of reciprocity. It begins with a description of early Christian communities and details how Christianity's attitude toward violence changed after it was made an official Roman state religion. The subsequent rise of the historical peace churches is reviewed, as well as William Penn's Holy Experiment in the colony of Pennsylvania. Martin Luther King Jr.'s Christian roots are explored, as well as the role of the ethic of reciprocity in Islam's founding and later history. Subsequent sections describe the nonviolent work of Abdul Ghaffar Khan, the Buddhist-inspired empire of Ashoka, and Mohandas K. Gandhi's use of Hindu beliefs in the development of his ideas of ahimsa, satyagraha, and shanti sena. The chapter closes with an exploration of the differences between principled and strategic nonviolence.

Key terms and people discussed include: Ethic of reciprocity; Emperor Constantine I; City of God; City of Man; peace churches; Petr Chelčický; Penn's Holy Experiment; Martin Luther King Jr.; Sufism; Abdul Ghaffar Khan; Ashoka; Mohandas K. Gandhi; ahimsa; satyagraha; shanti sena; unarmed civilian peacekeepers; principled nonviolence; and pragmatic nonviolence.

> The gods, it appears, have historically been among peacemakers' greatest friends, but paradoxically also among their greatest enemies.
>
> —ANTONY ADOLF (2009, 10)

Over half of the people in the world today belong to just a few religions. Christianity claims 2 billion members; Islam is not far behind with nearly 1.5 billion. Buddhism and Hinduism together account for another almost 1.5 billion believers. Though now strikingly different, these four world traditions all possess roots in what is often called the ethic of reciprocity or, almost as often, the Golden Rule.

The **ethic of reciprocity** directs people to care for everyone equally, without considering whether they are part of one's own family, tribe, or community. Confucius' *Analects* contains one of the oldest written formulations of this principle when it states, "Never impose on others what you would not choose for yourself." The Hindu god Krishna similarly instructs Arjuna in the *Bhagavad Gita*, "I love anyone who is incapable of ill will, and who returns love for hatred." Buddha asked his followers to embrace the ethic of reciprocity. He is reported in the *Dhammapada* to have said, "Putting oneself in the place of another, one should not kill nor cause another to kill." Jesus counseled, "And as ye would that men should do to you, do ye also to them likewise." Mohammed preached, "That which you want for yourself, seek for mankind."

Though the ethic of reciprocity is found in the traditions of over 4 billion believers, the idea of loving one's neighbor has not consistently inspired most believers to seek alternatives to violence and war. The causes of violence among and between Buddhists, Christians, Hindus, and Muslims are as varied as those among nonbelievers. Nonetheless, one historical trend has been especially consequential: Each of these religions increased their support for violence and war as it gained civil and political power. The Golden Rule of "treat others as you would like to be treated" thus often came to mean "treat those you like or who are useful to you as you would like to be treated. Others can be attacked, enslaved, and killed."

Christianity provides a vivid example of this shift.

EARLY CHRISTIAN COMMUNITIES OF CARE

Disagreements about what various religious founders really said, did, and meant have been debated for centuries. Arguments about what Jesus taught have been especially passionate, helping to spark thousands of schisms, hundreds of wars, and millions of deaths. Still, nonsectarian readers of Christianity's canonical four gospels generally agree that these texts endorse an expansive ethic of reciprocity. Loving all others seems central to what the Gospels report that Jesus taught.

Jesus' words in Luke are typical:

A man was going down from Jerusalem to Jericho, when he fell into the hands of robbers. They stripped him of his clothes, beat him and went away, leaving him half dead with no clothes. A priest happened to be going down the same road, and when he saw the man, and he passed by on the other side. So too, a Levite, when he came to the place and saw him, he too passed by on the other side. But a Samaritan, as he traveled, came where the man was; and when he saw him, he took pity on him. He went to him and bandaged his wounds, pouring on oil and wine. Then he put the man on his own donkey, took him to an inn and looked after him. The next day he took out two silver coins and gave them to the innkeeper. "Look after him," he said, "and when I return, I will reimburse you for any extra expense you may have." "Which of these three do you think was a neighbor to the man who fell into the hands of robbers?" The expert in the law replied, "The one who had mercy on him." Jesus told him, "Go and do likewise."

Most of the first Christians and their early converts understood Jesus' teachings as an exhortation for people to care for friend and foe alike. Harming others was forbidden, regardless of the circumstances. Most of the early Christians refused to serve in the Roman army. Early Christian history also offers many examples of believers following Jesus' advice to "resist not evil" but instead "turn the other cheek." For example, the Book of Acts describes Stephen, one of the most influential of the early Christians, crying out as he was being stoned to death, "Lord, do not hold this sin against them."

Similarly, though he had himself nearly been stoned to death for his faith, Paul subsequently wrote in his letter to the Corinthians, that Christians "are in rags, we are brutally treated, we are homeless. Yet when we are cursed, we bless; when we are persecuted, we endure it; when we are slandered, we answer kindly." Almost two hundred years after Paul's death, Clement of Alexandria, another influential pioneer of early Christianity, explained that "the church is an army of peace which sheds no blood." Three prominent early church theologians, Tertullian (160–220 CE), Origen (182–254 CE), and Lactantius (240–320 CE) also promoted this expansive nonviolent view.

Christianity's early emphasis on the ethic of reciprocity was one of the principle reasons it grew in just a few hundred years from perhaps a hundred believers at the time of Jesus' death to a massive movement with millions of adherents. The early Christians "ethic of concern," as sociologist Rodney Stark (1996) names it, generated communities that cared for one another and for their neighbors in ways that impressed outsiders and encouraged converts. Their Golden Rule practices helped Christian populations survive and grow proportionally larger during the Roman Empire's frequent deadly epidemics. Stark points out that the ethic of concern also led to women being valued significantly more within early Christianity than in the surrounding society. The early Christians rejected abortion, incest, infidelity, infanticide, polygyny, and divorce. These Christian practices were rare among the broader populatin at that time and so increased the well-being and fertility of Christian women relative to non-Christians. The higher proportion of women within early Christian communities also led these women to frequently marry non-Christian men, many of whom were then converted (Stark 1996).

Stark (1996) maintains that the early Christian communities of concern were especially attractive to residents of Roman cities where increasing proportions of the society resided. Crime, ethnic conflicts, fires, earthquakes, famines and, as mentioned, epidemics were more familiar to most people in these cities than were Roman order and largesse. Christianity's ethic of reciprocity represented an attractive alternative to the various other, generally more pessimistic, belief systems then available.

CHRISTIANITY'S TRANSFORMATION

Of course, there were divisions and disagreements even among these earliest Christian communities. Historical accounts of the lives of most early Christians are scant, but it is clear that some of the early faithful did accept work as Roman soldiers. Nevertheless, the Golden Rule and "shedding no blood" remained a central principle in faith—if not always in practice—for most followers of Jesus for almost three hundred years. Then, abruptly and unexpectedly, Christianity became one of the Empire's official religions and Christian rates of violence quickly became largely indistinguishable from that of the other groups around them.

In 312 CE, **Emperor Constantine I** transformed Christianity into an official and favored Roman state religion. Though not a Christian himself, Constantine dreamed one night that Jesus was commanding him to carry the sign of the cross into the next morning's battle. Constantine obeyed his dream and believed, just as the fight began, that he saw a flaming cross blazing in the sky. With it were the words, "In this sign thou shall conquer," words, as Kurlansky comments, "that were in complete contradiction to Christianity and would have been unutterable for Jesus" (2006, 25).

Constantine won the battle and concluded that Christian symbols and soldiers could help in his pursuit of greater power. He offered Christian men preferential treatment to entice them to join his armies. He promoted Christianity throughout his empire and built three spectacular churches, St. Peter's in Rome, Hagia Sophia in Constantinople, and the Holy Sepulchre (also known as the Church of the Resurrection) in Jerusalem. Constantine used state funds to support—and control—Christian congregations and priests. Constantine proclaimed that the Roman day of the Sun, Sunday, must be used as the weekly day of rest by all Roman subjects, whether Jewish, Christian, or pagan.

The many caring communities that had for centuries been associated with Jesus' ethic of reciprocity became part of a powerful religion associated with statecraft, executions, conquests, and wars. A religion that had long been antagonistic or, at least, indifferent to governments, became itself a government, focused like most other ancient dictatorial governments on power and control. Though it played little role in the iconography of early Christians, the fighting cross of Constantine's dream became the most common symbol of the faith.

A century after Constantine, Augustine justified the new Christian endorsement of violence with his influential distinction between the different moralities supposedly required in God's and in Man's realms. The ethic of reciprocity belongs only to the **City of God**, Augustine argued, and this realm of goodness is unattainable on Earth. Christians living on Earth in what Augustine labeled the **City of Man** should instead participate in slavery, torture, violence, and war. (As discussed in Chapter 2, Augustine even created guidelines for how just wars should be fought.) Every major subsequent Christian theologian has offered additional justifications to help Christians avoid thinking that Jesus' call for love was intended to apply universally to all human beings. And so since Constantine, Christian groups have frequently engaged in wars, most often against each other.

THE RISE OF THE HISTORIC PEACE CHURCHES

Jesus' expansive ethic of reciprocity was mostly forgotten among Christians in the centuries after Constantine but it never disappeared. Some sects and iconoclastic individuals insisted that the lesson of the Good Samaritan should be applied equally in the human City of Man as in the heavenly City of God. Many monastic orders were created to assist people who desired to imitate the original Christians while living with others in nonviolent communities. Later, after the Protestant Reformation, several of what are now called historic peace churches or simply **peace churches** emerged to practice the ethic of reciprocity and oppose the claim that harming others is acceptable Christian behavior. These historic peace churches continue their nonviolent work today in the denominations known as the Church of the Brethren, Mennonites, and Religious Society of Friends (Quakers).

Sectarian struggles flourished in the eleventh through thirteenth centuries in what today is called France. Many minority sects named themselves "good Christians," believers willing to disobey the official Church by opposing violence and killing. The good Christians argued that Jesus had forbidden governments to kill, even as a punishment for criminals. The Holy Roman Church and its supporters called these rebels "Cathars" and ruthlessly hunted, tortured, and executed them for almost two hundred years. The last known Cathar leader was killed in 1321. Soon after, however, yet more nonviolent Christian groups sprang up across Europe.

Most of these heretical groups are now forgotten but **Petr Chelčický**, the leader of one, deserves attention. As Mark Kurlansky (2006) points out, Chelčický's views, espoused in the fifteenth century in what is now the Czech Republic, predate by almost one hundred years the better known ideas of Martin Luther and Erasmus. In one of his last texts, *The Net of Faith*, written about 1443, Chelčický called the Pope and Europe's leaders "whales who have torn the net of true faith" by turning away from Jesus' law of love. Killing was always wrong, Chelčický believed, whether done by kings, popes, or ordinary people. The poor should refuse to serve in armies, just as the first Christians had. This would end wars and help create communities of loving equals, where property would be shared as it had been among Jesus' disciples.

Chelčický's influence grew even though his followers were driven underground (Kurlansky 2006). As many as 10,000 Chelčický supporters, known as the Unity of Brethren, were still active in the Czech region twenty years after Chelčický's death. A similar nonviolent, communitarian movement of "good Christians" emerged a little later in the German-speaking region of Switzerland. Known as Anabaptists, this movement spread rapidly across Europe in the sixteenth century even as multiple governments violently attacked its members. Anabaptists embraced the then-novel practice of consensual adult baptism, a ritual that remains prominent in many Protestant churches today. (Other Christian churches generally baptize infants or children before they are old enough to profess their belief.) The Anabaptists also claimed that Christians should not kill or assist governments and churches in killing. For these beliefs Anabaptists were still being murdered in many countries until late into the eighteenth century.

Two more new nonviolent Christian groups, the Mennonites and Waterlanders, appeared in Holland in 1572 where they also faced violent repression. A century later, England gave birth to the short lived True Levellers, subsequently known as "Diggers" because of their belief that the New Testament Acts of the Apostles required all Christians to join together to cultivate commonly held lands. The Diggers also opposed all violence and war. Gerrard Winstanley, a leading Digger, explained, "Victory that is gotten by the sword is a victory that slaves get one over another" (quoted in Kurlansky 2006, 73).

The Diggers survived persecution for only a couple of years but the Society of Friends, a related English movement born in the seventeenth century, has proven more enduring. The Society is now known by the name Quakers, originally meant as an insulting reference to the supposed gyrations of its founder, George Fox. Despite persistent efforts to kill and destroy them, the Quakers, along with Mennonite and—under various names—other Anabaptist churches, have survived into the twenty-first century. These nonviolent Christian denominations continue to practice an expansive interpretation of Jesus' Golden Rule.

PENN'S HOLY EXPERIMENT

Pennsylvania, one of America's earliest European colonies, was governed by the ethic of reciprocity for nearly half a century.

Charles II, the King of England, gave William Penn the territory that became Pennsylvania as payment for a debt owed to Penn's father. The elder Penn had captained the King's navies and, among other accomplishments, had won Jamaica for England from the Spanish. His son, William, however, was a convert to the Society of Friends and he resolved to govern his new colony while following George Fox's ideas. Penn himself referred to his plan as a "holy experiment" and so it is now often referred to as **Penn's Holy Experiment**. As Devin Kenny (2009) explains in *Peaceable Kingdom Lost*, Penn's experiment produced a society with little persecution or violence and with high levels of religious tolerance far beyond what was then practiced in Europe or the rest of the European imperial world.

Penn proclaimed that all sexes and races, as well as all religions, would be offered equal protection under the law. Penn was especially insistent that Pennsylvania's indigenous inhabitants, the Native Americans, be treated fairly. During a time when across the rest of the New World Indian lands were being stolen and Indians slaughtered, Penn vowed to Pennsylvania's native peoples that Jesus' Golden Rule also included them. In a letter to "his" Indians Penn explained that "one great God" had made all people alike. He continued:

> This great God has written his law in our hearts, by which we are taught and commanded to love and help and do good to one another, and not to do harm and mischief one unto another. Now this great God has been pleased to make me concerned in your parts of the world, and the king of the country where I live has given unto me a great province therein, but I desire to enjoy it with your friends, else what would the great God say to us, who has made us not to devour and destroy one another, but live soberly and kindly together in the world. (quoted in Soderlund and Dunn 1983, 88)

While Indian wars raged in other colonies, most Pennsylvania settlers and Indians peaceably negotiated their differences. There was no capital punishment and little slavery. Prisons were used to teach skills aimed at rehabilitating convicted criminals. Pennsylvania became the least violent and, by many measures, the wealthiest of all the new North American British colonies. So many immigrants arrived from England and elsewhere that, by the 1750s, Quakers made up only about a fifth of the colony's population. Many of the

A twentieth-century painting by J. L .G. Ferris depicts William Penn's arrival at his new colony.

newer residents and some of the old wanted Pennsylvania to reverse its Golden Rule policies and join with the British military in their wars against the French and Indians.

Benjamin Franklin was an influential advocate of these violence-promoting changes.
His 1747 pamphlet, *The Plain Truth* (containing the first political cartoon ever published in
the colonies), argued that a volunteer Pennsylvania-based militia could be legally assembled to join the fighting even if it did not receive authorization from any elected officials.
Finally, in 1756, after a seventy-four-year rule by an ethic of reciprocity, what Penn had
called his "precedent" came to a democratic end. A majority of the elected Assembly voted
to declare war on the Delaware Indians. Assembly Quakers immediately resigned in
protest.

Believers in an expansive interpretation of the ethic of reciprocity have not controlled
another government since.

MARTIN LUTHER KING JR.

The Society of Friends and other historic peace churches continued to promote their minority views in what became the United States of America and also elsewhere. Historic
peace church members helped lead both the antislavery and early women's suffrage movements in the nineteenth century and their influence grew even stronger in the twentieth

century. From books, lectures, and workshops in nonviolence sponsored by the Fellowship of Reconciliation (FOR) and other faith-based nonviolent Christian organizations, leaders in the American civil rights movement were taught nonviolent methods partly based on the expansive ethic of reciprocity.

Martin Luther King Jr. was a Baptist minister, as well as the son of a Baptist minister. He began his career preaching the orthodox Protestant interpretation of Christianity, that Jesus' ethic of care was meant mostly for one's own community. However, partly from the influence of the activist Quaker Bayard Rustin and other members of the historic peace churches, King's thinking gradually evolved to more resemble the views of the earliest Christians.

Signs of King's later views were evident even at the beginning of his career. His house had been bombed in 1955, not long after the then twenty-six-year-old found himself thrust into leadership of the Montgomery bus boycott. King's wife and baby, as well as King himself, were not injured but swarms of black people quickly assembled outside, eager for revenge. With the smell of the explosion still lingering, King walked onto the porch and said, "If you have weapons, take them home. He who lives by the sword will perish by the sword. Remember that is what Jesus said. We are not advocating violence. We want to love our enemies. I want you to love our enemies. Be good to them. This is what we must live by. We must meet hate with love" (quoted in Branch 1989, 166).

By the time of his death, King had expanded his understanding of Christian doctrine to include the promotion of economic equality and opposition to the American wars in Southeast Asia. In a famous speech at the Riverside Church in New York in 1967 near the end of his life, King explained why he agreed with the earliest Christians that his faith required him to oppose war:

> To me the relationship of this ministry to the making of peace is so obvious that I sometimes marvel at those who ask me why I am speaking against the war. Could it be that they do not know the good news was meant for all men, for communist and capitalist, for their children and ours, for black and white, for revolutionary and conservative? Have they forgotten that my ministry is in obedience to the One who loved His enemies so fully that He died for them? What then can I say to the Viet Cong or to Castro or to Mao as a faithful minister of this One? Can I threaten them with death, or must I not share with them my life? (King 2010)

Like the Cathars, Anabaptists, Mennonites, and Quakers who preceded him, King faced repeated threats to his life for preaching this expansive version of the ethic of reciprocity. Even the Federal Bureau of Investigation (FBI) tried to arrange for King's death (Frady 2005). The agency systematically defamed King to President Lyndon Johnson and to members of the U.S. Congress and the press. J. Edgar Hoover, the longtime head of the FBI, sent anonymous letters to King hoping to convince King that he should "save his honor" by committing suicide. Not long after, in 1968 as he was campaigning for a living wage for garbage workers in Memphis, King was assassinated.

ISLAM AND SUFISM

Christians did not commonly promote war and other forms of state-sponsored violence until almost three centuries after Jesus' death. By contrast, in his final decade Mohammed himself led troops in violent campaigns. However, earlier as he was first establishing his new religion, Mohammed had stressed the importance of nonviolence and peace. "Whoever kills a human being should be looked upon as though he had killed all mankind," Mohammed preached. "That which you want for yourself, seek for mankind" (Wattles 1996, 191–92). This message helped transform Mecca into a center of peace so renowned that it began to prosper as a regional center of trade.

After twelve years in Mecca, however, Mohammed led his believers away to settle in Medina. The new religion now had its own territory to defend and a different interpretation of the Golden Rule emerged, one that applied less to everyone and more to believers and allies. Finally, in 624, Mohammed led his followers in a surprise attack on a Meccan merchant caravan. This precipitated an even larger battle near Badr where, against great odds, Mohammed's followers emerged victorious. More violent battles followed until Mohammed died in 632.

Historians continue to argue over the links between Mohammed's mostly pacific twelve years in Mecca and his later more bellicose activities in Medina. This rich history provides Muslims with ample examples to support opposing interpretations of Islam's views on the morality of violence and war. Christian historians have typically emphasized the violent elements of Islam, making it easier to rally Christians to support anti-Muslim discrimination and crusades. For example, see Case 9-1, "Shia and Sunni Muslims." However, diverse pacific traditions have always been prominent, if not always dominant, among the Prophet's followers.

Sufism, for example, is an especially significant branch of Islam that has consistently promoted Mohammed's expansive message of peace. Sufism has played a role in Islam roughly like that played by the historic peace churches in Christianity. Sufism emerged soon after Mohammed's death at about the same time as the better known Shia-Sunni split. Much like the Protestants who later rose up to challenge medieval Catholicism, the first Sufis objected to Islam's endorsement of violence. Sufis, then and now, maintained that the Qur'an's fundamental teaching is that people should serve God through serving every human as a manifestation of God.

There are many texts associated with Sufism, but the tradition is customarily understood to require face-to-face teaching, to depend on transmission "from the heart of the teacher to the heart of the student." Such heart teachings are difficult to capture in prose, which may explain why Sufism has produced so many well-known songwriters and poets. Jelaluddin Rumi, probably the best known Sufi poet, presents a common Sufi perspective in "Love is a Stranger" when he writes, "I am neither Christian nor Jew, nor Magian, not Muslim." In another poem Rumi proclaims, "I have put duality away/and seen the two worlds as one." Strangers and enemies, givers and receivers of aid, are equally deserving of love in the Muslim tradition that Rumi represents.

Millions of Muslims on several continents embrace Sufism today. They commonly promote nonviolence and peacemaking but Sufism has become diverse enough to also include combative groups. For example, violent resistance to Russian colonization of the Caucasus in the nineteenth century was led by the Sufis Ghazi Mollah and Shaykh Shamyl. In the same region almost two hundred years later, Sufis led much of the violent resistance to Russian occupation of Chechnya. In general, however, Sufism promotes an expansive interpretation of the Golden Rule that governments tend to reluctantly tolerate in times of peace and to brutally repress during times of war.

CASE 9-1 SHIA AND SUNNI MUSLIMS

Religion is often mistaken to be the primal cause of violence when, in fact, other causes are at work. France and Germany fought several wars, but it was never primarily because of Catholic-Protestant differences. And so it is with contemporary conflicts between Shia and Sunni Muslims.

The division between these two major Muslim denominations began in disputes over who should lead Islam after the death of Mohammed in 632. Those who would go on to become known as Sunnis accepted Mohammed's father-in-law and friend, Abu Bakr. Others claimed the Prophet had instead intended that his cousin and son-in-law, Ali, take the lead. This faction became known as the Shia, a contraction of "shiaat Ali," the partisans of Ali. Through the centuries, these political differences spawned doctrinal differences so that today, though all Muslims accept the inerrancy of the Qur'an, Sunnis and Shiites commonly rely on different written collections of Islamic law and history (known as hadith).

Most contemporary Muslims are Sunni; only between 10 and 20 percent of all Muslims are Shia, but Shia make up the majority in several prominent countries, including Bahrain, Iran, and Iraq. In most places and eras, Sunnis and Shias have lived peaceably with one another, often intermarrying. They never spawned sectarian Muslim wars on the scale of the highly destructive Thirty Years War, which raged in Europe in the seventeenth century and was, at its beginning at least, a battle for dominance between Catholics and Protestants.

Tensions between Sunni and Shia began increasing in the middle of the twentieth century as many Muslim nations gained independence from Europe. Conflicts then and since have been mainly caused by postcolonial economic and political uncertainties like those also found in postcolonial Africa and previously in countries across the Americas. However, modern governments and rebel factions alike often try to inflame sectarian resentments and aspirations when this seems likely to gain them support.

As part of the 2011 Arab Awakening in Bahrain, for example, a popular campaign for democracy and an end to monarchy was for many subsequently transformed into a clash between the majority Shia and minority Sunni Bahraini. King Hamad bin Isa Al Khalifa rejected demands for free elections in part by claiming the protests arose not from his own citizens' political aspirations but for sectarian reasons associated with interfering Shia in Iran.

Much as they did in Bahrain, Sunni and Shia tensions also grew in Syria after nonviolent attempts to overthrow an autocrat failed. Initial demonstrations focused on calls for the resignation of Bashar al-Assad and free elections. Over time, however, the conflict became increasingly violent and sectarian. Foreign fighters, monies, and weapons from Shia in Iraq, Iran, and Lebanon were sent to assist Assad's forces, just as other foreign fighters, monies, and weapons from Sunnis in Saudi Arabia and Qatar were supplied to Assad's opposition.

The American war in Iraq also produced violent clashes among many Sunni and Shia who had previously lived mostly in peace. After Saddam Hussein's long-established government and political party was outlawed, tensions over sectarian differences increased as people struggled to establish a government and security institutions that all groups would accept.

Tensions and violence between Muslim sects may continue to rise in more countries as current governance forms are challenged. Religious differences may exacerbate these conflicts, but at root their causes are not religious but political and economic. And even now, as it was in the past, in most places Sunni and Shia still live peaceably together.

Sources: Diab 2013; Hamidaddin 2013; Hussain 2013.

RADICAL ISLAM

Contemporary Islam's ability to promote the Golden Rule was clearly demonstrated by the Sufi Amadou Bamba who led his followers in a nonviolent campaign against the French occupation of Senegal at the end of the nineteenth century. The Sunni Muslim Abdul Ghaffar Khan, sometimes referred to as "the frontier Gandhi," provides another, even better known example of modern Muslim nonviolence. **Abdul Ghaffar Khan** created a mass nonviolent movement against British colonialism that remained mostly nonviolent in the face of lethal repression even harsher than any Gandhi's movements faced (Banerjee 2000).

Khan was raised in what the nineteenth-century British colonizers called the North-West Frontier Province, a region that today includes portions of Pakistan and Afghanistan. The tribal people of this area, called Pashtuns or Pathans, had such a powerful reputation for violence that one early British commander exclaimed that for these "savages . . . civilized warfare is inappropriate" (Johansen 1997, 57). The British completed over one hundred burn-and-destroy campaigns during their period of colonization in the area. Public rights of assembly were restricted. Newspapers were censored and shut down.

Despite these measures, when the British finally left the subcontinent they acknowledged that they had never been able to subdue the "savage" Pashtuns. A similar failure would be repeated again in the 1980s and yet again in the first decade of the new century

Mohandas Gandhi with Abdul Ghaffar Khan at a Peshawar meeting with Khudai Khidmatgar activists.

as first Soviet and then American armies occupied this same region. Against these different invaders the Pashtuns repeatedly enhanced their reputation for fearlessness and independence.

In the 1930s Abdul Ghaffar Khan relied on these same characteristics of the Pashtuns to create a nonviolent army known as the Khudai Khidmatgar, that is, Servants of God. Khan taught this army that nonviolent resistance to evil—in this case, British occupation—was a moral obligation for every Muslim. Khan told his volunteers: "I am going to give you such a weapon that the police and the army will not be able to stand against it. It is the weapon of the Prophet" (quoted in Abu-Nimer 2003). Khan's work inspired Mahatma Gandhi to predict that it was not Indians but the "Frontier Pathans" who would demonstrate to the world "the priceless lesson of nonviolence" (Easwaran 2002, 155).

Khan's nonviolent army accepted the same Pashtun tribal code of Pashtunwali that had guided earlier generations. But Khan interpreted Pashtunwali as counseling a different sort of courage. Each new Khudai Khidmatgar was required to take a pledge that began, "In the presence of God I solemnly affirm," thus committing their honor as Pashtuns to ten declarations. These declarations included, "I shall always live up to the principle of nonviolence"; "I shall serve all humanity equally"; and "I promise to forgive those who oppress me or treat me with cruelty" (quoted in Johansen 1997, 59).

The movement grew swiftly. There were about one thousand trained Khudai Khidmatgar in 1930. A year later, the number had risen to 25,000 and then, at its peak in 1938, about 60,000 to 100,000 people had taken the oath and received some nonviolent training. Khan remained the leader but most growth came while he was silenced: The British jailed Khan from 1931 to 1934 and then, upon his release, forced him to remain in exile from his homeland for three more years. By the time Independence finally came in 1947, Khan had been imprisoned for a total of fifteen years of the previous twenty years.

Even with their leader in prison, the Khudai Khidmatgar remained steadfastly nonviolent as the British unleashed a reign of terror. All Khudai Khidmatgar meetings in towns and villages were banned; their efforts to start new schools, build roads, or undertake other such "unauthorized" improvement projects were outlawed. In Peshawar in April 1930, British soldiers killed about two hundred unarmed demonstrators. As Gene Sharp describes the scene, "When those in front fell down wounded by the shots, those behind came forward with their breasts bared and exposed themselves to the fire, so much so that some people got as many as twenty-one bullet wounds in their bodies, and all the people stood their ground without getting into a panic" (Sharp 1960, 110).

A few months later, in August in the Bannu District, British soldiers killed eighty unarmed demonstrators. Soon after other soldiers burned houses of suspected sympathizers and poured oil on grains stored for winter consumption. Entire villages were destroyed. Some Khudai Khidmatgar men were forced to disrobe and run along public streets through gauntlets of soldiers; other captured men were sexually abused; some were castrated (Banerjee 2000, 118–19). In all, over 10,000 Khudai Khidmatgar were imprisoned. When the jails grew too full, prisoners were taken to live at work sites where, sometimes with little food and no shelter, they were forced to labor at British projects.

Throughout, most of those who had undergone Khudai Khidmatgar training remained nonviolent. They enacted the ethic of reciprocity that Ghaffar Khan taught: "That man is a Muslim who never hurts anyone by word or deed, but who works for the benefit and happiness of God's creatures. Belief in God is to love one's fellowmen" (quoted in Easwaran 2002, 55). Gandhi believed that the spectacular successes of the Khudai Khidmatgar grew out of their fierce tribal traditions. He explained, "Nonviolence is not for cowards. It is for the brave, the courageous. And the Pathans are more brave and courageous than the Hindus" (quoted in Easwaran 2002, 195).

This nonviolent face of Islam is too little known.

ASHOKA'S BUDDHIST EMPIRE

Like Christianity and Islam, Buddhism also includes traditions that emphasize a broadly inclusive ethic of reciprocity. These traditions follow Buddha's teaching in the Dhamma-pada that "whoever would tend to me should tend to the sick." Buddha is also credited with saying, "hatred does not cease by hatred; hatred ceases by love." The emperor **Ashoka** (304 BCE–232 BCE) provides an example of an entire government organized by this interpretation of the Golden Rule, an example not repeated until Penn brought a similar vision to the New World.

Ashoka began like most other monarchs of his era, by leading troops into wars of conquest and causing the deaths of many thousands (Allen 2012). Some sources claim Ashoka even killed his own brothers to eliminate their competition for the throne. Eventually Ashoka's military campaigns created an immense empire stretching from present-day Bangladesh to Iran, dropping at its southern edge deep into the Indian peninsula. There would be no empire of equal size until the British conquered much of the same region almost two thousand years later.

Shortly after replacing his father as emperor, Ashoka put down a rebellion in the present-day Indian state of Orissa. According to Ashoka's own account, this campaign caused the death of 100,000 Kalinga and 10,000 of Ashoka's own soldiers. Hundreds of thousands more were injured and displaced. Witnessing this carnage transformed Ashoka so much that he resolved to change his approach to governance. He began ruling on the basis of what he understood to be Buddhism, a perspective then but a few centuries old. "All men are my children," Ashoka wrote to explain his perspective. "What I desire for my own children—and I desire their welfare and happiness both in this world and the next—that I desire for all men" (quoted in Singh 2009, 74).

Until his death thirty years later, the transformed Ashoka sought equal treatment for women, children, prisoners, and all social classes, as well as for neighboring tribes. He encouraged generosity to the poor and sick, improved roads and irrigation systems, and built schools and universities open to everyone who wanted to attend. Ashoka actively discouraged what he criticized as the many "vulgar and worthless ceremonies" some women in his empire were required by tradition to enact. Even those people who were considered to be "enemies," people living in what Ashoka described as "the unconquered territories" on the borders of his realm, were included within Ashoka's ethic of reciprocity.

Ashoka released prisoners and abolished capital punishment. Cruelty to animals was outlawed. Hunting for consumption was permitted but hunting for sport was banned and vegetarianism encouraged. Ashoka created wildlife and forest preserves and opened hospitals dedicated to the care of injured animals. He frequently traveled across his empire, making himself available to anyone who wanted to talk. He insisted that petitions from citizens be brought to his attention regardless of the time of day.

Much of Ashoka's approach to governance seems too utopian to be true. In fact, before the nineteenth century, Westerners widely considered stories about Ashoka to be mythical. Tales of his exploits were often included in collections of legends about the thousands of gods and spirits associated with Hinduism. Then, as Charles Allen explains in *Ashoka: The Search for India's Lost Emperor* (2012), European colonizers slowly and methodically began mapping and translating the many edicts and exhortations that Ashoka had left inscribed on rocks and pillars. Ashoka's messages have now been found scattered at thirty sites across what is present-day India, Nepal, Pakistan, and Afghanistan. Through multiple tests, twentieth-century archeologists and historians established that many of the legends about Ashoka are true. He used the Golden Rule successfully for decades to govern the premodern world's largest empire.

GANDHI'S *BHAGAVAD GITA*

Ghaffar Khan's ideas were drawn from Gandhi as well as from Islam. Gandhi in turn traced his views to the historic peace churches' interpretation of Christianity and, even more, to Hinduism. The *Mahabharata*, for example, contains this ethic of reciprocity admonition, "One should never do that to another which one regards as injurious to one's own self" (Mahabharata, Book 13). **Mohandas K. Gandhi** argued this principle is central to Hinduism. He relied on this religious understanding first in South Africa and then in India as he created the first, long-lasting mass nonviolent movement in modern history.

Although Christianity and Islam root their traditions in sacred texts, writing occupies a much less prominent role in Hinduism. This religion instead draws more on a rich cornucopia of customs, rituals, and traditions almost as diverse as its hundreds of gods. Still, Gandhi, a trained lawyer, based many of his views of Hinduism on just one book, the *Bhagavad Gita*.

The *Bhagavad Gita* is a surprising choice for a proponent of nonviolence as it recounts how the god Krishna persuades a reluctant Arjuna to slaughter his cousins and honored teachers. Arjuna has fled combat in horror and expresses his opposition to killing in arguments like those used by many contemporary conscientious objectors. The god Krishna then intervenes to refute Arjuna's objections one by one. Krishna even appeals to Arjuna's masculinity as he declares, "Do not yield to unmanliness. Arise and awake, and take up your bow." Arjuna is gradually convinced and the *Bhagavad Gita* concludes with Arjuna returning to the battlefield to kill whomever his superiors select.

Gandhi interpreted this story as an allegory that teaches, among other lessons, an expansive ethic of reciprocity. Gandhi argued that the battle discussed in the Gita is a metaphorical struggle between the lower and higher selves within each person. Krishna's real lesson, according to Gandhi, was that people should kill their base lower selves, including their attachment to desires and to the results of their actions. Conquering the lower self leads to the realization that all faiths and individuals are manifestation of the One. Gandhi thus advised people to treat friends and foes alike as they themselves would like to be treated. Jesus had offered similar counsel, Gandhi said, as did all the great world religions.

SATYAGRAHA PEACEKEEPERS

It is difficult to overestimate how very important Gandhi's thoughts and campaigns were to most of the nonviolent movements that became increasingly common across the last half of the twentieth century. Martin Luther King Jr.'s description of Gandhi highlights the religious roots of nonviolence that has more recently come to be considered by many as primarily a secular practice. King wrote:

> Gandhi was probably the first person in history to lift the love ethic of Jesus above mere interaction between individuals to a powerful and effective social force on a large scale. Love, for Gandhi, was a potent instrument for social and collective transformation. It was in this Gandhian emphasis on love and nonviolence that I discovered the method for social reform that I had been seeking. (King 2000, 478)

Gandhi used the word ahimsa to name what King here translates into the Christian idiom as love. **Ahimsa** means "do no harm" in the Jain religious tradition that helped Gandhi choose this word (Cortright 2008). Gandhi expanded the concept of ahimsa beyond merely avoiding harm to include a commitment to taking positive actions to support the well-being of all people. This active caring is what King described as "a potent instrument for social and collective transformation."

Gandhi believed seeking the truth would enable people to determine which actions are harming and which are not. Nonetheless, Gandhi reasoned, humans can never be sure they have really found the truth so everyone should refrain from violence even when they think it is right. Gandhi explained, "man is not capable of knowing the absolute truth and, therefore, not competent to punish" (Gandhi 2012, 3). Even decisions based on what people strongly believe to be true may be wrong, so conscientious people must make sure all their actions do no harm.

Gandhi coined the word **satyagraha** to name the practice of seeking truth in order to guide right action. Gandhi believed that deep truths, *satya* in Sanskrit, form a bedrock reality that can neither be created nor destroyed. Satyagrahis were people who sought to guide their lives through a continuing search for these eternal truths. Satya truths would endure once an individual's acts and life was done. As peace historian David Cortright explains, satyagraha is thus defined by Gandhi as "an ethical search for truth through nonviolent action. It is a method of testing truth and transforming conflict through the power of love" (Cortright 2008, 216).

Satyagraha is often translated as soul force or truth force, phrases that combine the invisible with the visible, the ideal with the material world. Gandhi intended his new term to contrast with the then well-known ideas of passive resistance and passivism, as well as with the abstract practices of philosophical and theological truth-seeking. Satyagraha and satyagraha-inspired institutions were to be robust and transformative. So, for example, Gandhi called for the formation in India of a satyagraha **shanti sena** or nonviolent peace army. Gandhi envisioned tens of thousands of well-trained, unarmed volunteers patrolling troubled communities to keep the peace and to bring quarreling groups together to work out their differences.

The Pashtun Khudai Khidmatgar described earlier helped inspire Gandhi's call for a shanti sena. With its one-time high of 60,000 to 100,000 members, the Khudai Khidmatgar remain the largest single example of a peace army the world has yet produced. A first shanti sena in India was formed after Gandhi's death in the late 1950s. It grew to include 6,000 trained volunteers by the mid-1960s and had some successes both in easing tensions during the Chinese-Indian war of 1962 and in calming sectarian rioting in Calcutta in 1964 (Cortright 2008).

Gandhi's idea of peace armies acquired a new life in the 1980s with the creation of several organizations of what today are often called **unarmed civilian peacekeepers** (Wallis 2009). Peace Brigades International, founded in 1981, and Witness for Peace, founded in 1983, both draw on the shanti sena model but extend it by sending volunteers across borders into distant conflict zones. Yet another group, Christian Peacemaker Teams, created in 1984, is a joint initiative of the historic peace churches and so continues work in new forms that the Cathars, Anabaptists, and other Christian groups began centuries ago. Christian Peacemaker Teams also send trained volunteers across borders and so far have mounted deployments in Bosnia, Canada, Chechnya, Colombia, Gaza and the West Bank, Haiti, Iraq, and the United States (Cortright 2008). An even newer group, the Nonviolent Peaceforce, launched in 2002, similarly emphasizes foreign deployments. (Some of the work of the Nonviolent Peaceforce is discussed in Case 13-3 in Chapter 13.) These and other unarmed civilian peacekeepers draw inspiration from the idea of an active, well-trained, nonviolent army that Gandhi first described.

TABLE 9.1   SOME PROMINENT UNARMED CIVILIAN PEACEKEEPEERS

Name	Deployment	Duration	Origins	Estimated Peak Participants*
Khudai Khidmatgars	British India	1929–1955	Pashtun Muslim	60,000 to 100,000
Shanti Sena	India	1957–1970s	Hindu	6,000
Peace Brigades International	Multiple international sites	1981–cont.	Secular	350
Witness for Peace	Multiple international sites	1983–cont.	Faith-based	40
Christian Peacemaker Teams	Multiple international sites	1984–cont.	Brethren, Quakers, Mennonites	201
Metta (formerly known as Michigan) Peace Team	Multiple international sites	1993–cont.	Catholic	259
Nonviolent Peaceforce	Multiple international sites	2002–cont.	Secular	Unknown
International Solidarity Movement	Palestine	2001–cont.	Secular	Unknown
Muslim Peacemaker Teams	Iraq	2005–2009	Muslim	<100

Sources: Cortright 2008; Lynch 2004; Wallis 2009.

*In a single year.

PRINCIPLED AND PRAGMATIC NONVIOLENCE

Some unarmed civilian peacekeeping groups draw their members primarily from religious believers but many do not. This difference in peace workers creates a conceptual distinction between principled and strategic nonviolence.

Principled nonviolence embraces an expansive interpretation of the ethic of reciprocity. It is usually associated with religion, as it was with the early Christians, Ashoka, Sufism, the historic peace churches, Gandhi, and King. King was describing principled nonviolence when he wrote, "Nonviolence is the truest sense is not a strategy that one uses simply because it is expedient at the moment; nonviolence is ultimately a way of life that men live by because of the sheer morality of its claim" (1986, 111).

Pragmatic nonviolence, also known as expedient, practical, or strategic nonviolence, employs the ethic of reciprocity as a tactic rather than as a moral imperative. While principled nonviolence promotes nonviolence because its practitioners believe violence is wrong, pragmatic nonviolence avoids violence because violence does not seem likely to work. Nonviolence in pragmatic nonviolence is thus a means to an end. On the other hand, most proponents of principled nonviolence treat nonviolence as an end as well as a means.

Because it is commonly associated with religion, principled nonviolence tends to ask for a greater commitment from its practitioners than does strategic nonviolence. Principled adherents attempt to integrate nonviolence principles into their inner and interpersonal lives. They aspire to love their enemies and seek to be good as well as do good. Pragmatic nonviolence practitioners are less ambitious; they aim to change external social and governmental forms without necessarily altering themselves and their relations with others.

Principled nonviolence is ambitious for its opponents as well as for itself. It seeks to create what Gandhi called "heart unity" and what King later named "the loving community," a condition of mutual recognition that all people are worthy of respect and dignity. "Whenever you are confronted with an opponent," Gandhi advised, "conquer him with love" (Gandhi 2001, 383).

By contrast, pragmatic nonviolent campaigns have no reluctance to use tactics that will force their opponents into changed actions and policies without altering their hearts. Pragmatic nonviolence does not aim to transform antagonists into better people but to coerce them into different actions. Table 9.2, "Principled and Pragmatic Nonviolence," provides a summary of some differences between principled and pragmatic nonviolence.

In both Gandhi and King's campaigns, people in positions of leadership were generally guided by principled views while those in the rank-and-file commonly understood nonviolence more pragmatically. However, there has been a shift since the American civil rights movement of the 1960s. As nonviolent campaigns have become more frequent and widespread, leaders as well as their followers more often consider nonviolence to be a pragmatic rather than a moral choice. The singing revolution across Estonia, Lithuania, and Latvia as well as the Velvet Revolution in Czechoslovakia about the same time adopted many of Gandhi and King's methods while generally ignoring their religious beliefs. Pragmatic nonviolence also guided later campaigns in Serbia, Georgia (the Rose Revolution), the Ukraine (the Orange Revolution), Lebanon (the Cedar Revolution), as well as the nearly dozen uprisings in 2011 known as the Arab Awakening or Arab Spring.

TABLE 9.2 PRINCIPLED AND PRAGMATIC NONVIOLENCE

Principled Nonviolence	Pragmatic Nonviolence
Positive peace	Negative peace
Guiding question: What is right?	Guiding question: What will work?
Means-oriented—nonviolent action is an end in itself	Goal-oriented—nonviolent action is a means toward an end
Grounded in morality, in ethical conviction—a way of life	Grounded in politics, in strategizing—a temporary choice
Radical and idealistic	Practical and strategic
Revolutionary—seeks to transform people and societies	Reformist—seeks to change particular policies and situations
Rejects all physical violence	Rejects physical violence as too costly or impractical in specific circumstances
Uses persuasion, avoids coercion, to strengthen relationships of involved parties	Uses persuasion and coercion as needed to defeat enemies
Struggle to end violence is good in itself—expect suffering in this morally correct work	Struggle and suffering is acceptable if it achieves goals or ends an intolerable situation
Committed participants train their inner selves to guide their actions	Temporarily mobilized participants train their actions
"The form is merely an expression of the spirit within. We may succeed in seemingly altering the form, but the alteration will be a mere make-believe if the spirit within remains unalterable."—Mohandas Gandhi	"Nonviolence is what people do, not what they believe." —Gene Sharp "Nonviolence is an alternative weapons system." —Gene Sharp

Sources: Burrowes 1996; Gan 2009; Stiehm 1968; Weber 2003.

The differences between principled and pragmatic nonviolent approaches are substantial but should not be exaggerated. Proponents of pragmatic nonviolence are often as concerned with doing good, with morality, as are faith-based proponents of principled nonviolence. Pragmatic nonviolence movements are also often as eager as principled movements to promote broad social transformations and positive peace; however, they may be more willing to settle for what is immediately possible, to be pragmatic.

Likewise, while principled nonviolent leaders are guided by religious and spiritual principles, they are frequently pragmatists. Gandhi and King undertook careful fact-gathering and made rational calculations about what would work best, even as both invoked religious principles when explaining their decisions to the media and their followers. Both Gandhi and King, too, were willing to settle for reform, for less than deep personal and societal transformations, when their more ambitious goals could not be met.

The historical examples described earlier in this chapter suggest that faith-based traditions that embrace an expansive ethic of reciprocity may be necessary to sustain nonviolent beliefs during periods of violent repression. Principled nonviolence may also be indispensable for its commitment to look beyond immediate circumstances and insist humans should strive to create transformed, better worlds. The expansive perspective associated with principled nonviolence can enrich pragmatic nonviolence's typical focus on short-term goals.

MAKING CONNECTIONS

There is no simple answer to the question of whether religion is more often a cause of violence or of peace. When religious groups such as the Sufis or historic peace churches support an expansive ethic of reciprocity, they tend to decrease violence and increase peace. However, when religious groups seek to acquire or maintain power, they tend to apply the Golden Rule restrictively, privileging members over outsiders. In these situations, the group selves created by religious affiliations often encourage more violence than is found among nonbelievers (Ginges and Atran 2011).

Modernity has changed religions in many ways. Though people continue to rely on religious stories to interpret their lives, they now increasingly also rely on science. For example, it is important for moderns to know whether archeologists and historians have established that Ashoka was a real person. His newly established historicity gives Ashoka's use of an expansive ethic of reciprocity a greater significance than it possessed when Ashoka was thought to be a mere legend. Similarly, it is possible that research that demonstrates the effectiveness of the ethic of reciprocity in modern life may help convince people today to apply the Golden Rule when older, mythic stories no longer seem relevant.

Much research reviewed in earlier chapters suggests that ethic of reciprocity strategies succeed more often than coercion and violence. Of course, much more research is needed before precise rates of effectiveness can be determined. And the use of nonviolence rather than violence may not always provide a valid operational measure of the Golden Rule. Still, this type of empirical work is just a few decades old. With enough time and resources there could one day be sufficient knowledge to make reliable claims about how often and under what conditions the ethic of reciprocity succeeds.

Science can strengthen religions, as the Dalai Lama says it has done to his. "If science proves some belief of Buddhism wrong," the Dalai Lama argues, "then Buddhism will have to change. In my view, science and Buddhism share a search for the truth and for understanding reality. By learning from science about aspects of reality where its understanding may be more advanced, I believe that Buddhism enriches its own worldview" (Gyatso 2005). Careful, cross-cultural research into the effectiveness of the Golden Rule may provide religions with support for some of their oldest beliefs.

FOR REVIEW

1. Explore the changing role that the ethic of reciprocity has played in any one of the world's major religions.
2. Examine the main factors that tend to transform nonviolent religions into supporters of violence.
3. Explain how the contemporary historic peace churches resemble the early Christian communities of care.
4. Describe one instance when an entire government was guided by an expansive ethic of reciprocity.
5. Adopt Gandhi and King's principled nonviolent perspective to evaluate the weaknesses in pragmatic nonviolence.

THINKING CRITICALLY

1. What are the principle obstacles that keep the early Christians' nonviolent communities of care from becoming a guide for contemporary Christians?

2. What likely caused the Holy Roman Church to vigorously suppress the Cathars, Petr Chelčický and his supporters, and the Anabaptists?

3. Why are Martin Luther King Jr.'s civil rights campaigns honored and remembered so much more than his anti-poverty and antiwar campaigns?

4. How can the same Sunni Muslim Pashtun tribal code of Pashtunwali encourage both nonviolence among the Khudai Khidmatgar in the 1930s and violence among the Taliban in the 1990s?

5. What difference would it make if future scientists determined that the stories about Ashoka's peaceful empire were myths?

6. Does Gandhi's allegorical interpretation of the *Bhagavad Gita* seem a legitimate way to understand Arjuna's story?

7. Can the concept of satyagraha and its religious equivalents still influence people in secularized contemporary societies?

8. What are the principle strengths and weaknesses of using unarmed civilian peacekeepers?

9. Are campaigns built on principled nonviolence more likely to build peaceful societies than are campaigns built on pragmatic nonviolence?

RECOMMENDED RESOURCES

The 5 Powers. Directed by Stuart Jolley and Gregory Kennedy-Salemi. Mindcloud Entertainment, 2014. An innovative documentary that uses animation, live-action interviews, and archival photos, documents, and footage to explore the faith-based peace work of Thich Nhat Hanh, Sister Chan Khong, and Alfred Hassler during and after the Vietnam War.

Christian Peace Witness. A contemporary North American Christian nonviolent organization that promotes an expansive ethic of reciprocity. The group also maintains links to "partners," other like-minded faith-based groups, on its website at http://christianpeacewitness.org/partners

Citizen King. Directed by Orlando Bagwell and Noland Walker. PBS Home Video, 2004. A documentary that focuses on King's last five years, using personal recollections and eyewitness accounts of friends, movement associates, journalists, law enforcement officers, and historians. Available on YouTube.

Fellowship of Reconciliation. One of the world's oldest peace-promoting organizations maintains links to more than forty other faith-based peace organizations under the heading "faith-based groups." Website at http://forusa.org

Gandhi. Directed by Richard Attenborough. Sony Pictures, 1982. A much acclaimed, fictional but generally accurate depiction of Gandhi's life as a nonviolence campaigner. The film begins in South Africa in 1893 and traces the major events that followed until Gandhi's assassination in 1948.

Gensler, Harry. Golden Rule Chronology. A historical review of ideas about the golden rule hosted on the Charter for Compassion website. Available at http://charterforcompassion.org/node/3983

I Am. Directed by Tom Shadyac. Homemade Canvas Productions, 2010. A documentary that offers interviews with scientists, religious leaders, environmentalists, and philosophers who explore two central questions: "What's wrong with the world?" and "What can we do about it?". Includes appearances by Desmond Tutu, Noam Chomsky, Lynne McTaggart, David Suzuki, Howard Zinn, and many others.

Juergensmeyer, Mark, Margo Kitts, and Michael Jerryson, editors. *The Oxford Handbook of Religion and Violence* (New York: Oxford University Press, 2013). A collection of forty original articles exploring the connection between religion and violence. The volume includes examinations of both historical and contemporary events, as well as analytical chapters describing patterns, themes, and theories associated with the study of religion and violence.

Rogers, Mark M., Tom Bamat, and Julie Ideh, editors. *Pursuing Just Peace: An Overview and Case Studies for Faith-Based Peacebuilders* (Baltimore, MD: Catholic Relief Services, 2008). Provides case studies and essays on faith-based peacebuilding from experienced practitioners. Available online at http://www.crsprogramquality.org/storage/pubs/peacebuilding/pursuing_just_peace.pdf

Romero. Directed by John Duigan. Vision Video, 1989. A fictional but generally accurate account of the life of Archbishop Oscar Romero, a Catholic bishop who led his church to oppose the repressive government in El Salvador in the 1970s.

Wattles, Jeffrey. *The Golden Rule* (New York: Oxford University Press, 1996). Provides a historical overview and philosophical analysis of the diverse meanings of the ethic of reciprocity, with a special emphasis on the relevance of the Golden Rule to modern life.

Weapons of the Spirit. Directed by Pierre Sauvage. Chambon Foundation, 1987. Re-released in 2014, this documentary tells how the Protestant villagers of the area of Le Chambon in France organized to protect Jews and others threatened by the Nazis during World War II. Includes moving interviews with members of the community and with some of the people that they helped.

PART

3

DISCIPLINARY
PERSPECTIVES

The three chapters in Part Three describe recent discoveries about peace, violence, and war associated with research in the natural and social sciences. Chapter 10 details investigations in biology, ethology, and anthropology which conclude that humans are fundamentally cooperative animals. Chapter 11 reviews psychological studies into why some situations encourage violence and why both being harmed and harming others is usually traumatic for humans. Chapter 12 spotlights sociological research into group dynamics as it further details why situational factors sometimes promote violence and sometimes peace.

CHAPTER 10

BIOLOGICAL FOUNDATIONS

CHAPTER OVERVIEW

This chapter surveys the biological basis of human social behaviors, with a special emphasis on evaluating claims that humans are genetically predisposed to violence. The chapter begins with a review of the myth of humans as killer apes before describing three types of evidence that suggest people do not have inborn violent tendencies. One line of evidence comes from primatologists who have found that levels of violence in several nonhuman primate species can be altered through social learning. Peaceful conflict resolution strategies of yet another primate, the matriarchal bonobos, are also described and contrasted with the often misrepresented behavior of chimpanzees. A second type of evidence is provided by anthropologists who study hunter-gatherers. Most conclude that frequent intratribal violence and intertribal war are not human universals. Neuroscience provides a third line of evidence. The discoveries of neuroplasticity and of the importance of early childhood and later experiences in structuring human brains demonstrate the human potential for peacefulness. The chapter concludes with consideration of how human genetic tendencies may shape future postindustrial, knowledge-based societies.

Key terms discussed include: Myth of the killer ape; Seville Statement on Violence; primate cultures of peace; bonobo peacemaking; chimpanzee violence; Australian Aborigine cultures of peace; contemporary hunter-gatherers; Yanomamö violence; and the neuroplastic revolution.

> Ultimately, our genes whisper within us; they do not shout. More than anything, they have made us capable of war and the most terrible violence under certain conditions, and of peace under others.
>
> —DAVID BARASH (2012)

From a biological perspective, *Homo sapiens* are a spectacular success. We have spread all across the planet and our population is rising.

Humans emerged as a separate species about 200,000 years ago and then lived for many thousands of years as nomadic hunter-gatherers on the savannahs of eastern Africa. Slowly, tentatively, our ancestors undertook a long series of emigrations out into other, more challenging ecosystems. About 10,000 years ago, before the development of agriculture, *Homo sapiens'* total population reached about 7 million. At the dawn of the modern age in 1600, there were probably half a billion people. The industrial revolution and its aftermath then sparked a population explosion without precedent in any other primate species. There were a billion humans by 1800, 2 billion by 1900, and over 7 billion now.

The biological foundation for these two successes of the human species, diverse ecosystem adaptation and population growth, has been difficult to determine. For a long time, many thinkers believed that *Homo sapiens* came to dominate other primates and much of Earth because humans are "naturally" aggressive and violent. This, view, influenced by social Darwinists, Freud, and others, was often accompanied by the associated claim that violence and war are core elements of "human nature." Violence and war might ebb and flow, it was thought, but they could never be eliminated.

This pessimistic view has now been rebutted by evidence indicating that *Homo sapiens'* success as a species depends more on cooperating with other humans than on harming them. As a recent series of articles in *Science* detailed, the current scientific consensus is that humans are more hardwired for collaboration than for violence and war (e.g., Boehm 2012; de Waal 2012; Esteban et al. 2012). Three types of research have been especially persuasive in establishing this consensus. One type looks at the social behaviors of nonhuman primates with near-human genomes. Another type focuses on hunter-gatherers during the tens of thousands of years before the development of agriculture. A third type of evidence is based on recent discoveries about the postnatal plasticity of the human brain. These lines of evidence respectively from biology, anthropology, and neuroscience support a similar conclusion that it is mostly through nourishing our social interdependence that humans are able to survive. This research in aggregate builds a strong case for rejecting the claim that humans are hardwired or in any way biologically predisposed for violence.

Before examining the evidence, it is useful to review the popular view that contemporary science refutes.

MYTH OF THE KILLER APE

Many people still accept the **myth of the killer ape**, the belief that humans are predisposed to murder their own kind and fight frequent wars. This belief is not innocent as it may sometimes work as a self-fulfilling prophecy, fostering violence where otherwise there might be none.

Some support their pessimistic views about violence with appeals to the book of Genesis where God promises Adam and Eve that he will punish them and their descendants in perpetuity. Cain's murder of Abel follows soon after, establishing a pattern of violence some believe God alone can stop. Protestant theologian John Calvin's interpretations of the Bible have been especially influential in supporting pessimism about human life. Even newborn babies contain "the seed of sin" within them, Calvin maintained, and babies are thus like their parents "abominable to God" and so destined to live lives full of violence and other forms of suffering (Calvin, 1956).

In the twentieth century, Sigmund Freud yoked this Old Testament pessimism to biology, claiming that his new "science" of psychoanalysis was based on "the fact" that violence and aggression are fundamental "drives" shaping all human behavior. With little evidence, Freud convinced many that violence is an inevitable part of human life. Freud and others often relied on oversimplified interpretations of Charles Darwin's theory of evolution to buttress their views. Many mistakenly maintained that Darwin's memorable phrase "the survival of the fittest" implies that the strongest and most violent are the fittest to live. "Fit" in Darwin's writing, in fact, just as correctly characterizes people with the ability to cooperate, build coalitions, and promote positive peace (Midgley 2010).

World Wars I and II helped persuade yet more people that humans have little potential for lasting peace. Then, in the 1960s, just as Freud's views were finally being recognized to have little factual basis, a new rash of pseudoscientific theories emerged claiming to prove that *Homo sapiens* are innately violent (Ury 2000). For example, the prominent zoologist Konrad Lorenz argued in his *On Aggression* (1966) that intra-species fighting is inevitable. Lorenz was later awarded a Nobel Prize in Medicine, partly in recognition of this work. Several other widely-read books during this period misinterpreted archeological discoveries to support claims that humans had climbed out of their primordial trees to become "killer apes," as Robert Ardrey phrased it in *African Genesis* (1961). Ardrey's bloody vision, amplified by Desmond Morris's equally popular *Naked Ape* (1967), helped shape 1960s popular culture. Both *Planet of the Apes* (1968) and *2001: A Space Odyssey* (1968), films now considered Hollywood classics, associated *Homo sapiens'* discovery of tools with the origins of organized killing.

There was never much solid empirical evidence that humans are innately killer apes, even during times when this view was most widely held. Edward O. Wilson, a founder of sociobiology, was often misinterpreted to be in support of the pessimistic view even though he concluded his magisterial survey of lower and higher animals with the assertion, "There is no evidence that a widespread unitary aggressive instinct exists" (1978, 103). In 1987 a group of prominent behavioral scientists from twelve countries published the **Seville Statement on Violence** in a further attempt to refute the myth that human violence is biologically determined. This declaration presented five core findings based on the research available a quarter of a century ago that social behaviors are learned. The Seville Statement declared, "It is scientifically incorrect to say that war or any other violent behaviour is genetically programmed into our human nature."

Much more has been learned about the bases of human behavior since the 1980s. We look now in turn at recent findings from primatology, anthropology, and neuroscience. (See Table 10.2, "Three Types of Evidence Humans are not Killer Apes," for an overview of these findings.)

PRIMATE CULTURES OF PEACE

Genetically, humans are very similar to our closest primate cousins. Studying these primates thus provides one way to investigate to what degree cooperation and violence may be part of our biological heritage.

Much early animal research assumed that primate social behaviors are determined primarily by instincts and by inherited predispositions. More recent studies have shown, however, that learning shapes behavior even in primates that are much less intelligent than humans. **Primate cultures of peace** are capable of producing increased cooperation among primates. Much aggression that was once thought to be genetically determined in fact depends on long chains of mutual interaction between genetics and learning, not on biology alone.

One particularly revealing experiment was completed with rhesus macaques, primates that usually live in rigidly hierarchical groups (de Waal 2005). Dominant males commonly maintain their status through high rates of aggression. These males harm other males and seldom attempt reconciliation following their frequent fights. Males of a closely related primate species, the stump-tailed macaques, are by contrast usually much less hierarchical. Stump-tailed macaques generally produce both lower rates of aggression and higher rates of reconciliation than do their rhesus macaque cousins.

In the early 1990s, primatologist Frans de Waal put males of these two different species of macaques together in the same enclosure for five months. At first, the male rhesus macaques enacted their usual aggressive behaviors while the stump-tails continued their own more peaceful customs, generally ignoring the rhesus monkeys' frequent angry displays. Often the stump-tails "didn't even look up. For the rhesus monkeys, this must have been their first experience with dominant companions who felt no need to assert their position" (de Waal 2005, 147).

The stump-tails continued their relaxed behaviors day after day and within a few weeks the rhesus macaques became less aggressive as well. After five months, both species of macaques were behaving equally like stump-tails, participating in mutual grooming more often than in displays of aggression. Rates of reconciliation for both groups now also mirrored those that were once common only to the more peaceful stump-tails. Perhaps most surprisingly, the researchers discovered that after the two species of males were separated again, "the rhesus monkeys continued to show three times more friendly reunions and grooming after fights than was typical of their kind. Jokingly, we called them our 'new and improved' rhesus monkeys" (de Waal 2005, 148).

A long-term study of baboons living in a reserve in Kenya provides a second demonstration of how primates can learn to alter what were previously mistaken to be genetically determined aggressive behaviors (Sapolsky 2006). In the early 1980s, half of the males in one closely observed baboon troop died. The males who survived lived only because they had been too timid to join the other males when they fought their way through the territory of other troops to feed on garbage left out beside a tourist lodge. The aggressive males made the journey successfully for many months but then all contracted a fatal disease when the lodge threw out meat infected with bovine tuberculosis.

The ratio of female-to-male adults in the troop abruptly shifted from one-to-one to about two females to one male. The surviving males were now not only outnumbered but were also males who had shown themselves to be atypically low in aggression. The troop's routine behaviors radically changed. Male interactions were no longer centered on maintaining dominance hierarchies. And, in one particularly significant behavior, the males

TABLE 10.1   GENETIC SIMILARITIES OF FOUR PRIMATE SPECIES

Species	Approximate Evolutionary Divergence from Humans	Genetic Match with Humans
Baboon (*Papio*; five species)	35 million years ago	97 percent
Macaque (*Macaca*; about twenty species)	25 million years ago	97.5 percent
Bonobo (*Pan paniscus*)	5 to 7 million years ago	98.7 percent
Chimpanzee (*Pan troglodytes*)	5 to 7 million years ago	98.7 percent

Sources: Gibbons 2012; Prüfer et al. 2012; Reinberg 2007.

began rushing to each other's defense when outside predators threatened. Such mutual assistance among baboon males had never been observed before.

Baboon aggression aimed at females also decreased while intersexual grooming and sitting together increased. Blood samples showed that indicators of risks for stress-related diseases decreased for both males and females.

If primate behaviors were determined primarily by genes, the previous aggressive male-male and intersex behaviors should have returned once time passed and the troop's sex ratios returned to normal. In fact, however, the new, less aggressive cultural patterns persisted. Even after all the baboons died that had been members of the troop when tuberculosis struck, the new, more peaceful behaviors continued (de Waal 2005). Each new generation taught the next.

The transgenerational changes exhibited by these baboons suggest that much primate aggression is not dictated by biological predispositions. A learned culture of peace can increase rates of cooperative behaviors in baboons, rhesus and stump-tailed macaques, and humans.

OUR PEACEFUL BONOBO COUSINS

Macaques and baboons are part of a group of primates that started down a different evolutionary path from humans over 20 million years ago. We are thus likely to learn even more about the genetic predispositions of *Homo sapiens* from studying two more closely related hominoids, the bonobos and chimpanzees. As Table 10.1 indicates, humans share common ancestors with these two species from around 5 million years ago. This is a relatively short time since Earth's mammals have been evolving for about 200 million years.

Though both bonobos and chimpanzees share 98.7 percent of their genes with humans, bonobos may tell us the most about *Homo sapiens'* biological predispositions since they resemble humans more than chimpanzees in several important ways (Gibbons 2012). Bonobos have longer legs and shorter arms than chimpanzees, which enable standing bonobos to see their environment much as standing humans do. Human and bonobo females also have sex throughout their cycle, not just during a short period of fertility, as do chimpanzees and all other primates. And, finally, human and bonobo females alone among primates have their genitalia located at the front of their bodies. These three similarities to humans seem to have helped bonobos develop a social life that is both female-dominated and significantly less violent than that of chimpanzees.

Two standing bonobos.

Frans de Waal (1998) argues that "make love, not war" could be a bonobo slogan, with the proviso that it is females who make most decisions about both love and war. **Bonobo peacemaking** depends on female-dominance and on the prominent use of sex as a technique for conflict management. As de Waal (1998, 32) summarizes his and other scientists' observations, although the "chimpanzee resolves sexual issues with power; the bonobo resolves power issues with sex."

The behavioral differences between bonobos and chimpanzees are especially surprising since their genes are 99.6 percent alike. Both species live in troops with a few dozen members and survive by foraging across relatively similar central African ecosystems. However, unlike male chimpanzees, male bonobos do not form same-sex groups, battle for power and status, or conduct raids on other primate troops. A male bonobo's status instead depends on his mother's rank. Adult males even sometimes rely on their mothers for protection from other males. Male bonobos never assume leadership positions. When their mothers die, orphaned male bonobos join other orphaned males in having no rank at all.

BONOBOS ARE FROM VENUS

Rank within bonobo troops is important as it determines who feeds first when food is found. Bonobo males of all ranks must wait for the females to be sated or to invite them to share. Even when female and male bonobos occasionally hunt meat together, females continue to assume the right to feed first (de Waal 2005). Occasional forest encounters with neighboring bonobo troops raise tensions, as such encounters also do for chimpanzee troops. Bonobo males do not, however, initiate mock or real fights, though they do vocalize excitedly in what seem to be anticipatory warning gestures. Simultaneously, females from the two troops usually begin intermingling, sometimes touching, and sometimes sharing food. Soon the females are relaxed together and males from the two troops begin to intermix as well. Females may have sex with other females across troop boundaries. After that, inter-troop heterosexual coupling may occur. Occasionally the newly joined troops travel together for a few days before returning to their separate roaming across the jungle canopy and floor (NOVA 2006).

Bonobos have sex with multiple partners with a frequency and in a range of positions that de Waal describes as "fully promiscuous and bisexual" (2005, 99). After discovering an especially rich new food source, bonobos often undertake five to ten minutes of intense sexual activity with different partners in their troop before beginning to eat. The excitement over the food may be sparking group sexual arousal or, some speculate, the sexual activity may allow the bonobos to reaffirm their bonds and relieve tensions that might otherwise arise in dividing up a limited food supply.

Bonobos sometimes use sex as a form of greeting. They turn to sex, too, after being scared by a predator. Juvenile bonobos have been observed practicing oral sex and using their tongues in vigorous mouth to mouth kissing. Actual copulation for young and old bonobos, however, lasts on average only about fourteen seconds, significantly less than the average duration for their human cousins.

Researchers have not determined the cause of the relative peacefulness found in bonobos. It may come from their matriarchal social system, frequent use of sex to defuse tensions, lack of ecosystem competition from gorillas (Wrangham and Peterson 1997), or from other reasons yet to be discovered. What is suggested from these observations of bonobo peacefulness is that neither bonobos nor their close human cousins are hardwired for patriarchal, aggressive, or violent behaviors.

ARE CHIMPANZEES NATURALLY VIOLENT?

In some ways, as de Waal (2005) declares, bonobos are from Venus and chimpanzees from Mars. And, as mentioned, though they are anatomically more like bonobos, humans also share 98.7 percent of their genes with chimpanzees. It is thus important to also look at the social behaviors of chimpanzees as we try to discover the biological predispositions of our species.

Much more is known about chimpanzees than bonobos largely because there are many more surviving wild chimpanzees and they are much easier to locate in the wild. Chimpanzees are, in addition, particularly boisterous, extroverted, and active. They reward animal researchers—and zoo-goers—with their frequently frenetic behaviors. Widely publicized reports of **chimpanzee violence** a few decades ago also brought new attention to this species, creating misunderstandings reinforced by prior beliefs about the supposed existence of "killer apes."

English researcher Jane Goodall was especially successful in publicizing the social behaviors of chimpanzees. Goodall published pathbreaking reports for several decades, sharing discoveries that included ample evidence that chimpanzees make and use tools with a sophistication prior researchers had thought possible only for humans. Goodall's early reports also emphasized the remarkable affection and peacefulness that the chimpanzees routinely offered to her and to each other.

Then, in the 1980s, Goodall announced that she had discovered that her affectionate chimpanzees were also "capable of very violent behavior" (quoted in Sponsel 1996, 101). Goodall reported that chimpanzee males rely on aggression to guarantee female submission and to establish and maintain status positions among each other. Goodall and other observers testified that packs of male chimpanzees in the wild sometimes even undertake sustained, violent attacks on neighboring troops. These skirmishes could last for hours, even days, and produce serious injuries and deaths. The victorious male raiders occasionally even murdered infants in the defeated troops.

These observations were seized upon by many popular writers to support their belief that humans are like chimpanzees and that both species carry genes predisposing them to violence. Goodall herself concluded differently. She wrote that the existence of occasional chimpanzee violence had surprised her but that the subsequent storm of publicity had created a distorted picture. Chimpanzee violent behaviors are rare, Goodall explained; that was why it had taken decades of careful observation before any such behaviors were spotted. Goodall concluded that her years of recording interactions demonstrated that chimpanzee cooperative behaviors "are far more frequent than aggressive ones; mild threatening gestures are more common than vigorous ones; threats per se occur much more often than fights; and serious, wounding fights are very rare compared to brief, relatively mild ones" (quoted in Sponsel 1996, 101).

Later researchers have even suggested that the chimp attacks that received so much publicity in the 1980s may have been unintentionally sparked by the primatologists themselves. Their practice of giving chimpanzees bananas in order to bring the troop closer for observation disrupted previously established feeding patterns (Power 1991).

Since male chimpanzees do occasionally organize themselves into small killing "armies," some analysts continue to claim that their biology makes them "naturally" violent. Some go even further to argue that humans are naturally violent as well. However, those familiar with bonobos could make a parallel argument that biology makes matriarchy, bisexuality, and promiscuity "natural" for humans. In fact, however, such simplistic attempts to explain complex social behaviors overlook the importance of primate learning. Genes alone cannot explain why some humans behave more like chimpanzees and some more like bonobos. Culture and circumstances like those described in Chapters 11 and 12 guide people to become altruists or murderers, lovers or batterers, and sometimes all of these within a single lifetime.

VIOLENCE IN PREMODERN HUNTER-GATHERER SOCIETIES

Although bonobos and chimpanzees offer clues about human biology, neither is genetically exactly like the primates that evolved into *Homo sapiens* about 200,000 years ago. Research into the behaviors of these earliest humans provides a second way to explore the possible biological roots of both cooperative and violent social behaviors in contemporary *Homo sapiens*.

Unfortunately, very few human artifacts survive from over ten thousand years ago. Scientists have thus struggled to determine just how prehistoric *Homo sapiens* hunter-gatherers lived day to day. Recent work along the southern coast of South Africa by archeologist Curtis W. Marean and others suggest that the earliest erect bipedal primates possessed much more complex thought and tools than had long been assumed. Marean and his colleagues reported in *Nature* in 2007, for example, that humans as early as 164,000 years ago had created a lunar calendar, were following multi-step processes using fire to transform poor-quality rocks into high-quality knives, and had begun using the ocean as a food source (Marean et al. 2007).

It is well established that *Homo sapiens* relied almost exclusively on gathering, fishing, and hunting for nearly 200,000 years before they became agriculturalists. Complex forms of cooperation were essential during that time to enable humans to emigrate successfully into ecosystems where the prey were often far larger and stronger than those these early humans had previously known. In many places, early humans were as often the hunted as the hunter. Plant foods remained their largest food source, except in extremely cold climates. Life for most of the time of human existence was thus like being "on a camping trip that lasted an entire lifetime" (Cosmides and Tooby 1997, 12). *Homo sapiens'* genetic makeup today evolved primarily from whatever biological adaptations helped humans perfect their gathering, hunting, and camping techniques.

Inter-species violence was likely quite uncommon in these genetically formative years. Many specialists believe, as Jonathan Haas (1996, 1360) writes in the *Encyclopedia of Cultural Anthropology*, "Archeologically, there is negligible evidence for any kind of warfare anywhere in the world before about 10,000 years ago," that is, in the approximately 200,000 years before the development of agricultural settlements. The archive of prehistoric art supports this view. Tens of thousands of instances of preagricultural hunter-gatherer art have been found and catalogued. None depicts clear scenes either of within-group violence or of war (Guthrie 2005; see Case 10-1, "Hunter-Gatherer Controversies"). Art created in later agricultural cultures does frequently show such acts, so it seems likely that inter-species violence and, especially, group violence would have been portrayed in early nomadic hunter-gatherer representations if this violence had been common. The persistent absence of these depictions in preagricultural art suggests to many experts that inter-species violence and war was "rare or absent for most of human prehistory" (Sponsel 1996, 104).

The archaeological record of preagricultural human life is so meager, however, that there is no way to establish with scientific precision exactly how often preagricultural hunter-gatherers were violent within their own clans or in intertribal conflicts. Analysts are thus forced to turn to other lines of evidence, including the study of rates of violence among hunter-gatherers whose practices continued into modern times. Ethnographies of Australia's native hunting-gathering peoples have proven valuable, as have global anthropological databases of several hundred modern indigenous cultures. Each of these types of research are described below and each tends to support the view that, as anthropologist William Ury writes, "A more fitting name for our species than the 'killer ape' would be the 'cooperative ape'" (Ury 2000, 40).

CASE 10-1 HUNTER-GATHERER CONTROVERSIES

As mentioned, the surviving archeological record left by prehistoric hunter-gatherers is sparse. Some analysts, including Azar Gat (2006) and Richard Wrangham (Wrangham and Peterson 1997), interpret this small archive as indicating that prehistoric war was common.

Historian Lawrence H. Keeley's *War Before Civilization* (1996) also argues this view and Keeley's claim was later popularized by psychologist Steven Pinker in *The Blank Slate: The Modern Denial of Human Nature* (2002) and again, more recently, in Pinker's *The Better Angels of our Nature* (2011). Unfortunately, both Keeley and Pinker's analysis seem to be built on several mistakes (Ferguson 2013; Ryan and Jethá 2010). Keeley and Pinker include later-appearing, more violent-prone horticulturalists that also did some foraging as examples of nomadic hunter-gatherers. The violence of these agriculturalists is then projected back upon authentic nomads. Keeley and Pinker also use evidence from present-day hunter-gatherers who have had extensive contact with neighboring agriculturalists as examples of prehistoric hunter-gatherers. Finally, Keeley and Pinker make the further mistake of viewing all instances of violence as instances of war, even when there is no evidence this violence was not actually between individuals within the same family or group.

This last mistake conflating interpersonal violence with group violence has been especially frequent. The archeological record clearly does include numerous artifacts of prehistoric weapons, wounded human skeletons, and art representing the use of weapons when multiple people are present. While a minority of researchers claim this evidence points to the presence of frequent wars between hunter-gatherer bands (e.g., Tacon and Chippindale 1994), many other interpretations are possible. The wounds found in skeletons could as easily have resulted from accidents, ritual sacrifice, or homicides as from war. The scenes shown in the art could be of hunting parties rather than of wars. As anthropologist Douglas P. Fry (2007, 134–35) points out, "Westerners tend to take war for granted," so some researchers may be projecting their own "martial conceptions onto indigenous situations."

All researchers agree that the archeological record of early humans likely includes instances of murder, vengeance killings, and feuds. Organized aggression intent on killing members of other groups, however, seems more likely to have arisen only once humans stopped being nomadic. As anthropologist Sarah Blaffer Hrdy (2009, 28) explains, "As groups grow larger, less personalized, and more formally organized, they would also be prone to shift from occasional violent disagreements between individuals to the group-wide aggression that we mistakenly take for granted as representative of humankind's naturally warlike state." Few hunter-gatherers likely had cause to experience or participate in what we moderns call war.

THE ABORIGINES OF AUSTRALIA

Nomadic hunter-gatherers first arrived in Australia at least 40,000 years ago. Their descendants spread out to inhabit that entire, immense continent, developing over two hundred distinct languages and reaching a population estimated to be between 300,000 and 700,000 when the first European arrived in 1788.

Though they were then common in the rest of the world, settled agricultural societies were nowhere present across Australia. The Aborigines instead relied on diverse types of nomadic gathering and hunting to survive within dozens of very different ecosystems. At the beginning of the nineteenth century, Australia thus presented to European explorers an undisturbed example of how earlier hunter-gatherers may have lived for many tens of thousands of years. The evidence amassed by European settlers and later anthropologists indicates some Aboriginal hunter-gatherers formed tribes that sometimes harmed one another while others formed tribes that refrained from such harming.

Some researchers have generalized the evidence that there was occasional group violence among some Aboriginal bands into a sweeping claim that frequent violence is an evolutionary human universal (e.g., Gat 2006). Others look at the same evidence from pre-European Australia and claim that it demonstrates "warfare was truly the exception to the well-established peace system of the Australian Aborigines" (Fry 2007, 15). One need not choose sides in this debate to conclude that the wide variance in rates of group violence among Australian hunter-gatherers undermines any broad claim that humans possess inborn violent predispositions. It seems more likely that cultural, historical, and environmental circumstances created the differences that led some Australian bands to behave more like chimpanzees and others more like bonobos.

One especially large Australian region, the Great Western Desert, held tribes that exhibited little pre-contact violence of any type. Research into this region and into other examples of **Australian Aborigine cultures of peace** thus provide researchers with multiple examples of how hunter-gatherers in other places and times might have resolved their conflicts without intra-group violence or intergroup war. Many such effective peacemaking techniques are detailed in Ronald and Catherine Berndt's *The World of the First Australians* (1999). The Berndts describe traditions of formal meetings in which disputants aired their grievances, systems of compensation for damages, ritualistic duels and contests, venues for public venting of grievances, and ceremonies that reconciled antagonists.

These and other peaceful conflict resolution customs enabled these Aboriginal bands to interact peacefully with other bands even as they continually roamed across wide regions in search of food. Most bands in the Great Western Desert region encouraged shifting band residence so that individuals could leave and return as often as they wished to the band of their birth. Most bands, too, were connected through marriage, religion, dialect, and trade with those they most often encountered. Rather than fight over resources, most of the Great Western Desert bands shared food with other bands, in times of plenty as well as in times of want. As an ethnographer of one group of contemporary Western Desert Aborigines reports, the Mardu "have no word for either 'feud' or 'warfare' and there is no evidence of the kinds of longstanding inter-group animosity one associates with feuding. . . . Everyone is mindful also of how much their survival rests on mutual hospitality and unfettered access to their neighbors' natural resources in both lean and bountiful times" (Tonkinson 2004, 101).

The existence of Australian Aborigine cultures of peace provides additional evidence that harming others is not built into human genes.

CONTEMPORARY HUNTER-GATHERERS

Studies of **contemporary hunter-gatherers** offer yet another way to try to determine what were the likely rates of violence and war among our oldest human ancestors. The Standard Cross-Cultural Sample, a database of 186 contemporary cultures created by George Peter Murdock and Douglas R. White, contains information on twenty-one hunter-gatherer societies that were still living in mostly traditional ways at least until a few decades ago (White 1986). Most of these hunter-gatherer societies spent their time "doing and reciprocating good deeds" (Fry 2011, xx). As another ethnographer concludes, these contemporary hunter-gatherers typically formed egalitarian communities where all members were expected to be generous and cooperative (Boehm 1999). For example, most hunter-gatherer bands in this sample regularly shared meat, their most valued food source, with all their community members. The contemporary Guayaki of South America even have a rule that hunters cannot eat any of the meat they kill.

Hunter-gatherers described in the Standard Cross-Cultural Sample frequently allowed other bands access to their resources during times of need, as well as in times of abundance. Local groups typically did not claim any natural resources or territories as their own. Those bands that host or supply others one year are likely to be the recipients of similar gifts the next.

Reciprocal sharing across bands was further supported by flexible patterns of mate selection and by family residency patterns. Hunter-gatherers in this sample were not male-dominated like chimpanzees or like most humans living in agricultural societies. Tracing ancestry through both the mother and father, bilateral descent, was more common than male, patrilineal descent. Only three of the twenty-one hunter-gatherer bands in the database had male-based kin groups of any kind. Heterosexual couples also had much flexibility in their choice of residency. The female seldom moved permanently to the male's home band. Most couples resided in multiple places, sometimes with the male's kin, sometimes with the female's, and sometimes with neither. This flexible pattern further encouraged intertribal peace and the sharing of resources as most of these contemporary hunter-gatherers had relatives in many bands.

Violence does sometimes occur. One recent review of the Standard Cross-Cultural Sample found that earlier ethnographers had recorded 148 incidents of fatal aggression in twenty-one hunter-gatherer bands (Fry and Söderberg 2013). The killers and victims were members of the same group in almost 85 percent of these incidents and nearly two-thirds of the incidents resulted from family feuds, disputes over or between mates, accidents, or group-sanctioned executions. Only one of the twenty-one hunter-gatherer groups, the Tiwi of Australia, has ever been recorded as participating in group violence against other groups.

In general, then, contemporary hunter-gatherers offer further evidence that neither evolution nor genetics predispose humans for violence.

CHAGNON'S CLAIMS ABOUT YANOMAMÖ VIOLENCE

For decades anthropologist Napoleon Chagnon's claims about **Yanomamö violence** have been cited to support the view that people are biologically predisposed for violence. Chagnon's influence began in 1968 with the publication of *Yanomamö: The Fierce People*, one of the most widely read anthropological books ever written. Chagnon argued that the Amazon-dwelling Yanomamö offer researchers a glimpse into premodern hunter-gatherer behaviors and that Yanomamö customs reveal that *Homo sapiens* are naturally more violent than most anthropologists are willing to believe.

Chagnon has now championed for five decades what he calls a "Darwinian approach" to human behavior. Acceptance of this approach much increased after Chagnon reported in the prestigious American magazine *Science* in 1988 that he had evidence to show that Yanomamö men who kill are more successful than those who do not (Chagnon 1988). Aggression and murder are evolutionarily adaptive behaviors, Chagnon declared, therefore humans are biologically predisposed to be violent.

Chagnon's argument was built on an analysis of Yanomamö males who had killed "enemies" in raids outside the borders of their own village. Chagnon claimed that these men, known as *unokais*, "had, on the average, more than two-and-a-half times as many wives as non-*unokais* and over three times as many children" (Chagnon 1990, 95). Such a disproportionate rate of reproduction among violent men would tend to breed increasingly more violence-prone Yanomamö men. And, if the Yanomamö are "typical of the pre-state societies in which humans evolved," as evolutionary psychologist Steven Pinker (2002, 116) later claimed, then their "strategic use of violence would have been selected over evolutionary time."

Chagnon has repeatedly asserted that his approach is "more scientific" than the approaches used by those who disagree with him. This appeal to science has helped keep Chagnon's Yanomamö claims in the forefront of discussions about whether humans are predisposed for violence. Chagnon's prominence is unfortunate, however, since independent examinations of Chagnon's data refute most of his central conclusions. Crucially, for example, while Chagnon and Pinker argue that the Yanomamö are representative of hunter-gatherers, the Yanomamö are in fact not typical of preagricultural humans. The Yanomamö live primarily as sedentary slash-and-burn agriculturalists, using modern era steel tools to cultivate crops such as bananas and plantains that are indigenous to Asia and were relatively recently imported to South America . Yanomamö customs are very different from those found among forager hunter-gatherers during *Homo sapiens'* first 200,000 years (Baker 2013 "Fight Clubs"; Fry 2007).

Re-examinations of Chagnon's data also indicate that even these Yanomamö slash-and-burn agriculturalists cultivating imported crops do not provide evidence of an evolutionary predisposition toward violence. Chagnon's sample population included 380 men age twenty and over. Sixty-four percent of these had never participated in any killings, suggesting there was no population-wide predisposition among them encouraging lethal violence (Fry 2007). Well over half of the adult males and none of the females demonstrated a killing tendency.

Chagnon's research has even more weaknesses. As R. Brian Ferguson pointed out in the *American Ethnologist* only a year after Chagnon published his own findings, Chagnon's case for the evolutionary power of violence depends on his assertion that Yanomamö killers had more wives and more children than non-killers who were *the same age*. But Chagnon's own data reveal that he did not control for age. His killer *unokais* are on average over ten years older than his non-killers. They are also more likely to be higher-ranking, to be headmen, independently of whether or not they have killed. In other words, Chagnon's Yanomamö data make clear only that older and higher ranking men tend to have more children and wives than their younger and lower ranking fellow tribesmen (Ferguson 1989). This finding does not warrant the claim that lethal male violence is a positive adaptation favored by human evolution.

TABLE 10.2 THREE TYPES OF EVIDENCE HUMANS ARE NOT KILLER APES

Evidence Type/Subject	Findings	Level of Support for No Violent Biological Predisposition
Biology		
Macaques	Capable of learning more peaceful behaviors	Strong
Baboons	Capable of learning more peaceful behaviors	Strong
Bonobos	Little in situ violence	Very strong
Chimpanzees	Frequency of violence exaggerated	Suggestive
Anthropology		
Prehistorical hunter-gatherers	Definitive evidence lacking	Suggestive
Australian Aborigines	Tribes and regions with little or no intertribal violence	Strong
Contemporary hunter-gatherers	Most studied groups commit little violence	Very strong
Yanomamö violence	Misinterpreted data	In dispute
Neuroscience		
Newborn brain structures	Walking and hand manipulations must be learned	Strong
Adult brain structures	Both peaceful and violent behaviors require extensive group- and language-based learning	Very strong

Though Chagnon's attention-grabbing assertions help keep his writing popular among researchers and the public alike, the Yanomamö do not in fact provide support for the view that humans are biologically predisposed for violence.

THE NEUROPLASTIC REVOLUTION

Recent discoveries in brain science provide yet a third distinct type of evidence supporting the conclusion that modern humans do not possess inborn predispositions encouraging violence.

People still speak of the brain being "hardwired" but new studies within what has been called the **neuroplastic revolution** show the brain contains few structures or "wires" at birth (Begley 2007). Postnatal experiences, not in-utero development, create almost all the neurological patterns found in adult primate brains. These neural patterns guiding adult social behaviors are not expressions of inherited genes (Doidge 2007). Humans do not come into the world wired to undertake any complex social acts whatsoever and certainly not to act violently with others in groups or to start wars.

The human brain at birth is like a computer hard drive that possesses an operating system but has few installed applications or programs. The newborn brain carries the potential for

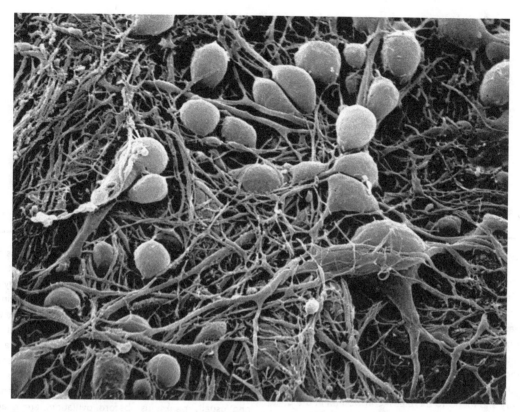

Human neuron cells and connecting synapses pictured through an electron microscope.

multiple installations but requires repeated, specific, complex post-birth experiences to acquire them. These postnatal learning experiences largely determine whether a brain will function like an Aztec or an Italian, and whether it will pursue peacemaking or killing.

Life's events form new synapses, patterns connecting—"wiring"—neurons into complex, interlinked structures. The density of neurons doubles in the first three months, signaling the importance of very early postnatal experiences. Adults end up with from 20 billion to 50 billion neurons and each of these neurons forms from two thousand to five thousand connections (synapses) with other neurons. The number of possible connections thus "exceeds the number of elementary particles in the universe" (Ramachandran 2012). And almost all of these connections result from learning, not from prenatal structures, genetics, or instincts.

Human brains are hardwired for surprisingly few behaviors. Infants instinctively search out nipples and suck when their lips touch nipple-like objects. Before age one, an instinct to swim may also appear, though it later disappears. Humans are also born with some simple reflexes. These include reactions like the startle reflex which, however, is triggered in the spinal cord and not the brain. No complex instinctual human behaviors have been found, nothing that hints at any hardwiring of neurons into synapses that could predispose people for aggression, violence, or peace.

Speech is yet another distinguishing behavior of *Homo sapiens* that our neurons are not at birth patterned to perform. An immense, new synaptic communication system must be forged in the postnatal brain before children begin to vocalize differently than our primate cousins. The neuron structures that distinguish speaking from nonspeaking human brains require a long series of repetitions of word-sounds to take place within a complex social network that steadily repeats these word-sounds. No complex social network of repetitions, no language.

Language acquisition and the synapses it creates are, in turn, prerequisites for most neuron activities that we associate with being human. Loving others, for example, as well as harming them, depends upon the existence of language processing brains. Little contemporary human cooperation or violence would be possible without the thinking, planning, and emotion that language enables. And language development is an outgrowth of

---

CASE 10-2   THE PHYSIOLOGY OF PEACE

Zoologists classify humans as an "obligatorily gregarious species," meaning that people seldom thrive by themselves. Physiologists have discovered multiple ways human bodies experience positive rewards when they participate in cooperative social relationships. Oxytocin, a hormone secreted by the pituitary gland, is especially important in promoting human social behaviors.

Oxytocin was initially isolated early in the twentieth century and found to be released in women in the onset of labor and in beginning the production of maternal milk. (Synthetic oxytocin, Pitocin and Syntocinon, are now often used to induce labor.) Scientists later discovered that males as well as females produce oxytocin and that surges in the body's supply of oxytocin increase rates of trust and cooperation in both men and women.

Paul J. Zak (2012) describes this process as an "oxytocin virtuous cycle," a positive feedback loop that encourages humans to feel good by doing good. Surges in oxytocin increase people's sensitivity to the needs of others. People then tend to become kinder, more generous, and more trusting; this leads both to decreases in fear and to increases in a willingness to cooperate. Further helping behaviors encourage further surges of oxytocin and additional caring behaviors.

Many studies have confirmed that levels of oxytocin rise in the human blood system when a person acts kindly toward another. The better a person knows or likes the recipient of their care or generosity, the more oxytocin they produce. Multiple receptors in the brain, heart, and vagus nerve spread oxytocin's positive reinforcements throughout the body.

The oxytocin virtuous cycle rewards people as they work and play together, and even as they talk, touch, text, and plan future social activities. However, many oxytocin repressors can block the production of oxytocin and so decrease rates of trust, cooperation, and levels of well-being. Potent oxytocin blockers include: anger, autism, cardiovascular stress, hostility, psychological trauma, ethnic, linguistic, or religious isolation, and testosterone.

Testosterone is an especially potent repressor of oxytocin. For example, female production of testosterone usually peaks just before ovulation, encouraging women to become less caring, empathetic, and cooperative and so, perhaps, providing women with the evolutionary advantage of tending to choose fathers for their children whom they trust. Males on average produce almost twenty times more testosterone than females, a variance that may help account for the differences in levels of violence and of caring behaviors found in females and males in many societies. Young males commonly produce twice as much testosterone as older males, a difference that is likely associated with the greater frequency of violence committed by younger males.

Human physiological processes are extremely complex and no social or violent behavior can be traced to the release of any single hormone or chemical. Nonetheless, people with high levels of oxytocin have repeatedly been shown to possess healthier immune systems and to live longer, happier lives. Producing oxytocin is evolutionarily adaptive and a major force in the physiology of peace.

Source: Zak 2012.

social experiences much more than of biology. As Piero P. Giogi (2009, 112) explains, "we are not born as human; we [learn to] become human after birth." (See Case 10-2, "The Physiology of Peace.")

The neuroplastic revolution is leading to a scientific understanding of the brain at a level of specificity undreamed of but a few decades ago. Much remains to be discovered but it is already established that humans are born with brains capable of acquiring neuron structures able to perform an almost inconceivably wide range of acts. New synaptic structures may form to enable people to act like bonobos or chimpanzees, or like Gandhi or Pol Pot. The possibilities are close to infinite since genes predetermine no specific social behaviors.

HUMAN NATURE IN THE INFORMATION AGE

Our genetic makeup did not change but humans did become more violent once they developed the patriarchal and hierarchical societies associated with large-scale agriculture (McNeill and McNeill 2003; Ury 2000). And now the five thousand to eight thousand year dominance of agricultural societies seems to be ending. For the first time in history, more people live in cities than in the country. Ever fewer people even in rural areas are directly involved in producing food. The shift in the United States is typical of similar shifts throughout the developed world. In 1790, about 90 percent of working adults in North America labored on farms. Two hundred years later the percentage had shrunk thirty-fold, to 3 percent (McNeill and McNeill 2003).

Globalization and information technologies may be encouraging a new type of human organization, one that diverse thinkers such as Manuel Castells (1996), Anthony Giddens (1990), and William Ury (2000) believe will generate societies as different from traditional agriculturally-based societies as these were from earlier nomadic hunter-gatherer bands. The current strengthening of the global peace network along with the increasing empowerment of women described in Chapter 5 may be among some of the most easily recognizable signs of an emerging radical social transformation.

Human genetics will not dictate whether future rates of violence in these new types of societies will most mirror those of hunter-gatherers or of agriculturalists. Human culture and learning will determine that.

MAKING CONNECTIONS

Nature and nurture, genes and learned behaviors, are not independent causes. As biologist Evelyn Fox Keller (2010, 7) explains, "Trying to determine how much of a trait is produced by nature and how much by nurture, or how much by genes and how much by environment, is as useless as asking whether the drumming we hear in the distance is made by the percussionist or his instrument." Biological predispositions provide the physical instrument upon which social learning "drums" human societies and relationships. Genetic predispositions cannot by themselves cause either peace or violence.

The following two chapters examine much of what is known about the cultural and social forces that do cause peace and violence. Chapter 11 describes findings from psychology that focus on micro, individual, and interpersonal causes, while Chapter 12 explores sociological, meso-level discoveries about group and situational drivers of peace and violence.

FOR REVIEW

1. Analyze the evidence that nonhuman primate behaviors are dependent on cultural learning.
2. Explain why bonobos are of special interest to researchers interested in peace and conflict.
3. Summarize the relevance of premodern hunter-gatherer bands for research into the biological bases of violence and war.
4. Describe the major weaknesses in Chagnon's claims about the evolutionary roots of Yanomamö violence.
5. Review the key implications for peace studies of recent discoveries associated with the neuroplastic revolution.

THINKING CRITICALLY

1. Why does the myth of humans as killer apes, as primates predisposed for violence, remain so widely believed?
2. What cautions should be kept in mind when using studies of nonhuman primates to draw conclusions about human behaviors?
3. Is matriarchy likely the principle reason bonobos live so peacefully?
4. Do modern humans seem to behave more like bonobos or chimpanzees?
5. Why are the patterns of violence found in hunter-gatherer societies different from the patterns found in agricultural societies?
6. What has made controversies about Yanomamö violence continue now for almost fifty years?
7. Is it mostly disconcerting—or liberating—to believe as Piero P. Giogi maintains that humans only become human after birth?
8. Which one of the types of evidence, respectively from biology, anthropology, and neuroscience, most strongly supports the claim that humans are not predisposed for violence? Which type of evidence provides the weakest support?
9. What signs are visible today to suggest that humans may be creating new societies that will become as different from agricultural societies as agricultural societies are from hunter-gatherer bands?

RECOMMENDED RESOURCES

de Waal, Frans. *The Bonobo and the Atheist: In Search of Humanism among the Primates* (New York: Norton, 2013). Draws on the most recent research to argue that there are biological sources for empathetic, cooperative, caring behaviors among all primates, including humans.

———. *Our Inner Ape* (New York: Riverhead, 2005). Summarizes primate research with a special focus on bonobos and chimpanzees.

Fine, Cordelia. *Delusions of Gender: How Our Minds, Society, and Neurosexism Create Difference* (New York: W. W. Norton, 2010). A methodical and effective review of claims that there are hardwired, biological differences between the sexes.

Fry, Douglas P. *Beyond War: The Human Potential for Peace* (New York: Oxford University Press, 2007). An anthropologist's survey of research into the causes and frequency of violence and war among nonhuman primates and human hunter-gatherers. Examines and debunks claims that violence among hunter-gatherers proves that humans are innately predisposed to wage war.

Keller, Evelyn Fox. *The Mirage of Space between Nature and Nurture* (Durham, NC: Duke University Press, 2010). A short, clearly written book that explains the connections between biological and social causes of gendered and other human behaviors.

Peaceful Societies. Provides information about twenty-five contemporary societies that successfully promote harmony, gentleness, and kindness while simultaneously devaluing aggressiveness and violence. Website at http://www.peacefulsocieties.org

Sapolsky, Robert M. "A Natural History of Peace." *Harper's* (April 2006): 15–22. A concise summary of the relevance of bonobo and chimpanzee studies for explanations of human violence and peace.

CHAPTER 11

PEACE PSYCHOLOGY

CHAPTER OVERVIEW

This chapter describes what psychologists have learned about the causes of violence. It begins with evidence that the need to belong is a fundamental human motivation. Next, after explaining the concept of the banality of evil, the chapter reviews Milgram's obedience experiment and the power of authoritarian situations. The importance of social roles and groups are then examined, followed by an analysis of Zimbardo's prison experiment. Next comes an analysis of groupthink in political decision-making, then individualistic explanations of violence are contrasted with situational explanations. The psychological effects of violence on both its perpetrators and victims are described, followed by a discussion of why research into these areas is often discouraged. Trends and causes of suicide are considered before the chapter reviews discoveries in positive psychology that establish the value of social relationships free from violence.

Key terms discussed include: Need to belong; banality of evil; Milgram's obedience experiment; group self; Zimbardo's prison experiment; deindividuation; groupthink; individualistic explanations of violence; antisocial personality disorder; post-traumatic stress disorder (PTSD); perpetrator-induced traumatic stress (PITS); social determinants of suicide; positive psychology; and benefits of social relationships.

> If you put good apples into a bad situation, you'll get bad apples.
>
> —PHILIP ZIMBARDO (quoted in Dreifus 2007)

William James launched the modern study of the psychology peace and violence in 1910 with the publication of his famous essay, "The Moral Equivalent of War." James argued that humans are not fallen angels, condemned to act sinfully, as most of his contemporaries believed. James said war and violence more often grow out of positive desires, from people's well-meaning attempts to do what they think is best for themselves and their communities.

Creating a more peaceful world does not require changing people or overcoming our animal nature, James concluded. Rather what is needed is more situations that offer people opportunities to help their own group without harming non-group members.

Contemporary behavioral science has reached a consensus that James was largely correct. As Chapter 10 makes clear, the biological evidence indicates that humans are not driven to harm others or to go to war because of inborn dispositions or traits. When violence erupts, it is usually because learning and circumstances—not genes, nature, or biology—have guided people toward ruin rather than resolution. While humans do possess the mental and physical ability to harm and kill, they also possess the ability to cooperate and sacrifice—even to yield their lives—to benefit others. As ample evidence in this chapter suggests, both violence and peacemaking are likely rooted in the same human need to belong.

THE NEED TO BELONG

Humans are profoundly social animals, what zoologists call an obligatorily gregarious species. Our young are entirely dependent on the care of other humans for the first five and more years of their lives. People's dependence on others remains strong even through adulthood as it is only through cooperating with others that humans are able to establish and maintain the friendships, families, occupations, groups, institutions, cultures, and societies that keep them alive.

Human evolution favored people who have the greatest ability to form and maintain robust connections with others. People with poor social skills have tended not to pass on their genes to later generations. As a result, much research suggests that the **need to belong is a fundamental modern human motivation.** This need to establish and maintain social relationships may be the underlying force that creates such other basic psychological needs as a need for achievement, affiliation, approval, intimacy, and power (Baumeister and Leary 1995; Fiske 2004; Yuval-Davis 2011).

Diverse types of evidence point to the strength and pervasiveness of the need to belong. Functional magnetic resonance imaging shows that the areas of the brain activated when people cooperate with one another are the same as those that respond to such stimuli as desserts, cocaine, and beautiful faces (Shermer 2005). When people experience positive social connections their brains release vasopressin and oxytocin, producing feelings of pleasure. Oxytocin seems to be especially important in guiding "the tend and befriend response," a behavior that humans exhibit much more frequently than its better known opposite, "the fight or flight response" (DeAngelis 2008). Tending and befriending encourages further release of oxytocin, and so yet more social bonding and even more release, until the hypothalamus is depleted. (See Case 10-2, "The Physiology of Peace," in Chapter 10.)

The need to belong manifests at every stage of the human life span. Infants show signs of bonding with the human voices they hear in utero, even before their need for familiar caretakers becomes so clearly evident in their early months. Toddlers and preschoolers spend much of their days practicing social relationships with stuffed animals, dolls, plastic action figures, and imaginary friends. Older children also, of course, demonstrate clear needs to connect to their caretakers, a need that shifts as they age until adolescents increasingly direct their need for belonging to peers and romantic partners. Adults continue that pursuit of romantic partners as they also tend to expand their group memberships into sometimes extraordinarily broad networks. Older adults are inclined to focus more on maintaining already established social bonds while focusing less than younger adults on creating new relationship bonds.

The ubiquity and strength of the need to belong can cause ordinary people to undertake heroic acts to create and maintain relationships. This same need can also persuade some people to complete violent, suicidal, and even genocidal acts, when they are placed in situations where doing so seems likely to help them satisfy their desire to belong.

THE BANALITY OF EVIL

The need to belong got new attention from social scientists after the horrors of World War II left many trying to understand how "civilized people" could commit such atrocities.

Some analysts suggested that flawed "national characters" were at fault, that, for example, the German people were "by nature" authoritarian and violent. However, as the jingoistic passions of war faded, it became increasingly difficult to maintain that the basic psychological makeup of Germans, Italians, or the Japanese was much different from the English, French, North Americans, and Russians who had opposed them.

Hannah Arendt helped inaugurate a new approach to understanding the social situational basis of violence in her 1963 book, *Eichmann in Jerusalem* (Arendt 2006). Arendt looked at the people who had maintained the Nazi death camps and concluded that most were normal people, doing their jobs. Their actions exhibited what Arendt called the **banality of evil**. The Holocaust had not been carried out by crazy or sadistic madmen, she concluded, but by ordinary people working in what was for them ordinary circumstances. Most were simply following procedures prescribed by their bosses, as employees do throughout the modern world. It was not that the perpetrators of the Nazi violence did not care about others but rather that they did in fact care very much about their families, friends, and communities.

Arendt's prescription for change was much like what William James had proposed: Decreasing violence would require altering human circumstances and situations. The need to belong and other basic human psychological characteristics need not—and probably could not—be changed.

MILGRAM'S OBEDIENCE EXPERIMENT

Arendt's then-radical perspective soon received strong experimental support from psychologist Stanley Milgram. **Milgram's obedience experiment** demonstrated that most ordinary people are willing to harm others when told to do so by an authority figure. Milgram (1974) told volunteers who answered a newspaper ad that they were participating in an important scientific study to determine how punishment affects learning. Volunteers were to work in pairs in a learning lab on the Yale University campus. One volunteer was to be the learner, required to memorize a set of word pairs. The other volunteer would act as the teacher, offering positive verbal responses to correct answers and administering an electric shock for wrong answers. The roles of learner or teacher appeared to the volunteers to be randomly assigned.

The researcher led both volunteers into a room. Those designated to be learner-volunteers were strapped into a chair with an electrode attached to one wrist. The teacher-volunteer was then taken into an adjoining room and shown a control panel with thirty-three switches, starting at a low of 15 volts and rising in 15-volt increments to 450 volts. This last, highest dose was marked with an ominous "XXX." An intercom connected the two rooms.

volt shockage   The researcher gave the teacher-volunteer a sample shock of 45 volts, to provide a sense of the pain created by a mild shock. The experiment began and the learner in the other room at first answered correctly. Gradually, however, his answers were more often wrong and the researcher advised the teacher-volunteer to keep increasing the voltage.

As the voltage rose so did the volume and intensity of complaints coming over the intercom. This complaining learner-volunteer was, in fact, a professional actor and not a volunteer at all, as the actual teacher-volunteer had been led to believe. With even larger doses, this learner-actor screamed and asked to be released from the experiment. Teacher-volunteers hesitated to increase the voltage further but the researcher instructed them to continue, reminding the teacher-volunteers that they had agreed to cooperate with science in completing this experiment. Once the teacher-volunteer pressed the 300-volt switch, the learner-actor ceased responding. The researcher reminded teacher-volunteers that a non-response counted as an incorrect answer, a procedure agreed to by the volunteers before the experiment began. Further, higher voltage shocks were thus required.

Silence followed each subsequent question, suggesting the volunteer was too injured to make further noises. Teacher-volunteers grew increasingly agitated and hesitant but the researcher exhorted them to follow the rules, to treat each absence of an answer as an incorrect answer. A further boost in voltage was required.

And so it went until teacher-volunteers pulled the switch to shock the long-silent actor-volunteer with a dose at the "XXX" level, seeming to suggest a possibly lethal shock. Two of every three teacher-volunteers administered shocks at the maximum 450-volt level. Even most of the "good" third who refused to administer this maximum dose stopped participating only after they had gone far enough to produce repeated protests and screams from the learner-actor.

Researchers have since completed many variations of Milgram's experiment, making it among the most replicated of all social science designs. Similar results recur across ages, gender, social class, and even across nine African, Asian, and European countries (Zimbardo 2007). These results indicate that most ordinary people everywhere will torture and risk killing innocent others when they are placed in situations where an authority directs them to do so. Situations can cause extreme violence, this experiment suggests, regardless of the different personality traits, social dispositions, religious memberships, or socioeconomic backgrounds people bring to these situations.

THE POWER OF GROUP SELVES

Subjects in Milgram's experiment had temporarily been assigned the role of teacher and so were acting in ways they thought appropriate for people in a Yale-based scientific experiment. Though they knew their work in the experiment would only last a short time, their brief embrace of the scientist-teacher role nonetheless produced extraordinary behavioral changes. The experiment suggests that longer lasting social roles likely produce even more profound effects.

People are assigned different roles within the various social groups to which they belong. Some of these group involvements begin at birth, for example, with memberships in gender, family, ethnic, religious, and national groups. Other group involvements are self-chosen later as people attempt to meet their needs to belong. So, for example, older children and adults embrace new roles through their participation in various political, professional, school, and sports groups. When adults form families they create still other new groups and roles that may or may not overlap with the family group into which they were born.

Group memberships provide people with a sense of a **group self** that shapes each person's self-understanding and their sense of what is real and right in the external world (Ellemers 2012). Studies show that the perceptions, goals, and judgments that come from groups are frequently more influential on people than the ideas associated with their own private, non-group selves. In this, as in so much else, the need to belong dominates more personal needs. Group self ideas do not to most individuals even seem to be coming from the group. Instead, brain studies using functional magnetic resonance imaging show that group perceptions, goals, and judgments directly shape their group members' personal experiences and emotions (Ellemers 2012). What the group believes and perceives overwhelmingly determines what its members believe and perceive.

People tend to follow the moral judgments of their own groups and to judge the morality of other groups to be inferior. The other groups' supposed inferiority can help make them into acceptable targets for exclusion and even violence, not only because the outgroup is thought to be worth less but also because the very existence of their alternative moral judgments can be seen as a rebuke and threat. The need to belong and the group selves that result can lead people to act altruistically and heroically, aggressively and violently, or all of these simultaneously, as when a soldier attacks an enemy position to save the lives of his platoon or a suicide terrorist detonates a bomb in a location he or she believes will help their group reach its goals.

Failing to acquire group membership and its accompanying group self can also create violence. People rejected by a group who then cannot meet their need to belong may respond by attacking the excluding group. Some political violence and school shootings have been explained this way, as acts that reflect the perpetrator's attempt to punish an excluding group (Leary et al. 2003).

ZIMBARDO'S PRISON EXPERIMENT

Many studies have explored how group selves shape individual actions. One especially important study, Philip **Zimbardo's prison experiment**, demonstrated that experimental subjects arbitrarily assigned to a violent social role will act violently even in the absence of an authority figure issuing orders (Zimbardo 2007).

Zimbardo advertised for volunteers and then used a battery of tests to select the twenty-four who seemed the most average on every trait. Half were randomly assigned to play the role of prisoner and half the role of prison guard. All were promised pay equivalent to about $100 a day in 2014 dollars.

Nine prisoner-volunteers were "arrested" at their homes, read their legal rights, and then taken by actual police officers to a realistic looking jail in the basement of the psychology building at Stanford University. Each prisoner was made to wear an ill-fitting uniform and stocking cap. They were addressed not by their names but according to numbers sewn on their uniforms. A chain around their ankles reminded them of their roles as prisoners. Three prisoners shared one windowless cell, with no clocks or windows to help keep track of time.

Three guard-volunteers stood duty on eight-hour shifts. The guards wore military-style khaki uniforms and dark glasses, making eye contact impossible. The guards carried clubs, whistles, handcuffs, and keys to the cells. They were given no explicit instructions about their duties, except that they were to "maintain order in the prison" without using physical violence.

Within two days, the prisoner-volunteers became withdrawn, depressed, and increasingly passive. Those playing at being guards also simultaneously changed their behaviors to fit their own new social roles. All the guards grew increasingly aggressive. At least once, and generally with greater frequency, each guard used his power to abuse and harass prisoners. Some guards woke prisoners late at night to force them to complete arbitrary chores. Prisoner rights to use the toilet, eat, wear glasses, and complete other mundane chores were redefined as privileges to be earned by pleasing the guards. The guards grew indifferent to the cameras they knew were recording them. They relished their power and competed with one another to discover new ways to humiliate the prisoners in their charge.

The experiment had been scheduled to last two weeks but was terminated on day six. Several of the prisoners had already been sent home after developing symptoms of an acute stress disorder, including crying, yelling, and disorganized thinking. One prisoner-volunteer developed a rash over his entire body. Still, only one prisoner tried to quit, though each prisoner and guard knew they were "only" volunteers.

Psychologists no longer conduct experiments like Milgram's and Zimbardo's that place volunteers in situations where their actions may harm themselves or others. Such research is now considered unethical. More recent evidence has been found, however, to support the conclusion that the need to belong promotes group selves which can generate both peaceful and violent behaviors.

DEINDIVIDUALIZATION AND GROUPTHINK

People in groups tend to agree to do things that they would reject were they making decisions by themselves. People usually strive to maintain their good standing as group members even when it means they must alter the judgments they would make were they not in the presence of other group members.

The possibility of violence increases the more individuals identify with a group. Psychologists call this **deindividuation**, the loss of a sense of separateness that develops in individuals as they begin to trust the group's judgment more than their own. People in groups tend to feel invisible and anonymous; they tend to replace their sense of an individual self with that of a group self. If the group declares that dangerous action, even violence or suicide, is necessary, deindividuated members commonly act as directed.

Deindividuation effects operate at the micro, interpersonal level but can also have monumental macro level effects. For example, most modern wars and policymaking are managed by groups safely stationed far from possible dangers. As members of these groups embrace a common group self, they tend to ignore their own private thinking so as to "go along" and remain members in good standing.

Social psychologists use the concept **groupthink** to describe the tendency of groups to suppress dissent, ignore counterevidence, and de-emphasize independent analyses. In his pioneering book, *Victims of Groupthink: A Psychological Study of Foreign-Policy Decisions and Fiascoes*, Irving I. Janis (1972; see also 2nd edition published in 1982) examined the groups responsible for the lack of American preparation for the attack on Pearl Harbor, the stalemate in the Korean war, the failed Bay of Pigs invasion, and the escalation of the Vietnam War. In each instance, Janis found individual needs to belong and to maintain a group self overrode individual judgments that would likely have led to better decisions. Janis concluded that groups frequently produce "instances of mindless conformity and collective misjudgment of serious risks" (Janis 1982, 3).

GROUPTHINK AS A CAUSE OF THE AMERICAN INVASION OF IRAQ

The Bush administration's decision to invade Iraq in 2003 seems to have largely been a result of groupthink (Badie 2010; Lobe 2004). Bush's inner circle felt great pressure to take some dramatic action in reaction to the September 11, 2001, attacks. Vice President Dick Cheney, Secretary of Defense Donald Rumsfeld, and several other key advisors believed the war on Afghanistan begun in October 2001 was an insufficiently impressive response. These advisors formed a core group to advocate for starting a war against a more formidable opponent, one that they thought would better increase global fears of the United States' military power.

The core group considered starting wars against Iran and Syria before settling on Iraq as the most suitable enemy. As detailed by Dina Badie (2010), for over a year this core group worked to convince the president and others in the Bush administration's foreign policy team that Saddam Hussein should be considered a primary target in the war on terror. Evidence amassed in the years since that war shows that most of the core group's claims about Iraq's level of military preparedness and its ties to terrorism were fundamentally wrong. Still, as Badie among others makes clear, it is a mistake to assume Cheney, Rumsfeld, and the other members of the core group were driven by dishonesty or immorality. They shared a common group self as hawkish neoconservatives. Their groupthink errors were rooted in their shared need to continue to belong to this powerful group.

The core group made it clear that those who did not agree with them about the need to invade Iraq would not be allowed to participate in further top-level discussions. So, for example, when CIA director George Tenet offered intelligence that did not support the claim that Saddam Hussein was connected to terrorism, the core group began questioning his and the CIA's competence and loyalty. When the Army chief of staff General Eric Shinseki predicted several hundred thousand soldiers would be needed to occupy Iraq, the core group publicly questioned both his intelligence and patriotism. Two separate, new intelligence services were created in the Department of Defense (the so-called Policy Counterterrorism Evaluation Group and the Office of Special Plans) and instructed to provide core team members Rumsfeld and Deputy Secretary of Defense Paul Wolfowitz with confirmation of what those two already believed.

Outsiders from the CIA, military services, and State Department who tried to bring more fact-based views to the core group were kept away by what Janis (1972, 198) calls groupthink's "mindguards." Using similar language, Bush's Secretary of the Treasury would later explain that a "praetorian guard encircled the president" (quoted in Suskind 2004, 293), shielding him from views that did not match what the core group wished him to hear.

Bush's core group also exhibited the groupthink symptom that Janis (1972, 197) named the illusion of invulnerability. They told each other that the Iraqis would likely treat the invading United States military as liberators and that ordinary Iraqis believed Saddam Hussein was as much of a menace to Iraq as the core group had convinced themselves he was to America. Thus, no plans were made for the post-invasion collapse of civil society or for how the occupying United States military might go about creating a new, functioning government.

Bush's core foreign policy group seems to have suffered the "deterioration of mental efficiency, reality testing and moral judgment" that Janis (1972, 9) identifies with group-think. Even as much of the rest of the world vigorously contested the evidence justifying an attack on Iraq, Bush's core decision-makers permitted nothing to disturb the self shared among members of their exclusive group. This group was, to their mind, making the choices necessary to maintain their country's security in the first decades of the twenty-first century.

INDIVIDUALISTIC EXPLANATIONS OF VIOLENCE

Many people continue to believe that it is "bad" people and not bad situations that cause most violence. Psychologists themselves helped foster this misunderstanding as for many decades they focused on individualistic explanations of violence while generally ignoring the importance of situations. These **individualistic explanations of violence** emphasized the role of internal mental states and dispositions in causing people to harm themselves and others. Much of the attention given to both Milgram's and Zimbardo's experiments arose in large part because their research offered dramatic demonstrations of the weakness of the individualistic explanations of violent behavior then dominating psychology.

Although most violence is a function more of social situations than of individual dispositions, psychologists believe a small percentage of perpetrators do commit violence in part because of their dispositional deficits in the normal need to belong. These people are popularly referred to as psychopaths or sociopaths, but neither of these labels points to mental disorders recognized in the Diagnostic and Statistical Manual (DSM-5), the American

Psychiatric Association's 2013 official guide to psychological disorders. The DSM-5 does recognize a related category, **antisocial personality disorder** (ASPD). The diagnosis of ASPD is associated with aggressiveness, a lack of respect for laws and social norms, frequent lying, a lack of guilt, and indifference to the mistreatment and injury of others. Those with ASPD have a diminished or impaired need to belong.

ASPD is estimated to be present in about 2 percent or nearly 6 million adults in the United States. Men are diagnosed with ASPD over twice as often as women (Blacks et al. 2010). Nonetheless, since few people with ASPD are more often violent toward others or themselves than are people without this diagnosis, ASPD is not a useful predictor or explanation for violence.

ASPD may provide some benefits for societies as people with ASPD tend to be more creative, goal-focused, and willing to take risks than those without ASPD. As Paul Babiak and Robert D. Hare explain in *Snakes in Suits: When Psychopaths Go to Work* (2007), many people with ASPD excel in occupations where it is useful to have extreme self-confidence, aggressiveness, and a willingness to push for results. Many business and prophetic religious leaders, as well as politicians, are thought to rely on their ASPD to secure and maintain their leadership positions. Antisocial personality disorder seems to lead more often to lofty achievements than to violence.

Nonetheless, despite the evidence, many people find it easier to believe that harmful behavior rises mostly from individual rather than from situational causes. Recognizing the causative potency of situations suggests social patterns and institutions would have to be changed to reduce violence, ambitious political projects that many people resist. It is generally easier to view perpetrators of violence as "bad people" who should be punished, perhaps even executed, than to seek to restructure a society so that violence-encouraging situations less often appear.

Individualistic explanations of violence also flourish because people in all cultures tend to remember and believe anecdotes more easily than data. This preference for stories further encourages individualistic explanations since individuals work better as protagonists in narratives about the causes of violence than situations do. The violent criminal and heroic police officer or soldier make good subjects for personal-interest news articles, documentaries, and movies. Statistical analysis that draws conclusions about the determinative power of unequal social structures depends on an abstract and, for most people, much less interesting point of view.

Nonetheless, public understanding of the situational origins of violence is slowly increasing. Many successes associated with the rise of the global peace network detailed in Chapter 3 have been built on projects to reduce violence and war through changing cultural, economic, political, and social institutions. Even some societies once widely thought to possess especially violent and militaristic national characters have shown themselves able to quickly become pacific once circumstances changed. Hawaiian chiefs warred regularly for centuries before abruptly ending their violent campaigns after Kamehameha unified the islands. Scandinavian cultures, once known as the most bellicose in Europe, are now widely thought to be the most peaceful. Germany and Imperial Japan rapidly eliminated their aggressive foreign policies after World War II. Europe, which experienced repeated wars for centuries, is now one of the most peaceful regions that modern humans have ever known. Such radical transformations were caused by new social institutions, not by sudden mutations in the psychological dispositions of Asians, Europeans, and Polynesians.

POST-TRAUMATIC STRESS DISORDER

Research into the psychological effects of violence took a leap forward in the 1970s after mental health professionals developed the category of post-traumatic stress disorder (PTSD), primarily to aid in the treatment of hundreds of thousands of returning American Vietnam veterans. PTSD became a formal diagnostic category in 1980 and subsequently has been used to study the effects of violence in many circumstances far beyond battlefields.

Post-traumatic stress disorder (PTSD) is a severe anxiety disorder that develops after exposure to psychological or emotional injury. People with PTSD have witnessed or have themselves experienced injury or death, either threatened or in actuality. The resulting symptoms include (1) repeated "reliving" of the events, e.g., in flashbacks, recurrent memories, or dreams; (2) erratic emotions, concentration, and awareness; and (3) avoidance of social groups and interpersonal relationships. Symptoms associated with anxiety, stress, and tension are also common. PTSD sufferers often "feel numb and emotionally disconnected from loved ones, yet also tense, irritable, and hypervigilant as if danger were forever present" (McNally 2012, 872).

A less serious diagnosis of acute stress disorder is given to those whose symptoms disappear in less than thirty days. Only symptoms that last longer are considered to warrant a diagnosis of PTSD. All the symptoms of PTSD reduce a person's ability to meet their basic need to belong, but people with a symptom that leads them to avoid social relationships or to be unable to form group selves are especially liable to fail to satisfy this basic need.

PTSD is not a reaction to violence of every type but mostly appears as a result of violence that weakens social bonds. Violence from nature—from earthquakes, tornadoes, tsunamis, et cetera—is thus not as likely to produce PTSD as is violence by humans. There is something especially traumatizing about knowing other humans are trying to sever social bonds, even when the perpetrators are members of so-called "enemy" groups.

PTSD symptoms are commonly worse the more that preexisting relationships and group selves are harmed by the threatened or actual violence. Violence that comes from one's immediate family, for example, is more likely to lead to PTSD than is violence from a person with whom the victim does not have frequent contact. Symptoms are worse, too, for those who directly witness violent events close up than for those who see these events from a distance. This is true for perpetrators who witness their own harming of others as well as for victims of violence. Snipers, for example, face extra stress as modern rifle telescopes provide them with close-up views of the faces of victims as bullets destroy them. As Jonathan Shay, a psychiatrist who specializes in PTSD, explains, "When you can see what you are killing, and know who you are killing, the emotional weight of that experience is likely to be way larger than when it is killing either from an airplane at thirty thousand feet or if you have only a general sense of where the enemy is" (quoted in Schmidle 2013, 34).

One study completed on Vietnam veterans found that 31 percent developed PTSD (Kulka et al. 1990). A RAND study of American military personnel who were deployed to

① don't let you serve anymore.

TBI's

② How many don't report or admit it.

Afghanistan and Iraq suggests they have somewhat lower rates, with an estimated 20 percent reporting symptoms of either PTSD or major depression (Tanielian and Jaycox 2008). Additional mental health problems such as alcohol abuse, suicide, and severe difficulties in adjusting to civilian life are also found in many Afghanistan and Iraq veterans who do not have PTSD. Rates for PTSD and other mental health problems will likely rise among these veterans in the years ahead as late-appearing symptoms begin to manifest.

PTSD develops more often in those who have had previous experiences of the sudden loss of social bonds. Earlier traumas increase negative reactions to new ones. Because children are especially dependent on social bonds, violent traumas in early life impair a young victim's ability to forge trusting relationships and group selves throughout their adult life. Even one early event is likely to linger as children "have little previous experience, less development of coping skills, and an unclear understanding of what is normal and what is unusual" (MacNair 2011, 35).

Violence shatters social bonds as well as bones, and physical wounds often heal even faster than do social wounds.

PERPETRATOR-INDUCED TRAUMATIC STRESS

Perpetrators of violence frequently suffer psychological harm because of what they have done to others. Rachel MacNair (2002) has proposed the diagnosis of **perpetrator-induced traumatic stress (PITS)** to identify psychological disorders associated with being the knowing agent of harm. PITS would become a subcategory of the PTSD diagnosis, recommended for use when PTSD-like symptoms occur not among victims or witnesses to direct violence but rather among people who have caused harm. Table 11.1 summarizes the differences between the diagnoses of PSTD and PITS.

Dave Grossman, a one-time Army Ranger and teacher at West Point, broke a long silence about the problems suffered by perpetrators of violence with publication in his widely-read book, *On Killing: The Psychological Cost of Learning to Kill in War and Society* (1995). Grossman pointed out that soldiers who kill, or try to kill, others in battle suffer more psychological disorders than do civilians who endure repeated bombing during warfare. Similarly, on the battlefield itself, support personnel who supply materials and weapons but do not directly aim to harm others suffer much lower rates of trauma. Medics, too, though they suffer physical injury and fatality rates almost equal to those suffered by battlefield soldiers, afterward manifest fewer symptoms of psychological trauma. From this and other evidence, Grossman concludes that soldiers suffer more psychological trauma because they have harmed others than because they have themselves been injured or seen their fellow soldiers injured.

Evidence from the Vietnam War supports Grossman's claim. American soldiers who report they killed while serving in Vietnam have higher rates of severe trauma than do those who say they did not (MacNair 2002). Even soldiers who killed while participating in only occasional light combat have more severe disorders than non-killing soldiers who experienced frequent, heavy combat.

Some evidence suggests that those who carry out government-sponsored executions and professional criminal "hit men" may also sometimes suffer from perpetrator-induced

TABLE 11.1 PTSD AND PITS

	PTSD	PITS
Full name	Post-traumatic stress disorder	Perpetrator-induced traumatic stress
DSM-5 status	Accepted disorder	Disorder proposed as a subcategory of PTSD
Cause	Witnessing, causing, or being the victim of harm produced by humans or natural disasters	Causing harm to others
Symptoms	A severe anxiety disorder, lasting over 30 days, often also associated with reliving the event, avoidance, arousal, and guilt	A severe anxiety disorder lasting over 30 days with symptoms like PTSD resulting from past violence caused by the person exhibiting the symptoms

Sources: American Psychiatric Association 2013; MacNair 2002, 2011.

trauma (MacNair 2002). Much is known about police officers who shoot others in the line of duty. There are occasional instances of unjustified shootings but usually police officers fire in dangerous situations to protect themselves, their partners, or the public. These officers commonly receive broad support for their actions from their peers, superior officers, and the communities that they serve. Nonetheless, police officers who harm others will frequently manifest symptoms of acute stress disorder or, less often, PTSD.

Laurence Miller (2006) estimates that about two-thirds of officers involved in shootings in the United States suffer moderate or severe psychological problems. Almost 70 percent leave the force within seven years after their critical incident. Most police departments now require mandatory counseling for all officers who shoot others in the line of duty, regardless of how justified or heroic the acts may be. It seems harming others is traumatizing even when strongly supported by the perpetrator's community.

OBSTACLES TO UNDERSTANDING PITS

As mentioned, thousands of combat soldiers returned home seriously traumatized from the American wars in Afghanistan and Iraq. By 2012, after eleven years of overseas combat, about as many soldiers had killed themselves as the estimated 6,500 that had been killed by others (Swofford 2012). Currently, the rate of suicide for all war veterans in the United States is about twice that for the adult population in general. If the rate of suicide by Afghanistan and Iraq veterans continues to rise, the disproportionately high rate of veteran suicide may further increase for years, perhaps decades.

Veterans who kill themselves suffer from disorders associated with three different conditions: From being harmed and seeing others harmed; from witnessing others perpetrate harm; and from the trauma produced by their own successes at injuring or killing others. Both Grossman and MacNair suspect that witnessing oneself cause harm is more damaging than the other two conditions. Unfortunately, however, very few studies have focused on the specific rates of trauma common to either government-approved or criminal violence perpetrators. The very acknowledgement that those who harm others frequently suffer severe negative psychological consequences troubles many. Some worry, for example, that examining the suffering of perpetrators of violence deflects attention away from the suffering of victims. Militaries, too, actively discourage this type of research. Learning more about the long-term psychological effects of perpetrating violence might discourage potential recruits from volunteering. More knowledge might also make it seem that the United States government should assume responsibility for treating and compensating the tens of thousands of veterans who followed orders to harm others and then suffered lasting mental disorders as a result.

MacNair speculates that researchers also hesitate to pursue questions about perpetrator-induced trauma in part from a fear of implying that soldiers who have harmed and killed are "at fault" for their own psychological injuries. The safer and more common research assumption is, instead, "that the veteran's suffering is due to the enemy rather than to what the soldier was expected to do" (MacNair 2011, 37).

These and other obstacles may discourage further research into perpetrator-induced trauma. Enough is known, however, to expect that people placed in situations where they are expected to hurt or kill other humans will frequently experience substantial stress, even if they have been carefully trained to harm others and are celebrated for their acts by their communities and countries.

Poster in the World Health Organization's campaign to prevent suicide.

SUICIDE AS A GLOBAL PROBLEM

With over 1 million fatalities a year, suicide is by far the largest cause of non-accidental violent deaths across the globe each year (World Health Organization 2011). Like all violence, suicide is also intimately associated with the difficulties many humans face in trying to meet their need to belong. As mentioned in Chapter 2, for decades peace studies researchers focused mostly on large-scale collective violence, ignoring the massive and probably growing problem of self-harming. Research and preventative efforts across the global peace network should be expanded to include more focus on the problem of suicide.

Consider, for example, that in 2000, the last year for which complete data are available, suicide accounted for 49 percent of all violent deaths across the globe. Homicide was responsible for 31 percent and wars for 19 percent (Krug et al. 2002). In the United States in 2009, there were an estimated 37,000 deaths from suicide and less than half that, 17,000, from murders. Many fewer American soldiers, about 650, died in combat that year even though the United States was fighting two foreign wars.

The worldwide suicide rate increased by about 60 percent over the last forty-five years (World Health Organization 2011). In the United States the estimated rate rose 50 percent, from 7.6 suicides for every 100,000 people in 1950 to 11 per 100,000 in 2005. Similarly, during the same period the rate of suicide per 100,000 rose from 6.7 to 9.5 in Great Britain

TABLE 11.2 SAMPLE COUNTRY SUICIDE AND HOMICIDE RATES

Country	Suicides per 100,000 (year)	Homicides per 100,000 (year)
Australia	8.2 (2006)	1.0 (2010)
Brazil	4.8 (2008)	21 (2011)
Canada	11 (2005)	1.6 (2010)
China	13.9 (1999)	1.0 (2011)
Colombia	4.9 (2007)	31.4 (2011)
Germany	12.3 (2010)	0.8 (2010)
France	16.3 (2007)	1.1 (2009)
India	10.5 (2009)	3.5 (2011)
Japan	24.4 (2009)	0.83 (2010)
Mexico	4.2 (2008)	23.7 (2011)
Netherlands	9.3 (2009)	1 (2007)
Russia	30.1 (2006)	10.2 (2010)
South Africa	0.9 (2007)	31.8 (2010)
Spain	7.6 (2008)	0.8 (2010)
Sweden	12.1 (2010)	1.0 (2011)
United Kingdom	6.9 (2009)	1.3 (2009)
United States	11 (2005)	4.8 (2010)

Sources: World Health Organization 2011; UNOCD 2014.

and from 19.6 to 24.2 in Japan. The WHO expects the rate to continue rising, unless effective prevention programs are established across the world. (See Table 11.2, "Sample Country Suicide and Homicide Rates.")

Self-inflicted violence is an even more serious problem than these high rates of fatalities suggest since most reported rates of suicide fatalities seriously undercount the actual rate. Autopsies and follow-up detective work in many possible suicides are often perfunctory or nonexistent. Rates are greatly underreported, too, since the cause of so many deaths—e.g., by automobile, drugs, poison, and pills—leave the victim's intent unclear.

Many more people attempt suicide than succeed. Most nonfatal suicide attempts are not reported to authorities so rates of increase in attempts are impossible to calculate. In the United States, for example, according to the U.S. Centers for Disease Control ("Suicide: Facts at a Glance" 2012) there are an estimated twenty-five nonfatal suicide attempts each year for every suicide death; in most recent years nonfatal suicide attempts led to nearly 500,000 emergency room visits and nearly 100,000 hospitalizations. Though nonfatal suicide attempts do not kill, they often create lasting physical disabilities.

CAUSES OF SUICIDE

Emile Durkheim, one of the founders of sociology, demonstrated in 1897 that suicide rates reflect shifting levels of social bonding. Durkheim (2007) showed that **social determinants of suicide** account for most of the variation found in suicide rates. Prominent social determinants include culture, region, gender, age, place of residence, employment and relationship status, and level of involvement with social groups. Changed social circumstances change rates of suicide.

Individual dispositions do play a role in suicide, but variations in frequencies of depression, anxiety, psychosis, and other internal traits do not mirror the persistent variations observed in suicide rates. Individual dispositions thus cannot be looked to as the principle cause of self-harming. Non-psychological, situational factors instead play the leading role. So, for example, the availability of guns, poisons, and other easy-to-use weapons of self-destruction often create particularly lethal suicide-enabling situations. In the United States, female military veterans are three times more likely to kill themselves than their non-veteran peers (McFarland et al. 2010). These female veterans are also much more likely to have easy access to and skill at using guns. This difference in the situational availability of guns, not individual psychological tendencies, probably explains most of the different rates of female civilian and veteran suicides.

Persistent gender differences across cultures further highlight the importance of social situational causes. Males kill themselves much more often than females in every part of the world (except in China) even though females and males exhibit a similar variance in their levels of mental illness and health (Krug et al. 2002). In the United States, women attempt suicide twice as often as men even though men kill themselves five times more often. There are no parallel differences between the sexes in rates of anxiety, depression, trauma, or other psychological dispositions. This suggests that differences in socially defined female and male group selves produce recurring gender differences in suicide rates.

The people most likely to commit suicide live in situations with weak or weakening social connections. These more likely suicides include: male adolescents; singles of both

LEARNING MORE BELONGING
AND WELL-BEING

Some of the best new work in psychology looks at brain activity and hormonal releases associated with behaviors that satisfy the need to belong. Functional brain imaging studies have found, for example, that a friendly touch and smile from others tends to activate the vagus nerve, calming the "fight-or-flight" cardiovascular response. Friendly touches and smiles also trigger the release of oxytocin, a powerful hormone that promotes trust and bonding, "the tend-and-befriend" response described in Case 10-2, "The Physiology of Peace." Studies at the U.S. National Institutes of Health found that just thinking about giving money to charity tends to trigger oxytocin's release, as does gazing at the picture of a baby. These and other studies suggest that bodies experience pleasure when people act or even merely imagine affirming their social connections to others.

Mental well-being positively effects physical health. Long-terms studies have shown that people with higher levels of life satisfaction have "lower death rates from cardiovascular disease, suicide, accidents, homicides, mental disorders, drug dependency, and liver disease related to alcohol" (Diener and Biswas-Diener 2008, 33).

Not surprisingly, more satisfied people also tend to live longer, though the exact number of years is far from established. Positive health benefits associated with strong feelings of well-being have been shown to persist across genders, ages, and educational levels.

It is important to note that despite claims to the contrary in many self-help books, people with higher positive emotions do not have higher rates of survival from life-threatening illnesses. People with high well-being scores do get sick less and live longer but the evidence shows that positive feelings do not influence the course of serious diseases. Some studies suggest the opposite, that people with the highest levels of life satisfaction die more quickly from serious diseases, perhaps because too often "highly positive people may fail to report symptoms of illness, a dangerous tendency that can lead to inadequate treatments" (Diener and Biswas-Diener 2008, 34). People with elevated senses of well-being may also be less willing than others to submit to the painful or invasive treatments that might prolong their lives while lowering its quality, including the quality of their social relationships.

Source: Diener and Biswas-Diener 2008.

sexes over seventy-five years of age; the recently divorced, widowed, and unemployed; and immigrants, prisoners and, as mentioned earlier, combat-experienced soldiers (Krug et al. 2002). Programs that decrease social isolation and increase the vitality of group selves significantly decrease the likelihood of self-harming. Unfortunately, modern industrial societies often make it difficult for people to maintain stable families, groups, friendships, communities, and jobs, the social relationships that most discourage self-harm. The WHO prediction that global suicide rates will continue to rise reflects the widespread belief that, as Durkheim said a century ago, modern life tends to decrease people's ability to satisfy their deep need to belong.

POSITIVE PSYCHOLOGY

It may be difficult but it is not impossible in the modern world to satisfy the human need to belong. Many psychologists in the last few decades have created a new field, positive psychology, in an effort to help people satisfy the need to belong and other basic needs.

Positive psychology researches mental health and well-being and also provides practical training in how best to achieve these states. Though it continues psychology's earlier emphasis on individualistic explanations of behavior, positive psychology also places much emphasis on how healthy people can best create and strengthen healthy group selves. In many ways, without intending to, positive psychology adopts peace studies' long-standing interest in researching and promoting positive peace. As explained in Chapter 2, positive peace refers to people cooperating for mutual benefit without being coerced by threats of violence or war. In positive psychology this mutual cooperation is associated with well-being.

One recurrent discovery is that genetics determine about half of each person's sense of well-being. This was first established by studies of thousands of identical twins, raised together and apart, and has been confirmed by later research, including one seventeen-year-long study of German men and women (Eid and Larsen 2008). Other studies indicate that approximately another 10 percent of each person's feelings of life satisfaction depend on immediate, short-term situations outside of personal control. These transient situations, for example, finding a good parking spot, passing a test, or arriving at a vacation retreat, elevate a person's mood. Negative transient situations, on the other hand, such as being cut off in traffic, failing a test, or being kicked off a vacation flight, can temporarily depress a person's feelings (Lykken 1999; Lyubomirsky 2007).

The remaining 40 percent of personal feelings of well-being depend on social situations that people can largely choose for themselves. The best choices for increasing a sense of life satisfaction within this 40 percent are choices that satisfy the need to belong. The **benefits of social relationships** are so great that they seem to be the single most effective way a person can increase his or her sense of well-being. Establishing satisfying group selves strengthens a person's mental health. On the other hand, breaking or weakening social bonds and group selves tends to decrease a person's sense of well-being. (See Figure 11.1, "The Three Determinants of Well-Being.")

Not all group selves have equally positive health effects. Studies show that giving support to others produces better health benefits than does receiving support (Brown et al. 2003).

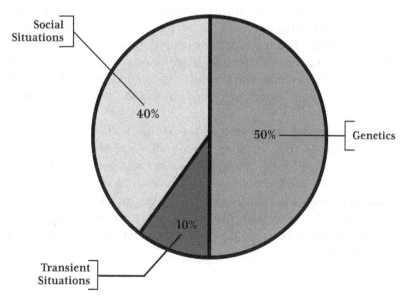

FIGURE 11.1 The Three Determinants of Well-Being.

The social role of giver is more satisfying than the role of receiver. In one study of 423 elderly individuals, people who reported providing help to spouses, relatives, or neighbors reduced their rate of dying within the following five years by half when compared to similar cohorts who reported providing no such help. Being a frequent recipient but not donor of support did not reduce mortality, suggesting that in some situations it is not the mere fact of social relationships but the social role of provider that most benefits health (Brown et al. 2003).

So far researchers have found only two social situations that commonly have long-term negative impacts on the sense of well-being. One is the loss of a job. It is not, however, the loss of income so much as the loss of social connections and an important group self that causes a diminution of life satisfaction. People also frequently become less satisfied with their lives for several years after the death of a spouse, a loss again associated with a deterioration of social bonds (Diener and Biswas-Diener 2008, 159).

In sum, positive psychologists have found that it is not what people possess either externally or internally but the quality of their social connections that most determines levels of fulfillment. As one leading researcher concludes, "time and time again . . . what makes us happy is the quality of our romantic bonds, the health of our families, the time we spend with good friends, the connections we feel to communities" (Keltner 2009, 13). Satisfying the need to belong is essential to human flourishing and, as is discussed in Chapter 13, is probably essential as well in helping to build positive peace.

MAKING CONNECTIONS

Though it is important to give people knowledge about techniques likely to increase their sense of personal peace, large scale social changes require new, large scale public policies. Legislators and policymakers must promote positive psychology's discoveries, especially since many of these discoveries contradict existing traditions and customs. Massive government-sponsored smoking cessation programs in the last half of the twentieth century decreased nicotine-associated deaths across much of the developed world. Similar government-led programs in many places cut automobile fatalities in half. Government-sponsored public health programs have also worked to increase the use of birth control, decrease infant and maternal mortality, prevent potentially cataclysmic pandemics, and implement mass vaccination programs.

Similar, evidence-based government programs are needed to lower rates of both other- and self-directed violence. The maturing behavioral sciences increasingly possess the knowledge necessary to help design such policies that could weaken and sometimes even eliminate violence-encouraging situations. Much is now known as well about what policies will best strengthen the positive social bonds that establish a sustainable positive peace. Chapter 12 describes some particularly important discoveries that sociologists have made about how to promote both healthy group selves and the social situations in which these selves can flourish.

FOR REVIEW

1. Summarize the evidence that there is a universal need to belong.
2. Explain the different ways that Milgram's and Zimbardo's experiments each raise doubts about individualistic explanations of human violence.
3. Evaluate how well the Bush administration's decision to invade Iraq illustrates the phenomenon of groupthink.
4. Describe the main differences between individual dispositional and social situational explanations of suicide.
5. Review the principal discoveries that positive psychology has made about how humans create a healthy sense of well-being.

THINKING CRITICALLY

1. How does the idea of the banality of evil help explain the behavior of Milgram's teacher-volunteers?
2. Which are the most influential group selves in your life? How does each of these different selves influence your perceptions and behavior?
3. What are the most prominent social roles that support violence in your society? What are the most prominent social roles that support nonviolence? Are violent and nonviolent roles valued differently?
4. What steps could a group take to minimize the chances it becomes the victim of groupthink?
5. Is it useful—or a mistake—to explain human behavior while relying equally on both individualistic and situational causes?
6. How might laws and punishments change if it were broadly believed that most criminal violence is produced more by situational than by individual dispositional causes?
7. Why does suicide commonly receive so much less attention than homicides and wars?
8. What are the likely main causes of the increase in suicides in contemporary societies?
9. Are there findings that positive psychology has made about how to increase an individual's sense of well-being that can be applied directly to your life?

RECOMMENDED RESOURCES

The Act of Killing. Directed by Christine Cynn and Joshua Oppenheimer. 2013. A documentary that examines how ordinary people in Indonesia during the 1960s became mass killers, murdering more than a million people as part of a government-encouraged anti-communist campaign.

Bok, Derek. *The Politics of Happiness: What Government Can Learn from the New Research on Well-Being* (Princeton, NJ: Princeton University Press, 2010). An ambitious attempt to detail how recent social science research into well-being should shape public policy and legislation in the United States.

Greater Good: The Science of a Meaningful Life. A rich site maintained by the Greater Good Science Center to teach skills that foster a thriving, resilient, and compassionate society. Website at http://greatergood.berkeley.edu

Lieberman, Matthew D. *Social: Why Our Brains Are Wired to Connect* (New York: Crown, 2013). Examines the neural mechanisms underlying the human need to belong and maintain social connections. Lieberman argues that the need to connect with other people is more basic than the human need for food or shelter.

MacNair, Rachel M. *The Psychology of Peace*, 2nd ed. (Westport, CT: Praeger, 2011). This pioneering book in the psychology of peace presents an overview of the micro-level causes and effects of violence.

Rifkin, Jeremy. "RSA Animate—The Empathic Civilisation." Reviews recent evidence that humans are hardwired to empathize and cooperate with other humans. Website at http://www.thersa .org/events/rsaanimate/animate/rsa-animate-the-empathic-civilisation

Seligman, Martin. "The New Era of Positive Psychology." TED Talk. February 2004. Seligman talks about psychology as a field of study that is moving beyond a focus on disorder to consider human well-being. Available at http://www.ted.com

Shoah. Directed by Claude Lanzmann. 1985. A classic documentary that examines how during the Holocaust ordinary people were able to participate in the systematic killing of over six million people.

The Soldier's Heart. Directed by Brian Delate. *Frontline*, PBS. 2005. A documentary that examines the psychological problems faced by United States soldiers who return home after fighting in the American war in Iraq.

The Wounded Platoon. Directed by Daniel Edge. *Frontline*, PBS. 2010. Examines the violence, depression, and stress exhibited by a platoon of Iraq War veterans whose members have committed murder, assault, and suicide. Available at http://video.pbs.org/video/1497566525

Yuval-Davis, Nira. *The Politics of Belonging: Intersection Contestations* (Thousand Oaks, CA: Sage, 2011). This book examines the role of group selves in partisan struggles across the world and argues that most analyses of national and ethnic groups misunderstand how gender and other social and economic factors are built upon the politics of belonging.

CHAPTER 12

THE SOCIOLOGY OF VIOLENCE

CHAPTER OVERVIEW

This chapter reviews what sociologists have learned about how situational factors promote violence. It begins with a description of discoveries made through direct observations of violent acts. Subsequent sections examine some common characteristics of violence-producing situations. Studies of the training of both soldiers and terrorists are then used to illustrate traits shared by most violence-promoting situations. The group discontinuity effect that promotes violence is discussed next. Subsequent sections describe actions individuals can take to keep themselves safe as well as important formal conflict resolution and conflict transformation programs that can alter potentially violence-promoting situations. The chapter concludes with a review of peace through health approaches that apply the medical model to violence reduction.

Key terms discussed include: Socially approved violence; violence-promoting situations; sequence of escalation; blame the victim; disproportionate ability to harm; audience-provoked violence; training suicide terrorists; discontinuity effect; conflict resolution; positions; interests; conflict transformation; and peace through health.

> Most of the time, the most dangerous, most violent persons are not doing anything violent.
>
> —RANDALL COLLINS (2009, 3)

No distinctive personal traits or cluster of individualistic factors have been found to explain why some people seek to harm others. It thus seems likely that violent situations, not violence-prone individuals, are the principle cause of most violence.

The importance of situations becomes evident when one considers that even the most frequently violent people spend most of their waking hours behaving like the ordinary peaceful people who surround them. Bullies, thugs, and hooligans, indeed, all of those thought to "like to fight," harm no one most days of their lives. Armed robbers and other violent criminals spend most of their time living with their families and friends as uneventfully as their victims live with theirs. Even most repeat rapists rarely attack more than a handful of victims a year. Few convicted murderers have killed more than one person. And serial killers, the worst of the worst, usually wait weeks, sometimes months, occasionally years, between murders. Something associated with a specific situation must occur to cause most periods of non-harming behavior to end.

Violence-promoting situations are the most common cause not only of criminal but also of socially approved violence. **Socially approved violence** is produced by government agents with government approval, or by people widely supported by the general public. Government-sponsored militaries, the police, prison guards, and state-sponsored executioners all perpetrate socially approved violence. So, too, do rebels and insurgents when their violence is endorsed by a majority of the population. Socially approved violence kills many more people each year than non-socially approved violence by criminals, insurgents, and political revolutionaries.

There is nothing unusual about the personalities, ethnicity, or educational and socioeconomic status of most perpetrators of socially approved violence; there is nothing about these people to indicate that they are more likely to harm others than are other people who never commit violent acts. And, like violent civilian criminals, soldiers and other socially approved agents of violence are not frequent agents of harm; their daily lives are generally indistinguishable from their nonviolent peers. Variations in social situations best explain eruptions of both criminal and socially approved violence.

CLOSELY OBSERVING VIOLENCE

Most people believe that they know much about violence even though most have seldom or never directly witnessed violence. Their "knowledge" comes primarily from reading about violence in books and magazines and likely even more often from watching violence portrayed on television, in movies, and video games, as well as in documentaries and news reports. Most people do not realize that these media systematically misled the public about both the causes and the actual practices of violence.

The media stereotype suggests that "bad people" and well-trained security forces often coolly, calmly, and efficiently attack and harm their targets. In fact, however, perpetrators of violence commonly experience emotional distress at the prospect of harming other human beings. As detailed in Chapter 11, most perpetrators must overcome internal resistance before they can shatter the implicit social bonds that they share even with people they have never met, even with people they consider enemies.

Randall Collins (2009) provided a breakthrough in the understanding of how violence actually occurs with the publication of *Violence: A Micro-sociological Theory*. Most studies of violence rely on statistics and second-hand reports. The resulting analyses are abstract and inferential. Collins instead turned to direct or near-direct observations of specific violent acts. His sources included video recordings, photographs, self-reports, witness and news accounts, interviews, and historical reconstructions both by professional historians and participants. In addition, unlike most earlier researchers, Collins reported on violence at all levels, from minor incidents among children on playgrounds and in the family car, through middling events like assaults, sports fan riots, and drive-by shootings, to gang wars and military campaigns.

Collins found the same phenomenon recurred at the micro, meso, and macro levels: People find that harming others is very difficult to conceive and carry out. Anticipating fatal violence, as a perpetrator as well as a victim, tends to produce involuntary urination, defecation, vomiting, sweating, and flight. Becoming a perpetrator thus requires very specific enabling circumstances. Even when these rare situations do allow people to bypass their inhibitions, afterwards people who have harmed others commonly find they have also harmed themselves. As explained in Chapter 11, even socially approved perpetrators of violence often suffer more psychological distress from their experiences of hurting others than from being harmed or from being threatened by harm themselves.

Collins' data showed that both civilian and military perpetrators typically look first for the best ways to escape physical threats. Running, hiding, bluffing, and pleading—not fighting—are by far the most common human responses to violent threats. This tendency to seek personal safety helps account for another myth-busting fact: Violent outbreaks seldom produce major physical damage. As Collins explains, most potentially violent situations at all levels typically result "in bluster and standoff, with little actually happening, or incompetent performance with mostly ancillary and unintended damage" (2009, 32).

Violent acts frequently results in little damage in part because actual violent behavior commonly lasts a very short time, especially when compared with the length of its typical representations in books, television, movies, and video games. Fistfights on screen often stretch on for several minutes although, in real life, these fights usually end with a punch or two in ten seconds or less. Onscreen gunfights are frequently drawn out, with extended stalking, chasing, and many bullets finding their mark. So, Collins points out, in the 1957 film *Gunfight at the O.K. Corral*, directed by John Sturges, the representation of the gunfight named

TABLE 12.1   MYTHS OF PERSONAL AND GROUP VIOLENCE

Myth	Reality
Mostly caused by bad people	Mostly caused by bad situations
Fighting is a typical first response	Fleeing is a typical first response
Generally easy for perpetrators to harm others	Generally difficult for perpetrators to harm others
Violence is usually seriously damaging	Violence is seldom seriously damaging
Perpetrators are typically competent	Perpetrators are typically incompetent
Perpetrators tend to view themselves as initiators	Perpetrators tend to view themselves as victims
Fighting commonly lasts for several minutes	Fighting commonly lasts for less than one minute
Violence erupts suddenly	Violence emerges slowly
Violent attacks come mostly from strangers	Violent attacks come mostly from family and friends

in the title takes up seven minutes while the actual fight in Tombstone, Arizona in 1881 was over in less than thirty seconds (Collins 2009, 14). Police chases in reality are also typically much shorter than their on-screen versions. Cars rarely cover more than a few blocks; the time elapsed from beginning to end of a mobile chase is seldom more than a minute.

While fighters, shooters, and knife wielders in books and on screen commonly hit their targets, in reality violent people usually miss or land blows that do little damage. The need for personal safety and to maintain social bonds creates immense inhibitions that most people rarely overcome. (See Table 12.1, "Myths of Personal and Group Violence.")

VIOLENCE-PROMOTING SITUATIONS

Of course, despite the obstacles, violence still too often occurs. Usually it is because a violence-promoting situation has driven one or more people to overcome their normal desire both to avoid being hurt and to avoid harming others. Social scientists have identified multiple conditions that tend to produce violence-promoting situations. Among the most prominent conditions are: A sequence of escalation, a way to "blame the victim," a perceived ability to inflict more harm than one will receive, the presence of guns, and an encouraging audience.

A SEQUENCE OF ESCALATION

Most violence at all levels emerges from situations of mutual, escalating provocations. It usually takes time for people to be convinced that their circumstances are becoming so bad that violence is a reasonable response. Persuading people to take violent action thus commonly requires a series of escalating communications. This in part explains why, despite the public's widespread misperception, the threat of being harmed comes much more often from friends and acquaintances than from strangers. It is mostly with friends and acquaintances that sufficient time together can pass to convince people that violence has now become "the only way." Isolated people are generally less violent. They have fewer connections and so do not harm or suffer harm from others as often as people with many relationships.

Since violence usually rises out of situations where people were previously involved in more or less harmonious communication, all parties contribute to some degree in the escalating steps that lead to physical harm (Stone et al. 2010). This perspective should not be thought to suggest that people who have been assaulted, raped, battered, murdered, or attacked "brought it on themselves." Recognizing the importance of escalating situations instead calls attention to the important fact that most relationships, even among long-time antagonists, are not violent most of the time. Violence rarely erupts in even the most chronically conflicted relationships and, when it does, that violence is usually preceded by warnings and preliminary hostile actions which provide one and sometimes both parties with opportunities to de-escalate the situation or to walk away.

BLAMING THE VICTIM

People who commit violence usually find a way to think of themselves as victims rather than as perpetrators (Baumeister 1999). "He started it!" children often exclaim when they are caught fighting with their siblings. Similarly, most people who are involved in assaults, street fights, domestic violence, and even wars maintain that they were "protecting themselves," even when their victims are much smaller, without weapons, and the more likely to suffer physical injuries.

In his classic study of law enforcement, Hans Toch (1969) showed that both the police and those they arrest commonly think of themselves as reasonable, peaceful people who were forced to act violently by the provocative aggression of the other. Terrorists, also, typically share a view of "themselves as victims, fighting back against an oppressive, intrusive, unjust state. In their view, they have been mistreated and denied legitimate means of expressing their views for so long that they have no recourse but to strike back" (Baumeister 1999, 55).

Countries at war similarly tend to present themselves as victims forced to use violence against their "civilized" inclinations because of the unreasonable actions of their enemy. So the Germans and Japanese in the 1930s each declared they were turning to violence "as a last resort" to protect themselves from enemies. Saddam Hussein similarly declared that he was acting in self-defense in invading Kuwait, as did George W. Bush when he justified the American wars against Afghanistan and Iraq.

Different types of situations encourage violence at the micro, meso, and macro levels but the belief that one is "right" and the enemy "wrong" is common across interpersonal, group, national, and international violent conflicts.

DISPROPORTIONATE ABILITY TO HARM

People do not want to be harmed themselves and so tend to avoid fights with equals, even sometimes at great cost to their wealth and prestige. In quarrels, the side that finds itself greatly outnumbered or without equal weaponry seldom initiates violence. Women batter men less often than men batter women, for example, in part because women less often find themselves able to attack in situations that are not likely to provoke an even more damaging response. Bullies, similarly, are notorious for avoiding fights with people possessing equal strength.

Wariness of being harmed also guides international policies. So, for example, in the first decade of the twenty-first century the United States declared itself to be in a fierce quarrel with three nations that formed a so-called "Axis of Evil." It then attacked only one, Iraq, the country with the least capability of harming the United States and its allies in return. The more formidable members of the axis, Iran and North Korea, were left alone.

GUN VIOLENCE

Easy access to weapons, especially firearms, is one especially potent instance of the **disproportionate ability to harm.** Guns are physically easy to fire, requiring much less effort or commitment than fighting with bare hands or, usually, even than fighting with other weapons such as arrows, bayonets, batons, knives, and swords. The presence of guns can quickly convert an ordinary conflict into a situation with lethal violence.

Many people who keep guns at home do so in an effort to increase their ability to harm unwanted intruders. They are often unaware of how easily the mere presence of personal weapons can introduce violence into ordinary domestic conflicts (Donohue 2003). For

gun
control.

example, a gun in a home in the United States is estimated to be about four times more likely to be involved in an accidental shooting than to be used in self-defense. The presence of these guns also makes it nearly three times more likely that someone will be murdered by a family member or intimate partner (Kellermann et al. 1993). Domestic guns also encourage attempted and successful suicides. Homes with guns in the United States are five times more likely to experience the suicide of a household member as are homes without guns (Kellerman et al. 1993). Family members less than eighteen years old are especially prone to become victims of gun accidents and to use easily accessible guns to harm themselves (Hemenway 2006).

Developed countries with a higher per capita gun ownership generally have higher rates of gun deaths. The United States, with the highest rate of gun ownership in the world, regularly has the highest rate of gun violence among the world's twenty-six richest countries (Hemenway and Miller 2000). Within the United States, those states with the highest per capita gun ownership have the highest rates of gun deaths (Miller et al. 2002). In addition, it is usually states with the strictest gun control laws that have the lowest per capita deaths by guns (Florida 2011).

[handwritten margin notes: ?? — England took guns away & then violence went down.]

Encouraging audiences are often necessary not only to begin but also to assure the continuance of face-to-face fights.

Of course, there are multiple reasons why gun deaths are three times more common in the United States (4.8 per 100,000) than in Canada (1.6 per 100,000), and six times more common in Louisiana (18 per 100,000) than in Hawaii (3 per 100,000). However, probably the single most potent cause of national and state differences is the ease with which the presence of a gun can transform ordinary life into a lethal situation.

ENCOURAGING AUDIENCES

The presence of group helpers can also turn disputes toward violence. **Audience-provoked violence** occurs when witnesses embolden others to fight. Encouraging audiences are the frequent cause when public quarrels become violent or in situations of civil unrest when many strangers find themselves thrust together roaming city streets. The behavior of witnesses is extremely consequential since, perhaps surprisingly, violence takes place in social situations with multiple attendees more often than in situations that include only a single perpetrator and victim. So, for example, Mike Planty (2002) found that in the United States about two-thirds of all violent acts are witnessed by one or more third parties.

Audiences can also be a decisive cause of terrorism and war. Citizens sometimes urge leaders to undertake violent campaigns that most of these citizens expect to witness via television and other media without themselves being harmed. Modern political decision-makers thus often feel pressure to use violence not because they calculate it will accomplish their goals but because they believe that is what the public demands.

Bar and schoolyard fights also sometimes erupt because witnesses encourage the quarrelling parties to trade blows. Similarly, two solitary gang members on a disputed street corner will fight more often if their respective gangs arrive to urge them on. Police who subdue an arrested suspect after he or she has resisted will similarly more likely escalate their violence if other officers shout them on.

Audience-provoked violence occurs both when the audience is unacquainted with the potential fighters and when the audience shares social bonds with those who may become either victims or perpetrators. Violence in the latter case can help satisfy the fighter's need to belong. An encouraging audience is thus especially effective when it is made up of family, friends, and acquaintances. Their exhortations can transform arguments and quarrels into violence even when the aggressor is inviting great harm to her- or himself. People may choose to fight even while expecting to lose if they believe that fighting will enhance their stature with the encouraging group.

A few groups repeatedly encourage their fellow group members to initiate violence, even when these actions are likely to bring harm to both the perpetrator and the group. Such seemingly irrational behavior is common among both soldier and terrorist groups, each of which is described below.

TRAINING SOLDIERS IN GROUPS

If a social situation encourages peacemaking, then group members will generally work for peace. And, as Milgram and Zimbardo's research discussed in Chapter 11 makes clear, if a social situation encourages violence, many people will become willing to commit

LEARNING MORE FOUR ARGUMENT STRATEGIES

All societies have multiple ways to conduct disagreements without resorting to physical force. In the United States, for example, Randall Collins (2009) found four common strategies many people use to deal with interpersonal conflicts without using violence. He names these four strategies: griping, whining, arguing, and quarrelling.

Griping is the least intense form of disagreement. Griping emphasizes complaints about an absent person that seldom lead to open conflict, much less violence. *Whining* is a more intense form of disagreement, involving complaints against someone who is present. Whining may lead to counter-complaining and, sometimes, to the building of even more tension. *Arguing* is a third and yet more extreme type of conflict where people actively express their disagreements. Arguing may satisfy the participants need to intensify the conflict or it may incite the disputants to grow yet angrier. Even though arguments may inflame emotions, few arguments lead to violence.

Quarrelling is the fourth and most dangerous of these four common forms of conflict. Arguments escalate into quarrels when one or both parties drop the initial focus of the conflict to begin disputing the grounds of the relationship itself. For example, at the micro level couples sometimes begin by arguing about some detail of household responsibilities and then escalate to quarrelling about their possible lack of love for or fidelity to each other. Similarly, at the meso level gang members may move from arguing with other gangs about individual behaviors to more serious disputes about rival territorial claims. At the macro level nations may argue about trading policies and then worsen their conflict by beginning to question the very legitimacy of the government they are opposing. Wars to create "regime change" may follow.

Before quarrelling, in the less dangerous condition of argument, disputants often explain themselves in detail, invoking logic, stories, and memories. Once arguments escalate to quarrels, however, people tend to speak in short sentences, rejecting reasoning for stark proclamations. Epithets and repetition may dominate as the quarrellers enact a well-recognized ritual that announces their growing emotional arousal, often of anger, sometimes of disappointment, embarrassment, or shame. Quarrelling commonly includes interruptions, inattention to the other's words, and people speaking abnormally loudly. Each of these behaviors breaks basic rules for normal, cooperative conversations and helps the quarrellers signal that they are growing increasingly serious about their disagreement.

Quarrellers shout, repeat, and curse to seize control of the conversation, warning their opponent that their now verbally disruptive actions may soon be followed by physically harmful acts. In most cases, however, quarrels do not escalate into physical violence. People "blow up" instead, with some final especially loud curses and pronouncements, before becoming silent or walking away "in a huff." Quarrellers also often become stuck in repetitions of the same claims, phrases, or curses so that one or both parties becomes bored and tension decreases. The quarrelling may de-escalate back into arguing or whining, or even into griping, if one quarreller introduces the name of a third-party scapegoat to blame for the conflict that has arisen.

Source: Collins 2009, 337–45.

violence. Modern militaries design their training programs to exploit this human tendency to conform to social roles.

Until recently, much military training was based on appeals to ideology, nationalism, or personal fear. However, this approach generally did a poor job of transforming ordinary people into willing killers. Brigadier General S. L. A. Marshall's *Men Against Fire* first published in 1947 surprised many with its finding that only about 15 to 20 percent of allied soldiers on battlefields in World War II fired their weapons at the enemy (Marshall 1947). Later researchers cast some doubt on Marshall's methods but most subsequent studies of actual combat units (rather than of idealized reports, often by commanding officers) have tended to support Marshall's conclusions that soldier fire rates in the first half of the twentieth century were surprisingly low.

Marshall's report led the United States military to try to improve its training procedures. As a result, the battlefield firing rate rose to 55 percent in the Korean War and reached a rate of between 80 and 95 percent among American soldiers during the Vietnam War (Grossman 1995). Contemporary military training focuses on building group selves, "unit cohesion," as well as on weapon proficiency. The once-prominent use of appeals to ideology, nationalism, and personal fear now play a secondary role.

Contemporary recruits begin their new lives by being transported to unfamiliar places for basic training. They are stripped of personal clothing, hairstyles, and personal space. Each is assigned a number and rank associated with their new group selves; these new identities compete with the previous nonviolent identities through which recruits have known themselves. Uniforms and haircuts reduce individual differences. Weeks of training then emphasize loyalty to the group, repetition of tasks to make firing automatic, and obedience to authority. Recruits attend classes, train, drill, eat, sleep, and play with their assigned cohort of similarly uprooted trainees. Later, recruits are assigned to new groups for further training and then to yet further new groups with whom they are periodically deployed to unfamiliar places where the group provides their primary interpersonal support. All is orchestrated to prepare the new soldiers to quickly, without reflection, harm others when so ordered, violent acts that they would have been highly unlikely to do before training.

In combat, difficult and dangerous circumstances help grow even stronger group selves as individual members are called upon to protect each other. Soldiers fight for their unit, for its survival, and for its glory, as together they constitute an encouraging audience exhorting each other to risk being killed. As Chris Hedges (2002, 38) reports, "A Marine Corps lieutenant colonel told me as he strapped his pistol belt under his arm before we crossed into Kuwait, 'none of these boys is fighting for home, for the flag, for all that crap the politicians feed the public. They are fighting for each other, just for each other.'"

In *On Killing*, ex-army officer Dave Grossman (1995) describes three military techniques that encourage soldiers to fire their weapons with genuine intent to harm. Each method is built on the human desire to maintain social bonds and to avoid harming people within one's own group. One technique is to create as many situations as possible that enable soldiers to fire while at a distance from their opponent. Knife and bayonet fights are hardest for soldiers as they must stand face to face with those they are supposed to harm. Soldiers find it easier to kill by dropping bombs from planes or firing artillery than when they must use weapons that bring them close enough to see their would-be victim's face.

Grossman also explains that firing and kill rates rise when a superior officer is near. As Milgram's experiment also demonstrates, the proximity of an authority figure changes the situation sufficiently to weaken most people's reluctance to kill. Additionally, soldiers have a higher firing rate when they work together in teams managing group-operated weapons such as tanks, machine-guns, rocket launchers, and mortars. Soldiers kill more easily in these situations that foster solidarity than in situations where they have no supporting audience and must fire a weapon alone. Some infantries are even trained to fire their solitary weapons in alternating turns in an effort to make it seem as if they are operating a group weapon.

The U.S. military now employs many psychologists who specialize in improving techniques to increase rates of killing. Psychological analysis begins even prior to enlistment as tests are used to eliminate potential enlistees with violent, antisocial, and other abnormal dispositions. Modern militaries reject recruits with personality disorders because they are likely not to form the group selves that soldiers are expected to possess. It is precisely because most soldiers in modern armies are ordinary people that they are so often traumatized when they successfully harm others in warfare. Chapter 11 earlier described some of the causes and consequences of these psychological wounds.

TRAINING TERRORISTS

The human need to belong and the creation of group selves also helps terrorist leaders recruit and train suicide bombers.

Terrorists are often popularly misconceived as fanatics, political extremists, or malcontents who lack economic or social opportunities. However, as Scott Atran (2003) reports, multiple researchers have found that terrorists are typically mostly indistinguishable from non-terrorists. For example, one study that looked at the psychological profile of 462 successful and thwarted suicide bombers found that "suicide attackers are rarely socially isolated, clinically insane, or economically destitute individuals but are most often educated, socially integrated, and highly capable people who could be expected to have a good future" (Pape 2005, 200).

Robert Pape (2005) also found that suicide terrorists are generally no more or less fanatical or religious than their peers. Most suicide terrorists are politically conscious individuals who are as likely to join civil society organizations as to become violent warriors. Like new volunteers in the U.S. military, terrorist recruits commonly begin their service with little more psychological inclination to harm others than do others of their age and gender in the populations from which they come. It takes a sophisticated social apparatus, what Ann Marie Oliver (2006) calls a "martyrdom machine," to strip people of their individual selves and prepare them to use their bodies as bombs.

Training suicide terrorists requires building group selves that accept violent social roles. Recruits undergo a careful sequence of group activities where terrorists-in-training are taught to view their proposed suicidal act as a necessary affirmation of their social bonds with their trainers, fellow recruits, co-religionists, and families.

More is known about the training of Palestinian terrorists than about any other group but this training is likely to be typical. Palestinian recruits are typically unmarried young men, of an age and status that leaves them especially eager to form new social bonds (Hassan 2001, 2006). An older, more experienced man commonly manages three to six recruits in a secret cell. The newer recruits work side-by-side with other members who are at varying stages in their training. All learn skills such as bomb-making, disguise, selecting and accessing targets, while they are simultaneously bonding with the group and with its leader. Repeated exercises over many weeks guide the recruits to believe that their small cell constitutes a family whose members must care for and protect one another.

As in-group affection grows so does an increasing emphasis on out-group hate. Multiple reasons to blame the potential bomb victims are repeated again and again. Once members seem ready to commit to harming the designated enemies, they are asked to compose a personal contract pledging to sacrifice their life, if necessary, to advance the group's goals. All the group members witness and celebrate the contract signing. Later, the leader presents recruits with a specific plan of action and the recruit is asked again to publicly declare his or her willingness to act for the good of the group. Recruits are told to write letters to family and friends, explaining their proposed actions. Commemorative photographs in heroic poses are taken. Members may also be videotaped, describing who they are and why they have chosen to become suicide terrorists.

The leader takes possession of the letters, photographs, and video files, to distribute to friends, family, and the media once the bombs have exploded. The creation of this package of martyr's memorabilia makes it less likely that any recruit will refuse orders. A large, valued future audience for the promised violence is guaranteed. "Being at that stage, a person sees himself as already dead," Ariel Merari explains. "There is no return for him without really losing any self-respect, the respect of others, but also because his mental state is already focused on killing himself, on being dead. He is already there, on the other side, actually" (quoted in Leung 2009).

The leader and other cell "family" members may accompany the suicide bomber as he or she begins his or her journey to the planned detonation site. The physical presence of others is generally not needed, however. By this stage ordinary nonviolent people have completely embraced their new group self and role. They sense a large audience is carefully watching and waiting. Ordinary people have become ready to use their bodies as weapons to kill others and themselves.

GROUP PATHWAYS TO VIOLENCE

Even the most violence-avoiding person will usually behave violently if he or she has an audience of fellow group members vigorously encouraging violence. Social psychologists label this the **discontinuity effect**, the tendency for groups to be "more antagonistic, competitive, and mutually exploitive than individuals" (Baumeister 1999, 193). Instances of otherwise peaceful groups initiating violence against outsiders has been observed repeatedly across a variety of cultures and circumstances.

Most people recognize the discontinuity effect when they are alone and meet a group. People then commonly experience some tension, knowing the likelihood of danger is greater than if they were facing individuals assembled alone. Like individuals, groups also tend to fear other groups more than they do individuals. This fear helps groups justify their violence against members of other groups, encouraging them to consider even first-strike violence as a form of self-defense.

Most group violence is aimed at outsiders and other groups, but group violence can also be directed at weak or discredited group members within the group. Members who question authority, hesitate to follow directions, or express a desire to leave a group frequently find themselves the targets of within-group hostility. Ex-members who no longer accept the expected group self are commonly perceived to be even greater threats than antagonistic external groups. So, for example, violent revolutionaries in France, Russia, China, and Cambodia eventually unleashed some of their fiercest punishments on their own discredited group members.

An approving crowd looks at a lynching victim in Waco, Texas, in 1916.

Modern armies operate similarly. Most train and deploy heavily armed, well-trained military police forces to ensure there is minimal wavering among soldiers. Long prison terms and a stigmatized dishonorable discharge without accrued benefits await soldiers who disobey. The Geneva Convention rules provide many more protections and rights for captured enemies than modern armies grant their own internal rule breakers. Prisoners of war are expected to be fed, clothed, and provided with medical care while military deserters and malingerers are often shot. Many contemporary terrorist groups and criminal gangs also have rules insisting that members remain obedient for life or face harsh punishments, including death.

The discontinuity effect is further intensified when groups adopt a division of labor. Most modern soldiers, for example, are seldom asked to directly harm anyone. Most soldiers instead work in supporting roles, loading and unloading supplies, operating computers and other devices, driving vehicles and planes that transport others who may fire. Similarly, terrorist cells will commonly include many members who assist but are never themselves asked to kill. Studies of the World War II German death camps discovered that the execution of millions was accomplished in so many, small, carefully organized separate steps that few individual Germans believed they were personally responsible. Each was only "doing his job," delivering orders from elsewhere, for example, or arresting "criminals," or driving a bus, or guarding prisoners, or filling a gas tank, or locking a door, or opening a valve. This created what Hannah Arendt named the banality of evil, discussed in Chapter 11.

A division of labor helps shield elite decision-makers from the frequent traumas faced by rank-and-file violence perpetrators. This division of labor increases the violence encouraged by the discontinuity effect as those asked to directly harm others need to know little about why specific victims have been chosen. Perpetrators thus face fewer difficult ethical choices. Humans—called "targets"—are selected for them by people higher in the hierarchy who are presumed by the rank-and-file to "know what they are doing." The lower-ranking perpetrator's loyalty to the group requires obedience to her or his role and to the established division of labor. It is not necessary for those who carry out most killing in modern warfare to be able to make informed decisions or to review the correctness of the lethal plans they are required to execute.

Meanwhile, the often isolated and distant circle of elite decision-makers also gains from the division of labor as its members can choose to have people killed without risking being harmed themselves. They do not even have to gaze upon the people they condemn to die. For example, the groupthink decision to wage war in Iraq discussed in Chapter 11 was made by a small core group of decision-makers in Washington, DC. They knew that their decision to send American planes and troops to invade Iraq would likely lead to the deaths of tens of thousands, perhaps hundreds of thousands, but they felt fairly certain that neither they nor their children would face any physical risks.

CONFLICT RESOLUTION PROGRAMS

Sociologists and other researchers now know more about violence-promoting situations and about the discontinuity effect than ever before. Governments, militaries, insurgents, and terrorists are using this knowledge in their efforts to increase the efficiency of their violence. Fortunately, this same knowledge can as well be used to reduce the incidence of violence-promoting situations. The rest of this chapter describes three especially prominent violence-reducing programs: Conflict resolution, conflict transformation, and public health violence abatement programs. Each draws from the maturing body of social science research into the causes of peace, violence, and war.

Social psychologist Morton Deutsch inaugurated the formal study of conflict resolution and management in the late 1940s. The field has since grown dramatically into an international movement that includes hundreds of research institutes spread across the world. **Conflict resolution** refers to a broad range of peacemaking approaches that attempt to end or reduce disagreements without violence. The label conflict resolution names both the academic field that studies resolution and management strategies as well as the actual practice of ending conflicts without violence. Some people involved in conflict resolution and management activities have not been formally trained, but there are also an increasing number of professionals with formal certification in the field. Conflict resolution strategies are today frequently used by educators, diplomats, lawyers and judges, and the business community. Commercial organizations have been especially active in spreading conflict resolution and management approaches through providing funds, credibility, and venues for training. Many large businesses in the developed world now provide conflict resolution and management programs to their managers, employees and, increasingly, customers.

Deutsch's pioneering insights continue to guide much contemporary research and training. Deutsch (1973) claimed that people in conflict usually adopt either a predominantly cooperative or competitive orientation and that cooperation more often achieves the desired results. A half century of research now supports Deutsch's once-controversial view. Much evidence shows, for example, that people in conflict who use mostly cooperative tactics (1) work more productively in groups, (2) have better interpersonal relations, (3) experience a stronger sense of well-being and self-esteem, and, probably most importantly, (4) more often successfully resolve their conflicts (Deutsch 2000, 29; see also Johnson and Johnson 1989). Successful conflict resolutions also tend to improve conditions for further, later successful resolutions.

Deutsch identifies three types of skills that are particularly useful to people in conflict (Deutsch 2000, 38–39). First are rapport-building skills. These are interpersonal behaviors that can reduce the tensions and suspicions that often thwart unskilled attempts at resolving conflicts. Second are skills to help identify problems, manage group dynamics, and facilitate decision making. These are skills commonly associated with effective managers. Finally, Deutsch points to the need for situation-specific conflict resolution skills.

Conflict resolution and management skills are now annually the focus of thousands of courses and workshops that increase the effectiveness of the global peace network. Hundreds of thousands of people across the globe have been trained in methods for dealing with conflicts, both small and large. The frequency, availability, and effectiveness of this training seems likely to continue expanding in the years ahead.

LEARNING MORE   KEEPING SAFE

Collins' 2009 pioneering study described earlier concludes with a list of actions his research suggests can increase levels of personal safety. Collins' recommendations include:

1. If you find yourself part of a potential audience to violence, try to disperse the crowd. If you find yourself in a confrontation surrounded by a violence-encouraging audience, strive to ignore or escape the crowd. Without emotional support from audiences, few public confrontations escalate into violence.

2. In public, be "streetwise." Avoid appearing off-guard or weak, especially when approached by strangers or individuals gathered in a group. Even frequently violent perpetrators usually seek to dominate an interaction before attacking. Would-be perpetrators will commonly try first to disrupt the

ordinary rhythms of communication. If potential victims avoid appearing vulnerable or ignore a first attempt to engage them in a sudden conversation, many would-be criminals will pass on, looking for easier targets.

3. Recognize that law enforcement officers and soldiers tend to panic and behave violently when they have been subjected to prolonged tension. Their inclination to use force rises with their numbers and with their perception that they themselves will not be harmed. People should take every opportunity to behave coolly and try to calm the security forces surrounding them, even when they stand as one against many.

4. Avoid escalations in verbal disagreements. Resist moving from arguing to quarrelling. Try to ease rising tensions. Stop the progression by "storming off," by de-escalating quarrelling to arguing, or by becoming boringly repetitive to allow time for emotions to subside.

UNDERSTANDING POSITIONS AND INTERESTS

Roger Fisher, William Ury, and Bruce M. Patton's *Getting to Yes* (2011) illustrates how widespread the interest in conflict resolution and management has become. *Getting to Yes* was an instant bestseller when first published in 1981 and has since been translated into over thirty languages and has sold nearly five million copies worldwide. Many ideas developed in *Getting to Yes* continue to guide conflict resolution and management programs. Fisher, Ury, and Patton advise, for example, that disputants should "separate the problem from the people" (2011, 17). People in disputes of all kinds are more likely to reach nonviolent resolutions if they focus on their disagreements rather than on personalities and personal histories.

Along with many others in the field of conflict resolution, Fisher, Ury, and Patton emphasize the importance of distinguishing between positions and interests. **Positions** are the beginning demands or requests that a person or group brings to a conflict. A position names what people say they want in order to end the conflict. **Interests,** by contrast, refer to the causes, goals, hopes, and fears that generate positions. An interest is a deeper, often unstated, and sometimes even unrecognized desire that has helped generate the position taken. Positions are like disease symptoms, while interests are the underlying cause of the symptoms.

Conflicts are resolved more effectively when interests and not positions are the focus for negotiation. For example, in a workplace dispute an employee might begin with the position that he requires a larger workspace while his manager counters with the position that no more space is available. The employee's underlying interest might turn out to be a desire to feel valued; the manager may be basing her position on an interest in appearing to be in control of workplace rewards.

Ury, Fisher, and Patton (1981, 41) offer an example of how positions and interests play out in international relations. In 1978, Egypt and Israel began negotiations over how to govern the Sinai Peninsula that Israel had captured and occupied in a war with Egypt a decade earlier. Both sides began with firm and incompatible positions. Egypt wanted the return of its ancient lost land while Israel took the position that it needed to keep the land that it had won. No suggestions for dividing the land seemed able to satisfy the initial positions each country presented.

Conflicting parties often believe they need to win acceptance of their positions but research shows that their deeper interests are generally more important. Trained conflict resolution facilitators use many techniques to help disputants recognize these important hidden interests. In the employee-manager example, a successful resolution based on interests might lead the manager to give the employee some tangible sign that she values his work. The manager could thus satisfy the employee's interest in being publicly recognized without either providing a larger workspace or sacrificing her own interest in asserting control.

In the example of the Sinai Peninsula, a historic settlement was reached once Israel recognized that its interest lay in increasing its security, not in possessing the Sinai itself. Similarly, Egypt went beyond its initial position to see that its deeper interest lay in reestablishing its national sovereignty over the land. An agreement was reached whereby Israel recognized Egyptian sovereignty over the Sinai Peninsula while Egypt guaranteed

Israel's security by demilitarizing large areas of the Peninsula where, otherwise, Israel-threatening tanks and missiles might mass.

The swift spread of conflict resolution and management programs in the last decades of the twentieth century illustrates how quickly the results of social science research can be embraced by a larger public. The frequent adoption of conflict resolution strategies by businesses, courts, schools, international organizations, and thousands of other groups also demonstrates how widely the public now shares with social scientists the belief that techniques exist to help make peace more common.

CONFLICT TRANSFORMATION PROGRAMS

Conflict resolution and management strategies have now been used in many cultures and circumstances for over half a century. Still, because it focuses mostly on specific situations, conflict resolution is sometimes faulted as mere "ambulance driving," as work that patches up conflicts while ignoring social structures that may keep producing new crises again and again.

Conflict resolution typically pursues what has been called the "no more shooting type" of peace mission. A second approach, conflict transformation, pursues a "no need for more shooting type" of mission (Arnson and Azpuru 2008). **Conflict transformation** works on specific crises with conflict resolution and management techniques as it simultaneously addresses more fundamental social institutional processes. While conflict resolution aims to produce negative peace, conflict transformation seeks to build positive peace.

John Paul Lederach, an influential proponent of conflict transformation, has refined this approach through three decades of work in crises on five continents, including in

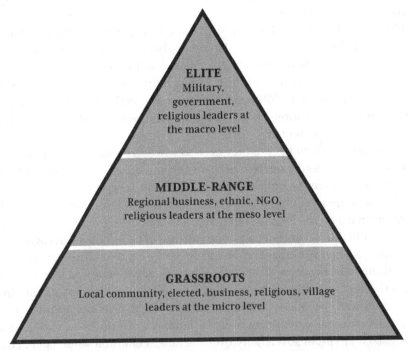

FIGURE 12.1 Pyramid of Relationships Among Change-Makers.

Colombia, the Philippines, Nepal, Nicaragua, Northern Ireland, and Somalia. Lederach maintains that conflict resolution is successful mostly in situations where the troubled parties have no long-term relationship with one another (Lederach 2003, 69). Often, however, disputants have ongoing associations and so, even though conflict resolution may ease the immediate crisis, larger problems will likely remain. Lederach's alternative requires mid- to long-range changes. As Lederach explains, "Rather than narrowly focusing on the single wave rising and crashing on the shore, conflict transformation starts with an understanding of the greater patterns, the ebb and flow of energies, times, and even whole seasons, in the great sea of relationships" (Lederach, 2003, 16).

Because it seeks to build positive peace, conflict transformation commonly requires widespread changes at multiple levels. Lederach pictures change-makers in a pyramidal structure containing three layers. The top level is composed of military, political, and elite business leaders with wide influence. The middle of the pyramid includes leaders of large organizations, public intellectuals, religious groups, and journalists. The wide base at the bottom is by far the largest. Here are grassroots community leaders such as local elected officials, village elders, community organizers, nonprofit directors, and influential local business owners and managers. (See Figure 12.1, "Pyramid of Relationships among Change-Makers.")

Lederach argues that an effective transformative process must alter relationships both within and between all three levels. Only these changes are likely to end the conditions that have produced recurrent violent situations for years. As Lisa Schirch points out, "It usually takes as long to end a conflict as it took to create it. Often this is a matter of decades rather than months or years" (Schirch 2004, 56.)

Table 12.2 provides a summary of some of the differences between conflict resolution and conflict transformation. The differences are numerous and so sometimes the two are considered to be opposing perspectives. However, it is probably more helpful to view conflict resolution and conflict transformation as associated processes with different goals. Conflict resolution techniques are best applied in crises to end direct violence and create negative peace. On the other hand, conflict transformation is better suited for long-term

TABLE 12.2 CONFLICT RESOLUTION AND TRANSFORMATION

Conflict Resolution	Conflict Transformation
Peacemaking—stop something not desired	Peacebuilding—create something that is desired
Create negative peace by solving the presenting problem	Create positive peace through transformation activities
"No more shooting"—end the crisis	"No need for more shooting"—end the underlying conditions producing crises
Specific, narrow, and product focused—this crisis is the problem	Holistic and broad process focused—this crisis is a symptom of a deeper problem
Immediate, short-term, specific time frame	Long-term, open-ended time frame
Aim for agreements	Focus on relationships
Create implementation instruments, e.g., written agreements, reforms of policies	Nourish long-lasting associations, e.g., build trust, diminish hatreds, prejudices, inequities, grievances, and fears

Sources: Arnson and Azpuru 2008; Coy 2009; Deutsch 1973; Lederach 2003; Schirch 2004.

projects, for building social structures able to nourish a sustainable positive peace. Conflict transformation requires restructuring social relationships, a more ambitious goal than most conflict resolution and management approaches are prepared to pursue.

SEEKING PEACE THROUGH HEALTH

Conflict resolution and transformation are but two of many new peace-promoting developments found within the global peace network. Many of these initiatives draw upon social science's maturing understanding of violence-promoting situations. A third prominent evidence-based development is known variously as medical peace work, health as a bridge to health, or peace through health, the phrase I will use here (Santa Barbara and Arya 2008). **Peace through health** refers to activities rooted in the health sciences that view violence as a particular type of treatable and preventable disease (Haegerich and Dahlberg 2011). Peace through health initiatives use heath science techniques to change behaviors and policies that will decrease the frequency and power of violence-promoting situations. Those using a peace through health approach often use the health science concepts of diagnosis, prognosis, and therapy to analyze conflict, violence, and war (Santa Barbara and Arya 2008; Wiist et al. 2014).

CASE 12-1 PEACE THROUGH HEALTH CREATES CEASEFIRES

The desire for physical health is common across cultures and political factions. So, too, usually is the desire to keep children healthy. These two desires have been used to broker ceasefires in several countries over the last few decades.

A first success came during the civil war in El Salvador in the 1980s. Childhood mortality levels had risen terribly during the war years as access to health services plummeted. Health workers associated with UNICEF and the Pan American Health Organization joined with the Roman Catholic Church to broker a ceasefire during the Christmas season in 1985 so that children across the country could be immunized. The effort was successful and subsequently expanded into "days of tranquility" that were observed three times each year. About 300,000 children were immunized at many hundreds of locations each year until a permanent ceasefire was established in 1992. By then polio had been eliminated throughout the country and the incidence of such previously fatal diseases as measles and tetanus had dropped dramatically. The public health effort worked not only at greatly improving childhood survival rates but in showing the warring factions and their civilian supporters in El Salvador that they shared and could achieve common goals. The days of

tranquility seemed likely to have helped to speed this civil war's end.

Success in El Salvador has inspired similar, mostly successful health-based temporary ceasefires in nearly twenty countries. These humanitarian pauses have included efforts in Lebanon in 1987, the Philippines from 1988 to 1993, Afghanistan from 1994 to 1997 and again in 2001, the Democratic Republic of Congo in 1999 and 2000, and in Iraq several times after 1996.

Health-oriented ceasefires draw upon each population's common interest in good health but then simultaneously create time for people to experience again for a while what it is like to live in peace. This experience can reawaken and strengthen people's resolve to find a way forward to create a more permanent peace. Temporary health-based ceasefires also demonstrate that cooperation among factions can produce benefits for everyone, without creating winners and losers. In El Salvador, for example, everyone's children—regardless of their caregivers' politics—became less likely to contract polio or die from a treatable disease. Establishing and maintaining temporary ceasefires also creates new channels of communication that can then be used to negotiate a longer lasting peace.

Source: Arya 2007.

The idea that violence is a disease has a long history, going back at least to Augustine over 1,500 years ago (Nagler 2004, 34–42). However, humans learned how to plan and implement effective health science initiatives only recently. These newly possible public health programs have saved hundreds of millions of lives over the past fifty years and seem likely to save even more as programs improve and are more widely implemented (Levine 2004). Some of the more successful initiatives so far include: Mass vaccination initiatives for such once-cataclysmic diseases as polio, measles, and smallpox; preventing HIV/AIDS and many other sexually transmitted infections; smoke cessation and highway safety campaigns; and the dissemination of birth control knowledge and devices.

There was insufficient knowledge until recently to adopt a similar health sciences approach to launch effective violence abatement programs. More research is still needed to determine the most effective diagnostic and therapeutic strategies. And most governments typically remain much more willing to fund research aimed at improving their police, security, and military forces than to fund health sciences research aimed at preventing the formation of violence-promoting situations. Nonetheless, financial support for health sciences–based violence reduction initiatives is rising (Arya and Santa Barbara 2008).

The health sciences have already proven decisive in several well-publicized antiwar campaigns. For example, in the 1980s the International Physicians for the Prevention of Nuclear War (IPPNW) changed how many people thought about the probable consequences of nuclear war (Arya 2007). Ex-Soviet premier Mikhail Gorbachev credited IPPNW with altering his own as well as world opinion. Gorbachev wrote in his memoir, *Perestroika*, that IPPNW was convincing because they relied on "accurate knowledge" and used "strictly scientific data" so that politicians such as himself could no longer ignore the truth that a great power nuclear war would create an unacceptably large global catastrophe (quoted in Arya 2007, 370).

The prestige and methods of the health sciences played a prominent role in the campaigns against land mines that led to the 1997 Convention on the Prohibition of the Use, Stockpiling, Production and Transfer of Anti-Personnel Mines and on Their Destruction (also known as the Ottawa Convention or Ottawa Treaty). This agreement has now been adopted by 161 countries (though not by the United States). Many of the arguments against the continuing manufacture and use of land mines emphasized medical studies of the frequent suffering that land mines bring to noncombatants and, especially, to children. The opinions of health professionals and their frequent emphasis on what is required for human health helped sway global opinion in ways that other types of arguments did not (Arya 2007). (See also Case 12-1, "Peace through Health Creates Ceasefires.")

The health sciences and peace studies have a natural affinity. Both seek to end unnecessary human suffering and both value health more than any particular ethnicity, ideology, or nation. As Johan Galtung and Charles Webel (2007) suggest, the health sciences and peace studies may become increasingly active partners in forming a single human science of well-being. Table 12.3 provides a list of some the most prominent peace through health organizations.

TABLE 12.3 PROMINENT PEACE THROUGH HEALTH ORGANIZATIONS

Name	Mission
Doctors Without Borders, at www.msf.org	An international, medical humanitarian organization that delivers emergency aid to people affected by armed conflict, epidemics, natural disasters, and exclusion from health care
Health and Human Rights, at www.who.int/hhr/en	Unit within the World Health Organization advocating for the view that health is a universal human right
Health as a Bridge for Peace, at www.who.int/hac/techguidance/hbp/en	Supports health workers in delivering health programs in conflict and post-conflict situations
International Committee of the Red Cross, at www.icrc.org	Works worldwide to provide humanitarian help for people affected by conflict and armed violence and to promote laws that protect victims of war
International Physicians for the Prevention of Nuclear War, at www.ippnw.org	Global network of health professionals seeking a more peaceful and secure world free from the threat of nuclear annihilation
Pan American Health Organization (PAHO), at http://www.paho.org/hq/ and www.disaster-info.net	Aims to strengthen national and local health systems and improve the health of the peoples of the Caribbean and Americas
Physicians for Human Rights, at physiciansforhumanrights.org	Uses medicine and science to stop mass atrocities and human rights violations
UNICEF, at www.unicef.org	United Nations–sponsored agency to promote health, education, gender-equity, and security for children
WHO Violence and Injury Prevention, at www.who.int/violence_injury_prevention/violence/en	World Health Organization projects to reduce direct and indirect violence and injury

Source: Arya 2007.

MAKING CONNECTIONS

Research into violence reduction will never produce findings with the certainty common to the natural or, even, to the life sciences. Proof of the cause of an absence is extremely difficult to produce so it will likely never be possible to determine what specific conflict reduction techniques stopped violence that never occurred. For example, experiments cannot be run on two similarly dangerous real life situations with one serving as a control and allowed to run its course into potentially deadly violence.

Still, as in all complex scientific research, there are ways to analyze data to produce hypotheses that can be tested against other data sets. Future research is likely to provide increasingly accurate estimates of the probable success rates for conflict resolution, conflict transformation, peace through health, and other violence reduction programs. Then, as additional research is completed, the public will learn yet more about the benefits of different evidence-based strategies for reducing violence. A better informed public is, in turn, likely to further support the global peace network and increases in peace research and, simultaneously, to push for a wider use of those techniques that best keep people safe.

One hundred years ago, in the heyday of Freudian and social Darwinian mythologies, human violence was considered inevitable. The scientific understanding that violence is caused more by bad situations than by bad people is just now beginning to be translated into practical programs. An era of widespread, conscious violence reduction may lie ahead.

FOR REVIEW

1. Review which forms of socially-approved violence are most, and least, encouraged by the majority of people in your community.
2. Assess which characteristics of violence-promoting situations are most likely to cause violence.
3. Explore the similarities between the training of soldiers and the training of suicide bombers.
4. Review how conflict resolution programs distinguish between positions and interests.
5. Explain how "peace through health" approaches to violence reduction differ from a reliance on security forces and other traditional coercive attempts to decrease violence.

THINKING CRITICALLY

1. What are the principle obstacles to conducting research like that pioneered by Randall Collins which is based on direct or near direct observations of violent acts?
2. What difference might it make if all adults were required to own a handgun?
3. Can you draw upon your own experience to explain why encouraging audiences are often able to convince people to fight?
4. What actions could a group take to reduce its own discontinuity effect?
5. What are the central differences between how volunteer soldiers and suicide terrorists are trained?
6. Describe how a real or imagined disagreement might escalate from griping, to whining, arguing, quarrelling, and finally, interpersonal violence.
7. Why have commercial enterprises become one of the main global promoters of conflict resolution training?
8. How does the distinction between positions and interests apply to ordinary conflicts among family members, friends, and partners? Can you offer examples from your own experience where confusion between positions and interest produced conflict?
9. How could peace through health violence abatement programs one day become as common as public health programs aimed at reducing diseases, smoking, and highway deaths?

RECOMMENDED RESOURCES

"Dealing Constructively with Intractable Conflicts." This free online course focuses primarily on long-lasting, difficult-to-resolve conflicts, but it also offers basic instruction in conflict resolution techniques. Available at http://www.beyondintractability.org/educationtraining/dealing-constructively-intractable-conflicts

Fisher, Roger, William Ury, and Bruce M. Patton. *Getting to Yes: Negotiating Agreement Without Giving In* (New York: Penguin, 2011). An updated and revised edition of an immensely influential book about negotiation and conflict resolution.

Lederach, John Paul. *The Little Book of Conflict Transformation* (Intercourse, PA: Good Books, 2003). Succinctly explains why conflict transformation is more effective than conflict resolution in ending the recurrence of group and state violence. Based on Lederach's twenty years of work in peacebuilding on five continents.

Peacemakers Trust. Dedicated to research and education on conflict transformation and peace-building. This robust site offers its own original materials and also provides a well-designed portal to conflict resolution and transformation resources across the Internet. Website at http://www.peacemakers.ca

"Violence and Injury Prevention." This site describes efforts by the World Health Organization to reduce violence across the world. It also provides excellent research reports and global data sets. Website at http://www.who.int/violence_injury_prevention/en

"Violence Prevention: Injury Center." Sponsored by the United States Centers for Disease Control and Prevention, this site provides reports on violence as a public health problem. It includes summaries of ongoing violence abatement programs and descriptions of the most recent research and data. Website at http://www.cdc.gov/violenceprevention

Wiist, William H. et al. 2014. "The Role of Public Health in the Prevention of War: Rationale and Competencies." *American Journal of Public Health* 104(6): 34–47. An ambitious and pioneering effort by the American Public Health Association to describe how public health organizations can best moderate the political, economic, social, and cultural causes of war.

Zimbardo, Philip. *The Lucifer Effect: Understanding How Good People Turn Evil* (New York: Random House, 2007). Describes Milgram's as well as Zimbardo's experiments while offering a clear explanation of how social roles and situations shape behavior.

CHAPTER 13

INNER AND OUTER PEACE

CHAPTER OVERVIEW

This chapter describes opportunities for both volunteer and paid work in support of peace. It begins by exploring personal and inner peace, then examines the idea that peace workers should first focus on themselves before committing to help others. The chapter next points to the increasing number of job opportunities associated with tens of thousands of peace-promoting organizations. Direct peace work, focused mostly on creating negative peace, is distinguished from indirect peace work, focused mostly on creating positive peace. A section describes opportunities for peacemaking, a form of direct peace work aimed at ending or at least decreasing physical violence. This is followed by a survey of careers in peacekeeping and conflict resolution. Further sections review work opportunities in peacebuilding and conflict transformation. The chapter concludes with separate descriptions of the work done by entrepreneurial peacebuilders, peace educators, and peace researchers.

Key terms discussed include: Personal peace; inner peace; direct peace work; indirect peace work; peacemaking; peacekeeping; peacebuilding; shared value capitalism; corporate social responsibility; socially responsible investing; social enterprise; social entrepreneurs; peace education; and peace research.

> You may never know what results come from your action.
> But if you do nothing, there will be no results.
>
> —MOHANDAS GANDHI (attributed)

Everyone helps maintain peaceful relations as they coordinate with friends, family, acquaintances, coworkers, and strangers. This daily peace work negotiates life's many ordinary conflicts without violence most of the time. Professional peace workers often differ from ordinary people, then, not in what they do so much as in the self-awareness and levels of skill they bring to their jobs.

The contemporary world offers ample opportunities for peace-promoting activities on both a small and large scale. There is also important peace work people can do by focusing on themselves, on the type of personal peace discussed in Chapter 2. We will look at this inner work once more before surveying the breadth of career and volunteer opportunities associated with peacemaking, peacekeeping, peacebuilding, and other jobs.

INNER AND PERSONAL PEACE

Disagreements persist in peace studies over how much emphasis should be placed on inner peace and personal well-being. However, no one disputes that micro level violence, especially suicide, is by far the largest source of violence in most countries year after year. Peace studies researchers and workers thus have a strong reason to make individual misery and self-harming central to their concerns.

Personal peace is commonly identified with psychological well-being, a condition discussed in Chapter 11. A related concept, **inner peace**, is more often associated with a special type of religious or spiritual understanding. Some of the best-known careers associated with peace studies include counselors, psychologists, psychiatrists, public mental health workers, and social workers who aim to increase levels of personal peace. There are as well many careers associated with religious or spiritual traditions that encourage the development of inner peace. These jobs include clergy as well as martial arts, meditation, and yoga instructors.

Personal and inner peace workers sometimes specialize in assisting people with careers in peacemaking, peacekeeping, and peacebuilding, people who often witness violence and its lingering horrors. The psychological costs of these job-related experiences can be immense and so some people (e.g., the Metta Center for Nonviolence) advise peace workers to seek first their own personal or inner peace before beginning to work for the peace of others.

Some monotheistic religious traditions also maintain that people should first discover God inside themselves before trying to work on behalf of other people. Some non-theistic spiritual traditions embrace a related view. For example, the Buddhist teacher Geshe Kelsang Gyatso writes, "Without inner peace, outer peace is impossible. We all wish for world peace, but world peace will never be achieved unless we first establish peace within our own minds" (Gyatso 2001, 11).

Unfortunately, some people who begin their peace work by first focusing on themselves may find that they never achieve sufficient self-knowledge, inner peace, or well-being to begin serving others. Meanwhile, concrete opportunities to decrease direct violence or increase positive peace may be disregarded.

A primary emphasis on personal or inner peace can sometimes also have additional drawbacks. Much peace work requires quick action, a willingness to seize possibilities in unexpected moments. Most of the successful nonviolent movements of the past century flourished because masses of ordinary citizens suddenly followed other ordinary citizens and leaders into the streets. Few in the masses or among their leaders had achieved advanced levels of inner peace or elevated states of well-being. It often would have been a mistake to wait to try to make social change until more people became personally or spiritually advanced. Extraordinarily effective peace work has been accomplished by people with many personal flaws.

CASE 13-1 TEAM RUBICON

About two million Americans participated in the American wars in Afghanistan and Iraq. Many of these veterans then faced multiple difficulties after they left the military. Jobs were scarce, especially jobs where veterans could make use of skills they had learned in the military. Many veterans also wished to find ways to help others that did not require the use of fatal force. The nongovernmental organization Team Rubicon was created to meet these needs.

Team Rubicon provides relief immediately after catastrophes, an organizational mission chosen because natural disasters present many of the same problems that soldiers confront in combat. One Team Rubicon volunteer on site after Hurricane Sandy explained, "This is what combat veterans do best, chaos management, personnel management, and logistical management" (Golden n.d.).

Team Rubicon's mission statement includes this principle, "We will always be motivated solely by the altruistic desire to help those in demonstrable need." Since its creation in 2010, Team Rubicon has assisted in disaster relief in Burma, Chile, Haiti (twice), Mozambique, Pakistan, Sudan, Turkey, and in thirteen states in the United States. Many U.S. military veterans have found a renewed sense of purpose through working with Team Rubicon.

For more information see Team Rubicon at http://teamrubiconusa.org

Sources: Golden n.d.; Team Rubicon, 2013.

Emphasizing personal or inner peace before beginning outer peace work also suggests that personal or spiritual gains cannot be made through serving others. In fact, however, one of the best ways to learn about one's own strengths and weaknesses is through caring for others, especially in challenging situations like those that outer peace work often presents. Well-being itself, as discussed in Chapter 11, is often strongest in those who regularly assist people in need.

Many religious, spiritual, and secular organizations encourage a path to personal peace through serving others. The historic Christian peace churches described in Chapter 9 have promoted this approach, but comparable commitments to peace outreach are found in most of the world's religions.

It is thus probably not necessary to choose between inner and outer peace work. Those with healthy levels of well-being or inner peace will generally work better with others and avoid the compassion fatigue that frequently haunts careers in peacemaking, peacekeeping, and peacebuilding. Concurrently, those who pursue opportunities to help others will find these activities often enrich their personal lives. The pursuit of inner and outer peace can be mutually supporting.

DIRECT AND INDIRECT PEACE WORK

As David J. Smith (2011) points out, peace workers can promote peace either directly or indirectly. **Direct peace work** tends to focus on ending physical violence through conflict resolution and creating negative peace. Examples of direct peace workers include nonviolent campaigners who target abuses of human rights, police and social workers confronting domestic violence, diplomats and mediators intervening in dangerous disputes, and UN peacekeepers deployed to stop civil and ethnic wars.

By contrast, **indirect peace work** focuses on ending indirect structural violence through conflict transformation and creating positive peace. Examples of indirect peace workers

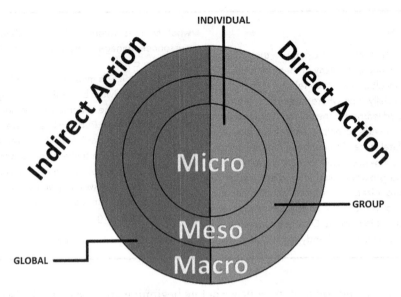

FIGURE 13.1 Levels of Peace Work.

include nonviolent campaigners seeking to increase awareness of human rights, journalists publicizing dangerous situations, social entrepreneurs building community-based businesses, and trainers offering instruction in conflict resolution skills. Indirect work that builds positive peace can also be mostly unplanned, but still impactful. Such is the work of many teachers, of health and social workers, and of numerous others.

As Smith (2011) also makes clear, both direct and indirect peace work takes place at many levels. Efforts may focus on the individual, group, regional, and international levels, stretching across the continuum of micro, meso, macro, and ecological activities discussed throughout this book. Most peace workers emphasize one level but many shift back and forth over the course of their careers. A social worker who has spent years focusing on domestic violence perpetrators and victims at the micro level may also work at the meso level as a policy advocate or campaigner for legislation. International diplomats and mediators also frequently shift levels by working on national policies and by teaching individuals and groups aspiring to become international diplomats and mediators.

Peace workers may shift between direct and indirect action as well as between levels. Figure 13.1 suggests one way to visualize these possibilities. Careers can be made in peacemaking, peacekeeping, peacebuilding, social enterprise, research, and education. A brief review of each of these important types of work will illustrate the diversity of opportunities available.

PEACEMAKING

Peacemaking aims to end or at least decrease direct physical violence. Effective peacemakers try to remain neutral, refusing to choose sides while insisting that physical violence immediately end.

Peacemaking usually takes place in an emergency when people are being hurt and the hurt will continue, perhaps escalate, if peacemakers do not intervene. Arbitrators, diplomats, and mediators frequently act as peacemakers in ongoing violent disputes. The best peacemakers are able to work calmly in crises. Most people require training and practice to become effective peacemakers, but the opportunities to learn these skills have dramatically increased in recent decades. Successful peacemakers have the satisfaction of seeing their work result in an immediate reduction of physical harm.

Career opportunities in peacemaking at the macro, international level increased almost fourfold after the end of the Cold War as United Nations peacekeeping missions became much more common (see Table 6.5, "UN Peace Missions"). The UN depends on its member nations for troop deployments, since it has no permanent troops of its own. The Department of Peacekeeping Operations within the UN provides coordination and support. This permanent department provides employment for people unable or reluctant to work as military peacemakers. Many UN member nations also contribute staff to assist with specific peacemaking campaigns.

The North Atlantic Treaty Organization (NATO), European Union, and African Union sometimes mount peacemaking operations independently from the United Nations. These efforts offer additional career opportunities for people wishing to specialize in international peacemaking.

CASE 13-2 RACHEL CORRIE

Rachel Corrie was a twenty-three-year-old student at Evergreen State College in Washington state when she created a senior year project that took her to Gaza, part of the Palestinian territories under occupation by Israel. Corrie became a volunteer with the International Solidarity Movement, a nonviolent group supporting the rights of Palestinians. For several months, Corrie lived as a guest of Palestinians and joined protests against the Israeli army's efforts to demolish Palestinian houses.

On March 16, 2003, Corrie and eight other International Solidarity Movement volunteers attempted to block two Israeli army bulldozers that were preparing to destroy the home of a Palestinian pharmacist. Corrie was wearing a bright orange fluorescent jacket and, for much of the time, using a megaphone that called attention to her presence. After about three hours, Corrie was run over twice by a Caterpillar DR9 armored bulldozer. She died soon after from a fractured skull, shattered ribs, and punctured lungs.

Non-Israeli witnesses maintained Corrie was intentionally killed by the soldier driving the bulldozer but an official inquiry by the Israeli government ruled the death accidental. The circumstances of her death remain in dispute, but Corrie's commitment to nonviolence has since been frequently celebrated. A play exploring her life, *My Name is Rachel Corrie*, premiered in London in 2005 and has been produced in dozens of venues across the world. *Let Me Stand Alone*, a collection of Corrie's writings, including diaries, letters, and e-mails, was published in 2008. Both the play and book have been met with protests organized by supporters of Israel.

In her last e-mail four days before dying, Corrie wrote to her father:

Hi Papa,

Don't worry about me too much, right now I am most concerned that we are not being effective. I still don't feel particularly at risk. Rafah [the city where Corrie was living and would die] has seemed calmer lately, maybe because the military is preoccupied with incursions in the north. Still shooting and house demolitions, one death this week that I know of, but not any larger incursions. I can't say how this will change if and when war with Iraq comes.

More information can be found at the Rachel Corrie Foundation for Peace & Justice website at http://rachelcorriefoundation.org

Peacemaking is also frequently required at both the meso and micro levels. For example, community police officers are often called to intervene in violent situations. Many schools have designated peacemakers, often both staff and students, trained to interrupt fights. People who are mostly concerned with the other types of peace work described in later sections are also likely to be thrust sometimes into the role of peacemaker; peacemaking skills are thus often taught to every type of peace worker. (See Case 13-2, "Rachel Corrie.")

PEACEKEEPING AND CONFLICT RESOLUTION

Effective peacemakers stop direct violence but it is the responsibility of other types of peace workers to help belligerents create conditions for a positive peace that will keep violence from breaking out again.

Peacekeeping comes after or simultaneous with peacemaking and seeks to sustain pauses in direct violence. Macro, international peacekeepers enforce and monitor truces and ceasefires while meso and micro level peacekeepers maintain negative peace between groups and individuals. International peacekeepers often work at food distribution, electoral assistance, refugee return and reintegration, civilian protection, prevention of gender-based violence, restoration of transportation and other basic services, and establishing safe havens.

United Nations peacemaking operations often metamorphose into peacekeeping operations. So, for example, UN peacekeepers have now been maintaining truces with various levels of success in the Middle East since 1948, in Cyprus since 1964, and in the Congo since 1999. Like peacemaking, peacekeeping works best when the antagonistic parties agree to the process. This is not always the case, however, and so UN and other peacekeepers have sometimes defended their presence with force against local factions trying to drive them way. The UN missions in Somalia in 1993–1994 and in Bosnia in 1993–1995 were marred by especially long and intense uses of deadly military fire (Findlay 2002).

Though international and regional peacekeeping is done by national militaries and supporting governmental agencies, volunteer civilian organizations are also increasingly involved in peacekeeping campaigns. These groups use nonmilitary methods and peace workers who do not wish to be associated with weapons or force. Peace Brigades International has placed unarmed civilian peacekeepers on missions in the Balkans, Colombia, El Salvador, Guatemala, Haiti, Indonesia, Mexico, Nepal, Nicaragua, and Sri Lanka. A second large global organization, the Nonviolent Peaceforce, is discussed in Case 13-3. An actively managed database of all unarmed civilian peacekeeping activities since 1990 is available online at the Selkirk College Mir Center for Peace.

Unarmed peacekeepers typically live alongside the people threatened by civil disturbances. They act as the eyes and ears of the world, ready to draw global attention to any harm they witness or that they themselves suffer. Because civilian peacekeepers are outsiders and remain neutral, they are often able to talk to all sides and to encourage dialogue among belligerents that can lead to long-term solutions.

The number of people deployed as unarmed peacekeepers totals only a few thousand at any one time. Nonetheless, each deployed peacekeeper requires supporting communities so this widens the career opportunities for people wanting to support direct international peace work without going into the field themselves. Mostly volunteer organizations such as Amnesty International and Human Rights Watch also do peacekeeping as they monitor and publicize human rights abuses in countries across the world. Case 13-1, "Team Rubicon," provides an example of yet another type of unarmed peacekeeping.

Peacekeeping is also much needed at the meso and micro levels, within people's home nations and communities. There are many opportunities for careers in this work, especially in the field of conflict resolution. Chapter 12 describes some of principles of conflict resolution, a type of work associated with peacemaking as well as peacekeeping. There are many more undergraduate and graduate programs offering training and certification in conflict resolution and management than in any other form of peace work.

People trained in conflict resolution and management work in legal and justice systems and in government bureaucracies, as well as in nonprofit and nongovernmental organizations. Some conflict resolution practitioners have independent practices, as mediators and arbitrators. Conflict resolution managers are also employed in human resource departments in commercial businesses and in advising and counseling divisions of educational institutions. Many other people hold positions in which formal training in conflict resolution and management is valued but not required.

Peace Brigades International volunteers accompany members of the Dalit Feminist Uplift Organization (DAFUO) in Nepal.

CASE 13-3 NONVIOLENT PEACEFORCE

The Nonviolent Peaceforce (NP), with headquarters in Brussels, was established in 2002 and has quickly become one of the world's most active unarmed civilian peacekeeping organizations. NP has sponsored substantial projects in Kyrgyzstan, the Philippines, Myanmar, South Caucasus, South Sudan, and Sri Lanka. The experience of two NP teams in one region of Sri Lanka illustrates the strengths and weaknesses of civilian peacekeeping.

NP began working in Sri Lanka in 2003 during the long civil war between the government and the Liberation Tigers of Tamil Eelam, commonly referred to as the LTTE or Tamil Tigers. The government defeated the rebels in the Eastern Province in 2007 and tense provincial elections were held the following year. New violence erupted soon after these elections near Batticaloa Town.

The NP team has been working in this area since 2006 and helped convene a meeting of key people from the government, rival political parties, and religious leaders from both Christian and Muslim communities. This group issued a widely publicized call for an end to the violence but, a few days later, attacks and kidnappings began again. Many people left their homes in hopes of finding safety. Meanwhile, the NP team continued promoting an end to the violence by working as neutral mediators among various untrusting ethnic and religious communities. The NP team encouraged trans-party meetings and agreements and visited with displaced people to try to increase their sense of security and to communicate their needs to government and humanitarian agencies.

Violence continued for a few weeks before tapering off enough for the displaced people to return home. Though the NP proved unable to stop the violence, most of the key groups in the area wanted the NP team to remain in the area to help strengthen community networks that might decrease future violence. The NP's neutrality, growing network of relationships, and ability to broker meetings impartially was considered important by Sri Lankans for building a lasting, positive peace.

During this period, a NP team based further north in Valaichchenai had even more success. The NP had been working in this area even longer, since 2003. It had built relationships and trust through its work after the disastrous 2004 tsunami. Goodwill was further increased through later efforts to secure the release and rehabilitation of child soldiers, obtain humanitarian aid for people in displaced persons' camps, and promote community organizations trying to end ethnic and religious conflicts.

The NP team in Valaichchenai began working with its community partners to prevent the eruption of violence as soon as reports arrived of the post-election fighting in Batticaloa Town. Muslim and Tamil shopkeepers in Valaichchenai were encouraged to band together for mutual support. The NP team sponsored joint activities for diverse youth groups that might be prone to attack each other. NP members also worked with the army, police, and local political parties to improve patrols that might deter violence. Tensions rose with reports of worsening violence in Batticaloa Town, but no one was hurt or driven from their homes in Valaichchenai. Many local observers agreed with the government's divisional secretary for the area that it was because of the NP that no violence erupted in Valaichchenai.

NP's work in Sri Lanka shows that success requires substantial investments in time and personnel. The failure to prevent violence in Batticaloa Town was probably related to the relatively short period—two years—that the NP team had been working in that area. The greater success in Valaichchenai likely depended on the five years of efforts NP invested in that town. Such long-term commitments require substantial monies but are cheap when compared to the cost of violence or to the much higher and often less effective cost of deploying and maintaining coercive, armed peacekeepers.

Source: Furnari, n.d.

PEACEBUILDING AND CONFLICT TRANSFORMATION

Both peacemaking and peacekeeping aim to create negative peace, to stop direct violence or defuse conflicts that could escalate into violence. Peacebuilding, a third type of peace work, functions at a more ambitious level. **Peacebuilding** promotes positive peace by strengthening conditions that discourage coercion and violence. While peacemaking and peacekeeping oppose violence directly, peacebuilding operates more incrementally. It is often difficult to determine how well peacebuilding is working since its effects are indirect and may not manifest for years.

Peacebuilding is desperately needed in war-torn countries. Once peacemakers and peacekeepers establish a truce, post-conflict peacebuilders provide for basic needs, such as housing, food, and medicine. Peacebuilders must often also try to disarm combatants, clear land mines, restore public services, repair infrastructure, return refugees, and provide psychological trauma services. The greater the war damage, the harder it is to complete this initial post-conflict stage. In most cases, large groups of peacebuilders are required.

Even more peacebuilders are needed in the second post-conflict stage. Then peacebuilders assist in programs to revive and improve the economy, resettle and employ former fighters, build or rebuild governmental, legal, and judicial systems, and—in many cases—decrease the domination of one segment of the society over others. This is the work of conflict transformation, the building of positive peace, described in Chapter 12.

Peacebuilding to improve economies, decrease poverty and hunger, and foster power sharing are also often needed even in societies that are not recovering from war. The majority of peacebuilders make their careers in these situations, working in their own societies at the meso and micro levels to decrease indirect cultural and structural violence and to build positive peace. The ambition of these goals is reflected in the broad range of peacebuilding-related jobs, which include careers aimed at improving the economic prospects, health, human rights, and well-being of disadvantaged groups.

Meso and micro peacebuilders include: Community organizers; advocates for youth protection, rights, and services; promoters of interfaith, interethnic, and intercultural dialogue; workers for restorative justice and prison reform; campaigners for human and gender rights, fair policing, and equitable justice administration policies; supporters of violence victims; public health workers; and many others.

ENTREPRENEURIAL PEACEBUILDING

Because a healthy and inclusive economy helps build positive peace, many peacebuilders work to create equitable economies. The growth of socially engaged forms of capitalism over the last few decades has created tens of thousands of new peace-related jobs that were unknown but a generation ago. **Shared value capitalism** is market-based commerce that manages a "double-bottom line" as it seeks to generate social benefits at the same time as profits. Shared value capitalism provides diverse careers, including work in corporate social responsibility, socially responsible investing, social enterprise, and new types of revenue-producing philanthropy.

Corporate social responsibility is also sometimes known as corporate conscience or corporate citizenship. It is a form of corporate self-regulation in which businesses aim to meet high ethical standards and to promote positive social and environmental change. Corporate social responsibility pressures businesses to act to benefit a triple bottom line that includes people and the planet, as well as shareholder profit. Some businesses use their corporate social responsibility plans as public relations gimmicks but many others genuinely try to operate for the benefit of stakeholders as well as shareholders. Stakeholders include consumers, employees, and the communities that produce, distribute, and sell the company's products and services. Managing corporate social benefit plans provide careers for peace workers prepared to work in medium and large businesses.

The growth of shared value capitalism has helped create a rapid expansion of socially responsible investing. **Socially responsible investing**, also known as socially conscious, green, or ethical investing, is a strategy of investing for profit while also seeking to promote social good. Socially responsible investors avoid businesses involved in alcohol, gambling, pornography, military preparedness, tobacco, and weapons while seeking out businesses that promote environmental stewardship, consumer protection, human rights, and social justice. Almost one out of every $8 under professional financial control in the United States in 2010 was invested with some socially responsible principles, a 34 percent increase since 2005 (Social Investment Forum Foundation 2010). Managing this approximately $3 trillion provides jobs for people with dual training in finance and peacebuilding.

The rise of social enterprise is also creating many jobs. Traditional businesses with corporate social responsibility policies view social benefits as an optional addition to their primary commercial activities. **Social enterprise**, on the other hand, makes social benefits the business's primary focus. Social enterprises aim to generate commercial revenues in order to sustain social benefit activities that promote human and environmental well-being. Though almost unheard of a generation ago, most cities across North America and Europe now host networks of successful and aspiring **social entrepreneurs**. Classes and degrees in social enterprise have become commonplace in business schools across the developed world. Formal course work is often useful, but social enterprise is open to any peacebuilder ready for the challenge of managing a commercial enterprise that places social benefits at the center of its business plan.

LEARNING MORE   B CORPORATIONS

Several different initiatives are underway to help the public recognize which companies are doing more than simply issuing false claims about their shared value benefits. One especially promising development is the establishment of B corporations, officially certified for-benefit companies, usually referred to simply as B Corps.

Currently only two types of commercial organizations are recognized under the U.S. federal tax code, "S" and "C" corporations. Both of these are legally required to serve the financial needs of their shareowners above all else. A shareowner can sue a board of directors of an S or C corporation, for example, if the board tries to benefit a country or local community more than its financial bottom line. If a board's choice were between the survival of the corporation and the survival of the United States, by law the board would be expected to favor the corporation.

B corps are, by contrast, legally constituted to serve stakeholders. Registering as a B Corp makes it possible for companies to seek to maximize both benefits and profits or, if they choose, to maximize benefits over profits. B Lab, the independent organization that created the legal structure of B corporations, administers a set of standards to determine whether a company qualifies as an authentic for-benefit corporation. Certification is based on ratings on multiple factors, including measures of the candidate company's impact on local communities, degree of transparency in corporate reporting, treatment of employees, and the level of sustainability of its business activities.

In its first five years, B Lab certified 990 companies in thirty-two countries and 60 industries. Many more candidate B corps may be certified as the concept becomes better known.

Sources: B Lab, 2013.

The success of for-benefit businesses is provoking a transformation in much of the nonprofit sector. These hundreds of thousands of organizations have traditionally supported themselves through gifts and grants. They thus find themselves vulnerable to the fluctuating resources of their private and governmental benefactors. Becoming a social enterprise can help nonprofit organizations move toward economic self-sufficiency. There are thus increasing career opportunities for entrepreneurial peacebuilders who can help nonprofits generate their own revenue streams and so escape some of the challenges of fundraising.

PEACE EDUCATION

Peace education has grown quickly in many countries across the past few decades. **Peace education** teaches alternatives to violence as it tries to build positive peace and decrease both direct and indirect violence. The Global Campaign for Peace Education helped spark global interest with its launch in 1999. UNESCO provided effective publicity and resources through sponsorship of the International Decade for a Culture of Peace from 2001 to 2010. UNESCO continues to provide resources to promote both peace curriculum development and practical peace training throughout the world. Because of the efforts of the Global Campaign for Peace Education, UNESCO, and many others, there are now dozens of peace education associations worldwide.

Peace educators sometimes teach peacemaking skills separately but they also often integrate peace education into traditional academic subjects such as literature, history, language, civics, and the arts. Teaching students the conflict resolution skills of active listening, negotiation, and mediation is especially common. Some peace education trains students to participate more effectively in their own civil societies and yet other peace education programs focus more on promoting international human rights.

Elements of peace education are now found in schools throughout North America and Europe. The Peace Education Foundation in Miami, Florida, for example, has by itself supplied peace-related curriculum materials to more than 20,000 schools. Jobs in peace education for teachers and for curriculum developers are likely to continue to grow.

Peace education is also expanding at post-secondary institutions. About 450 programs provide degrees or certificates in peace studies at about 390 different four-year institutions of higher learning across the world (Hansvick and Harris 2007; McElwee et al. 2009). There are also independent educational peace organizations. For example, The National Peace Academy was created in 2009 to provide inexpensive training in peacebuilding for people outside of university degree programs. The National Peace Academy currently offers dozens of free or inexpensive courses and multiple certificate programs mostly online each year. It was at the National Peace Academy's founding summit in 2009 that this book was conceived.

While growth in new undergraduate programs has slowed, new graduate programs increased 58 percent to a total of 156 between 2000 and 2007 (Hansvick and Harris 2007). Many additional colleges and universities also offer stand-alone courses as part of other disciplines and majors. Peace studies related courses are common within teacher education

TABLE 13.1 PEACE WORK CAREERS

Career Type	Actions	Sample Jobs
Inner and Personal Peace	Achieve inner peace and improve individual well-being	Clergy; meditation and stress-reduction teachers; therapists
Negative Peace: Peacemaking	Halt the fighting; decrease the violence	Arbiter; conciliator; diplomat; mediator; negotiator
Negative Peace: Peacekeeping	Enforce, monitor, and manage truces; restore governments and civil society; create conditions for conflict resolution	UN security forces; human rights watch; international protective accompaniment; community police; domestic violence workers
Positive Peace: Peacebuilding	Create conditions for conflict transformation; minimize indirect and structural violence	Constitution and judiciary creators; community organizers; humanitarian and public health workers; social workers; trauma and reconciliation workers; restorative justice consultants
Positive Peace: Shared Value Commerce	Peacebuilding through commerce; diminish indirect and structural violence	Corporate social responsibility managers; social entrepreneurs and managers; for-benefit venture capitalists and philanthropists
Education	Teach peace enhancing skills	Professors; teachers; trainers
Research	Evaluate peace and violent practices	Biologists; historians; neuroscientists; social scientists

See also: Strategic Peacebuilding Pathways, at http://kroc.nd.edu/strategic-peacebuilding-pathways

programs and, as mentioned, teachers increasingly consider educating students for peace an important objective of their work. Significant growth in peace studies courses at community colleges in the United States has also begun. David J. Smith (2013) lists over twenty established programs, with many more in development. There are, in addition, many courses and programs at both the secondary and post-secondary level that focus specifically on conflict resolution, management, and mediation training, allied fields sometimes considered to be separate from peace studies.

PEACE RESEARCH

Careers for peace and conflict researchers are also available. **Peace research** takes place across disciplines in the humanities and health, natural, and social sciences. Most researchers studying peace, violence, and war identify more with their disciplines than with the field of peace studies. Though efforts to create a unified disciplinary research program have so far met with scant success, this book is purposefully interdisciplinary. It aims to weaken the barriers between disciplines and to encourage a broad, integrated research approach.

Dozens of research institutes were created in the last half century to generate and disseminate empirical knowledge about the causes of peace, violence, and war. For example, the United States Congress created the United States Institute of Peace (USIP) in 1984. USIP now operates from an architecturally impressive building prominently situated on the Washington Mall. USIP works with an annual budget of about $40 million, pursing its mission "to prevent and mitigate international conflict without resorting to violence."

The Appendix lists some of the world's more prominent peace and conflict research institutes. These and hundreds of other organizations provide jobs for peace researchers. Table 13.1, "Peace Work Careers," provides an overview of the most common contemporary peace-associated careers.

GETTING STARTED WORKING FOR PEACE

Your personal journey as a self-aware peace promoter has begun, by reading this book, if not before. How you now proceed depends on your interests and opportunities. More education and training may be needed but, happily, these are now widely available, both at traditional educational institutions and at many online sites.

Volunteering and pursuing internships can be especially valuable. These activities commonly make formal education and training more meaningful and can help guide choices about what further education and training are most needed.

The rise of the global peace network and much else has made many regions of the contemporary world less violent than people could have imagined just a century ago. Whether our descendants will live in an even more peaceful world depends on much that is beyond any one person's control. And yet, much about the future will be shaped by individual decisions made today. Most peace promoters do their jobs because they believe they are simultaneously serving both their communities and themselves. Their peaceful means nurture their peaceful ends.

FOR REVIEW

1. Support the claim that people should first seek personal or inner peace before they undertake peace work on behalf of others.
2. Describe the major differences between indirect and direct peace work.
3. Describe the strengths and weaknesses of each of the three main types of peace work: Peacemaking, peacekeeping, and peacebuilding.
4. Evaluate the probable effectiveness of shared value capitalism as a promoter of peace.
5. Explain which type of peace work best fits your own interests and future plans.

THINKING CRITICALLY

1. Do you agree or disagree with Gyatso's claim that "without inner peace, outer peace is impossible"?
2. How can serving others increase a peace worker's sense of personal peace?
3. Is direct or indirect peace work more likely to increase levels of world peace in the decades ahead?
4. Should the jobs associated with shared value capitalism be considered comparable to other types of peacebuilding activities?
5. Does the work sponsored by the United States Institute of Peace likely conflict with the work undertaken by the United States' five military academies?
6. What are the most consequential instances of peace research presented in the earlier chapters in this book?

7. Do some types of peace work careers listed in Table 13.1 seem more important than others?

8. Among the many organizations listed in the Appendix, are there one or two with whom you would particularly like to serve an internship or begin a professional career?

RECOMMENDED RESOURCES

Career Resources of the Peace and Collaborative Development Network (PCDN). Provides resources for employers, job seekers, and interns focused on international development, peacebuilding, humanitarian relief, social entrepreneurship, international affairs, and more. Website at http://www.internationalpeaceandconflict.org

Global Campaign for Peace Education. Portal for educators seeking to include peace education in all forms of education. Includes curricula in multiple languages as well as teacher training manuals. Website at http://www.peace-ed-campaign.org

Graduate Programs in Conflict Resolution and Peace Studies. Offers one list of graduate programs in the United States and another for the rest of the world. Website at http://www.conflict-resolution.org/sitebody/education/grad.htm

The Interrupters. Directed and produced by Steve James. *Frontline*, PBS, 2012. A documentary that tells the story of three violence interrupters, members of CeaseFire, a grassroots organization working to stop street violence in Chicago. Available at http://www.pbs.org/wgbh/pages/frontline/interrupters

Peace, Peacebuilding, and Peacelearning: A Holistic Introduction. A free curriculum created by the National Peace Academy to help people create change in their personal lives, their communities, and the world at large. Available at http://nationalpeaceacademy.us/edresources/study-guide

Religion, Peace and Reconciliation Resources. A rich source of links to universities, research institutes, and training resources, with an emphasis on the United Kingdom and Europe. Available through the York St John University Faculty of Education and Theology, at http://www.yorksj.ac.uk/education--theology/faculty-of-etrs/our-departments/theology--religious-studies/centres-and-resources/cris/cris-resources/religion-peace--reconciliatio.aspx

Smith, David J. editor. *Peacebuilding in Community Colleges: A Teaching Resource* (Washington, DC: United States Institute of Peace, 2013). Twenty-three contributors join Smith to offer case studies, sample activities, and syllabi to help guide peace studies and conflict resolution programs at community colleges.

Strategic Peacebuilding Pathways. Offers a visually attractive, detailed list of occupations for volunteer and professional peace workers, divided into three main categories: Justice and healing, change and development, and violence prevention, conflict response and transformation. Available at the Kroc Institute for International Peace Studies, at http://kroc.nd.edu/strategic-peacebuilding-pathways

Unarmed Civilian Peacekeeping. Online video. Eighteen-minute introduction to the training, goals, and projects of the Nonviolent Peaceforce in several locations across the world. Available at http://vimeo.com/44641646

University-Based Conflict and Peace Research and Educational Programs. A robust list of over one hundred links to programs across the world maintained at Peacemakers Trust. Website at http://www.peacemakers.ca/education/educationlinks.html#univ

UN Cyberschoolbus Peace Education. UN-maintained site with resources for teaching peace education, human rights, and several other related curriculum areas. Includes interactive games and quizzes. Website at http://www.un.org/cyberschoolbus

SELECTED SECULAR PEACE ORGANIZATIONS

Secular Organizations That Emphasize Training and Action			
Name	Founded	Mission	Website
Women's International League for Peace and Freedom	1915	To create a transformed world at peace	wilpf.org/International
War Resisters' International	1923	To resist war through nonviolent revolution	wri-irg.org
Peace Action (formerly SANE)	1957	To abolish war and assure all live in health and dignity	www.peace-action.org
Campaign for Nuclear Disarmament	1957	To rid the world of all weapons of mass destruction	www.cnduk.org
Amnesty International	1961	To promote human rights	www.amnesty.org
Doctors without Borders	1971	To provide medical assistance to victims of violence	www.doctorswithoutborders.org
International Physicians for the Prevention of Nuclear War	1980	To create a world freed from the threat of nuclear annihilation	www.ippnw.org
Peace Brigades International	1981	To support human rights through protective accompaniment	www.peacebrigades.org
Search for Common Ground	1982	To build a sustainable peace through dialogue, media, and communnity	www.sfcg.org
The Albert Einstein Institution	1983	To advance the use of nonviolent action	www.aeinstein.org
Witness for Peace	1983	To support peace, justice, and sustainable economies in the Americas	www.witnessforpeace.org
The Open Society Foundations	1984	To build societies accountable to their citizens	www.soros.org

Secular Organizations That Emphasize Training and Action			
Name	Founded	Mission	Website
United States Institute of Peace	1984	U.S. Congress–funded center aimed at mitigating international conflict without violence	www.usip.org
rtc: Responding to Conflict	1991	To coordinate and train support for local peace transformation initiatives	www.respond.org
Transcend International	1993	To use action, education/training, dissemination and research to transform conflicts nonviolently	www.transcend.org
International Crisis Group	1995	To prevent and resolve conflicts through field-based analysis, practical policy prescriptions, and high-level advocacy	www.crisisgroup.org
Women Peacemakers Program	1997	To empower gender-sensitive women and men as nonviolent peacemakers	www.womenpeacemakersprogram.org/
Global Youth Action Network	1999	To facilitate youth participation in global decision-making	gyan.tigweb.org
Swiss Peace	1999	To analyze the causes of violent conflicts and develop strategies for their peaceful transformation	www. swisspeace.ch
Lawyers without Borders	2000	To support the rule of law and peacebuilding in the legal sector	www.lawyerswithoutborders.org
International Center for Transitional Justice	2001	To help societies in transition address legacies of human rights violations and strengthen civic and state institutions	www.ictj.org
The International Center on Nonviolent Conflict	2002	To encourage the study and use of nonmilitary strategies	www.nonviolent-conflict.org
Nonviolent Peaceforce	2002	To implement unarmed civilian peacekeeping	www.nonviolentpeaceforce.org
Alliance for Peacebuilding	2003	To promote collaborative action to prevent and mitigate violent conflicts	www.allianceforpeacebuilding.org
Global Partnership for the Prevention of Armed Conflict	2003	To promote regional partnerships that increase human security	www.gppac.net
The Centre for Applied NonViolent Action and Strategies (CANVAS)	2003	To provide practical information for nonviolent activists	www.canvasopedia.org
The Peace Alliance	2005	To network and support peacebuilding across the U.S.	www.thepeacealliance.org
3P Human Security	2005	To foster human security and conflict prevention in U.S. policy	3phumansecurity.org

Secular Organizations That Emphasize Training and Action

Name	Founded	Mission	Website
Mediators Beyond Borders International	2007	To build conflict resolution capacity in underserved areas across the world	www.mediatorsbeyondborders.org
World Beyond War	2014	To end the institution of war and establish a just and sustainable peace	www.worldbeyondwar.org

Selected Secular Organizations That Emphasize Education and Research

Name	Founded	Mission	Website
Rotary Peace Centers	1905	To educate leaders in international cooperation, peace, and conflict resolution	www.rotary.org
Peace Research International (PRIO)	1959	To conduct research on the conditions of peaceful relations between states, groups, and people	www.prio.org
Peace Science Society (International)	1963	To encourage the development of peace analysis and conflict management	pss.la.psu.edu/
Stockholm International Peace Research Institute (SIPRI)	1966	To research conflict, armaments, arms control, and disarmament	www.sipri.org
Tampere Peace Research Institute (TAPRI)	1970	To research the causes of war, nonviolent resolution of conflicts, and conditions for peace	www.uta.fi/yky/en/research/tapri/index.html
Uppsala University Department of Peace and Conflict Research	1971	To research the causes and dynamics of conflict, including maintenance of the Uppsala Conflict Data Program	www.pcr.uu.se
Alternatives to Violence Project	1975	To empower people to live nonviolent lives	avpinternational.org
University for Peace	1980	To provide an international institution of higher education for peace	www.upeace.org
Canadian Peace Alliance	1985	To coordinate Canadian voices for peace	canadianpeace.org/
International Center for Cooperation and Conflict Resolution (ICCCR)	1986	To develop knowledge and practice to promote conflict resolution, cooperation, and social justice	icccr.tc.columbia.edu/
The International Peace Research Association Foundation (IPRAF)	1990	To provide a worldwide network for peace researchers seeking nonviolent ways to resolve conflict	www.iprafoundation.org
Heidelberg Institute for International Conflict Research (HIIK)	1991	To distribute knowledge about the emergence, course, and settlement of interstate and intrastate political conflict	www.hiik.de

Selected Secular Organizations That Emphasize Education and Research			
Name	Founded	Mission	Website
Training for Change	1992	To educate people to use strategic nonviolence for social change	www.TrainingforChange.org
Berghof Foundation	1993	To investigate and develop innovative and pragmatic approaches to conflict transformation	www.berghof-conflictresearch.org/en/
Instituto Universitario General Gutiérrez Mellado (IUGM)	1997	To research and teach about the search for peace, security, and defense	iugm.es/who-we-are/?L=2
Conflict Resolution Information Source	1999	To provide an up-to-date site for conflict and alternative dispute resolution resources	www.crinfo.org
Earth Charter Initiative	2000	To promote ethical principles for building a just, sustainable and peaceful global society	www.earthcharterinaction.org
Global Partnership for the Prevention of Armed Conflict	2003	To promote a global shift in peacebuilding from solely reacting to conflict to preventing conflicts from turning violent	www.gppac.net/
Human Security Report Project (HSRP)	2007	To track trends in organized violence, their causes, and consequences	www.hsrgroup.org
Waging Nonviolence	2009	To provide a source for news, analysis, and reporting on contemporary nonviolent campaigns	wagingnonviolence.org
National Peace Academy	2010	To promote peace learning and action	www.nationalpeaceacademy.us
Global Nonviolent Action Database	2011	To provide information on all major cases of nonviolent action, from BCE to the present	nvdatabase.swarthmore.edu
SUMMIT: The Sustainable Mountain Development and Conflict Transformation Global Knowledge and Action Network	2015	To empower people by connecting them through information, technology, collaborative partnerships, and resources	www.summitglobaldatabase.org

For lists of North American faith-based peace organizations, see the website compilations at Christian Peace Witness <http://christianpeacewitness.org/partners> and at the Fellowship of Reconciliation <http://forusa.org/groups/religious-peace-fellowships>.

Thanks for suggestions from Anne Meyer Byler, Joanie Connors, Gordon Fellman, Douglas Fry, John Filson, Jorgen Johansen, George Lakey, Barbara Woods Langlais, Edward W. Lollis, Bill McConochie, Tuomo Melasuo, Paul A. Olson, David J. Smith, Eric Stoner, and Michael True.

GLOSSARY

AGE OF PEACEBUILDING The last few decades during which the United Nations and other nongovernmental organizations undertook an unprecedented wave of projects to end interstate and intrastate violence.

AHIMSA A Sanskrit word sometimes translated as love, Gandhi expanded the usual meaning of this term from merely avoiding harm so that it included taking positive action to support the well-being of all.

ANTISOCIAL PERSONALITY DISORDER (ASPD) A psychiatric diagnosis with symptoms of aggressiveness, a lack of respect for laws and social norms, frequent lying, a lack of guilt, and indifference to the mistreatment and injury of others. Those with ASPD are sometimes popularly called psychopaths and sociopaths. Their disorder may as often lead to lofty achievements as to violence.

ASHOKA Ruled an immense empire in Asia for decades guided by the ethic of reciprocity. Ashoka promoted equal treatment of women, children, prisoners and all social classes, as well as neighboring tribes.

ATTITUDES TOWARD WAR The acceptance of war as an inevitable and natural human occurrence has declined significantly, especially across the last one hundred years.

AUDIENCE-PROVOKED VIOLENCE A frequent cause of violence-promoting situations associated with the power of witnesses to convince others to fight. *See also* Violence-promoting situation.

AUSTRALIAN ABORIGINE CULTURES OF PEACE Suggest that preagricultural humans were probably not frequent killers and that they used multiple, effective cultural practices for resolving conflicts without violence.

BACKFIRE *See* Paradox of repression.

BANALITY OF EVIL Hannah Arendt's phrase for the ordinary situations in which most workers carried out the mundane tasks that led to the Holocaust. Most workers followed procedures prescribed for them by their bosses, as employees do throughout the modern world.

B CORPS Form a third type of legal organization, in addition to "S" and "C" types, that is legally constituted to serve stakeholders. Also known as B corporations, B corps can maximize both benefits and profits or, if they choose, maximize benefits over profits.

BELOVED COMMUNITY Term used by Martin Luther King Jr. to describe an association of caring social equals like that created by the early Christian and like the state that many Christians believe awaits them after death.

BENEFITS OF SOCIAL RELATIONSHIPS Fulfilling the human need to belong is the single most effective way a person can voluntarily improve their mental health and increase their sense of well-being.

BIOLOGICAL AND CHEMICAL WEAPONS Human-made agents capable of killing millions, perhaps even billions, of people.

BLAME THE VICTIM A frequent cause of violence-promoting situations, associated with the tendency of violence perpetrators to think of themselves as reasonable, peaceful people who were forced to act violently by the provocative aggression of the other. *See also* Violence-promoting situation.

BONOBO PEACEMAKING Depends on female-dominance and the polymorphous use of sex as a technique for conflict management. Bonobos display few of the aggressive behaviors sometimes associated with their genetic close cousins, the chimpanzees.

CAPITALIST PEACE The claim that increased peace among democracies is caused more by economic than by political or normative forces since capitalist systems emphasize laws, negotiations, and contracts and so deter interstate wars. *See* Democratic peace.

CHELČICKÝ, PETR Influential medieval founder of the Unity of Brethren. Chelčický taught an expansive ethic of reciprocity while rejecting the authority of the Roman Catholic Church in terms that Martin Luther would echo almost one hundred years later.

CHILDREN'S CRUSADE In the American civil rights campaign in Birmingham, Alabama, the prominent use of children in nonviolent actions likely to provoke violent government reactions.

CHIMPANZEE VIOLENCE Exaggerated and misinterpreted in many widely publicized reports. Chimpanzees are not as peaceful as bonobos but neither are they frequently violent, as some writers claim.

CITY OF GOD The spiritual, heavenly realm in Christian theology that Augustine claimed was the proper place for the practice of an expansive ethic of reciprocity. *See also* City of Man.

CITY OF MAN The human, earthly realm in Christian theology that Augustine claimed was not a proper place for the practice of an expansive ethic of reciprocity. *See also* City of God.

CIVIL DISOBEDIENCE Nonviolent, sometimes illegal, acts undertaken by individuals or groups to obstruct government actions that they judge unjust or immoral. *See also* Constructive program; Obstructive program; Nonviolent action.

CIVIL SOCIETY ORGANIZATIONS Voluntary associations that seek to advance common economic, political, social, or religious interests. They include educational and research institutions, faith-based associations, labor unions, local community groups, not-for-profit organizations, philanthropic foundations, and professional associations.

CIVILIAN CASUALTIES Despite some well-known claims to the contrary, the rate of non-combatant civilian casualties in wars has probably remained about the same—approximately 50 percent—for several centuries.

CLIMATE WARS Violent conflicts caused by disruptions in the availability of food, water, and other vital resources that could increase as Earth warms in the decades ahead.

CONFLICT RESOLUTION A broad range of peacemaking approaches aimed at ending or reducing disagreements without violence. Conflict resolution names both the academic field that studies resolution strategies as well as the actual practice of ending conflicts.

CONFLICT TRANSFORMATION An alternative to conflict resolution that uses a broad range of peacemaking approaches at the micro, meso, and macro levels to resolve crises through changing fundamental social structural processes.

CONSENT THEORY OF POWER Political theory that state power ultimately depends not on violence but on the collaboration of ordinary citizens.

CONSTRUCTIVE PROGRAM Mohandas Gandhi's term for the creation of alternative social forms to replace the social, political, and economic institutions being opposed through nonviolent action. *See also* Obstructive program.

CONTEMPORARY HUNTER-GATHERERS Typically form egalitarian communities where all members are expected to be generous and cooperative, providing support for the view that rates of violence and war were probably low in most pre-agricultural human societies.

CORPORATE SOCIAL RESPONSIBILITY A form of corporate self-regulation in which businesses aim to meet high ethical standards and to benefit a triple bottom line that includes people and the planet, as well as shareholder profit.

CRITICAL MASS OF WOMEN Sufficiently large minority of female participants to produce shifts in discussions, policies, and legislation.

CULTURAL AND TECHNOLOGICAL CLUSTER OF THE GLOBAL PEACE NETWORK Associated elements of the network that further strengthen the international and national clusters. Elements include changed public attitudes toward violence and war, the accumulation of knowledge, the rising use of social media, as well as others. *See also* Global peace network.

CULTURAL VIOLENCE A type of indirect violence caused by aspects of culture that justify or normalize direct and structural violence. *See also* Structural violence.

CYBER WARFARE Acts sponsored by nation-states, international organizations, or other non-state sponsored groups aimed at damaging or destroying their opponents' information networks and communication capabilities.

DALAI LAMA A Tibetan Buddhist, exiled from Tibet since 1959, who promotes global interfaith dialogues aimed at promoting nonviolence and reducing sectarian and ethnic conflicts.

DEINDIVIDUATION The loss of a sense of separateness developed by individuals in groups as they begin to trust the group's judgments and norms more than their own. Deindividuated members will tend to act as directed by their group, even when they would not have taken such an action alone. *See also* Groupthink.

DEMOCRATIC PEACE Democracies fight wars as often as non-democracies but rarely, if ever, go to war against each other. *See* Capitalist peace.

DIGITAL ACTIVISM The use of electronic technologies, especially social media such as Facebook, Twitter, and YouTube, to create political and social change. Digital technologies enable activists to speed up communication among citizens at the same time that they make it easier and cheaper to share information with large audiences.

DIRECT PEACE WORK Occupations that tend to focus on ending direct physical violence through conflict resolution and creating negative peace. *See also* Indirect peace work.

DIRECT VIOLENCE Human-initiated physical harm inflicted without social structural intermediaries. This is the violence of interpersonal and intimate partner violence, rapes, assaults, suicide, armed insurrections, police states, and wars.

DISPROPORTIONATE ABILITY TO HARM A frequent cause of violence-promoting situations, associated with the finding that those with a greater ability to harm are more likely to initiate and continue violence. *See also* Violence-promoting situations.

DISCONTINUITY EFFECT The tendency for groups to be more antagonistic, competitive, and violent than individuals. The more valued a group membership, the more likely group members are to act violently even though they would not on their own.

DOMESTIC VIOLENCE *See* Gender-based violence.

DRONE WARFARE The use of unmanned aerial autonomous weapons to kill either combatants or non-combatants or both.

EMPEROR CONSTANTINE I Transformed Christianity from a nonviolent, peripheral cult into an official and favored Roman state religion whose members were free to participate in state-sponsored violence.

ETHIC OF RECIPROCITY Directs people to care for everyone equally, without considering whether they are part of one's own family, tribe, or community group. Also known as the Golden Rule.

FAITH-BASED PEACE STUDIES Practiced by those whose religious or spiritual beliefs suggest that not harming others is a moral good. Until the final decades of the twentieth century, most peace leaders and peace movements had roots in faith traditions.

FEMALE INFANTICIDE Violent activities or neglect that leads to the death of many more female than male babies through direct and indirect infanticide.

FOREIGN DIRECT INVESTMENT Monetary investment in buildings, machinery, or equipment in another country, including joint ventures and alliances, as well as investments in management services, technology, and intellectual property. Unlike indirect portfolio investments in stocks or bonds. Thought by some to contribute to the capitalist peace.

GANDHI, MOHANDAS K. In South Africa and India over several decades, created the first, mass nonviolent civil resistance movements in modern history, in part by claiming that the ethic of reciprocity is a central doctrine of Hinduism. *See also* Satyagraha.

GENDER-BASED VIOLENCE Physical or mental harm directed at people on the basis of their gender role, social-sexual characteristics, or sexual orientation. *See* Sex-based violence.

GENDER-EQUITY PROFITS Businesses with a critical mass of females in positions of power tend to make larger profits than businesses with no influential groups of females.

GENDER PERSPECTIVE Uses gender as a master lens through which to foreground the differences between men and women's customs, expectations, experiences, roles, status, and power. A gender perspective recognizes that gender is an important element in every aspect of economic, social, and private life.

GENDER ROLES Sets of expectations held by groups about how females and males should behave because of their actual or assumed primary and secondary sex characteristics.

GHONIM, WAEL A leader in the campaign for regime change in Egypt in 2010–2011 who used electronic images and social media to help mobilize tens of thousands of citizens.

GLOBAL NONVIOLENT ACTION DATABASE A searchable online resource that aims to describe every nonviolent campaign throughout history, from every part of the world. The database currently contains information on over 1000 campaigns.

GLOBAL PEACE INDEX An objective measure of a country's level of peace based on twenty-three indicators associated with both internal and external peace-related factors. Used to monitor trends and make comparisons among countries, as well as to measure how peace and violence influence national and world economies.

GLOBAL PEACE NETWORK A non-hierarchical grid that currently links hundreds of thousands of peace-promoting organizations and millions of individuals spread across the globe. *See also* International cluster, National cluster, and Cultural and technological cluster of the global peace network.

GLOBALIZATION OF MARKETS The tendency for companies to seek to sell their products and services all over the world. Thought by some to contribute to the capitalist peace.

GLOBALIZATION OF PRODUCTION Dispersing the creation of goods and the outsourcing of services across multiple borders. Thought by some to contribute to the capitalist peace.

GOLDEN RULE *See* Ethic of reciprocity.

GREAT POWER WARS Violent conflict among nations that have the ability to exert significant influence beyond their own geographical region.

GROUP SELF Points to how individual self-understandings, perceptions of reality, and personal goals and judgments are often derived from the group(s) to which people belong.

GROUPTHINK The tendency of groups to suppress dissent, ignore counter-evidence, and de-emphasize independent analyses. Group members are apt to elevate their loyalty above their commitment to making sure that the group makes the objectively best decision. *See also* Deindividuation.

HACKTIVISM A form of civil disobedience in which citizens access government websites and conduct virtual-sits, institute website redirections, and create look-alike website parodies.

HARD POWER Indicates a foreign policy emphasis on military power, coercion, and force. *See also* Smart power; Soft power.

HETERONORMATIVITY A worldview usually supported by laws and customs that promote heterosexuality and dichotomous gender relations as the single acceptable form of gender and sexual expression.

HUMAN RIGHTS Fundamental moral or legal entitlements that people possess at birth, regardless of nationality, sex, or ethnic origin, race, religion, language, or other social status.

HUMAN SECURITY Focuses on protecting and expanding human rights through increasing cooperation among citizens. Includes attention to the basic human needs for food, shelter, and health care.

HUMAN TRAFFICKING Recruiting, transporting, harboring, or employing a person through the use of force, coercion, or other means, for the purpose of exploiting them. Increasingly common in sweat shops, on agricultural plantations, and among domestic laborers.

INDIRECT PEACE WORK Occupations that focus on ending indirect, structural violence through conflict transformation and creating positive peace. *See also* Direct peace work.

INDIRECT VIOLENCE Physical and mental harm caused by social systems and cultures. Instances include inequitable childhood mortality and malnutrition rates, hunger in societies with plenty, mass incarceration, slavery, segregation, and any other systematic discrimination based on age, gender, ethnicity, income, religion, or race. Also sometimes known as structural violence.

INDIVIDUALISTIC EXPLANATIONS OF VIOLENCE Emphasize the role of internal mental states and dispositions in causing violent behaviors.

INDUSTRIALIZATION OF WARFARE The use of modern technology, industrial production, and bureaucratic organization to increase the rate of both battlefield and civilian deaths.

INNER PEACE A psychological state associated with a special religious or spiritual understanding. *See also* Personal peace.

INTERESTS In the field of conflict resolution, interests refer to causes, goals, hopes, and fears that generate disputes. Interests are deeper, often unrecognized desires that produce positions. *See also* Positions.

INTERNATIONAL CLUSTER OF THE GLOBAL PEACE NETWORK Institutions and organizations working across national borders to promote peace. These include aid agencies, human rights promoters, international courts and treaties, peacekeepers, as well as others. *See also* Global peace network.

INTERNATIONAL TRIBUNALS AND COURTS Apply the rule of law to the adjudication of human rights disputes, often in places where the local judicial system is either weak or corrupt. These institutions include the Commission on Human Rights, World Court, and International Criminal Court.

INTERSTATE CONFLICTS Violent disputes that take place between nation-states.

INTIMATE PARTNER VIOLENCE Physical harm directed against a family member or romantic partner, including battering, assault, murder, rape and other types of sexual coercion, as well as forms of controlling behaviors such as isolating a partner from family and friends or restricting access to information and assistance.

INTRASTATE CONFLICTS Violent uprisings that take place between groups within countries.

JUST WAR DOCTRINE Specifies the conditions under which it is ethical to wage war and also establishes criteria for the manner in which a just war should be fought.

KANT, IMMANUEL An eighteenth-century German philosopher who argued that world peace would be possible if nations were democratic, entered into an international association, and were led by people with a cosmopolitan perspective.

KHAN, ABDUL GHAFFAR A Pashtun and Sunni Muslim who created a mass nonviolent movement against British colonialism based in Islamic teachings. Khan's movement remained mostly nonviolent in the face of lethal repression harsher than any Gandhi's movements faced.

KING JR., MARTIN LUTHER A Baptist minister and leader of the civil rights movement in the United States. In the 1960s, King expanded his earlier emphasis on domestic issues to include opposition to the American wars in Southeast Asia.

LETHAL AUTONOMOUS WEAPONS Unmanned devices, such as armed robots and drones, designed to carry out killing missions with little or no human intervention.

MACRO LEVEL OF PEACE ANALYSIS Focuses on conflict and violence associated with international relations and foreign policy. The broadest unit of analysis used in the social sciences.

MATERNAL MORTALITY Death during pregnancy or through childbirth complications; frequencies vary greatly from country to country and among ethnic groups within countries.

MESO LEVEL OF PEACE ANALYSIS Focuses on conflict and violence between groups and regions. The mid-level unit of analysis used in the social sciences.

MICRO LEVEL OF PEACE ANALYSIS Focuses on individual and interpersonal conflict and violence, the level where about 80 percent of all fatal violence is found. The smallest unit of analysis used in the social sciences.

MILGRAM'S OBEDIENCE EXPERIMENT Demonstrated that most experimental subjects are willing to follow orders to harm others when told to do so by an authority figure.

MILITARY-INDUSTRIAL COMPLEX Phrase popularized by President Dwight D. Eisenhower to describe the influence of professional soldiers and members of the defense and security business sector on the United States' domestic and foreign policies.

MISSING WOMEN The estimated over 100 million females absent from the world population due to female infanticide, gendered health care neglect, sex-specific abortions, unnecessary maternal mortality, and other causes.

MOTIVES FOR WAR Leaders choose war to gain (1) resources, (2) security, (3) prestige, and (4) revenge, with prestige by far the most common motive.

MOVEMENT OF MOVEMENTS Naomi Klein's label for the recent explosion of new civil society organizations that now likely includes a million or more nongovernmental, noncommercial groups spread across the world.

MYTH OF THE KILLER APE The belief that humans are universally predisposed to be violent by biology, genetics, or divine forces. This myth often works as a self-fulfilling prophecy, fostering violence where otherwise there might be none.

NATIONAL CLUSTER OF THE GLOBAL PEACE NETWORK Organizations and groups within countries that promote peace. These include peace, human rights, and environmental groups, as well as pro-democracy and women's rights organizations, and others. *See also* Global peace network.

NATIONAL SECURITY Focuses on protecting national borders through the use of threats, coercion, and force.

NEED TO BELONG A basic human motivation to maintain social bonds with other humans. Perhaps the broadest and most dominant need, from which many other needs are derived.

NEGATIVE PEACE The coerced absence of direct human-initiated physical harm. Negative peace can be achieved through ceasefires and treaties, as well as by putting violent people into restraints or prisons, or some other form of social isolation. *See also* Positive peace.

NEUROPLASTIC REVOLUTION A change in perspective to the understanding that the postnatal human brain is shaped as much by its lived experiences as by its biological inheritance.

NEW WARS Aim to mobilize civilian populations more than to capture their territory or resources.

NONVIOLENT ACTION A term popularized by Gene Sharp to replace the terms "nonviolence" and "passive resistance," to emphasize the active way that nonviolent campaigns wage conflict without violence. *See also* Civil disobedience.

NONVIOLENT METHODS Specific nonviolent activities that enable people to oppose government actions and policies through protests, resistance, and interference. Choices of methods are often guided by nonviolent strategies.

NONVIOLENT STRATEGIES Plans, policies, and schemas that guide decisions about which methods to use in conducting protests, resistances, and interventions.

OBSTRUCTIVE PROGRAM Michael Nagler's term for nonviolent action that uses protests, resistance, and interventions to express disapproval with customs, laws, and policies. *See also* Constructive program.

PARADOX OF REPRESSION When oppressive violence by government forces or their allies backfires and increases support for a nonviolent movement. Also known as backfire, backlash, and political jiu-jitsu.

PEACE Built through right relationships and harmonious associations; more than the mere absence of violence.

PEACEBUILDING Works indirectly and incrementally to promote positive peace by strengthening conditions that discourage coercion and violence. Activities may include aiding in economic reconstruction, establishing nonviolent modes of resolving conflicts, fostering reconciliation, protecting human rights, providing humanitarian relief and trauma healing services, repatriating refugees, resettling internally displaced persons, and supporting broad-based education.

PEACE CHURCHES Denominations founded after the Protestant Reformation whose members practiced the ethic of reciprocity in opposition to claims that some violence is acceptable for Christians. The Church of the Brethren, Mennonites, and Religious Society of Friends (Quakers) continue this tradition today. Also known as the historic peace churches.

PEACE ECOLOGY A holistic perspective that focuses on the interdependencies that connect the separate elements found at the macro, meso, and micro levels of human activity.

PEACE EDUCATION Teaches alternatives to violence in an effort to build positive peace and decrease direct and indirect violence.

PEACEKEEPING Maintains pauses in direct violence, often after or simultaneous with peacemaking. Peacekeeping work includes food distribution, electoral assistance, refugee return and reintegration, civilian protection, prevention of gender-based violence, restoration of transportation and other basic services, and establishing safe havens.

PEACEMAKING Aims to end or at least decrease direct physical violence. Arbitrators, diplomats, and mediators frequently act as peacemakers. May include military coercion and violence.

PEACE RESEARCH The formal study of conflict, peace, violence, and war, undertaken with little coordination or communication across disciplines in the humanities and health, natural, and social sciences.

PEACE STUDIES A diverse field built on the belief that more peace is possible when people possess the necessary knowledge and will; includes specialties in research, practical action, and education that all aim to help create a more peaceful world.

PEACE THROUGH HEALTH Initiatives that view violence as a particular type of treatable and preventable disease; often analyzes conflict, violence, and war in terms of diagnosis, prognosis, and therapy.

PEACE THROUGH PEACE A foreign policy strategy of relying on nonviolent actions such as diplomacy and negotiation as a principle means for creating peace. *See also* Peace through strength.

PEACE THROUGH STRENGTH A foreign policy strategy of preparing for and sometimes starting wars as a principle means for creating peace. *See also* Peace through peace.

PENN'S HOLY EXPERIMENT William Penn's English colony, Pennsylvania, governed on the basis of the ethic of reciprocity. The experiment lasted for decades and produced a society with little persecution or violence and with levels of religious tolerance then unknown in Europe or the rest of the European imperial world.

PERPETRATOR-INDUCED TRAUMATIC STRESS (PITS) A severe anxiety disorder with symptoms like those associated with post-traumatic stress disorder; caused by being an active participant in causing physical or mental harm.

PERPETUAL PEACE An idea first formulated by Immanuel Kant that lasting peace on earth would be possible if nations were democratic, entered into an international association, and were led by people with a cosmopolitan perspective.

PERSONAL PEACE A state of psychological well-being. *See also* Inner peace.

POPULATION IS THE PRIZE The goal of foreign and military policy to enhance commercial and social relations between countries through winning the cooperation of citizens.

POSITIONS In the field of conflict resolution, positions refer to the beginning demands or requests that a person or group brings to a conflict. A position names what people say they want. *See also* Interests.

POSITIVE PEACE Conditions of right relationships and harmonious associations in which people flourish in a sharing and equitable community, with no or few instances of direct or indirect violence. *See also* Negative peace.

POSITIVE PSYCHOLOGY Researches mental health and well-being and provides practical training in how best to achieve these states.

POST-TRAUMATIC STRESS DISORDER (PTSD) A severe anxiety disorder that develops after exposure to psychological or emotional injury. Symptoms last for more than one month and cause significant loss in ordinary coping skills. *See also* Perpetrator-induced traumatic stress.

PRAGMATIC NONVIOLENCE Views nonviolent action as a means to an end that may be abandoned if it does not work. Also known as expedient, practical, or strategic nonviolence. *See also* Principled nonviolence.

PRIMATE CULTURES OF PEACE Show that much of what was once thought to be genetically-triggered aggression is rooted in primate cultural learning. New cooperative behaviors can be learned by primates and passed on to later generations.

PRINCIPLED NONVIOLENCE Adopts an expansive interpretation of the ethic of reciprocity, viewing nonviolent action as a moral absolute, as well as a practical means. Often associated with religious faith. *See also* Pragmatic nonviolence.

REVOLUTION IN THE MINDS OF THE PEOPLE John Adams's explanation of the transformation of the American colonists into independent citizens able to view themselves as a new sovereign nation before the violent revolution began.

RISE OF DEMOCRACY Citizens are increasingly participating in the governance of their countries and international forums are increasingly adopting democratic principles.

SATYAGRAHA A term created by Mohandas Gandhi to name the spiritual attitude of seeking truth through nonviolent action. Satyagraha is sometimes translated as "soul force" or "truth force." *See also* Ahimsa.

SEQUENCE OF ESCALATION A frequent cause of violence-promoting situations associated with a temporal series of interactions and communications that increase tensions between disputants. *See also* Violence-promoting situation.

SEVILLE STATEMENT ON VIOLENCE Public declaration of five core findings by prominent social scientists published in 1987 to refute the widespread misbelief that organized human violence is biologically determined.

SEX-BASED VIOLENCE Physical or mental harm directed at people because of their biological appearance—or assumed appearance—as either female or male. *See* Gender-based violence.

SEX-SELECTIVE ABORTION Many more female than male fetuses are terminated through selective abortion.

SHANTI SENA A term Gandhi invented to name his vision of a well-trained, nonviolent peace army that would live within communities and act as impartial peacekeepers in times of trouble.

SHARED VALUE CAPITALISM Market-based commerce that seeks to generate social benefits at the same time as profits. Manages a "double bottom line." Includes corporate social responsibility, socially responsible investing, social enterprise, and new types of revenue-producing philanthropy.

SHARP, GENE A ground-breaking historian and theorist of nonviolent action. Sharp developed a consent theory of power and was a pioneer in describing the many methods used by nonviolent movements.

SMART POWER Indicates a foreign policy that relies first and foremost on soft power—persuasion, cooperation, negotiation, and mediation—while retaining the capability and willingness to use hard power, if necessary. *See also* Hard power; Soft power.

SOCIAL DETERMINANTS OF SUICIDE Factors that account for most of the persistent variation in aggregate suicide rates. Culture, region, gender, age, employment and relationship status, and level of involvement with social groups account for most of the variation in aggregate suicide rates.

SOCIAL ENTERPRISE A business that makes social benefits its primary focus. Social enterprises aim to generate commercial revenues in order to sustain social benefit activities that produce improvements in human and environmental well-being.

SOCIAL ENTREPRENEURS Creators of mission-based enterprises who use business principles to create social value, often financially self-sustaining organizations that address social or environmental problems.

SOCIALLY APPROVED VIOLENCE Physical harm produced by government agents with government approval, or by people widely supported by the general public. Government-sponsored militaries, the police, prison guards, and state-sponsored executioners all sometimes perpetrate socially approved violence. So, too, do rebels and insurgents when their violence is endorsed by a majority of the population.

SOCIALLY RESPONSIBLE INVESTING A strategy of investing for profit while also seeking to promote social good. Socially responsible investors avoid businesses involved in alcohol, gambling, pornography, military preparedness, tobacco, and weapons while seeking out businesses that promote environmental stewardship, consumer protection, human rights, and social justice.

SOFT POWER Indicates a foreign policy that stresses persuasion, cooperation, negotiation, and mediation. *See also* Hard power; Smart power.

STATE MONOPOLY ON THE USE OF VIOLENCE Political theory that governments maintain their power by claiming that they alone can legitimately use physical harm and coercion.

STRUCTURAL VIOLENCE Physical and mental harm caused by inequitable customs, traditions, systems, and laws. Instances include inequitable childhood mortality and malnutrition rates, hunger in societies with plenty, mass incarceration, slavery, segregation, and any other systematic discrimination based on age, gender, ethnicity, income, religion, or race. Also sometimes known as indirect violence. *See also* Cultural violence.

SUCCESS RATES OF NONVIOLENCE Found both by case studies and by numerical analysis to be higher than success rates for violence. Nonviolence also is more likely than violence to produce later positive results even when it leads to short-term failure.

SUFISM Form of Islam that has consistently promoted an expansive understanding of the ethic of reciprocity much like the historic peace churches in Christianity.

TERRORISM Premeditated violence directed primarily at non-combatants that aims to produce fear and advance a political cause. *See also* Terrorism from above; terrorism from below.

TERRORISM FROM ABOVE Government-based violence aimed at producing fear and insecurity in non-combatants. Terrorism from above may aim at domestic or international audiences.

TERRORISM FROM BELOW Citizen-based violence aimed at producing fear and insecurity in non-combatants. Terrorism from below may aim at domestic or international audiences.

THOREAU, HENRY DAVID A nineteenth-century American writer who influentially argued that citizens are obligated to commit civil disobedience to government actions that they judge unjust or immoral.

TRAINING SUICIDE TERRORISTS A careful sequence of group activities to teach recruits how to use their bodies as bombs and to view their violence as an affirmation of their social bonds with their trainers, fellow recruits, co-religionists, and families.

UNARMED CIVILIAN PEACEKEEPERS Based on Gandhi's idea of shanti sena or peace armies, these groups of trained volunteers deploy to conflict zones where they work to prevent, reduce, and stop violence.

VIOLENCE-PROMOTING SITUATION Required to enable most people to overcome their desire both to avoid being hurt and to avoid harming others. Different types of situations encourage violence at the micro, meso, and macro levels.

VIOLENT WOMEN Women are not genetically passive or nonviolent, and have participated in violent conflicts on all continents for at least the last few hundred years.

WAR RAPE Sexual violation and assault of women and girls who reside in or are refugees from a conflict zone.

WOMEN IN PEACEBUILDING Including women in equal proportions to men and bringing a gender perspective to ceasefire and post conflict negotiations. Mandated by UN Security Council Resolution 1325.

WOMEN IN THE RESEARCH SCIENCES Beginning in the health sciences and spreading now to the social sciences and peace studies, a critical mass of females are changing research priorities and policies.

YANOMAMÖ VIOLENCE This South-American tribe was once thought to provide evidence for the claim that violence is a biologically adaptive behavior. Later studies of the Yanomamö rebutted this claim.

ZIMBARDO'S PRISON EXPERIMENT Demonstrated that experimental subjects assigned to the social role of prison guard would act violently even in the absence of an authority figure giving them orders.

REFERENCES

Aafijes, Astrid. 1998. *Gender Violence: Hidden War-Crime.* Washington, DC: Women, Law, and Development International.

Abrahms, Max. 2006. "Why Terrorism Does Not Work." *International Security* 31 (2): 42–78.

Abu-Nimer, Mohammed. 2003. *Nonviolence and Peace Building in Islam: Theory and Practice.* Tallahasee: University Press of Florida.

Ackerman, Peter, and Christopher Kruegler. 1994. *Strategic Nonviolent Conflict: The Dynamics of People Power in the Twentieth Century.* Westport, CT: Praeger.

Ackerman, Peter, and Jack Duvall. 2000. *A Force More Powerful: A Century of Nonviolent Conflict.* New York: Palgrave.

Adam, Karla. 2011. "Occupy Wall Street Protests Go Global." *Washington Post.* October 15. Online.

Adams, John. 1856. *The Works of John Adams,* vol. 10. Edited by Charles Francis Adams. Boston: Little Brown.

Adolf, Antony. 2009. *Peace: A World History.* Malden, MA: Polity.

Ahlström, Christer. 1991. *Casualties of Conflict: Report for the World Campaign for the Protection of Victims of War.* Uppsala, Sweden: Department of Peace and Conflict Research, Uppsala University.

Allen, Charles. 2012. *Ashoka: The Search for India's Lost Emperor.* New York: The Overlook Press.

Altincekic, Ceren. 2009. *FDI Peace: Which "Capitalism" Leads to More Peace among Dyads?* Broomfield, CO: One Earth Future Foundation Working Paper.

American Psychiatric Association. 2013. *Diagnostic and Statistical Manual of Mental Disorders DSM-V,* 5th ed. Washington, DC: American Psychiatric Association.

Amnesty International USA. 2013. *Making Love a Crime: Criminalization of Same-sex Conduct in Sub-Saharan Africa.* June. Online.

Amster, Randall. 2009. "Pax Gaia: The Ecology of War, Peace, and How to Get from Here to There." In *Building Cultures of Peace: Transdisciplinary Voices of Hope and Action,* edited by Randall Amster and Elavie Ndura-Ouédraogo, 240–57. Newcastle upon Tyne, UK: Cambridge Scholars Publishing.

Amster, Randall, and Elavie Ndura, editors. 2013. *Exploring the Power of Nonviolence: Peace, Politics, and Practice.* Syracuse, NY: Syracuse University Press.

Anderlini, Sanam Naraghi. 2007. *Women Building Peace: What They Do, Why It Matters.* Boulder, CO: Lynne Rienner.

Anderson, Ross. 2012. "Cyber and Drone Attacks May Change Warfare More Than the Machine Gun." *The Atlantic.* March. Online.

Ardrey, Robert. 1961. *African Genesis: A Personal Investigation into the Animal Origins and Nature of Man.* New York: Atheneum.

Arendt, Hannah. 2006 [1963]. *Eichmann in Jerusalem: A Report on the Banality of Evil.* New York: Penguin Classics.

Arnson, Cynthia J., and Dinorah Azpuru. 2008. "From Peace to Democratization: Lessons from Central America." In *Contemporary Peacemaking: Conflict, Peace*

Processes and Post-war Reconstruction, 2nd ed., edited by John Darby and Roger MacGinty, 271–88. New York: Palgrave Macmillan.

Arthur L. Kellerman, et al. 1992. "Suicide in the Home in Relation to Gun Ownership." *New England Journal of Medicine* 327 (7): 467–72.

Arya, Neil. 2007. "Peace through Health?" In *Handbook of Peace and Conflict Studies,* edited by Charles Webel and Johan Galtung, 367–94. New York: Routledge.

Arya, Neil, and Joanna Santa Barbara. 2008. *Peace Through Health: How Health Professionals Can Work for a Less Violent World.* Herndon, VA: Kumarian Press.

Atran, Scott. 2003. "Genesis of Suicide Terrorism." *Science* 299 (5612): 1534–39.

B Lab. 2013. *Certified B Corporation.* March 4. http://www.bcorporation.net

Babiak, Paul, and Robert D. Hare. 2007. *Snakes in Suits: When Psychopaths Go to Work.* New York: HarperBusiness.

Babst, Dean V. 1972. "A Force for Peace." *Industrial Research* 14 (4): 55–58.

Bacevich, Andrew J. 2010. "No Exit." *The American Conservative.* February 1. Online.

———. "The End of (Military) History? The United States, Israel, and the Failure of the Western Way of War." *Huffington Post.* July 29. Online.

Badie, Dina. 2010. "Groupthink, Iraq, and the War on Terror: Explaining US Policy Shift toward Iraq." *Foreign Policy Analysis* 6 (4): 277–96.

Baker, Peter. 2013. *Days of Fire: Bush and Cheney in the White House.* New York: Doubleday.

Baker, Peter C. 2013. "Fight Clubs: On Napoleon Chagnon." *Nation* (June 1): 11–18.

Bales, Kevin. 1999. *Disposable People: New Slavery in the Global Economy.* Berkeley, CA: University of California Press.

Banerjee, Mukulika. 2000. *The Pathan Unarmed: Opposition and Memory in the North West Frontier.* London: James Currey.

Barash, David P. 2002. "Evolution, Males, and Violence." *The Chronicle Review* (May 24): B7.

———. 2012. "The End of War?" *Chronicle of Higher Education Blogs.* January 5. Online.

Barash, David P., and Charles P. Webel. 2008. *Peace and Conflict Studies.* 2nd ed. Los Angeles: Sage.

Barber, Lucy G. 2002. *Marching on Washington: The Forging of an American Political Tradition.* Berkeley: University of California Press.

Barry, Kathleen Lois. 2010. *Unmaking War, Remaking Men: How Empathy Can Reshape Our Politics, Our Soldiers and Ourselves.* Santa Rosa, CA: Phoenix Rising Press.

Bartkowski, Maciej J. 2013. "Recovering Nonviolent History." In *Recovering Nonviolent History: Civil Resistance in Liberation Struggles,* edited by Maciej J. Bartkowski, 1–30. Boulder, CO: Lynne Rienner Publishers.

Baumeister, Roy F. 1999. *Evil: Inside Human Violence and Cruelty.* New York: W. H. Freeman.

Baumeister, Roy F., and Mark K. Leary. 1995. "The Need to Belong: Desire for Interpersonal Attachments as a Fundamental Human Motivation." *Psychological Bulletin* 117 (3): 497–529.

BBC World Service. 2008. "World Views US 'More Positively.'" *BBC News Front Page.* April 2. Online.

Bear, Julia B., and Anita Williams Woolley. 2011. "The Role of Gender in Team Collaboration and Performance." *Interdisciplinary Science Reviews* 36 (2): 146–53.

Becker, Jo, and Scott Shane. 2012. "Secret 'Kill List' Proves a Test of Obama's Principles and Will." *New York Times.* May 29. Online.

Begley, Sharon. 2007. *Train Your Mind, Change Your Brain: How a New Science Reveals Our Extraordinary Potential to Transform Ourselves.* New York: Ballantine.

Benjamin, Medea. 2012. *Drone Warfare: Killing by Remote Control.* New York: OR Books.

Berndt, Ronald Murray, and Catherine Helen Berndt. 1999. *The World of the First Australians: Aboriginal Traditional Life, Past and Present.* Canberra, Australia: Aboriginal Studies Press.

Black, Donald W., Tracy Gunter, Peggy Loveless, Jeff Allen, and Bruce Sieleni. 2010. "Antisocial Personality Disorder in Incarcerated Offenders: Psychiatric Comorbidity and Quality of Life." *Annals of Clinical Psychiatry* 22 (2): 113–20.

Bloom, Mia. 2007. "Female Suicide Bombers: A Global Trend." *Daedalus* 136 (1): 94–102.

Bloom, Sandra L. 2001. "Conclusion: A Public Health Approach to Violence." In *Violence: A Public Health Menace and a Public Health Approach,* edited by Sandra L. Bloom, 83–101. New York: Karnac Books.

Bock, Joseph G. 2012. *The Technology of Nonviolence: Social Media and Violence Prevention.* Cambridge, MA: MIT Press.

Boehm, Christopher. 1999. *Hierarchy in the Forest: The Evolution of Egalitarian Behavior.* Cambridge, MA: Harvard University Press.

———. 2012. "Ancestral Hierarchy and Conflict." *Science* 336 (6083): 844–46.

Bornstein, Daniel. 2004. *How to Change the World: Social Entrepreneurs and the Power of New Ideas.* New York: Oxford University Press.

Bott, Sarah, Andrew Morrison, and Mary Ellsberg. 2005. *Preventing and Responding to Gender-Based Violence in Middle- and Low-Income Countries: A Global Review and Analysis.* World Bank: Online Elibrary, WPS3618.

Boulding, Elise. 1992. *The Underside of History: A View of Women Through Time, Revised Edition.* Newbury Park, CA: Sage.

———. 2000. *Cultures of Peace: The Hidden Side of History.* Syracuse, NY: Syracuse University Press.

Boulding, Kenneth. 1977. "Twelve Friendly Quarrels with Johan Galtung." *Journal of Peace Research* 14 (1): 80–83.

Branch, Taylor. 1989. *Parting the Waters: America in the King Years 1954–63.* New York: Simon and Schuster.

Brauer, Jurgen, and John Tepper Marlin. 2009. "Nonkilling Economics." In *Toward a Nonkilling Paradigm*, edited by Joám Evans Pim, 125–48. Honolulu: Center for Global Nonkilling.

Brizendine, Louann. 2007. *The Female Brain.* New York: Broadway.

———. 2010. *The Male Brain.* New York: Broadway.

Brooks, Stephen. 2005. *Producing Security: Multinational Corporations, Globalization, and the Changing Calculus of Conflict.* Princeton, NJ: Princeton University Press.

Brown, Stephanie L., Randolph M. Nesse, Amiram D. Vinokur, and Dylan M. Smith. 2003. "Providing Social Support May Be More Beneficial Than Receiving It: Results from a Prospective Study of Mortality." *Psychological Science* 14 (4): 320–27.

Brownmiller, Susan. 1993. *Against Our Will: Men, Women, and Rape.* New York: Ballantine Books.

Buchanan, Tom. 2012. *Europe's Troubled Peace: 1945 to the Present.* New York: Wiley.

Bueno de Mesquita, Bruce, James D. Morrow, Randolph M. Siverson, and Alastair Smith. 1999. "An Institutional Explanation of the Democratic Peace." *American Political Science Review* 93 (4): 791–807.

Burgess, Jim. 2011. "Spectators Witness History at Manassas." *Hallowed Ground Magazine.* Spring. Online.

Burke, Jason. 2011. *The 9/11 Wars.* New York: Penguin Books.

Burrowes, Robert J. 1996. *The Strategy of Nonviolence Defense: A Gandhian Approach.* New York: State University of New York Press.

Calvin, John. 1956. *On God and Man.* Edited by F. W. Strothmann. New York: Fredrick Ungar.

Caprioli, Mary, and Mark A. Boyer. 2001. "Gender, Violence, and International Crisis." *Journal of Conflict Resolution* 45 (4): 503–18.

Caprioli, Mary. 2000. "Gendered Conflict." *Journal of Peace Research* 37 (1): 51–68.

———. 2003. "Gender Equality and State Aggression: The Impact of Domestic Gender Equality on State First Use of Force." *International Interactions* 29 (3): 195–214.

———. 2005. "Primed for Violence: The Role of Gender Inequality in Predicting Internal Conflict." *International Studies Quarterly* 49 (2): 161–78.

Carter, April. 2005. *Direct Action and Democracy Today.* Malden, MA: Polity.

Caryl, Christian. 2011. "Predators and Robots at War." *New York Review of Books.* September 29. Online.

Castells, Manuel. 1996. *The Rise of the Network Society: The Information Age, Economy, Society and Culture.* Culture, vol. 1. New York: Wiley-Blackwell.

Catalyst. 2010. *Statistical Overview of Women in the Workplace.* Catalyst Online.

Chagnon, Napoleon. 1968. *Yanomamö: The Fierce People.* New York: Holt, Rinehart & Winston.

———. 1988. "Life Histories, Blood Revenge, and Warfare in a Tribal Population." *Science* 239 (4843): 985–82.

———. 1990. "Reproductive and Somatic Conflicts of Interest in the Genesis of Violence and Warfare among Tribesmen." In *The Anthropology of War*, edited by J. Haas, 77–104. Cambridge: Cambridge University Press.

Chang, Iris. 2011. *The Rape of Nanking: The Forgotten Holocaust of World War II.* New York: Basic Books.

Chenoweth, Erica, and Maria J. Stephan. 2011. *Why Civil Resistance Works: The Strategic Logic of Nonviolent Conflict.* New York: Columbia University Press.

Churchill, Winston S. 1991 [1932]. *Thoughts and Adventures.* New York: Norton.

Clawson, Heather J., Nicole Dutch, Amy Solomon, and Lisa Goldblatt Grace. 2009. *Human Trafficking Into and Within the United States: A Review of the Literature.* Washington, DC: U.S. Department of Health and Human Services.

CNN. 2001. "Gulf War Facts." *The Unfinished War: A Decade Since Desert Storm.* Online.

CNN Wire Staff. 2012. "Drone Strikes Kill, Maim and Traumatize Too Many Civilians, U.S. Study Says." Septermber 25. Online.

Coleman, Susan W., and Ellen Raider. 2006. "International/Intercultural Conflict Resolution Training." In *Sage Handbook of Conflict Communication*, edited by John G. Oetzel and Stella Ting-Toomey, 663–690. Thousand Oaks, CA: Sage Publications.

Collins, Randall. 2009. *Violence: A Micro-sociological Theory.* Princeton, NJ: Princeton University Press.

Condry, J. C., and S. Condry. 1976. "Sex Differences: A Study of the Eye of the Beholder." *Child Development* 47 (3): 812–19.

Conetta, Carl. 2008. "Forceful Engagement: Rethinking the Role of Military Power in US Global Policy." *Project on Defense Alternatives.* December. http://www.comw.org/pda/fulltext/081201Force fulEngagement.pdf

Conser Jr., Walter H. 2013. "The United States: Reconsidering the Struggle for Independence, 1765–1775." In *Recovering Nonviolent History: Civil Resistance in Liberation Struggles*, edited by Maciej Bartkowski, 299–318. Boulder, CO: Lynne Rienner Publishers.

Cooper, Tara, Sebastian Merz, and Mila Shah. 2011. "A More Violent World? Global Trends in Organised Violence." *Berghof Handbook of Conflict Transformation.* Online.

Cortright, David. 2008. *Peace: A History of Movements and Ideas.* New York: Cambridge University Press.

———. 2009. *Gandhi and Beyond: Nonviolence for a New Political Age.* Boulder, CO: Paradigm Publishers.

Cosmides, Leda, and John Tooby. 1997. "Evolutionary Psychology: A Primer." Center for Evolutionary Psychology, University of California, Santa Barbara. January 13. http://www.psych.ucsb.edu/research/cep/primer.html

Coy, Patrick G. 2009. "Conflict Resolution, Conflict Transformation, and Peacebuilding." In *Peace, Justice, and Security Studies: A Curriculum Guide*, 7th edition, edited by Timothy A. McElwee et al., 63–78. Boulder, CO: Lynne Rienner.

Crews, Robin J. 2002. "A Modest Proposal for Peace Studies." *Peace Review: A Journal of Social Justice* 14 (1): 73–80.

Cumings, Bruce. 2010. *The Korean War: A History.* New York: Modern Library.

Daly, Martin, and Margo Wilson. 1988. *Homicide.* New Brunswick, NJ: Transaction Publishers.

D'Anjou, Leo. 1996. *Social Movements and Cultural Change: The First Abolition Campaign.* New York: Aldine de Gruyter.

DasGupta, Sumona, and Meenakshi Gopinath. 2005. "Women Breaking the Silence: The Athwaas Initiative in Kashmir." In *People Building Peace II: Successful Stories of Civil Society*, edited by Paul van Tongreren, Malin Brenk, Marte Hellema and Juliette Verhoeven, 111–16. Boulder, CO: Lynn Rienner Publishers.

DeAngelis, Tori. 2008. "The Two Faces of Oxytocin." *Monitor on Psychology* 39 (2): 30.

"Debasing Dissent." 1967. *New York Times.* November 16, 46. Online.

Deutsch, Morton. 1973. *The Resolution of Conflict: Constructive and Destructive Processes.* New Haven, CT: Yale University Press.

———. 2000. "Cooperation and Conflict." In *The Handbook of Conflict Resolution*, edited by Morton Deutsch and Peter T. Coleman, 23–40. San Francisco: Jossey-Bass Publishers.

de Waal, Frans B. M. 1998. *Bonobo: The Forgotten Ape.* Berkeley: University of California Press.

———. 2005. *Our Inner Ape.* New York: Riverhead.

———. 2012. "The Antiquity of Empathy." *Science* 336 (6083): 874–76.

de Waal, Frans B. M., and D. Johanowicz. 1993. "Modification of Reconciliation Behavior through Social Experience: An Experiment with Two Macaque Species." *Child Development* 64: 897–908.

Diab, Khaled. 2013. "Syria's Sunni vs. Shia Myth." June 30. *Huffington Post.* Online.

Diener, Ed, and Robert Biswas-Diener. 2008. *Happiness: Unlocking the Mysteries of Psychological Wealth.* Malden, MA: Blackwell.

Dobbins, James, Seth G. Jones, Keith Crane, Andrew Rathmell, Brett Steele, Richard Teltschik, and Anga R. Timilsina. 2005. *The UN's Role in Nation-Building.* Santa Monica, CA: Rand Corporation.

Dodson, Howard. 2005. "Slavery in the Twenty-First Century." *UN Chronicle.* September–November: 28–29.

Doidge, Norman. 2007. *The Brain that Changes Itself.* New York: Viking.

Donnelly, Jack. 1986. "International Human Rights: A Regime Analysis." *International Organization* 40 (3): 599–642.

Donohue III, John J. 2003. "The Final Bullet in the Body of the More Guns, Less Crime Hypothesis." *Criminology and Public Policy* 2 (3): 397–410.

Douglass, Frederick. 1999. *Frederick Douglass: Selected Speeches and Writings*. Edited by Phillip S. Foner and Yuval Taylor. Chicago: Lawrence Hill Books.

Dreifus, Claudia. 2007. "Finding Hope in Knowing the Universal Capacity for Evil." *New York Times*. April 3. Online.

Durant, Will. 1950. *The Story of Civilization*, vol. 4. New York: Simon and Schuster.

Durkheim, Emile. 2007. *On Suicide*. New York: Penguin.

Dutton, Mary Ann, Dean G. Kilpatrick, Merle Friedman, and Vikram Patel. 2003. "Violence Against Women." In *Trauma Interventions in War and Peace: Prevention, Practice, and Policy*, edited by Bonnie L. Green, et al., 155–84. New York: Springer.

Dyer, Gwynne. 2011. *Climate Wars: The Fight for Survival as the World Overheats*. London: Oneworld Publications.

Earle, Ethan. 2012. "A Brief History of Occupy Wall Street." *Rosa Luxemburg Stiftung*. http://www.rosalux-nyc.org/a-history-of-occupy

Earth Charter Initiative. 2012. "The Earth Charter." http://www.earthcharterinaction.org/content/pages/Read-the-Charter.html

Easwaran, Eknath. 2002. *Nonviolent Soldier of Islam: Badshah Khan, A Man to Match His Mountains*, 2nd ed. Tomales, CA: Nilgiri Press.

Eckhardt, William. 1992. *Civilization, Empires and Wars: A Quantitative History of War*. Jefferson, NC: McFarland.

Ehrenreich, Barbara. 1998. *Blood Rites: Origins and History of the Passions of War*. New York: Macmillan.

Eid, Michael, and Randy J. Larsen. 2008. "Ed Diener and the Science of Subjective Well-Being." In *The Science of Subjective Well-Being*, edited by Michael Eid and Randy J. Larsen, 1–13. New York: Guilford Press.

Einstein, Albert. 1968. *Einstein on Peace*. Edited by Otto Nathan and Heinz Norden. New York: Schocken.

Eisner, Manuel. 2003. "Long-Term Historical Trends in Violent Crime." *Crime and Justice* 30: 83–142.

Eliot, Lise. 2009. *Pink Brain, Blue Brain: How Small Differences Grow Into Troublesome Gaps—And What We Can Do about It*. New York: Houghton Mifflin Harcourt.

Ellemers, Naomi. 2012. "The Group Self." *Science* 336 (6083): 848–52.

Ellsberg, Mary, Henrica A. F. M. Jansen, Lori Helse, Charlotte H. Watts, and Claudia Garcia-Moreno. 2008. "Intimate Partner Violence and Women's Physical and Mental Health in the WHO Multi-Country Study on Women's Health and Domestic Violence." *The Lancet* 371 (9619): 1165–72.

Ember, Carol. 1978. "Myths about Hunter-Gatherers." *Ethnology* 17 (4): 439–48.

Enloe, Cynthia. 1983. *Does Khaki Become You? The Militarization of Women's Lives*. Boston: South End Press.

———. 1990. *Bananas, Beaches and Bases: Making Feminist Sense of International Politics*. Berkeley: University of California Press.

Esteban, Joan, Laura Mayoral, and Debraj Ray. 2012. "Ethnicity and Conflict: Theory and Facts." *Science* 336 (6083): 858–65.

European Commission. 2012. "The EU in the World—Economy and Finance." July. http://epp.eurostat.ec.europa.eu/statistics_explained/index.php/The_EU_in_the_world_economy_and_finance

Feith, Douglas J. 2009. *War and Decision: Inside the Pentagon at the Dawn of the War on Terrorism*. New York: HarperCollins.

Fellman, Gordon. 1998. *Rambo and the Dalai Lama: The Compulsion to Win and Its Threat to Human Survival*. Albany, NY: SUNY Press.

Ferguson, R. Brian. 1984. *Warfare, Culture, and Environment*. Orlando: Academic Press.

———. 1989. "Do Yanomamö Killers Have More Kids?" *American Ethnologist* 16 (3): 564–65.

———. 2013. "Pinker's List: Exaggerating Prehistoric War Mortality." In *War Peace, and Human Nature: The Convergence of Evolutionary and Cultural Views*, edited by Douglas P. Fry, 112–31. New York: Oxford University Press.

Filkins, Dexter. 2010. "New Model for Afghan War: 'Population is the Prize.'" *New York Times*. February 13. Online.

Findlay, Trevor. 2002. *The Use of Force in UN Peace Operations*. New York: Oxford University Press.

Fine, Cordelia. 2010. *Delusions of Gender: How Our Minds, Society, and Neurosexism Create Difference*. New York: W. W. Norton.

Fischer, Louis. 1954. *Gandhi: His Life and Message for the World*. New York: New American Library.

Fisher, Roger, William Ury, and Bruce M. Patton. 2011. *Getting to Yes: Negotiating Agreement Without Giving In*. New York: Penguin.

Fisk, Robert. 2006. *The Great War For Civilisation: The Conquest of the Middle East*. New York: Alfred A. Knopf.

Fiske, Susan. 2004. *Social Beings: A Core Motives Approach to Social Psychology*. Hoboken, NJ: Wiley.

Florida, Richard. 2011. "The Geography of Gun Deaths." *The Atlantic*. January 13. Online.

Frady, Marshall. 2005. *Martin Luther King, Jr.: A Life.* New York: Penguin.

Freire, Pablo. 2007. *Pedagogy of the Oppressed.* New York: Continuum.

Friedman, Benjamin M. 2005. *The Moral Consequences of Economic Growth.* New York: Knopf.

Fry, Douglas P. 2006. *The Human Potential for Peace.* New York: Oxford University Press.

———. 2007. *Beyond War: The Human Potential for Peace.* New York: Oxford University Press.

———. 2011. "Human Nature: The Nomadic Forager Model." In *Origins of Altruism and Cooperation,* edited by Robert W. Sussman and C. Roberts Cloninger, 227–48. New York: Springer.

Fry, Douglas P., and Patrik Söderberg. 2013. "Lethal Aggression in Mobile Forager Bands and Implications for the Origins of War." *Science* 341 (6143): 270–73.

Furnari, Ellen. n.d. "Nonviolent Peaceforce in Action: A Study in Violence Prevention and Related Theory." *Western Institute for Social Research.* https://docs.google .com/file/d/0B1rHbE2cUcqPQ2lpN3hTLVFiUFU/edit

Galtung, Johan. 1964. "An Editorial." *Journal of Peace Research* 1 (1): 1–4.

———. 1969. "Violence, Peace, and Peace Research." *Journal of Peace Research* 6 (3): 167–91.

———. 1985. "Twenty-Five Years of Peace Research: Ten Challenges, and Some Responses." *Journal of Peace Research* 22 (2): 141–58.

———. 1990. "Cultural Violence." *Journal of Peace Research* 27 (3): 291–305.

Galtung, Johan, and Charles Webel. 2007. "Peace and Conflict Studies: Looking Back, Looking Forward." In *Handbook of Peace and Conflict Studies,* edited by Charles Webel and Johan Galtung, 397–99. New York: Routledge.

Gan, Barry. 2009. "The Relationship of Peace Studies to Nonviolence." In *Peace, Justice, and Security Studies: A Curriculum Guide,* edited by Timothy A. McElwee et al., 79–90. Boulder, CO: Lynne Rienner.

Gandhi, Arun. 2004. "Foreword." In *The Search for a Nonviolent Future,* edited by Michael N. Nagler, ix–x. Makawao, HI: Inner Ocean.

Gandhi, Mohandas. 1996. *The Essential Writings of Mahatma Gandhi.* Edited by Raghavan Iyer. New Delhi: Oxford University Press.

———. 2006. "Constructive Programme: Its Meaning and Place and Related Writings." In *Gandhi's Experiments with Truth: Essential Writings by and about Mahatma Gandhi.* Edited by Richard Johnson, 92–103. Lanham, MD: Lexington Books.

———. 2007. *Ahimsa: The Way To Peace.* Rediscovering Gandhi, vol. 2. New Delhi, India: Concept Publishing Company.

———. 2012. *Non-Violent Resistance.* Dover: Courier Dover Publications.

Garcia-Moreno, Claudia, Henrica A. F. M. Jansen, Mary Ellsberg, and Charlotte H. Watts. 2006. "Prevalence of Intimate Partner Violence: Findings from the WHO Multi-Country Study of Women's Health and Domestic Violence." *The Lancet* 368 (9543): 1260–69.

Gartzke, Erik. 2005. "Economic Freedom and Peace." In *Economic Freedom of the World: 2005 Annual Report,* edited by James Gwarthney and Robert Lawson, 29–44. Free the World, Fraser Institute. Online.

———. 2007. "The Capitalist Peace." *American Journal of Political Science* 51 (1): 166–91.

———. 2012. "Could Climate Change Precipitate Peace?" *Journal of Peace Research* 49 (1): 177–92.

Gat, Azar. 2006. *War in Human Civilization.* New York: Oxford University Press.

Gates, Gary J., and Frank Newport. 2012. *Special Report: 3.4% of U.S. Adults Identify as LGBT.* Williams Institute. http://www.gallup.com/poll/158066/special-report-adults-identify-lgbt.aspx

Gates, Robert M. 2008. "U.S. Global Leadership Campaign." July 15. U.S. Department of Defense, Speeches. Online.

Gbowee, Leymah. 2011. *Mighty Be Our Powers: How Sisterhood, Prayer, and Sex Changed a Nation at War, a Memoir.* New York: Beast Books.

Geneva Declaration on Armed Violence and Development. 2008. *Global Burden of Armed Violence.* Online.

———. 2011. *When the Victim is a Woman.* Online.

Ghiglieri, Michael P. 1999. *The Dark Side of Man.* Cambridge, MA: Perseus Publishing.

Ghonim, Wael. 2012. *Revolution 2.0: The Power of the People is Greater Than the People in Power.* New York: Houghton Mifflin Harcourt.

Gibbons, Ann. 2012. "Bonobos Join Chimps as Closest Human Relatives." *Science Now.* June 30. Online.

Giddens, Anthony. 1990. *The Consequencies of Modernity.* Malden, MA: Polity.

Ginges, Jeremy, and Scott Atran. 2011. "Psychology Out of the Laboratory: The Challenge of Violent Extremism." *American Psychologist* 66 (6): 507–19.

Giorgi, Piero P. 2009 . "Nonkilling Biology." In *Toward a Nonkilling Paradigm*, edited by Joám Evans Pim, 95–123. Honolulu: Center for Global Nonkilling. Online.

Giroux, Henry A. 2007. *The University in Chains: Confronting the Military-Industrial-Academic Complex*. Boulder, CO: Paradigm Publishers.

Global Nonviolent Action Database. 2009. "Pashtuns campaign against the British Empire in India, 1930–1931." Online.

Golden, Harry. n.d. *Why Team Rubicon Exists*. YouTube Online.

Golding, J. M. 1999. "Intimate Partner Violence as a Risk Factor for Mental Disorders." *Journal of Family Violence* 14 (2): 99–132.

Goldstein, Joshua. 2007. *The Role of Digital Networked Technologies in the Ukranian Orange Revolution*. Cambridge, MA: Bechman Center Research Publication No. 2007-14.

Goldstein, Joshua, and Juliana Rotich. 2008. *Digitally Networked Technology in Kenya's 2007-2008 Post-Election Crisis*. Cambridge, MA: Bechman Center Research Publication No. 2008-09.

Goldstein, Joshua S. 2012. *Winning the War on War: The Decline of Armed Conflict Worldwide*. New York: Plume.

Goodall, Jane. 1986. *The Chimpanzees of Gombe: Patterns of Behavior*. Cambridge, MA: Harvard University Press.

Goodell, Jeff. 2010. "Meet America's Most Creative Climate Criminal." *Rolling Stone*. July 7. Online.

Gregg, Richard B. 1966. *The Power of Nonviolence*. New York: Schocken.

Grossman, Dave. 1995. *On Killing: The Psychological Cost of Learning to Kill in War and Society*. Boston: Little Brown.

Guevara, Ernesto Che. 2009. *Socialism and Man in Cuba*. New York: Pathfinder Books.

Guilmoto, Christopher Z. 2007. *Sex-Ratio Imbalance in Asia: Trends, Consequences and Policy Responses*. Paris: LPEDA/IRD. http://www.unfpa.org/gender/docs/studies/summaries/regional_analysis.pdf

Guthrie, Charles, and Michael Quinlan. 2007. *Just War: The Just War Tradition*. New York: Walker & Co.

Guthrie, R. Dale. 2005. *The Nature of Paleolithic Art*. Chicago: University of Chicago Press.

Gyatso, Geshe Kelsang. 2001. *Transform Your Life: A Blissful Journey*. London: Tharpa.

Gyatso, Tenzin, the 14th Dalai Lama. 2005. "Our Faith in Science." *New York Times*. November 12. Online.

Haas, Jonathan. 1996. "War." In *Encyclopedia of Cultural Anthropology*, vol. 4, edited by D. Levinson and M. Ember, 1357–61. New York: Henry Holt.

Haegerich, Tamara M., and Linda L. Dahlberg. 2011. "Violence as a Public Health Risk." *American Journal of Lifestyle Medicine* 5 (5): 392–406.

Hamidaddin, Abdullah. 2013. *Six Rules of Thumb for Writing on Sunni/Shiite Concepts*. May 31. http://english.alarabiya.net/en/views/news/middle-east/2013/05/31/Six-rules-of-thumb-for-writing-on-Sunni-Shiite-concepts-.html

Hand, Judith L. 2006. *A Future without War: The Strategy of a Warfare Transition*. San Diego: Questpath Publishing.

Hansvick, Christine L., and Ian M. Harris. 2007. "Peace and Conflict Programs within Higher Education: Changes Observed Since the Year 2000." *Proceedings of the International Education for Peace Conference*. 276–88. Vancouver: International Education for Peace Institute.

Hassan, Nasra. 2001. "An Arsenal of Believers: Talking to the Human Bombs." *The New Yorker*. November 19, 36–41.

———. 2006. "Suicide Terrorism." In *The Roots of Terrorism*, edited by Louise Richardson, 29–44. New York: Routledge.

Hawken, Paul. 2007. *Blessed Unrest: How the Largest Social Movement in History is Restoring Grace, Justice, and Beauty to the World*. New York: Penguin Books.

Hedges, Chris. 2002. *War is a Force that Gives Us Meaning*. New York: Anchor Books.

Helvey, Robert L. 2004. *On Strategic Nonviolent Conflict: Thinking about the Fundamentals*. Boston, MA: Albert Einstein Institution.

Hemenway, David. 2006. *Private Guns, Public Health*. Ann Arbor: University of Michigan Press.

Hemenway, David, and Matthew Miller. 2000. "Firearm Availability and Homicide Rates across 26 High-Income Countries." *Journal of Trauma* 49: 985–88.

Hewitt, J. Joseph. 2011. "Trends in Global Conflict, 1946–2009." In *Peace and Conflict 2012*, by J. Joseph Hewitt, Jonathan Wilkenfeld, Ted Robert Gurr and Birger Heldt. Boulder, CO: Paradigm Publishers.

Hewitt, J. Joseph, and Jonathan Wilkenfeld. 1996. "Democracies in International Crisis." *International Interactions* 22 (2): 123–42.

Hoare, Joanna, and Fiona Gell. 2009. *Women's Leadership and Participation*. Oxford, GB: Oxfam GB.

Hodge, David R. 2008. "Sexual Trafficking in the United States: A Domestic Problem with Transnational Dimensions." *Social Work* 53 (2): 143–52.

Hoffman, Bruce. 2002. *Lessons of 9/11*. Santa Monica, CA: RAND Corp. http://www.rand.org/content/dam/rand/pubs/testimonies/2005/CT201.pdf

Horgan, John. 2012. *The End of War*. San Francisco: McSweeney's Books.

Horvitz, Leslie Alan, and Christopher Catherwood. 2006. *Encyclopedia of War Crimes and Genocide*. New York: Facts on File.

Howard, Michael. 2000. *The Invention of Peace: Reflections on War and International Order*. New Haven, CT: Yale University Press.

Hrdy, Sarah Blaffer. 2009. *Mothers and Others: The Evolutionary Origins of Mutual Understanding*. Cambridge, MA: Harvard University Press.

Hudson, Valerie M. 2012. "What Sex Means for World Peace." *Foreign Policy*. April 24. http://www.foreignpolicy.com/articles/2012/04/24/what_sex_means_for_world_peace

Hudson, Valerie M., Bonnie Ballif-Spanvill, Mary Caprioli, and Chad F. Emmett. 2012. *Sex and World Peace*. New York: Columbia University Press.

Human Security Centre. 2005. *Human Security Report 2005: War and Peace in the 21st Century*. New York: Oxford University Press.

Human Security Report Project. 2005. "What is Human Security?" *The Human Security Report*. http://www.hsrgroup.org/docs/Publications/HSR2005/2005HumanSecurityReport-WhatIsHumanSecurity.pdf

Human Security Report Project. 2011. *Human Security Report 2009/2010: The Causes of Peace and the Shrinking Costs of War*. New York: Oxford University Press.

Hussain, Murtaza. 2013. "The Myth of the 1,400 Year Sunni-Shia War." *Al Jazeera*. July 9. http://www.aljazeera.com/indepth/opinion/2013/07/2013719220768151.html

Hyde, Janet Shibley. 2005. "The Gender Similarities Hypothesis." *American Psychologist* 60 (6): 581–92.

Institute for Economics & Peace. 2008. *The Study of Industries that Prosper in Peace—The 'Peace Industry.'* Sydney: Institute for Economics and Peace. Online.

———. 2009. *Peace, Its Causes and Economic Value*. Sydney: Institute for Economics and Peace. Online.

———. 2011. *GPI: 2011 Methodology, Results & Findings*. Sydney: Institute for Economics and Peace. Online.

International Security. 2014. "Drone Wars Pakistan: Analysis." http://securitydata.newamerica.net/drones/pakistan/analysis

Inter-Parliamentary Union. 2010. *Women in National Parliaments*. July 30. http://www.ipu.org/wmn-e/arc/world310710.htm

Iraq Body Count. 2013. *Iraq Body Count*. http://www.iraqbodycount.org

Iraq Coalition Casualty Count. 2013. "Operaton Enduring Freedom." http://icasualties.org

Janis, Irving L. 1972. *Victims of Groupthink: A Psychological Study of Foreign-Policy Decisions and Fiascoes*. Boston: Houghton Mifflin.

———. 1983. *Groupthink: Psychological Studies of Policy Decisions and Fiascoes*, 2nd ed. Boston: Houghton Mifflin.

Jenkins, Tony, and Betty A. Reardon. 2007. "Gender and Peace: Towards a Gender-Inclusive, Holistic Perspective." In *Handbook of Peace and Conflict Studies*, edited by Charles Webel and Johan Galtung, 209–31. New York: Routledge.

Jenkins, Tony, and National Peace Academy. 2012. "Peace, Peacebuilding and Peacelearning: A Wholistic Introduction." *National Peace Academy*. http://nationalpeaceacademy.us/edresources/study-guide

Johansen, Robert C. 1978. *Toward a Dependable Peace*. New York: Institute for World Order.

———. 1997. "Radical Islam and Nonviolence: A Case Study of Religious Empowerment and Constraint Among Pashtuns." *Journal of Peace Research* 34 (1): 53–71.

John A. Vasquez, editor. 2012. *What Do We Know about War?* 2nd ed. Lanham, MD: Rowman & Littlefield.

Johnson, D. W., and R. T. Johnson. 1989. *Cooperation and Competition: Theory and Research*. Edina, MN: Interaction.

Johnston, Ian. 2013. "Malala Yousafzai: Being Shot by Taliban Made Me Stronger." July 12. NBC News Online.

Joiner, Thomas. 2005. *Why People Die by Suicide*. Cambridge, MA: Harvard University Press.

Jones, Seth G., and Martin C. Libicki. 2008. *How Terrorist Groups End: Lessons for Countering Al Qa'ida*. Santa Monica: RAND Corporation.

Joy, Lois, Nancy M. Carter, Harvey M. Wagner, and Sriram Narayanan. 2007. *The Bottom Line: Corporate Performance and Women's Representation on Boards*. http://www.catalyst.org/system/files/The_Bottom_Line_Corporate_Performance_and_Womens_Representation_on_Boards.pdf

Joyce, Mary. 2011. "The 7 Activist Uses of Digital Tech: The Case of Popular Resistance in Egypt." April 12. International Center on Nonviolent Conflict webinar. Online.

Judt, Tony. 2006. *Postwar: A History of Europe since 1945.* New York: Penguin.

———. 2011. *Ill Fares the Land.* New York: Penguin.

Kaldor, Mary. 2003. *Global Civil Society: An Answer to War.* New York: Polity.

———. 2007. *New and Old Wars: Organized Violence in a Global Era,* 2nd ed. Palo Alto, CA: Stanford University Press.

Kano, Takayoshi. 1990. "The Bonobo's Peaceable Kingdom." *Natural History* 11: 62–71.

Kant, Immanuel. 2006. *Toward Perpetual Peace and Other Writings on Politics, Peace, and History.* New Haven: Yale University Press.

Karatnycky, Adrian, and Peter Ackerman. 2005. *How Freedom Is Won: From Civic Resistance to Durable Democracy.* Washington, DC: Freedom House.

Keegan, John. 1993. *A History of Warfare.* New York: Vintage Books.

Keeley, Lawrence H. 1996. *War Before Civilization.* New York: Oxford University Press.

Keller, Evelyn Fox. 2010. *The Mirage of Space between Nature and Nurture.* Durham, NC: Duke University Press.

Kellermann, Arthur L., et al. 1993. "Gun Ownership as a Risk Factor for Homicide in the Home." *The New England Journal of Medicine* 329 (15): 1084–91.

Keltner, Dacher. 2009. *Born to Be Good: The Science of a Meaningful Life.* New York: W. W. Norton.

Kennan, George F. 1987. "Containment 40 Years Later: The Sources of Soviet Conduct." *Foreign Affairs* 65 (4). Online.

Kennedy, David. 2004. *The Dark Sides of Virtue: Reassessing International Humanitarianism.* Princeton, NJ: Princeton University Press.

———. 2012. "The International Human Rights Regime: Still Part of the Problem?" In *Examining Critical Perspectives on Human Rights,* edited by Rob Dickinson et al., 19–34. New York: Cambridge University Press.

Kenny, Kevin. 2009. *Peaceable Kingdom Lost: The Paxton Boys and the Destruction of William Penn's Holy Experiment.* New York: Oxford University Press.

Khatchadourian, Haig. 1998. *The Morality of Terrorism.* New York: Peter Lang.

Kimura, Doreen. 1999. *Sex and Cognition.* Cambridge, MA: MIT Press.

———. 2002. "Sex Differences in the Brain." *Scientific American Special Edition* 267 (3): 32–37.

King Jr., Martin Luther. 1986. *Stride Toward Freedom: The Montgomery Story.* New York: Harper & Row.

———. 2000. *Symbol of the Movement, January 1957–December 2008,* vol. 4 in the Papers of Martin Luther King, Jr. Berkeley, CA: University of California Press.

———. 2005. *Threshold of a New Decade, January 1959–December 1960,* vol. 5 in the Papers of Martin Luther King, Jr. Berkeley, CA: University of California Press.

———. 2010. "Beyond Vietnam." In *Landmark Speeches on the Vietnam War,* edited by Gregory Allen Olson, 92–113. College Station, TX: Texas A&M Press.

Kirilenko, Anastasia, and Daisy Sindela. 2012. "Remaining Members of Pussy Riot: 'We're Stronger Than the State.'" http://www.rferl.org/content/pussy-riot-members-secret-interview-russia/24690799.html

Klare, Michael T. 2001. *Resource Wars: The New Landscape of Global Conflict.* New York: Macmillan.

Klasen, Stephen, and Claudia Wink. 2003. "Missing Women: Revisiting the Debate." *Feminist Economics* 9 (2–3): 263–300.

Klein, Naomi. 2004. "Reclaiming the Commons." In *A Movement of Movements: Is Another World Really Possible?,* edited by Tom Mertes, 219–29. New York: Verso.

Kraft, Kenneth. 1992. "Introduction." In *Inner Peace, World Peace: Essays on Buddhism and Nonviolence,* edited by Kenneth Kraft, 1–10. Albany, NY: SUNY Press.

Kristof, Nicholas D., and Sherry L. WuDunn. 2009. *Half the Sky: Turning Oppression into Opportunity for Women Worldwide.* New York: Alfred A. Knopf.

———. 2009. "The Women's Crusade." *The New York Times Magazine.* August 23. Online.

Krug, Etienne G., et al. 2002. *World Report on Violence and Health.* Geneva: World Health Organization.

Kulka, R. A., et al. 1990. *Trauma and the Vietnam War: Report of Findings from the National Vietnam Veterans Readjustment Study.* New York: Brunner/Mazel.

Kurlansky, Mark. 2006. *Nonviolence: Twenty-Five Lessons from the History of a Dangerous Idea.* New York: Modern Library.

Kurzman, Charles. 2004. *The Unthinkable Revolution in Iran.* Cambridge, MA: Harvard University Press.

LaFree, Gary, and Laura Dugan. 2012. "Trends in Global Terrorism, 1970–2008." In *Peace and Conflict 2012,* edited by J. Joseph Hewitt, Jonathan Wilkenfeld, and Ted Robert Gurr, 39–52. Boulder, CO: Paradigm Publishers.

Lane, Jan-Erik, and Uwe Waqschal. 2011. *Culture and Politics*. New York: Routledge.

Leary, M. R., R. M. Kowalski, L. Smith, and S. Phillips. 2003. "Teasing, Rejection, and Violence: Case Studies of the School Shootings." *Aggressive Behavior* 29 (3): 202–14.

Lebow, Richard Ned. 2010. *Why Nations Fight: Past and Future Motives for War*. New York: Cambridge University Press.

Lederach, John Paul. 1997. *Building Peace: Sustainable Reconciliation in Divided Societies*. Washington, DC: United States Institute of Peace.

———. 2003. *The Little Book of Conflict Transformation*. Intercourse, PA: Good Books.

Leitenberg, Milton. 2006. *Deaths in Wars and Conflicts in the 20th Century*, 3rd ed. Ithaca, NY: Cornell University Peace Studies Program. Online.

Lentin, Ronit. 1997. "Introduction: (En)gendering Genocides." In *Gender and Catasrophe*, edited by Ronit Lentin, 2–17. New York: Zed Books.

Leung, Rebecca. 2009. "Mind of the Suicide Bomber." *CBS News*. February 11. Online.

Levine, Ruth, and the What Works Working Group. 2004. *Millions Saved: Proven Success in Global Health*. Washington, DC: Center for Global Development.

Levy, Jack S., and William R. Thompson. 2010. *Causes of War*. New York: Wiley-Blackwell.

Lewis, David L. 2013. *King: A Biography*. Chicago: University of Illinois Press.

Libicki, Martin C. 2009. *Cyberdeterrence and Cyberwar*. Santa Monica: RAND Corporation. Online.

Lobe, Jim. 2004. "POLITICS-U.S.: Chickenhawk Groupthink?" *International Press Service*. May 11. http://www.ipsnews.net/2004/05/politics-us-chickenhawk-groupthink

Lorenz, Konrad. 1966. *On Aggression*. New York: Routledge.

Lykken, David. 1999. *Happiness: What Studies on Twins Show Us about Nature, Nurture, and the Happiness Set Point*. New York: Golden Books.

Lynch, Damon. 2004. "Three Peace Forces: The Khudai Khidmitgars, Shanti Sena and Nonviolent Peaceforce." *Asian Reflection*. December. http://asianreflection.com/npsskk.pdf

Lyubomirsky, Sonja. 2007. *The How of Happiness*. New York: Penguin.

Lyubomirsky, Sonja, David Schkade, and Kenneth M. Sheldon. 2005. "Pursuing Happiness: The Architecture of Sustainable Change." *Review of General Psychology* 9 (2): 111–31.

Mackay, Mairi. 2012. "Gene Sharp: A Dictator's Worst Nightmare." *CNN*. June 25. http://www.cnn.com/2012/06/23/world/gene-sharp-revolutionary/index.html

MacNair, Rachel M. 2002. *Perpetration-Induced Traumatic Stress: The Psychological Consequences of Killing*. Westport, CT: Praeger.

———. 2011. *The Psychology of Peace*, 2nd ed. Westport, CT: Praeger.

Malone, Thomas W., and Anita Williams Woolley. 2011. "Defend Your Research: What Makes a Team Smarter? More Women." *Harvard Business Review* (June): 32–33.

Mao, Zedong. 1972. *Quotations from Chairman Mao*. San Francisco, CA: China Books.

Marean, Curtis W., et al. 2007. "Early Human Use of Marine Resources and Pigment in South Africa during the Middle Pleistocene." *Nature* 449: 905–08.

Marshall, Monty G., and Ted Robert Gurr. 2005. *Peace and Conflict 2005*. College Park, MD: Center for International Development and Conflict Management.

Marshall, S. L. A. 1947. *Men Against Fire*. New York: William Morrow.

Martin, Brian. 1989. "Gene Sharp's Theory of Power." *Journal of Peace Research* 26 (2): 213–22.

———. 2005. "How Nonviolence Works." *Borderlands e-journal* 4 (3). http://www.bmartin.cc/pubs/05borderlands.html

Matheu, Maite. 2009. "Advocacy and National Elections: Women's Political Participation in Honduras." In *Women's Leadership and Participation: Case Stuides in Learning for Action*, edited by Joanna Hoare and Fiona Gell, 81–92. Rugby, United Kingdom: Oxfam Practical Action Publishing.

Mayer, Jane. 2011. "Taking It to the Streets." *New Yorker* (November 28): 19.

Mayton II, Daniel M. 2001. "Gandhi as Peacebuilder: The Social Psychology of Satyagraha." In *Peace, Conflict and Violence: Peace Pyschology for the 21st Century*, edited by Daniel J. Christie, Richard V. Wagner, and Deborah DuNann Winter, 307–13. Upper Saddle River, NJ: Prentice-Hall.

Mazurana, Dyan, and Susan McKay. 2001. "Women, Girls, and Structural Violence: A Global Analysis." In *Peace, Conflict, and Violence: Peace Pyschology for the 21st Century*, edited by Daniel J. Christie,

Richard V. Wagner, and Deborah DuNann Winter, 130–38. Upper Saddle River, NJ: Prentice-Hall.

McCarthy, Ronald M., and Christopher Kruegler. 1993. *Theory Research and Theory Building in the Study of Nonviolent Action.* Cambridge, MA: The Albert Einstein Institution.

McElwee, Timothy A. 2003. "Instead of War: The Urgency and Promise of a Global Peace System." *Crosscurrents* 53 (2). Online.

McElwee, Timothy A., B. Welling Hall, Joseph Liechty, and Julie Garber. 2009. *Peace, Justice, and Security Studies: A Curriculum Guide,* 7th ed. Boulder, CO: Lynne Rienner.

McFarland, Bentson H., Mark S. Kaplan, and Nathalie Huguet. 2010. "Datapoints: Self-Inflicted Deaths among Women with U.S. Military Service: A Hidden Epidemic?" *Psychiatric Services* 61 (12). Online.

McGann, James G. 2012. "2012 Global Go-To Think Tanks Index." *The Think Tanks and Civil Societies Program.* January 21. http://repository.upenn.edu/cgi/viewcontent .cgi?article=1006&context=think_tanks

McGuire, Danielle. 2010. *At the Dark End of the Street.* New York: Alfred A. Knopf.

McKay, Susan. 1998. "The Effects of Armed Conflict on Girls and Women." *Peace and Conflict* 4 (4): 381–92.

McKibben, Bill. 2012. "Global Warming's Terrifying New Math." *Rolling Stone.* July 19. Online.

McKnight, Gerald D. 1998. *The Last Crusade: Martin Luther King, Jr., the FBI, and the Poor People's Campaign.* New York: Basic Books.

McNally, Richard J. 2012. "Are We Winning the War Against Posttraumatic Stress Disorder?" *Science* 336 (6083): 872–75.

McNeill, J. R., and William H. McNeill. 2003. *The Human Web: A Bird's-eye View of World History.* New York: W. W. Norton.

McNeill, William H. 1982. "The Industrialization of War." *Review of International Studies* 8 (3): 203–13.

Merari, Ariel. 1990. "The Readiness to Kill and Die: Suicidal Terrorism in the Middle East." In *Origins of Terrorism: Psychologies, Theologies, States of Mind,* edited by Walter Reich, 192–209. Washington, DC: Woodrow Wilson Center Press.

Merari, Ariel. 2010. *Driven to Death: Psychological and Social Aspects of Suicide Terrorism.* New York: Oxford University Press.

Mertus, J. 1995. "State Discriminatory Family Law and Customary Abuses." In *Women's Rights, Human Rights: International Feminist Perspectives,* edited by J. Peters and A. Wolper, 135–48. New York: Routledge.

Middelaar, Luuk van. 2013. *The Passage to Europe: How a Continent Became a Union.* New Haven, CT: Yale University Press.

Midgley, Mary. 2010. *The Solitary Self: Darwin and the Selfish Gene.* Durham, England: Acumen.

Milgram, Stanley. 1974. *Obedience to Authority.* New York: Harper & Row.

Miller, Laurence. 2006. "Law Enforcement Traumatic Stress." *American Academy of Experts in Traumatic Stress.* http://www.aaets.org/article87.htm

Miller, Matthew, Deborah Azrael, and David Hemenway. 2002. "Household Firearm Ownership Levels and Homicide Rates across U.S. Regions and States, 1988–1997." *American Journal of Public Health* 92: 1988–93.

Mirovalev, Mansur. 2012. "A Guide to Pussy Riot's Oeuvre." *Newsvine.* August 18. Online.

Mitchell, Sara McLaughlin. 2012. "Norms and the Democratic Peace" In *What Do We Know About War,* 2nd Edition, edited by John A. Vasquez, 167–88. Lanham, MD: Rowman and Littlefield.

Morris, Desmond. 1967. *The Naked Ape: A Zoologist's Study of the Human Animal.* New York: McGraw-Hill.

Moser-Puangsuwan, Yeshua. 2013. "Burma: Civil Resistance in the Other Indian Anti-Colonial Struggle, 1900–1940." In *Recovering Nonviolent History: Civil Resistance in Liberation Struggles,* edited by Maciej Bartkowski, 183–98. Boulder, CO: Lynne Rienner Publishers.

Moufakkir, Omar, and Ian Kelly. 2010. *Tourism, Progress, and Peace.* Cambridge, MA: CAB International.

Mousseau, Michael. 2012. "A Market-Capitalist or a Democratic Peace?" In *What Do We Know About War,* 2nd Edition, edited by John A. Vasquez, 189–211. Lanham, MD: Rowman and Littlefield.

Moyn, Samuel. 2012. *The Last Utopia: Human Rights in History.* Cambridge, MA: Harvard University Press.

Mullen, Michael G. 2010. "Admiral Mullen's Speech on Military Strategy." *Council of Foreign Relations.* March 3. Online.

Mutua, Makau. 2002. *Human Rights: A Political and Cultural Critique.* Philadelphia, PA: University of Pennsylvania Press.

Nagler, Michael. 2004. *The Search for a Nonviolent Future.* Makawao, HI: Inner Ocean Publishing.

———. 2006. "Constructive Programme." In *Gandhi's Experiments with Truth: Essential Writings by and about Mahatma Gandhi*, edited by Richard Johnson, 253–60. Lanham, MD: Lexington Books.

———. 2011. "Is This the Movement We've Been Waiting For?" *Waging Nonviolence*. November 9. Online.

Nanda, B. R. 1958. *Mahatma Gandhi*. Woodbury, New York: Barron's Educational Series.

National Center for Injury Prevention and Control. 2011. *The National Intimate Partner and Sexual Violence Survey, 2010 Summary Report*. Atlanta: Centers for Disease Control and Prevention. Online.

Nepstad, Sharon Erickson. 2011. *Nonviolent Revolutions: Civil Resistance in the Late 20th Century*. New York: Oxford University Press.

Nonviolent Peaceforce. 2012. *2012 Annual Report*. Bruxelles, Belgium: Nonviolent Peaceforce. http://www.nonviolentpeaceforce.org/sites/nonviolentpeaceforce.org/files/attachments/NP%202012%20AR_FINAL.pdf

Nye Jr., Joseph S. 1991. *Bound to Lead: The Changing Nature of American Power*. New York: Basic Books.

———. 2005. *Soft Power: The Means to Success in World Politics*. New York: PublicAffairs.

———. 2006. "Think Again: Soft Power." *Foreign Policy*. February 23. Online.

———. 2009. "Get Smart: Combining Hard and Soft Power." *Foreign Affairs* 88 (4): 160–63.

Oliver, Anne Marie. 2006. "Brides of Palestine." *Salon*. July 20. Online.

OneWorld South Asia. 2010. "India: More NGOs than Schools and Health Centres." *OneWorld International*. July 7. http://southasia.oneworld.net/news/india-more-ngos-than-schools-and-health-centres#.UfLW-o19Dh4

Pape, Robert. 2005. *Dying to Win: The Strategic Logic of Suicide Terrorism*. New York: Randon House.

Parekh, Bhikhu. 2001. *Gandhi: A Very Short Introduction*. New York: Oxford University Press.

PBS Frontline. 2003. "The War Behind Closed Doors." February 20. http://www.pbs.org/wgbh/pages/frontline/shows/iraq/view

Pellegrino, Greg, Sally D'Amato, and Anne Weisberg. 2010. *Paths to Power: Advancing Women in Government*. March. https://www2.deloitte.com/content/dam/Deloitte/global/Documents/Public-Sector/dttl-ps-pathstopower-08082013.pdf

Philpott, Daniel. 2010. "Introduction: Searching for Strategy in an Age of Peacebuilding." In *Strategies of Peace: Transforming Conflict in a Violent World*, edited by Daniel Philpott and Gerard F. Powers, 3–18. New York: Oxford University Press.

Pinker, Steven. 2002. *The Blank Slate: The Modern Denial of Human Nature*. New York: Viking.

———. 2005. "The Science of Gender and Science." *Edge: The Third Culture*. Online.

———. 2010. *The Better Angels of Our Nature: Why Violence Has Declined*. New York: Penguin.

Planty, Mike. 2002. *Third Party Involvement in Violent Crime, 1993–1999*. Washington, DC: Bureau of Justice Statistics Special Report.

Plastas, Melinda. 2011. *A Band of Noble Women: Radical Politics in the Women's Peace Movement*. Syracuse, NY: Syracuse University Press.

Popovic, Srdja, Andrej Milvojevic, and Slobodan Djinovic. 2006. *Nonviolent Struggle: 50 Crucial Points*. Centre for Applied Nonviolent Action and Strategies. Online.

PollingReport. 2013. "President Bush: Job Ratings." *PollingReport*. http://www.pollingreport.com/BushJob1.htm

Power, Margaret. 1991. *The Egalitarians—Human and Chimpanzee; An Anthropological View of Social Organization*. New York: Cambridge University Press.

Prüfer, Kat, et al. 2012. "The Bonobo Genome Compared with the Chimpanzee and Human Genomes." *Nature* 486 (June 13). Online.

Purdy, Heather. 2004. "Marital Rape." In *Encyclopedia of Rape*, edited by Merril D. Smith, 122–24. Westport, CT: Greenwood Publishing.

Pussy Riot. 2013. *Pussy Riot! A Punk Prayer For Freedom*. New York: The Feminist Press at CUNY.

Raider, Ellen, Susan Coleman, and Janet Gerson. 2006. "Teaching Conflict Resolution Skills in a Workshop." In *Handbook of Conflict Resolution: Theory and Practice*, edited by Morton Deutsch and Pete T. Coleman, 499–521. San Francisco: Jossey-Bass Publishers.

Ramachandran, Vilayanur. 2012. "Adventures in Behavioral Neurology—or—What Neurology Can Tell Us about Human Nature." *Edge*. February 21. Online.

Raqib, Mohammad. 2005. "The Muslim Pashtun Movement of the North-West Frontier of India—1930–1934." In *Waging Nonviolent Struggle*, edited by Gene Sharp, 113–34. Boston: Porter Sargent Publishers.

Reagan, Ronald. 1986. "Address to the Nation on National Security." *Federalism and the New Conservatism*.

February 26. http://reagan2020.us/speeches/address_on_national_security.asp

Reardon, Betty A. 1985. *Sexism and the War System.* New York: Teachers College Press.

———. 1988. *Comprehensive Peace Education.* New York: Teachers College Press.

———. 1993. *Women and Peace.* Albany, NY: State University of New York Press.

Reinberg, Steven. 2007. "Macaque Genome Sequenced." *ABC News.* April 12. Online.

Reuveny, Rafael, and Aseem Prakash. 1999. "The Afghanistan War and the Breakdown of the Sovet Union." *Review of International Studies* 25: 693–798.

Rice, Condoleezza. 2011. *No Higher Honor: A Memoir of My Years in Washington.* New York: Crown.

Riley, James C. 2005. "Estimates of Regional and Global Life Expectancy, 1800–2001." *Population and Development Review* 31 (3): 537–43.

Roudi-Fahimi, Farzaneh, and Valentine M. Moghadam. 2003. *Empowering Women, Developing Society: Female Education in the Middle East and North Africa.* Washington, DC: Population Reference Bureau.

Russett, Bruce. 2010. "Democractic Peace." In *Oxford International Encyclopedia of Peace,* edited by Nigel Young, 559–62. New York: Oxford University Press.

Russett, Bruce, and John R. Oneal. 2001. *Triangulating Peace: Democracy, Interdependence, and International Organization.* New York: W. W. Norton.

Ryan, Christopher, and Cacilda Jethá. 2010. *Sex at Dawn: The Prehistoric Origins of Modern Sexuality.* New York: Harper.

Sanger, David E. 2011. "The Price of Lost Chances." *New York Times.* September 8. Online.

———. 2012. *Confront and Conceal: Obama's Secret Wars and Surprising Use of American Power.* New York: Crown.

Santa Barbara, Joanna, and Neil Arya. 2008. "Introduction." In *Peace through Health: How Health Professionals Can Work for a Less Violent World,* edited by Neil Arya and Joanna Santa Barbara, 3–13. Boulder, CO: Kumarian Press.

Sapolsky, Robert M. 2006. "Social Cultures among Nonhuman Primates." *Current Anthropology* 47 (4): 641–48.

Sarkees, Meredith Reid, and Frank Whelon Wayman. 2010. *Resort to War: A Data Guide to Inter-State, Extra-State, Intra-State, and Non-State Wars, 1816–2007.* Washington, DC: CQ Press.

Scheffran, Jürgen, et al. 2012. "Climate Change and Violent Conflict." *Science* 336 (6083): 869–71.

Schell, Jonathan. 2003. *The Unconquerable World: Power, Nonviolence, and the Will of the People.* New York: Henry Holt.

Schirch, Lisa. 2004. *The Little Book of Strategic Peacebuilding.* Intercourse, PA: Good Books.

Schirch, Lisa, and Manjrika Sewak. 2005. "The Role of Women in Peacebuilding." Working Paper. The Hague, Netherlands: Global Partnership for the Prevention of Armed Conflict.

———. 2005. "Women: Using the Gender Lens." In *People Building Peace II: Successful Stories of Civil Society,* edited by Paul van Tongreren, Malin Brenk, Marte Hellema, and Juliette Verhoeven, 111–16. Boulder, CO: Lynn Rienner Publishers.

Schmidle, Nicholas. 2013. "In the Crosshairs." *The New Yorker.* June 3, 33–45.

Schock, Kurt. 2005. *Unarmed Insurrections: People Power Movements in Nondemocracies.* Minneapolis: University of Minnesota Press.

Sen, Amartya. 1990. "More Than 100 Million Women Are Missing." *New York Review of Books.* December 20.

———. 2003. "Missing Women—Revisited." *British Medical Journal* 327 (7427): 1297–1298.

Shanker, Thom. 2011. "Warning Against Wars Like Iraq and Afghanistan." *New York Times.* February 26. Online.

Sharp, Gene. 1960. *Gandhi Wields the Weapon of Moral Power: Three Case Histories.* Ahmedabad, India: Navajivan Publishing House.

———. 1973. *The Politics of Nonviolent Action: Part One: Power and Struggle.* Boston: Porter Sargent.

———. 1979. *Gandhi as a Political Strategist.* Boston: Peter Sargent.

———. 2005. *Waging Nonviolent Struggle: 20th Century Practice and 21st Century Potential.* Boston: Porter Sargent.

———. 2012. *Sharp's Dictionary of Power and Struggle.* New York: Oxford University Press.

Shea, Christopher. 2008. "Violence, Up Close and Personal." *The Chronicle Review.* February 22: B15.

Shenon, Philip. 1995. "20 Years After Victory, Vietnamese Communists Ponder How to Celebrate." *New York Times.* April 23. Online.

Shermer, Michael. 2005. "Unweaving the Heart." *Scientific American* 293 (4): 36.

Shifferd, Kent D. 2011. *Exploring Peace: Resource Materials in the Christian Tradition.* Eau Claire, WI: Exploring Peace Commission of the Episcopal Diocese.

————. 2011. *From War to Peace: A Guide to the Next Hundred Years.* Jefferson, NC: McFarland.

Singh, Indra Narain. 2009. *Buddhism in South-East Asian Countries,* vol. 2. Delhi, India: Prashant Publishing House.

Small Arms Survey. 2012. "Weapons and Markets." http://www.smallarmssurvey.org/weapons-and-markets.html

Smith, David J. 2011. "Starting a Career Building Peace." *National Career Development Association.* Online.

————, editor. 2013. *Peacebuilding in Community Colleges: A Teaching Resource.* Washington, DC: United States Institute of Peace.

Smith, Jackie, and Ernesto Verdeja. 2013. *Globalization, Social Movements, and Peacebuilding.* Syracuse: Syracuse University Press.

Smith, Rupert. 2007. *The Utility of Force: The Art of War in the Modern World.* New York: Knopf.

Smithey, Lee A., and Lester R. Kurtz. 1999. "'We Have Bare Hands': Nonviolent Social Movements in the Soviet Block." In *Nonviolent Social Movements,* edited by Stephen Zunes et al., 96–124. Malden, MA: Blackwell.

Social Investment Forum Foundation. 2010. *2010 Report on Socially Responsible Investing Trends in the United States.* Washington, DC: Social Investment Forum Foundation. http://www.ussif.org/files/Publications/10_Trends_Exec_Summary.pdf

Soderlund, Jean R. 1983. *William Penn and the Founding of Pennsylvania: A Documentary History.* Philadelphia: University of Pennsylvania Press.

Sponsel, Leslie E. 1996. "The Natural History of Peace: The Positive View of Human Nature and Its Potential." In *A Natural History of Peace,* edited by Thomas Gregor, 95–125. Nashville, TN: Vanderbilt University Press.

————. 2009. "Reflections on the Possibilities of a Nonkilling Society and a Nonkilling Anthropolgy." In *Toward a Nonkilling Paradigm,* edited by Joám Evans Pim, 35–59. Honolulu, HI: Center for Global Nonkilling.

Stark, Rodney. 1996. *The Rise of Christianity: A Sociologist Reconsiders History.* Princeton, NJ: Princeton University Press.

Steinberg, Blema S. 2008. *Women in Power: The Personalities and Leadership Styles of Indira Gandhi, Golda Meir, and Margaret Thatcher.* Quebec, Canada: McGill-Queen's University Press.

Stephan, Maria J., and Erica Chenoweth. 2008. "Why Civil Resistance Works: The Strategic Logic of Nonviolent Conflict." *International Security* 33 (1): 7–44.

Stiehm, Judith. 1968. "Nonviolence Is Two." *Sociological Inquiry* 38 (1): 23–30.

"Still Lonely at the Top." 2011. *The Economist.* July 23, 61–62.

Stockholm International Peace Research Institute. 2011. *SIPRI Yearbook 2011: Armaments, Disarmament and International Security.* Online.

Stolberg, Sheryl Gay. 2002. "War, Murder and Suicide." *The New York Times.* October 3. Online.

Stone, Douglas, Bruce Patton, and Sheila Heen. 2010. *Difficult Conversations: How to Discuss What Matters Most.* New York: Penguin.

"Suicide: Facts at a Glance." 2012. *Centers for Disease Control and Prevention.* http://www.cdc.gov/violence-prevention/pdf/Suicide_DataSheet-a.pdf

Sundquist, Eric J. 2009. *King's Dream.* New Haven, CT: Yale University Press.

Suskind, Ron. 2004. *The Price of Loyalty.* New York: Simon and Schuster.

Swofford, Anthony. 2012. "We Pretend the Vets Don't Even Exist." *Newsweek* (May 28): 27–32.

Tacon, Paul, and Christopher Chippindale. 1994. "Australia's Ancient Warriors: Changing depictions of fighting in the rock art of Arnhem Land, N.T." *Cambridge Archaeological Journal* 4: 211–48.

Tanielian, Terri, and Lisa H. Jaycox, editors. 2008. *Invisible Wounds of War: Psychological and Cognitive Injuries, Their Consequences, and Services to Assist Recovery.* Westport, CT: Rand Pubishing.

Team Rubicon. 2013. "Mission Statement." http://www.teamrubiconusa.org/our-mission

Terry, Geraldine, and Joanna Hoare. 2007. *Gender-Based Violence.* New York: Oxfam Publishing.

Thoreau, Henry David. 1980. *Walden and "Civil Disobedience."* New York: Signet Classics.

Tirman, John. 2012. "Why Do We Ignore the Civilians Killed in American Wars?" *Washington Post.* January 6. Online.

Toch, Hans. 1969. *Violent Men.* Chicago: Aldine Publishing Company.

Tol, Richard S. J., and Sebastian Wagner. 2010. "Climate Change and Violent Conflict in Europe over the Last Millennium." *Climatic Change* 99 (1–2): 65–79.

Tonkinson, Robert. 2004. "Resolving Conflict within the Law: The Mardu Aborigines of Australia." In *Keeping* the Peace: Conflict Resolution and Peaceful Societies, edited by Graham Kemp and Douglas P. Fry, 89–104. New York: Routledge.

Torres, Sasha. 2003. *Black, White, and in Color: Television and Black Civil Rights.* Princeton, NJ: Princeton University Press.

Troop, Don. 2012. "Robots at War: Scholars Debate the Ethical Issues." *The Chronicle of Higher Education.* September 14, A1, A10–A13.

Turse, Nick. 2013. *Kill Anything That Moves: The Real American War in Vietnam.* New York: Metropolitan Books.

Tutu, Desmond. 1999. *No Future Without Forgiveness.* New York: Doubleday.

UNICEF. 2013. *Female Genital Mutilation/Cutting: A Statistical Overview and Exploration of the Dynamics of Change.* July. http://www.unicef.org/media/files/FGCM_Lo_res.pdf

UNODC. 2014. *Global Study on Homicide 2013.* Vienna: United Nations Office on Drugs and Crime. http://www.unodc.org/documents/gsh/pdfs/2014_GLOBAL_HOMICIDE_BOOK_web.pdf

United Nations Secretary-General. 2006. *The Secretary-General's In-depth Study of All Forms of Violence Against Women.* New York. Online.

UN Conference on Trade and Development. 2011. *World Investment Report 2011.* New York United Nations. http://www.unctad-docs.org/files/UNCTAD-WIR2011-Full-en.pdf

UN Department of Public Information 2013. "United Nations Peacekeeping Operations Fact Sheet 30 June 2013." New York: United Nations. http://www.un.org/en/peacekeeping/documents/bnote0613.pdf

UN Office for the Coordination of Humanitarian Affairs. 2010. "Women UN Peacekeepers—More Needed." *IRIN.* May 20. Online.

Urgel, Aurora, and Gaynor Tanyang. 2008. *Creating the Space to Empower Women Fishers.* Oxfam GB. February. Online.

Ury, William. 2000. *The Third Side: Why We Fight and How We Can Stop.* New York: Penguin Books.

U.S. Department of State. 2009. *Trafficking in Persons Report 2009.* Washington, DC: United States Department of State.

———. 2012. "Fact Sheet: Non-Governmental Organizations (NGOs) in the United States." *HumanRights.Gov.* January 12. Online.

"US Launched Cyber Attacks on other Nations." 2012. *RT Question More.* January 24. www.rt.com/usa/news/us-attacks-cyber-war-615/

Verdonk, Petra, Yvonne W. M. Benschop, C. J. M. de Haes, and Toine L. M. Lagro-Janssen. 2009. "From Gender Bias to Gender Awareness in Medical Education." *Advances in Health Science Education* 14 (1): 135–52.

Wallensteen, Peter. 2012. "Future Directions in the Scientific Study of Peace and War." In *What Do We Know about War?* 2nd ed., edited by John A. Vasquez, 257–70. Lanham, MD: Rowman & Littlefield.

Wallerstein, Immanuel. 2006. "The Curve of American Power." *New Left Review* 40 (July–August): 77–94.

Wallis, Claudia. 2005. "The New Science of Happiness." *Time.* January 9. Online.

Wallis, Timmon. 2009. "Civilian Peacekeeping." In *The Oxford International Encyclopedia of Peace,* edited by Nigel Young, 302–05. New York: Oxford University Press.

Wattles, Jeffrey. 1996. *The Golden Rule.* New York: Oxford University Press.

Weber, Max. 2004. *The Vocation Lectures.* Indianapolis, IN: Hackett Publishing.

Weber, Thomas. 2003. "Nonviolence is Who? Gene Sharp and Gandhi." *Peace & Change* 28 (2): 250–70.

Welzer, Harald. 2012. *Climate Wars: What People Will Be Killed For in the 21st Century.* Polity: Malden, MA.

Wiist, William H. et al. 2014. "The Role of Public Health in the Prevention of War: Rationale and Competencies." *American Journal of Public Health* 104 (6): 34–47.

White, Douglas R. 1986. "Focused Ethnographic Bibliography for the Standard Cross-Cultural Sample." *World Cultures* 2 (1): 1–126. (Reprinted 1989 *Behavior Science Research* 23:1–145.)

White, Matthew. 2011. *Source List and Detailed Death Tolls for Man-made Multicides throughout History.* http://necrometrics.com/warstats.htm

Wikipedia. 2013. "Pussy Riot." September 2. Online.

Wilson, Edward O. 1978. *On Human Nature.* Cambridge, MA: Harvard University Press.

"Women Weaving Bougainville Together: Leitana Nehan Women's Development Agency in Papua New Guinea." 2005. In *People Building Peace II: Successful Stories of Civil Society,* edited by Paul van Tongreren, Malin Brenk, Marte Hellema and Juliette Verhoeven, 122–26. Boulder, CO: Lynn Rienner Publishers.

Wood, Gordon. 1993. *The Radicalism of the American Revolution.* New York: Vintage Books.

Wood, Houston. 2014. "The Global Peace Network." *Peace Review: A Journal of Social Justice* 26 (2): 258–64.

World Bank. 2012. "Four Million Missing Women." Gender Equality and Development. http://go.worldbank.org/GPLFFB9PQ0

World Health Organization. 2010. "Injuries and Violence: The Facts." Geneva: WHO Department of Violence and Injury Prevention and Disability. http://www.who.int/violence_injury_prevention/key_facts/en/

———. 2011. "Suicide Data." Mental Health. http://www.who.int/mental_health/prevention/suicide/suicideprevent/en/index.html

———. 2012. *Trends in Maternal Mortality: 1990 to 2010.* Geneva: World Health Organization. http://whqlibdoc.who.int/publications/2012/9789241503631_eng.pdf

———. 2013. *Global and Regional Estimates of Violence against Women: Prevalence and Health Effects of Intimate Partner Violence and Non-Partner Sexual Violence.* Geneva: World Health Organization. http://www.who.int/iris/bitstream/10665/85239/1/9789241564625_eng.pdf

Wrangham, Richard W., and Dale E. Peterson. 1997. *Demonic Males: Apes and the Origins of Human Violence.* New York: Houghton Mifflin Harcourt.

Xu, Xiao, Fengchuan Zhu, Patricia O'Campo, Michael A. Koenig, Victoria Mock, and Jacquelyn Campbell. 2005. "Prevalence of and Risk Factors for Intimate Partner Violence in China." *American Journal of Public Health* 95 (1): 78–85.

Young, Marilyn B. 2008. "Bombing Civilians from the Twentieth to the Twenty-First Centuries." In *Bombing Civilians: A Twentieth Century History*, edited by Yuki Tanaka and Marilyn B. Young, 154–74. New York: New Press.

Yunus, Muhammad. 2011. "Sacrificing Microcredit for Megaprofits." *The New York Times.* January 14, A23.

Yuval-Davis, Nira. 2011. *The Politics of Belonging: Intersectional Contestations.* Thousand Oaks, CA: Sage.

Zak, Paul J. 2012. *The Moral Molecule: The Source of Love and Prosperity.* New York: Dutton.

Zarkov, Dubravka. 2006. "Towards a New Theorizing of Women, Gender, and War." In *Handbook of Gender and Women's Studies*, edited by K. Davis, M. S. Evans, and J. Lorber, 214–33. Thousand Oaks, CA: Sage.

Zhang, David, C. Y. Jim, George Lin, Yuan-Qing He, James Wang, and Harry Lee. 2006. "Climatic Change, Wars, and Dynastic Cycles in China over the Last Millennium." *Climatic Change* 76 (3–4): 459–477.

Zimbardo, Philip. 2004. "A Situationist Perspective on the Psychology of Evil." In *The Social Psychology of Good and Evil*, edited by Arthur Miller, 21–50. New York: Guilford.

———. 2007. *The Lucifer Effect: Understanding How Good People Turn Evil.* New York: Random House.

Zimring, Franklin. 2007. *The Great American Crime Decline.* New York: Oxford University Press.

Zunes, Stephen. 1994. "Unarmed Insurrections against Authoritarian Governments in the Third World: A New Kind of Revolution?" *Third World Quarterly* 15 (3): 403–426.

———. 2009. "Terrorism and Security in a Post-9/11 World." In *Peace, Justice, and Security Studies*, edited by Timothy A. McElwee et al., 13–25. Boulder, CO: Lynne Rienner Publications.

Zunes, Stephen, and Lester R. Kurtz. 1999. "Conclusion." In *Nonviolent Social Movements: A Geographical Perspective*, edited by Stephen Zunes, Lester R. Kurtz, and Sarah Beth Asher, 302–22. Malden, MA: Blackwell Publishing.

CREDITS

INDEX